ISLAMIC COMMERCIAL LAW

An Analysis of Futures and Options

OTHER TITLES BY M. H. KAMALI
AVAILABLE FROM THE ISLAMIC TEXTS SOCIETY

Principles of Islamic Jurisprudence

The Dignity of Man: An Islamic Perspective

Equity and Fairness in Islam

Freedom, Equality and Justice in Islam

Freedom of Expression in Islam

The Right to Life, Security, Privacy and Ownership in Islam

The Right to Education, Work and Welfare in Islam

Citizenship and Accountability of Government: An Islamic Perspective

Mohammad Hashim Kamali

ISLAMIC COMMERCIAL LAW

An Analysis of Futures and Options

ISLAMIC TEXTS SOCIETY

First published in 2000 by
The Islamic Texts Society
Miller's House
Kings Mill Lane
Great Shelford
Cambridge CB22 5EN, U.K.

Reprint 2002, 2003, 2004, 2006, 2010

British Library Cataloguing-in-Publication Data.
A catalogue record for this book is
available from the British Library.

ISBN 978 0946621 79 8 cloth
ISBN 978 0946621 80 4 paper

ABOUT THE AUTHOR

Dr. Mohammad Hashim Kamali is currently Professor of Law at the International Islamic University of Malaysia, where he has been teaching Islamic law and jurisprudence since 1985. Born in Afghanistan in 1944, he studied law at Kabul University, where he was later appointed Assistant Professor. Following this he worked as Public Attorney with the Ministry of Justice in Afghanistan. He completed his LL.M. and his doctoral studies at London University, where he specialised in Islamic law and Middle Eastern Studies. Dr. Kamali then held the post of Assistant Professor at the Institute of Islamic Studies at McGill University in Montreal, and later worked as a research Associate with the Social Science and Humanities Research Council of Canada. He is the author of *Law in Afghanistan. A Study of the Constitutions, Matrimonial Law and the Judiciary* (Leiden: E.J. Brill, 1985); *Principles of Islamic Jurisprudence* (second edition, The Islamic Texts Society: Cambridge, 1991); *Freedom of Expression in Islam* (Kuala Lumpur: Berita, 1994; new edition, The Islamic Texts Society: Cambridge, 1997); *Punishment in Islamic Law: an Enquiry into the Hudūd Bill of Kelantan* (Kuala Lumpur: Institute for Policy Research, 1995); *Istihsan (Juristic Preference) and its Application to Contemporary Issues* (Jeddah: Islamic Research and Training Institute, Eminent Scholars Lecture Series No. 20, 1997) and numerous articles in reputable international journals. He is twice recipient of the Ismāʿīl al-Faruqi Award for Academic Excellence in 1995 and 1997.

بسم الله الرحمن الرحيم

Contents

ACKNOWLEDGEMENTS ix
INTRODUCTION xi

PART ONE

FUTURES TRADING IN THE MARKET-PLACE

I. The Futures Contract 1
II. Uses of Futures 15
III. Futures Contracts and Conventional Contracts 22
IV. The Futures Market 30
V. Risk Reduction Strategies 43
VI. The Futures Markets of Alexandria and Kuala Lumpur 49

PART TWO

FUTURES TRADING AND CONVENTIONAL SALES: A DISCOURSE IN *FIQH*

Introductory Remarks 65
VII. The *Sharīʿah* Perspective on Commercial Transactions (*Muʿāmalāt*) 66
VIII. Uncertainty and Risk-Taking (*Gharar*) in Islamic Law 84
IX. The Subject-Matter of a Sale 99
X. 'Sell Not What is Not With You' 110

XI. Sale Prior to Taking Possession (*Qabḍ*) 117
XII. Debt Clearance Sale (*Bay^c al-Dayn bi'l-Dayn*) 125
XIII. Deferred Sale (*Bay^c al-Mu'ajjal*) 131
XIV. Speculation or Gambling 146
XV. A Summary of Modern Opinion 159

PART THREE

OPTIONS

Introductory Remarks 181
XVI. A Market Analysis of Options 183
XVII. Options (*al-Ikhtiyārāt*) from the Islamic Legal Perspective 191

CONCLUSION 206
GLOSSARY 220
BIBLIOGRAPHY 227
INDEX 235

ACKNOWLEDGEMENTS

It is my pleasant duty to thank the research centre of the International Islamic University, Malaysia for providing me with a research grant to cover the cost of travelling and data collection at the preliminary stages of my research. Dr. Abdul Hamid Abu Sulayman, Rector of the I.I.U., Malaysia, and Professor Ahmad Ibrahim, Dean of the Faculty of Laws, were both supportive in granting my request for research leave on two occasions during the summer vacations of 1992 and 1993 and I take this opportunity to thank them both for their generous support. I would also like to thank Dr. Frank Vogel, Director of the Islamic Legal Studies Program of Harvard Law School, for inviting me to conduct a seminar on 'Futures Trading from the Islamic Legal Perspective' at Harvard in October 1994. Mr. David Harding, Director of AHL Futures Investments, invited me to observe the operational aspects of futures trading at his company headquarters in London and continued sending me his periodical publications, which proved beneficial to my research; I take this opportunity to thank him for his generous advice and assistance. I also thank Sayyd M. Syeed, former Chief Editor of the *American Journal of Islamic Social Sciences*, who obtained and made available to me copies of unpublished documents which proved to be useful. Fadlullah Wilmot, Special Assistant to the Rector of I.I.U., Malaysia, and Dr. Ubiyatholla Ismath Bacha, Head of the Business Studies Department of the Faculty of Economics and Management, read the manuscript and made valuable suggestions for its improvement and I take this opportunity to thank them both for their contributions. Lastly, I thank the secretarial staff at the Faculty of Laws, I.I.U., Malaysia, especially Siti Rohaya Zakaria, who were all very helpful and always courteous in giving me assistance with the typing and preparation of the manuscript.

Mohammad Hashim Kamali
International Islamic University, Malaysia
August 2000

Introduction

Islamic commercial law has often been singled out as the most important area of contemporary research in relevant Islamic studies and has, in terms of overall priority, been given an even higher rating than research in applied sciences and medicine. This is due to the critical importance of commercial transactions in the generation of wealth and the prospects of productivity in contemporary Muslim countries. New research on issues of the conventional law of commercial transactions (*muʿāmalāt*) is essential for the viability and success of economic development programmes in Muslim countries. In recent decades, research interest in the law of *muʿāmalāt* has increasingly focussed on specific themes and the development of new operative formulas to stimulate profitable business in the market-place. Futures trading is one such theme wherein original, independent juristic reasoning (*ijtihād*) is evidently required to enhance the prospects of economic success, especially in farming and agro-based industries, in developing Muslim countries.

Large-scale futures trading is a relatively new phenomenon which emerged in the early 1970s and has rapidly expanded ever since. New products and trading formulas in the various sectors of trading in commodities, options, financial futures and stock index futures, etc., have increased so much that futures contracts are currently available in over eighty commodities, ranging from foodgrains, oil and oil seeds, sugar, coffee, livestock, eggs, orange juice, cotton, rubber, precious metals and currencies. In terms of trading volume, futures trading has far exceeded trading levels in conventional stocks, and it is currently the single most voluminous mode of commerce on the global scale.

Futures trading is economically beneficial because it facilitates better production planning in the agriculture and agro-based industries. In these sectors it is also utilised as a hedging device against violent movement in the price of commodities over a period of time which, in the case of agricultural produce, stretches over crop seasons, often from sowing to harvesting time. Futures trading is also used by food processors, merchants and manufacturers as a means of ensuring sales and purchases in advance, without them having to face the uncertainties of marketing at a later occasion, that is, after harvesting or production, as the case may be.

Furthermore, there is a manifest need for trading and investment vehicles in Muslim countries that could ensure that surplus funds are absorbed and utilised in local/regional markets. One of the most discouraging phenomena of recent decades, namely, that of a flow of surplus funds from the oil-rich countries of the Middle East to the West, is largely due to the absence of adequate investment facilities. In spite of recent developments that have already affected the financial situation of most Muslim/Arab oil-producing countries, such as the loss of revenues due to the decline in the price of oil and the enormous expense of the Gulf War on the countries of the Gulf, this flow of funds to the West continues to threaten the vitality and survival of Muslim economies. In a recent article in *The Financial Times* of London, Roula Khalaf wrote that 'acceptance of Islamic banking is growing', but that the Qur'ānic prohibition against receiving or paying interest has meant that 'about 75 per cent of Islamic banking funds are invested in short term commodity (futures) trades'. The same report estimated that 'funds invested in an Islamic way in the Arab world may amount to $50 billion–much of it is used for commodity trades'. To give an indication of the place of investment and where the money goes, we further read that commodity trading is conducted 'in return for a fee by a middleman–often a western bank, like Citybank– that arranges for a trader to buy goods on an Islamic bank's behalf ... and the western banks have always been happy to oblige'.[1]

In view of this, and in the light of the *Sharīᶜah* principle of permissibility (*ibāḥah*) that renders all commercial transactions permissible in the absence of a clear prohibition, the verdicts of not only the Mecca-based Fiqh Academy but also of many Muslim scholars who have proscribed futures trading and declared it totally forbidden is a most discouraging form of imitation (*taqlīd*). This body of opinion is mainly founded on the analysis that futures trading does not fulfil the requirements of the conventional Islamic law of sale–and turns a blind eye to the fact that futures trading is a new phenomenon which has no parallel in the conventional law of *muᶜāmalāt*, and should therefore be governed by a different set of rules. This imitative approach also fails to relate the issues at hand to the normative guidance of the Qur'ān and *Sunnah*, which can support a different calibre research and an affirmative ruling on the subject. The title of

Roula Khalaf's article, 'An Inherent Contradiction', portrays the concern on the part of Islamic banks and investment institutions to observe the letter of the Qur'ānic ruling on usury, but also underscores their failure to act for the benefit and prosperity of the Muslim masses. The nature of the problem must be that the Islamic legal advisors to these institutions have limited their understanding of the Qur'ān to the literal meaning of the text alone, and have not applied any juristic insight or imagination to the task of alleviating the dismaying economic predicament faced by Muslims. In answer to the question of whether Islamic banks may invest in futures or not, Khalaf tells us that this 'depends on the bank's Sharia board, whose members are experts in the Koran but less so in the field of bank options ... It is up to each institution to say what is Islamic'.[2] This is, of course, an expected result of what Khalaf called 'the absence of a standard interpretation of the Sharia', and if allowed to continue it 'will dampen further development of the industry'[3] as a whole and slow down efforts to enable financial institutions in the Muslim world to enhance and diversify their own resources.

This enquiry shall review the existing literature on the subject and then proceed to develop a fresh perspective on it. The central feature of this research will be to offer a different interpretation of the source materials of the *Sharīʿah* as to how an issue of vital importance to the economic viability of the Muslim community should be tackled, namely, not through facile reliance on the negative positions of *taqlīd*, but through bold yet upright approaches to research on issues of Islamic commercial law.

An Outline of the Issue

The juristic debate over the validity or otherwise of futures revolves around five points. Firstly, that the countervalues in these sales are both non-existent at the time of contract: no goods are delivered at the time and no price is paid. The contract that is concluded is, therefore, said to be no more than a paper transaction and not a genuine sale. Consequently, futures sales consist merely of an exchange of promises made for the sole purpose of speculative profit-making. To validate a sale from the perspective of the *Sharīʿah*, it is necessary that at least one, if not both, of the countervalues should be present at the time of the contract. Either the price or delivery of the subject matter may be postponed to a future date, but not both. Secondly, the proponents of the prohibitive argument also state that futures trading is invalid in the eyes of the *Sharīʿah* as it consists of short-selling in which the seller neither owns nor possesses the commodity he sells. The reason given for the prohibition is that the essence and purpose of a sale is to transfer ownership of the object of sale to the buyer; if the seller does not own the underlying commodity in the first place, he cannot transfer ownership. Thirdly, that futures sales fall short of meeting the requirements of *qabḍ*, that is, the taking into possession of the subject-matter prior to resale. A fourth issue has been raised over the deferment of both of the countervalues to a future date, which effectively turns futures sales into what is known in jurisprudence as the sale of one debt for another (*bayᶜa'l-kāli' bi'l-kāli'*), which is said to be forbidden. And lastly, that futures trading partakes of speculation that verges on gambling and consists of uncertainty and risk-taking (*gharar*). The element of gambling in futures is also said to be that it causes volatility with the cash market prices of commodities. Most of these issues proceed entirely from an Islamic juristic perspective on the validity of a conventional sale, except for the issue of gambling, which features in Islamic law as well as other literature on the subject. Some early studies on futures recorded the view that futures encourage price volatility and tend to destabilise the market. More recent research has actually supported the opposite view: that futures tend to reduce price volatility and have a stabilising influence on the market.

A trader who enters a futures contract, whether as a buyer or seller, is required to pay an initial deposit of about ten per cent of the contract value. The actual price is paid upon delivery, that is, when the buyer wishes to take delivery, at which time the countervalues change hands. But actual delivery only takes place in about two per cent of all contracts. As for the rest, traders usually enter a reverse transaction prior to maturity, and settle their accounts with the clearing-house. In this way the trader terminates his contract. He may take a profit or a loss, but the offsetting of transactions prior to maturity is a unique feature of futures trading that enables traders to move in and out of contracts and seize the opportunity to make a profit. To give an example, the owner of a bakery feels that wheat prices are likely to rise within the forthcoming months, so he decides to lock-in the current market price of wheat at $2.50 per bushel and buys four June contracts of 5,000 bushels each for December delivery. He instructs his broker accordingly, who concludes the transaction on his behalf and pays a margin deposit of $5,000 in a segregated account in his own name. The trader is now long four wheat contracts that are due to mature in December. There are two possibilities: either the buyer remains in the open position until maturity and takes delivery in December or, alternatively, he decides, some time during the interval, to offset his position by selling four wheat contracts of the same quantity and delivery month for $2.55 a bushel and make a profit of $1,000. This is what usually happens: the parties to a futures contract generally prefer to offset their positions since this saves on transaction costs, storage fees and administrative difficulties; they prefer to enter a reverse transaction at a time when they can realise a profit. After reversing the trade, the buyer's net position is zero. The clearing-house recognises this and the party concerned is absolved from any further obligation.

A trader who chooses to enter a futures contract may be a genuine hedger, as is shown to be the case in our example, who may buy or sell a futures contract in order to protect himself against drastic fluctuations in the price of commodities. The other, and more likely possibility is that the trader is a speculator who enters the market with the sole intention of making a profit out of the price movements of commodities during the contract period. Upon closer examination, however, we may find that the distinction which we have just attempted between hedgers and speculators is more conceptual than real, for it is difficult to distinguish the two in categorical terms: hedgers are also speculators who take a certain risk and speculate over the likely movement of prices. Even a trader who enters the market in order to hedge a position may well decide to sell later, when the price moves in his favour, and then buy again when the prices go down—in which case he has, to all intents and purposes, become a speculator. Since futures sales do not involve the physical movement of commodities, and trading takes place on the basis of a low margin deposit of only about ten per cent of the actual price, they remain wide open to financial speculation and excessive risk-taking, which is often said to resemble gambling. The main reason for having a low margin is to keep hedging inexpensive because higher margins would mean more funds tied up, and add to the cost of hedging.

Literature Review

Among the commentators who have discussed futures, I refer firstly to ʿAbd al-Raḥmān al-Jazīrī, who described a voidable sale (*bayʿ al-fāsid*) as being one in which a movable object is resold prior to taking possession. Thus when a person buys a quantity of cotton or cloth and then sells the same back to the original owner or a third party before taking delivery, the sale is voidable. 'This also applies', al-Jazīrī added, 'to the well-known sale of [futures] contracts in our time ... When someone buys cotton, for example, and then sells it prior to taking delivery from the seller—whether the second sale is at the same price or lower—the sale is voidable.'[4] However, the sale of immovable objects, such as houses and gardens, prior to taking them into possession, is valid as there is no fear of destruction or loss—unless they too are exposed to danger, for instance if the house is located on the sea shore, in which case the sale would be subject to the same rules that apply to movable objects.

It is thus clear that the basic rationale behind taking possession prior to selling is to prevent *gharar*, that is, uncertainty over the seller's ability to deliver in the event of destruction or loss. If the *gharar* in question can be removed effectively, then it would follow that the requirement of taking into possession before selling may be relaxed or even totally omitted.

Umar Chapra is critical of short selling stocks and securities primarily because 'it is a kind of speculation which has no beneficial economic purpose'. This is in contrast, Chapra adds, to short selling in forward and futures sales which involve 'sales of certain agricultural commodities or manufactured goods that perform an economic function ... providing producers as well as users with the assurance that they can sell or receive the goods when ready or needed'.[5] Notwithstanding the 'beneficial economic purpose' that Chapra has identified in futures, he does not pursue the theme and reverts, somewhat unexpectedly, to the stereotypical prohibitive opinion of others when he writes that 'it is generally felt that trading in futures contracts is for purposes other than the exchange of titles'.[6] It seems as though Chapra himself is not convinced of the soundness of what is 'generally felt', but he does not explore the issues and turns to other matters relating to stock market transactions.

This imitative (*taqlīdī*) tendency is also evident in Akram Khan's statement that 'futures trading is alien to Islamic law as it involves trading without actual transfer of the commodity or stock to the buyer, which is explicitly prohibited by the Prophet ﷺ'.[7] The Prophetic *ḥadīth* that Khan has quoted in support of his view was addressed to a Companion, Ḥakīm ibn Ḥizām, and states simply: 'Sell not what is not with you.' As I shall later elaborate, Khan has not taken this *ḥadīth* to its logical conclusion, nor has he explored the juridical meaning of the word 'transfer' (and '*qabḍ*'—'taking possession') which has a bearing on the substance of his statement. Khan has not touched, for example, on the Mālikī opinion on *qabḍ* (which they confine to foodstuffs only) or to Ibn Qayyim al-Jawziyyah's critique of the majority position on the issues of delivery and transfer. Khan has shown no awareness of the juristic discourse of the Muslim jurists (*fuqahā*) and commentators on the issues he has raised, and yet he has spoken in such categorical terms as to say that 'all the transactions in this chain are unlawful' and that 'the Islamic position on futures market is quite clear'.[8]

In his 1983 publication on Islamic law of obligations, Ṣubḥi Mahmassānī stated in passing that 'contracts concerning future things (*al-ashyā' al-mustaqbalah*) are basically invalid, for such things are non-existent at the time of contract—except for the fact that the majority of the jurists have exceptionally permitted certain contracts such as *salam* (forward sale) and *istiṣnā*ᶜ (the contract of manufacture).'[9] It is further stated that proprietary contracts (*ᶜuqūd al-tamlīk*) which seek to postpone transfer of ownership of the object of contract to a future date partake of gambling, which is why they are prohibited.[10]

In his 1982 article entitled 'Ra'y al-Tashrīᶜ al-Islāmī fī Masā'il al-Burṣah'—'The Sharīᶜah Perspective on Bourse-related Issues', Aḥmad Yūsuf Sulaymān reviewed the rules of Islamic jurisprudence on issues such as the sale of objects that the seller does not own, sale prior to taking possession, deferred sales, and sales of the non-existent. Sulaymān directly applied the Islamic juristic rules of conventional sale on these issues to futures and passed prohibitive judgements on almost every issue he considered. In support of his views, Sulaymān has, like Akram Khan and others, relied mainly on the Ḥadīth quoted earlier, namely, that one must not sell what is not with one. Sulaymān too has not looked into the meaning and rationale of this Ḥadīth but instead told us that the *Sharīᶜah* has validated *salam* (forward sale in which the price is paid at the time of the contract but delivery is postponed to a future date) and that this is the only framework within which a deferred sale involving a future delivery can be validly concluded.[11] This is also the position taken by another commentator, Badr al-Mutawalli ᶜAbd al-Bāsiṭ, *Sharīᶜah* advisor to the Finance House of Kuwait, whose prohibitive views on futures are entirely based on *salam*. Since futures fail to fulfil all the requirements of a *salam* sale, they are prohibited. The point is, of course, that in a *salam* sale, one of the countervalues, that is, the price, is paid on a prompt basis although delivery of the subject matter is postponed to a future date. This is the extent, according to both Sulaymān and ᶜAbd al-Bāsiṭ, of the flexibility that the *Sharīᶜah* provides concerning the idea of deferment in a sale. A sale, in other words, in which both the countervalues are deferred to a future date is *ultra vires* and the *Sharīᶜah*, in their views, is totally closed to the prospect of validating futures. To discuss these arguments in details would be beyond the scope of this essay, but I note here that the views of both Sulaymān and al-Bāsiṭ were challenged and refuted by two prominent commentators, Professor ᶜAlī ᶜAbd al-Qādir and Majd al-Dīn ᶜAzzām respectively. ᶜAdb al-Qādir's commentary, written in refutation of Sulaymān's, article was published in the same volume of the *Encyclopedia of Islamic Banks* (in Arabic) which carried Sulaymān's article, and so was Majd al-Dīn ᶜAzzām's response to ᶜAbd al-Bāsiṭ, which appeared in the same collection of legal verdicts (*fatāwā*) that was published by the Finance House of Kuwait. Both these commentators criticised the basic approach that Sulaymān and al-Bāsiṭ took to the issues, and emphasised, in turn, the fact that futures trading was a new mode of trading that called for a fresh response which needed to be formulated in the light of the operative procedures of futures markets.[12] A similar analysis of futures has been advanced by yet another author, ʿAbd al-Karīm al-Khāṭib, who admitted that although futures contracts did not fulfil all the requirements of a conventional contract, they were carefully regulated and they satisfied the basic purpose and rationale of those rules.[13] Al-Khāṭib, ʿAzzām and ʿAbd al-Qādir share the view that the registration and clearance procedures as well as the guarantee functions of the clearing-house are precise, and trading in futures is conducted by trained professionals in a highly centralised and controlled market. In addition, the contract specifications and its related procedures are such that the prospects of uncertainty and risk-taking (*gharar*) are virtually eliminated. The conclusion is thus drawn that futures contracts are valid from the Islamic legal (*Sharīʿah*) perspective.

In its 1985 resolution on stocks and commodities markets, the Mecca-based Fiqh Academy takes a somewhat ambivalent view of futures. The resolution is ambivalent in that it acknowledges the benefits of futures to farmers and commodity traders, but then fails to reflect that evaluation in its final verdict on the subject. The Fiqh Academy also acknowledges that futures trading has developed into a variety of different transactions and that, therefore, each case should be viewed and evaluated on an individual basis. But then this view too is not reflected in its final resolution, which is prohibitive on futures as a whole, without any attempt to address individual issues. Futures trading in stock indices and currencies, for example, is governed by a different set of rules from futures trading in commodities. Furthermore, options and options on futures that are traded on commodity exchanges are different modes of trading altogether, which need to be addressed separately. The Fiqh Academy has not done this, notwithstanding its clear acknowledgement of the availability of a variety of different trading formulas in the futures markets. It has, in sum, taken a similar approach to futures as that taken by Yūsuf Sulaymān and ʿAbd al-Bāsiṭ, and has drawn, not surprisingly, the same conclusion: futures transactions are forbidden because they involve the sale of things which the seller does not own or possess; futures transactions are also concluded over things which do not exist at the time of contract. The Academy's resolution states that most futures sales are not genuine sales in that the parties are not interested in making or taking delivery, and instead aim at making profits from the price movement of commodities. The conclusion is also drawn that the buying and selling of futures contracts is closer to gambling than trading.[14]

A typical example of the approach that western scholars have taken on the issues I have raised is perhaps Rayner's 1991 publication (originally a Ph.D. dissertation), *The Theory of Contracts in Islamic Law*, where she wrote in a broad sweep that, 'the institution of mortgages and insurance, and the combined concepts of share trading, financial futures and spot commodity purchases would clearly be *bāṭil* on several grounds, according to the strict tenets of the *Sharīʿah*'.[15] Rayner continued to specify these 'strict tenets', as far as they related to futures, to include, 'leaving open the payment terms ... not taking possession of objects before resale', and stated that the speculative nature of futures trading brought this line of commerce close to gambling.[16] This is about all that can be found in this work of over 440 pages on the futures contract. Apart from the absence of any specific investigation to support her conclusions, Rayner's comment that futures contract leaves open the payment terms is factually incorrect. The fact is that the previous day's closing prices of all futures contracts are regularly quoted in the press and the exact 'exercise price' is determined when the deal is struck on the trading floor. The delivery month is specified by the maturity date and it is usually the third week of that month. There is a certain mechanism involved in the daily adjustment of the price which is due to a clearance procedure, known as marking-to-market, or daily settlement, but this is simply a clearance procedure which does not change the substance of our statement that the payment terms are, on the whole, adequately specified and guaranteed by the clearing-house procedures.

Lastly, Rodney Wilson exhibited a similar attitude when he wrote that 'forward, futures and options dealings are viewed as potentially corrupting by modern specialists in Islamic finance'.[17] Apart from any attempt to enquire into the details of his statement, Wilson's observation is also inaccurate in so far as it places forward sale (of *salam*) on the same footing as futures and options, for *salam* is clearly valid in Islamic law and it does not therefore qualify for the description 'potentially corrupting'.

Broadly speaking, the methodology I propose to follow in conducting this enquiry is to acquire, first of all, an adequate understanding of the mechanism of futures and the relevant market procedures since only then will we be able to determine the nature of the issues before us in each case and specify the purpose of our enquiry and its hypotheses. I have devoted the whole Part One to an exposition of futures trading at the market-place. In Part Two, I refer to the established rules of Islamic law of contract and verify their application to the proposed issues and determine whether the necessary answers can be obtained from the existing rules of Islamic law. Part Three is devoted to market analysis of options and to a discussion on the permissibility of options from the Islamic legal perspective. I shall ascertain whether or not my hypotheses can be supported by the rulings of the established schools of law (*madhāhib*)—or the independent reasoning (*ijtihād*) of individual scholars, as the case may be—failing which I resort back to the sources of *Sharīʿah*, namely the Qur'ān and *Sunnah*, and ascertain whether the necessary solutions can be obtained through the interpretation and analysis of the sources.

This procedure is expected to apply mainly to issues on which the conventional Islamic law might have something to say. I shall normally follow the established rulings of law if they engender the desired solutions, otherwise I may depart from them and provide the necessary justification for doing so, in which case I may need to advance a fresh perspective on issues which have no precedent in the established law of *muᶜāmalāt*. With regard to matters on which the existing law is altogether silent, the last step in the foregoing procedure is likely to become the first. This would mean that we refer to the Qur'ān and *Sunnah* in the first place and attempt a solution that can be ascertained in the wording, purpose and objectives of these sources. There may be issues which are best determined by recourse to the original principle of permissibility (*ibāḥah*). I have discussed this principle in some detail in a subsequent chapter, where I have traced its Qur'ānic origin and stated that it applies mainly to civil transactions and customary matters. In applying *ibāḥah*, our main task would be to ascertain the absence of specific prohibition in the sources of the *Sharīᶜah*, and not necessarily to search for affirmative evidence to prove the validity of a certain transaction. The test of the validity of a solution that is obtained in this way will remain its proximity to the Qur'ān and *Sunnah*. The answers may be speculative (*ẓannī*) or consist of a mere interpretation but they must be guided by the principles and objectives of the *Sharīᶜah*. In areas where no ruling or precedent can be found in the textual sources or the existing law, the issue will be referred to the prevailing custom and the requirement of considerations of public interest (*maṣlaḥah*). This last is indeed one of the principles of the *Sharīᶜah* which is likely to have a greater bearing on the objectives of this research, especially when no specific guidance of direct relevance can be found in the textual sources and the law of *muᶜāmalāt*. The relevance of *maṣlaḥah* to the subject of our concern should be obvious when it is noted that this enquiry is motivated by consideration of social utility and the identification of legitimate benefits to the community within the framework of the *Sharīᶜah*. Opening the way to *maṣlaḥah*, and obstructing the means (*sadd al-dhara'iᶜ*) which lead to social mischief, backwardness and degradation, constitute the guiding motive and ultimate objective of this research.

I take this opportunity to refer briefly to Muṣṭafā Shalabī's observation concerning new financial transactions on which no precedent is found in the existing works of Islamic law and jurisprudence. Shalabī discusses the two approaches that Muslim scholars have often taken with regard to such issues. One of these is to ascertain a prohibitive ruling or opinion in the works of the jurists of early Islam and then to extend it by way of analogy to the new issue. There are instances, for example, where the jurists of the past have declared certain transactions to be forbidden on grounds of uncertainty and lack of knowledge (*al-gharar wa'l-jahālah*) and so forth.

The second approach taken by many contemporary researchers is to identify an affirmative ruling or opinion in the works of the jurists and then to extend it to the new issue because of certain similarities that are observed between the old and the new cases. Shalabī then tells us that both these approaches are erroneous: experience has often shown that new commercial transactions are often a creation either of statutory legislation which has its origin in non-Islamic sources, in which case they would resemble non-Islamic customs and practices which might combine both benefit and harm. We ought therefore to take this ambivalence into consideration and ascertain their benefits and harms as the case may be and take each on its individual merit, and in doing so attempt original *ijtihād* in the light of the general principles of the *Sharīʿah*. The attempt to project new transactions back into the works of medieval jurists who lived in a different period of history and never encountered the problems we are faced with is bound to be hazardous and fraught with inaccuracy. The Prophet ﷺ has left us with the best example to which we must aspire: he left some pre-Islamic customs of the Arabs, which were deemed beneficial, intact, and overruled others because the harm in them was greater than the benefit. We ought to follow the same approach: instead of holding on to questionable analogies, our approach to new commercial transactions should be guided by either the legitimate public interest (*maṣlaḥah*) which they serve or the manifest harm that can be perceived in them.[18]

We face the question of whether the Islamic law of contract is resourceful enough to cover the vast varieties of contemporary commercial contracts, or whether it only contemplates some limited forms of transactions that were practised in early Muslim communities. How should the Muslim scholar face the commercial reality of the market-place of the present day and age? In responding to these questions, the other commentators, Noor Mohammed and Muḥammad Yūsuf Mūsā, have both expressed the view that the theory of contract in Islamic law should be guided by 'the state of the time, public interest, and overriding spirit of *Sharīʿah*'. Noor Mohammed adds that: had the Islamic scholarship gone through the Industrial Revolution, it would surely have attempted the necessary changes to the conventional law of contract in order to meet the realities of contemporary commerce.[19] We do not welcome change for its own sake, of course, but nor do we forsake it merely for the sake of conforming to outdated juristic constructs. The *Sharīʿah* provides us with the necessary tools (*maṣlaḥah* being one of them) and if the change that is needed can be effected within its given parameters, then it must surely be attempted and secured.

NOTES

1. Roula Khalaf, 'An Inherent Contradiction', *The Financial Times*, December 15, 1994, p.42.
2. Ibid.
3. Ibid.
4. Abd al-Raḥmān al-Jazīrī, *al-Fiqh ʿalā al-Madhāhib al-Arbaʿah*, 5th edn, Cairo, Maktabah al-Tijāriyyah al-Kubrā, n.d., III, p. 191.
5. Umar Chapra, 'The Role of the Stock Exchange in an Islamic Economy', in Sheikh Ghazali *et al.* (eds), *An Introduction to Islamic Finance*, Kuala Lumpur, Quill Publishers, 1992, p. 356.
6. Ibid.
7. M. Akram Khan, 'Commodity Exchange and Stock Exchange in an Islamic Economy', *The American Journal of Islamic Social Sciences*, 5 (1998), p. 91.
8. Ibid, p. 99.
9. Ṣubḥī Mahmassānī, *al-Mawjibāt wa'l-ʿUqūd fi'l-Sharīʿah al-Islāmiyyah*, 3rd edn, Beirut, Dār al-ʿIlm li'l-Malāyin, 1983, p. 327.
10. Ibid, p. 475.
11. Aḥmad Yūsuf Sulaymān, 'Ra'y al-Tashrīʿ al-Islāmī fī Masā'il al-Burṣah', in *al-Mawsūʿah al-Fiqhiyyah al-Iqtisadiyyah*, vol. V, pp. 387ff.
12. For the text of Yūsuf Sulaymān's opinion and ʿAlī ʿAbd al-Qādir's response to it, see their respective articles in *al-Mawsūʿah*, n. 15, p. 387ff. and 438ff. The text of ʿAbd al-Bāsiṭ's opinion and the response to it by Majd al-Dīn ʿAzzām can both be found in Bayt al-Tamwil al-Kuwaiti, *al-Fatāwā al-Sharʿiyyah fī Masā'il al-Iqtiṣādiyyah*, 2nd edn, Kuwait, 1405/1985, pp. 113-130.
13. ʿAbd al-Karīm al-Khāṭib, *al-Siyāsah al-Māliyyah fi'l-Islām wa Sillatuha bi'l-Muʿāmalāt al-Muʿasarah*, 2nd edn, Cairo, Dār al-Fikr al-ʿArabī, 1976, p. 170ff.
14. Majlis al Majmaʿ al-Fiqhī al-Islāmī, 'Sūq al-Baḍā'iʿ al-Burṣah', in *Qarārāt Majlis al-Majma al-Fiqhī al-Islāmī*, Mecca, Rabitah al-ʿAlam al-Islāmī, 1985, pp. 120-5.
15. S. E. Rayner, *The Theory of Contracts in Islamic Law*, London, Graham & Trotman, 1991, p. 297.
16. Ibid.
17. Rodney Wilson, 'Islamic Financial Instruments', *Arab Law Quarterly*, 6 (1991), p. 209.
18. Muṣṭafā Shalabī, *al-Fiqh al-Islāmī bayn Mithāliyyah wa'l-Wāqiʿiyyah*, Cairo, Dār al-Jāmiʿiyyah, 1982, p. 244.
19. Noor Mohammed, 'Principles of Islamic Contract Law', *Journal of Law and Religion*, 6, (1988), p. 115; see also Muhammad Yusuf Musa, 'The Liberty of Individual in Contracts and Conditions According to Islamic Law', *Islamic Quarterly*, 2 (1955), p. 70.

PART ONE

FUTURES TRADING IN THE MARKET-PLACE

CHAPTER ONE

The Futures Contract

I. History in Brief

From very early times and in many lines of trade, buyers and sellers have found it advantageous to enter into forward or futures contracts and agree on deferred delivery of a certain commodity at a mutually convenient time in the future. Whenever something is ordered, instead of being purchased on the spot, a forward or future contract is involved. The price is usually determined at the time of contract but the merchandise is delivered later. For some items, the time-lapse may be only a few days; for others, such as houses, it may be several months before they are manufactured and ready to be delivered.

Market historians have attempted to trace back the history of futures trading to early commercial practices in Europe, Japan and the United States. There are accounts of trade fairs in medieval Europe which were initially seasonal events and then became permanent as trust was established among traders and they were consequently able to conduct forward trading. A bill of exchange known as the 'Fair Letter', which indicated that payment and delivery were to occur at a later date, came into use. Permanent markets developed in Europe, and the year 1570 saw the opening of the Royal Exchange of London for both spot and forward trading.

There are also accounts of contracts for forward delivery of rice in the late seventeenth century in Japan, a practice which was associated with feudalism. The Shogunate rulers of Japan issued a decree that feudal lords should spend half of the year in Edo (now known as Tokyo), the Shogunate seat of government. The feudal landowners were therefore absentee landlords for half of the year. Many were used to an extravagant lifestyle and, in order to meet their expenses in the city environment of

Edo, they issued warehouse receipts to wholesale and retail merchants against their anticipated crops. The merchants bought the receipts against their anticipated needs, a practice which is synonymous with modern-day hedging.[1]

Historical records indicate that the Arabs preceded the rest of the world by several centuries in forward trading and the use of commercial papers. It is particularly interesting to note that soldiers and government officials during the early Umayyad rule (late seventh century/first century *Hijra*—when many of the leading Companions were still alive) were issued commodity coupons (*ṣukūk al-badā'iᶜ*) in lieu of the pay. Imam Mālik has thus stated in his *Muwaṭṭa'* that *ṣukūk al-badā'iᶜ* found currency among people and they were brought and sold prior to maturity. Then Zayd ibn Thābit and 'another man from the Companions of the Prophet ﷺ called on Marwān ibn al-Ḥakam and said: Are you permitting usurious sale, O Marwān? To this he said: I seek refuge in God, what is this? Then they said: People buy these *ṣukūk* and then sell them prior to maturity. Marwān then sent his guards to chase up the coupons and return them to the original owners.' The episode is also recorded in *Ṣaḥīḥ* Muslim on the authority of the Companions, Abū Hurayrah and Salmān bin Yāsar. According to this report, Marwān then addressed the people and declared these sales prohibited.[2]

The issue was evidently over the sale of foodstuffs prior to taking possession (*qabḍ*), in that the coupon holder should have taken possession of the foodstuffs prior to resale. Many jurists have proscribed the transaction in question just as there are others who held that the government issued these coupons to its employees in lieu of their pay, and they basically represented a debt on the part of the government. As the Shāfiᶜī jurist al-Nawawī stated, although this may have some irregularity with regard to *qabḍ*, the sale of *ṣukūk* was, nevertheless, lawful according to the Shāfiᶜī school of law. The papers in question were issued as credit notes to facilitate payment to the employees, and the latter were within their rights to sell them and 'this degree of departure from the rule on the grounds of *maṣlaḥah* and leniency (*al-rifq*) to the soldiers was tolerable'.[3] I have elsewhere addressed the juristic issue over *qabḍ* (taking possession) and its relevance to futures. The point here is that *ṣukūk al-badā'īᶜ* were identical to what we know as warehouse receipts, and the basic concept thereof is present in the contemporary futures contract. The reason that this kind of commercial practice—and certain other related ones such as the letter of credit (*ḥawālah*), bills of exchange (*safātij*) and promissory notes (*ruqᶜ al-ṣayārifah*)[4]—found acceptance so early in the history of commerce is due to the Qur'ānic approval of deferred liability transactions, that is the concept of *mudāyanah* (see Qur'ān 2:282) and the explicit validation of forward sale (*salam*) in the *Sunnah* of the Prophet ﷺ. I shall discuss these in some detail later. The basic purpose of the present discussion is to give a glimpse of the early history of the commercial practices of the Arabs, something that is often overlooked in the relevant literature in English. In more recent times, however, it is the midwestern city of Chicago that has been widely acclaimed as being the largest centre of futures trading in the world.

Chicago's location at the base of the Great Lakes and in the north-eastern corner of the Great Plains made it a logical market centre for grain farmers to meet with merchants from the populous East Coast. In around 1848, railroads were built into Chicago from all directions, and then the Illinois-Michigan Canal was opened, all of which contributed to Chicago's potential as a major trading centre. The grains market was, however, susceptible to price volatility, due partly to climatic factors, a lack of adequate storage facilities and the absence of practical methods of determining the grading, delivery and payment terms of agricultural produce. In 1848, a group of local merchants founded the Chicago Board of Trade (CBOT) with a relatively small membership of 82, in order to minimise abuse in the grain trade, and to promote orderly methods and uniformity in commercial practices. In 1858, the CBOT restricted trade to members of the exchange, and new rules were subsequently adopted in the 1860s which evolved the ad hoc system of forward contracting into futures trading in a centralised market. These rules include the deposition funds for guaranteed performance, standardised contract terms, procedures to be followed in the event of delivery failure, standard delivery procedures and more reliable methods of payment.

Historically, the futures contract represents an outgrowth of the forward contract. In America, until the mid-nineteenth century, the farmer usually bore the brunt of market fluctuations, with the natural pattern of seasonal crops generally encouraging fluctuation in commodity prices. This was because most farmers were ready, almost all at the same time, to sell soon after the harvest. The supply was well in excess of demand at that particular time, which resulted in lower prices for the new crops. The farmer could either sell at a low price, or store his crops, which naturally involved additional costs and exposure to risk.

The opposite situation was experienced at the end of the crop year. As the season's crops were consumed, supply diminished and this resulted in higher prices. The grain merchants were often forced to buy the bulk of the year's supply during the harvest period so as to avoid paying high prices later in the year. In order to keep their mills running, manufacturers too competed with each other for the dwindling supplies.

To protect themselves against seasonal price fluctuations, producers and consumers of agricultural commodities began to buy and sell for forward delivery. These transactions, which became known as 'to-arrive contracts', involved a binding sale by a farmer to a buyer for a quantity of grain to arrive 10, 20, 30 or 60 days later. For example: a miller agrees on 1 April to buy 5,000 bushels of corn from a farmer for $2.20 per bushel. The corn is to be delivered on 1 June. The buyer and the seller have agreed on a price for a product 'to arrive' two months later—hence the term 'to arrive'.

Although trading forward went a long way to protect buyers and sellers against the risk of price fluctuations, forward contracts did not eliminate the risk of financial loss and could easily prove disadvantageous to the parties: if the price of the underlying commodity in a forward contract rose before delivery was due, the seller would stand to lose out on profit. The buyer too remained apprehensive of a price decrease, and would incur a loss if the price of the commodity in question fell during the interval.

Furthermore, the possibilities of failure to deliver, or consignments of sub-standard quality, and of buyers who default or are unable to pay, exposed both the buyers and sellers in forward contracts to risks that they naturally wanted to avoid. To provide protection against loss, insurance houses began to establish themselves in and around the various exchanges and met the demand for insurance against possible defaults. Due to the time-lapse between the dates of agreement and delivery, the forward traders required a deposit to be paid to an independent third party as earnest money. The introduction of deposits of good faith money created a demand for borrowing, to which the banks were quick to respond by extending credit, charging interest from the date of deposit to the date of delivery. The added costs of both interests on loan and insurance were naturally reflected in the forward selling price. These developments eventually led to the standardisation of contracts. The market participants organised themselves into an exchange and set up the necessary rules to establish strict standards of size, quality and grade; among themselves they mutually guaranteed performance on all contracts. This was to avoid the cumbersome process of negotiating the specific terms of each and every contract. The exchange was also a central meeting place and, eventually, the only place where trading was done, in contradistinction to forward trading, which was not confined to any particular place. This development marked the formation of the first commodity futures exchange which reflected the interests not only of farmers and grain merchants but also of all those associated with the production and marketing of commodities.

Eventually, these to-arrive contracts were bought and sold many times prior to contract maturity and physical delivery. Many other people who were not in the grain trade were willing to assume the risk but were not willing to take actual delivery. These were speculators who were interested in a possible gain from the price movement of the underlying commodities. The merchant with a contract who did not want to absorb the risk at all could thus transfer ownership of the contract to a third party, namely, the speculator who was willing to take a chance solely in the hope of making a profit.

Although the first to-arrive contracts were not transferable, the printed documents that were developed to specify the grade, quantity and time of delivery of the goods soon began to be traded as valuable instruments. These alterations to the initial to-arrive contracts resulted in the creation of a futures market in which a contract was readily tradable before delivery. The contract thus became a negotiable instrument on its own and represented a viable addition to the actual trading of commodities in the cash market. A set of additional rules that were introduced to ensure orderly trading in futures also included the following:

a) the commodity selected for trading had to be easily gradable;

b) prices had to be reported openly and be equally accessible to all traders;

c) buyers and sellers were required to establish financial responsibility and comply with a set of rules to that effect.

Subsequent developments along these lines led to the formation of clearing-houses and their elaborate procedures, as discussed below, which guaranteed the performance of contracts and ensured the smooth settlement of contracts by offset or eventual delivery.[5]

The commodity futures market differs from the forward market in that physical delivery hardly takes place in futures, whereas actual delivery does take place in forward market transactions. The non-delivery aspect of the futures market evolved gradually in response to the actions of certain large buyers who would continue buying large quantities of the same maturity date. Ultimately, the sellers were 'cornered' because of shortages in cash market supplies. To redress this situation, the sellers were allowed to deliver a different grade of the same commodity, but to protect the buyers who did not wish to receive delivery, they were allowed to re-sell the futures contract without getting delivery. In this way, manipulations by buyers led to sellers being given a certain option to vary the grade, and this in turn resulted in buyers being given the choice not to accept delivery by entering an offset or a reverse transaction.[6]

The principle upon which commodity futures markets have always been based is that like may be exchanged with like if readily and reliably available in large or 'bulk' amounts of identical quality. This transferable quality of the standardised futures contract also meant that the contract itself commanded a price, just as the actual or 'physical' goods did when traded in the cash market.

The flexibility that the futures contract offered, compared to the forward contract, can be illustrated as follows: consider a grain farmer who wishes to sell his August crop ahead of time in April; if he sells a forward contract, delivery is obligatory whether it be taken from his own crops or someone else's. If between April and August, his crops fail due to bad weather, he has a real exposure to risk for he must fulfil the terms of his forward contract on the agreed date. If he sold futures contracts rather than contracting forward, his risk from this exposure could be reduced. He could 'sell' his August crop in April by selling an August delivery futures contract. If by late June he considered that he had little chance of harvesting his anticipated crop, he could offset a part, or all, of his commitment in the futures market simply by purchasing an August contract at the price for such contracts that prevailed in June. In August, after the crop harvest, he could let the futures contract go into the delivery process or, more commonly, offset his obligation in the futures market by purchasing a reciprocal 'buy' contract and then sell his actual crop in the cash market. If prices had risen, the loss on his futures contract would be offset by the additional price gain in the cash market in August. In this way the grain farmer, as well as the miller, manufacturer and hedgers, could all protect themselves in the futures market against possible price changes in the spot market.[7]

II. Contract Specifications

A futures contract is an agreement to buy or sell a specific amount of a commodity or financial instrument at a particular price on a stipulated future date. The price is determined between buyer and seller on the floor of the exchange, and the contract obliges the buyer to purchase the underlying commodity and the seller to sell the commodity unless the contract is sold to a third party before the settlement date. In *SFC Finance Co. Ltd. v. Masri*,[8] J. Leggat defined a futures contract as 'a legally binding commitment to deliver at a future date, or take delivery of, a given quantity of a commodity, or a financial instrument at an agreed price'. The contract, if allowed to run to its termination, is fulfilled by a cash payment on the delivery date based on the settlement price for that day, and actual delivery of the underlying commodity. By definition, every contract has two principals: a buyer and a seller. The buyer, known as 'long', agrees to take delivery of the underlying asset and the seller, known as 'short', agrees to make delivery. The parties do not negotiate the terms of their agreement as these are all standardised except for the price, which is settled on the floor of the exchange. The delivery months are normally standardised, but the actual day of delivery is determined by the seller and the exchange: when the seller gives notice of his intention to deliver to the clearing-house, the latter assigns that delivery to the oldest long position. The buyer is thus uncertain of the time and place of delivery until the moment he is notified by the clearing-house. Relatively few contracts (about two to three per cent) end in actual delivery, but the fact that delivery is a possibility makes a contract's value in the delivery month differ only slightly, if at all, from the cash market price. Contracts are thus standardised in regard to the type of commodity, the size of the contract, the pricing unit, the exchange on which trading takes place, the last quoted price and the delivery month. The contract information also determines the grade and size of the underlying commodity, but the seller is nevertheless allowed to make delivery of a different grade of the same commodity. For significant variations in the grade and place of delivery, however, the seller may have to discount the price.[9]

Unlike securities, where a company may offer a set number of stocks for sale, a commodity contract exists whenever there is a buyer and a seller. Contracts exist when both the buyer and seller mutually agree to transact business at a given price. Thus there is no limit to the number of futures contracts that can be created. The process of contract creation can theoretically go on as long as buyers find sellers and vice versa. This is a feature of the commodities market which makes the establishing of a position easier, when compared, for example, to the stock market. 'Going long' in the stock market means buying stock and paying for it, whereas 'going long' in commodities means buying a futures contract that involves the possibility of accepting delivery. 'Selling short' in the stock market means selling the stock one does not own. In commodities, however, since contracts can be created indefinitely, selling may involve two situations: selling short for the purpose of making delivery, or selling to liquidate a position.[10]

III. Registration of Contracts

Except for the screen-based computerised exchanges, trading is generally conducted by open outcry auction on the market floor and deals are struck through a series of shouts and hand signals. The details of commodities on offer are already known and advertised and all that is needed is agreement in principle and specification of the type and number of contracts. Upon conclusion of a contract, a record of the transaction is made, and a trading slip is signed by both the seller and buyer or their agents. The contract is then registered with the clearing-house following the various checks to confirm that the trade actually took place. Once a contract is duly registered, it becomes legally binding and the registration statement, or contract note, serves as legal proof of the parties' rights and obligations.

As long as the contract is outstanding, the seller is under obligation to deliver the stated amount of the commodity, and the buyer is similarly under obligation to accept delivery and pay for it. However, both the buyer and seller are at liberty to terminate their obligations, almost unilaterally, by offsetting and liquidating the contract. Thus a futures contract to sell can be satisfied by delivery or by offsetting it with a buy transaction. Similarly, a futures contract to buy can be satisfied by taking delivery or by an offsetting transaction in the opposite direction: if A sells 5,000 bushels of wheat for delivery in December, he can liquidate the sale by purchasing 5,000 bushels of wheat for delivery in the same month. Since the clearing-house is a party to both these contracts, the purchase would offset the sale. After the reversing trade, the net position of the seller or buyer is zero, and the party concerned is absolved of any further obligation.

IV. Commission Fees

Unlike stock market transactions, brokerage commission in commodities are paid only after both the buying and selling transactions are completed. Commissions are incurred on a round turn basis. This is the practice of charging a single commission to both buy and sell a futures contract. Thus when a contract is bought, the commission may not be charged until it has been liquidated by a subsequent sale in the same delivery month, or until delivery is taken. Commissions paid are usually less than those in land, precious goods and securities. Commission rates are usually based on the number of contracts bought or sold and are unrelated to the amount of money involved in a transaction. Less active customers tend to come under house rates, but for high volumes of trade, a lower rate may be negotiated. The 'house rate' in the United States can be $40 to $80 per contract, but for active participants, the rates can be as low as $15 to $25 per contract. A day-trade commission, charged when a position is established and closed the same day, may be half that of the normal round-turn rate.

There are other convenient aspects to futures trading when compared to trading in stocks. The commodity trader is not concerned with dividends, interest payment, handling certificates, rights offerings, proxies, ex-dividend dates, conversions, or any other of the host of factors that might burden a security trader. The market mechanisms of futures concerning delivery are also such that the trader has less to worry about as regards deliveries than the security traders. If he is short, he cannot get delivery; if he is long, he can avoid delivery by simply selling his position before the delivery month arrives.[11]

V. Margin

All commodity transactions in the futures market are margin transactions in which the trader, whether buyer or seller, is required to deposit a margin ranging from two to ten per cent of the face value of the contract. This is not a partial payment of the price but a good faith deposit to guarantee the fulfilment of a contract. It is intended to protect the seller against the buyer's default, should prices fall, and the buyer against the seller's default, should prices rise. Margin money is normally deposited in the buyer's own account, but a general power of attorney is granted to the broker to withdraw money whenever necessary from the account, or in the event of default to close the account. The broker will have the authority to sell out or buy in because the customer will have signed a consent form when the account was opened. But if the money is not used and the trader has fulfilled his commitments, it is returned to him. The investor is also entitled to withdraw any balance in the margin account in excess of the initial margin.

There are two types of margins, namely, original margin and maintenance margin. Original margin is the deposit that must be made when a futures position, long or short, is initiated. The precise amount of this margin is often determined on the basis of the price volatility of the underlying commodity and other factors. It is usually ten per cent of the contract value, which is roughly equal to the maximum daily price fluctuation permitted for the contract in question. Margin requirements are set by the commodity exchanges, but they cannot be below the minimum established by the Commodity Exchange Authority. Maintenance margin is an additional margin required by the broker from the client. When there has been a price decline or advance on the contract that effects a paper loss in the margin account, the client must deposit additional, or maintenance, margin. Most exchanges set maintenance margin at about seventy-five per cent of the initial margin and, when this level of price movement occurs, the broker demands additional deposits from the trader to bring the position back to the initial margin level.[12] Under normal circumstances, minimum original margin requirements for a given item might be adjusted up or down only several times in the course of a year. In periods of rapid price changes, margin requirements might be adjusted on a weekly, or even daily, basis.

Futures exchanges are guided by two opposing considerations when determining the appropriate levels for margin requirements. On the one hand, margins must be low enough to allow the broad participation, which is essential for market liquidity. On the other, they must be high enough to ensure the financial integrity of the market. The relative smallness of the initial margin is justified partly because there is another safeguard built into the system, known as marking-to-the-market, which is discussed below in Chapter Five.

VI. Delivery

As mentioned earlier, very few futures contracts actually lead to delivery of the underlying asset. The rest are closed up prior to the delivery date. Delivery is nevertheless an important factor, and it is the possibility of eventual delivery that determines the prices of futures. The three salient aspects of delivery in futures are the delivery notice, delivery grades, and the delivery period.

(a) Delivery Notice. When the seller decides to make delivery, his broker issues a 'notice of intention to deliver' to the exchange clearing-house. This notice declares how many contracts will be delivered and, in the case of commodities, the grade of the commodity, its price, the place of delivery and the day on which delivery will be made. One point which it does not clarify, however, is the name of any specific individual to whom delivery should be made. The exchange then chooses a party with a long position to accept delivery. This is usually a buyer who has remained in the long position for the longest period. The delivery date is most often the business day following the issuance of the notice. Parties with long positions must accept delivery notices. However, if the notices are transferable, they have a short period, usually half an hour, to find another party with a long position who is prepared to accept the notice from them.[13]

(b) Delivery Grades. In the early twentieth century in the United States, legislation was introduced authorising the federal supervision of grain grading and inspection. This establishment of standard grades is said to have been the single most important development to facilitate futures trading. Because of this, a customer does not actually have to view the physical commodity before accepting delivery. The buyer can be confident of a product that will be delivered several months down the road because of the consistencies specified by the standard grades.

The seller has the option of delivering any grade within a range of grades as permitted by the exchange rules. Sellers are given this choice in order to enable a steady supply at stable prices. Variation in grades may, however, be compensated for with premiums for higher grade or discounts in price for inferior grades. Premiums and discounts are normally determined by differences that are observed in the cash market between the various grades.

In some futures contracts, such as those concerned with financial instruments or gold, there is normally only one deliverable grade, and no question of grading is therefore expected to arise. This also means that the problem of premium or discount versus grade does not arise in the trade of these contracts.

(c) Delivery Period. The period during which delivery can be made is defined by the exchange, and varies from contract to contract. Commodities are traded up to twelve or eighteen months ahead of delivery. Some are traded only in selected months which take account of the harvest and market times. The selection of a few months for trading is practical because this method adds to market liquidity. Financial futures, on the other hand, almost always trade in a regular pattern of months, ninety days apart (i.e., March, June, September and December). Most futures contracts expire in the second half of their delivery month. December corn, for instance, expires about one week before the last day of that month. Two to three weeks before the termination of the contract in question, the delivery period usually begins. It is during this two to three weeks that most contracts must be settled by delivery. The seller holds a negotiable receipt issued by the authorised warehouse, where the underlying commodity is stored, certified as to grade and prepared for delivery. Delivery is made by the transfer of the endorsed receipt from the seller to the buyer. At this time the buyer hands over a certified check and the delivery is complete. The party taking delivery is then responsible for all warehousing costs. In the case of livestock futures, there may be costs associated with feeding and looking after the animals. In the case of financial futures, delivery is usually made by wire transfer. For all contracts, the price paid is usually based on the previous day's settlement price adjusted for grade, the delivery location and so on. The whole delivery procedure, from the issuance of the notice of intention to deliver to the delivery itself, takes two to three days.[14]

As stated earlier, the seller in a futures contract is allowed the flexibility to choose to deliver at any time during a certain period. It is generally optimal for the seller to deliver as early as possible. This is because the future prices tend to decrease nearer maturity, and also because the interest that can be earned on the cash received outweighs the benefit of holding the asset. It is therefore reasonable to assume that delivery will often take place at the beginning of the delivery period.[15]

VII. Types and Subject-Matter

The types of futures contracts that are traded fall into five categories. The underlying goods traded may be agricultural or metallurgical commodities, interest-earning assets, foreign currencies or stock indices. In the agricultural sector, contracts are traded in grain (corn, oats and wheat), oil and meal (soybeans, soy meal and soy oil, sunflower seed and oil and palm oil), livestock (cattle, including live hogs), poultry (eggs and live broilers), forest products (lumber and plywood), foodstuffs (coffee, cocoa, orange juice, potatoes and sugar) and cotton. For many of these, several different contracts are available for different grades or types of the commodity in question. Most of the goods have more than one delivery month. For some relatively inactive contracts, there may be trading in only one or two delivery months in the year, whereas active commodities may have trading in up to eight delivery months. In addition to metals, the metallurgical category includes petroleum contracts, since they share an important attribute, namely, that they are both indefinitely storable. Contracts are thus traded on gold, silver, silver coins, platinum, palladium, copper, heating oil, crude oil, gasoline and propane.

Futures contracts on interest-bearing assets only began in 1975, but trading in them has rapidly increased since then. Contracts are traded on Treasury bills, notes and bonds, on bank certificates of deposit, Eurodollar deposits and GNMAS, which are government-backed single family mortgages. A number of contracts are traded on instruments with a three-month maturity period (the T-bill, Eurodollar and CD contract). This makes it possible for trading based on anticipated interest rate differentials for the same maturity to take place.

Active futures trading of foreign currencies dates back to the inception of freely floating exchange rates in the early 1970s. Contracts are traded on the British pound, the Canadian dollar, the Japanese yen, the Swiss franc and the German mark. Contracts are also listed on French francs, Dutch guilders and the Mexican peso, but these have met with only limited success. The foreign exchange futures market represents the one case of futures trading which still enjoys a very active forward market.

Futures contracts for stock indices began in 1982, and have proved fairly successful. Four different exchanges in the United States began to trade contract on three indices: the Standard and Poor's 500, the New York Stock Exchange Index and the Value Line Index. Many new entries in this market are being planned, including one by the Kuala Lumpur Options and Futures Exchange (KLOFFE), which is scheduled to begin trading in stock index futures in the near future. One of the peculiarities of trading in stock index contracts is that they are generally cash-settled, and do not admit the possibility of actual delivery. A trader's obligation must consequently be fulfilled by a reversing trade or a cash settlement at the end of trading.

For some commodities, there are contracts on a number of exchanges, in which case they usually differ in contract specification. Wheat contracts, for example, are traded on the Chicago Board of Trade, the Kansas City Board of Trade, the Mid-America Commodity Exchange and the Minneapolis Grain Exchange. Whereas the standard contract size in wheat is 5000 bushels for most exchanges, the Mid-America Exchange trades a contract for 1000 bushels, which appeals more to the smaller trader. There are also differences in the kinds of wheat contracts that are traded on these exchanges and, more importantly perhaps, their delivery destinations are different, and this can make a particular contract more appealing than others.[16] When a commodity contract is traded on more than one exchange, it tends to encourage inter-market spreading and arbitrage activities. Some financial futures, the Nekkei 225 index for example, are listed on more than one exchange internationally, so as take advantage of time zone differentials, and hence the existence of round the clock trading. Positions taken on one exchange, say, the CME in Chicago, are often reversed out on another exchange, such as the SIMEX in Singapore.

NOTES

1. Hussin, 'Glimpse at the Futures Markets Then and Now', *New Straits Times*, January 20, 1985, p. 20.

2. Abū al-Ḥusayn ibn al-Ḥajjāj al-Nīshāpūrī Muslim, *Mukhtaṣar Ṣaḥīḥ Muslim*, ed. Muḥammad Nāṣir al-Dīn al-Albānī, 4th edn, Beirut, al-Maktab al-Islāmī, 1402/1982, Kitāb al-Buyūʿ; *Tanwīr al-Hawālik*, II, 141; see also *Sirāj al-Niẓām al-Maṣrafī*, p. 27ff.

3. Yaḥyā b. Sharaf al-Nawawī, *al-Majmūʿ Sharḥ al-Muhadhdhab*, Cairo, Idarah al-Tabaʿah al-Munīriyyah, 1345/1925, IX, 267; see also Aḥmad Ḥassan, *ʿAmal Sharikāt al-Istithmār al-Islāmiyyah fī al-Sūq al-ʿAlamiyyah*, Jeddah, al-Dār al-Saʿudiyyah li'l-Nashr wa'l-Tawziʿ, 1407/1986, p. 286.

4. For details see *Sirāj al-Niẓām al-Maṣrafī*, pp. 20-9.

5. New York Institute of Finance, *Futures. A Personal Seminar*, New York, New York Institute of Finance, 1989, pp. 2-5; R. J. Teweles and F. J. Jones, *The Commodity Futures Game*, 2nd edn, New York, McGraw Hill Book Co., 1987, p. 10; Robert E. Fink and Robert B. Feduniak, *Futures Trading. Concepts and Strategies*, New York, New York Institute of Finance, 1988, p. 10; David and Bettelheim Courtney, *An Investor's Guide to the Commodity Futures Markets*, London, Butterworths, 1986, p. 8; Hussin, 'Futures Markets', p. 20.

6. Khan, 'Commodity Exchange', AJSS, 5 (1988), p. 98.

7. Courtney, *Investor's Guide*, p. 12.

8. *SFC Finance Co. v. K. Masri*, All England Law Reports (1986) 1, p. 44. Teweles

(*Commodity Futures*, p. 22) also describes the futures contract as a firm legal agreement between a buyer or seller, and an established commodity exchange or its clearing-house in which the trader agrees to deliver or accept, during a designated period, a specified amount of a certain commodity that adheres to the particular quality and delivery conditions prescribed by the commodity exchange on which that commodity is traded. For a similar definition, see Fink, *Futures Trading*, p. 28 and Azzah Mahidin, 'Still Far to Go', *Malaysian Business*, December 1-15, 1990, p. 38.

9. Teweles, *Commodity Futures*, pp. 23-4; NYIF, *Futures*, p. 8.

10. Lawrence J. Gitman and Michael D. Joehnk, *Fundamentals of Investing*, 3rd edn, New York, Harper and Row, 1988, pp. 516ff; Robert W. Kolb, *Understanding Futures Markets*, Glenview, Scott Foresman & Co., 1985, pp. 2-3; NYIF, *Futures*, pp. 4-7; Benton Gup, *The Basics of Investing*, 3rd edn, New York, John Wiley, 1986, p. 487ff.

11. NYIF *Futures*, p. 18; Teweles, *Commodity Futures*, pp. 18-19.

12. NYIF *Futures*, p. 52 ff; Teweles, *Commodity Futures*, p. 55; Gitman, *Fundamentals*, p. 523; Kolb, *Understanding Futures*, p. 7; John Hull, *Introduction to Futures and Options Markets*, Englewood Cliffs, New Jersey, Prentice Hall, 1991, p. 24.

13. Frank K. Relly, *Investment Analysis and Portfolio Management*, 2nd edn, Chicago, The Dryden Press, 1985, p. 765; Teweles, *Commodity Futures*, p. 61.

14. NYIF, *Futures*, pp. 84-86; Hull, *Introduction to Futures*, p. 31; Fink, *Futures Trading*, p. 52; Kolb, *Understanding Futures*, p. 54.

15. Hull, *Introduction to Futures*, p. 72.

16. Kolb, *Understanding Futures*, pp. 9-12.

CHAPTER TWO

Uses of Futures

This discussion attempts to provide the basis of an assessment as to whether the benefit and public interest (*maṣlaḥah*) that is likely to be served by trading in futures would justify its availability to the public, specifically in Muslim countries. A verdict in favour or against futures trading on grounds of utility and *maṣlaḥah* is, in the final analysis, bound to partake of value judgement. The aim here is to provide relevant data for a considered judgement based on an adequate knowledge of the material advantages of this area of modern commerce. The *maṣlaḥah* will in due course be evaluated by the available guidance in the sources of *Sharīʿah*. The main point of the evaluation, discussed in Part Two of this work, is whether the *maṣlaḥah* in question conflicts with any of the clear rulings of the *Sharīʿah* on *gharar*, gambling and *ribā'*, or whether it violates any principle of the existing law. The uses of futures may be summarised under six headings as follows.

I. A Regular Market

Because of the introduction of futures trading, agricultural crops need not be traded on traditional seasonal patterns of availability at only certain times of the year any longer. Conventional trade in such commodities was the victim of seasonal factors such as over-supply at harvesting time and shortages towards the end of season, each affecting prices accordingly. The futures market, however, facilitates regular, permanent and centralised trading in commodities. This is a function of market liquidity and the regular presence of a large number of traders in the market at any given time. Commodity contracts are bought and sold at all times on the basis of descriptions of grade and quality. The market mechanism guarantees the fulfilment of a contract, and provides regular access to trading in a range of commodities and financial instruments which perform important economic functions. The fact that contracts are concluded on the basis of description only contributes to the continuity and presence of a regular market in futures.[1]

II. Better Planning

Futures and options enable producers, merchants and suppliers to plan their production and marketing activities ahead of time. One person may want to deliver wheat nine months hence but not know anyone who wishes to receive it, while someone else may want wheat for delivery at that time and not know a seller. A commodity exchange that establishes a standard futures contract for a specified amount and type of wheat makes it possible for traders to execute their transactions on the floor of the exchange without personal contact. A textile factory that is about to sign a contract with a cloth merchant would face uncertainties, on the one hand, over determining the price of sale and time of delivery of the finished goods to the merchants, and on the other over the quantity and timing of cotton supply from the cotton growers. All parties in the chain can use the futures market to co-ordinate their production and marketing activities to remove uncertainty and to be able to conclude definitive agreements with one another.[2] From a social point of view, the farmers who often belonged to the poorer class hitherto had to suffer the ravages of price fluctuation. Futures encourage price stability and thereby alleviate some of these injustices.

Ever since its inception in the early 1970s, more and more people have turned to futures as a way of combating inflation. Although high rates of inflation drastically affect other investments like stocks and bonds, the opposite is true of commodity futures. Commodities tend to do well in periods of high inflation. Whenever wheat and rice double in price, futures contracts in these commodities reflect a similar trend. This positive correlation between commodity futures and inflation rates means that they are a better hedge against inflation than common stocks.[3] Trading in futures thus offers the advantage of fighting inflationary pressures, and it appeals especially to suppliers and contractors who undertake to use or deliver large quantities of commodities within a certain period of time.

III. Futures as Insurance

Futures and options are generally seen as important tools for risk management. Traders use the futures market to limit their exposure to loss on account of the price volatility of commodities. Farmers, producers and manufacturers are all exposed to the risk of price fluctuation of the commodity they produce or have on their inventories. The futures markets provide them with the opportunity to hedge themselves against possible losses. As one of the principal uses of the futures market, hedging consists of entering an equal but opposite position in both the cash and the futures markets. The possible loss in one is then likely to be offset by a gain in the other.[4]

Futures contracts provide a useful means of reducing risk because they are highly liquid instruments that can be entered into or liquidated on short notice at almost any time. They are also 'paper' transactions which do not involve the immediate transfer of the underlying assets or of any certificates, which means that they have the added convenience of saving the customer from having to worry about safe-keeping and the timely delivery of papers. The credit exposure is always to a futures clearing-house, which is also an advantage since it means that traders do not have to worry about the credit-worthiness of their opposite numbers in a transaction. Finally, low margin rates and commissions make futures trading relatively inexpensive when compared to trading in stocks and shares. By providing risk reduction techniques, futures trading helps to reduce the possibility of bankruptcy and provides the hedger with the least expensive means of insurance against adverse price movements.[5]

IV. Cost-Efficiency

Futures are cost-efficient and enable traders and producers to finance their supply requirements more efficiently. For example, in an attempt to ensure its raw material requirements for several months ahead, a textile factory may find that futures prices for the commodity it needs are lower than the cash market prices. It would, therefore, be cost-efficient for the factory to utilise the futures market for its purposes, and ensure necessary supplies at the right time. The alternative to this might be to purchase very large quantities in the spot market and face transportation, storage and insurance costs. Only the futures market provides this facility. Suppose also that the same textile factory owner has a large inventory of a certain commodity in store, but fears a drop in the prices in the future; in this case, the futures market would enable him to sell a futures contract for a certain delivery month and protect himself against possible losses.[6]

V. Futures as Price Indicators

The futures market provides a means of price discovery. Since the prices in the futures markets provide information that is not readily available elsewhere, the markets serve people's needs by enabling them to ascertain the future prices of commodities. One need not be a trader in the market to receive this information, for it is available in the newspapers, and may be used by traders and non-traders alike.

Under normal circumstances of adequate supply, the price of a physical commodity for future delivery will be approximately equal to the present cash price, adjusted by the amount it costs to carry or store the commodity from the present time to the month of delivery. It is due in large measure to this pattern of relationship between the cash and futures prices of commodities that futures tend to serve as market barometers and indicators of the direction in which cash prices are likely to move. They determine prices for the present and project them into the future, thereby serving as a directional force, guiding the movement of goods into market channels. Because of a close connection between futures prices and expected future spot prices, individuals and organisations can obtain information on the price trends of commodities. The mechanism involved here is known as the 'random walk approach': the closer a futures delivery month comes to the cash month, the narrower the difference in price should become, until it is extinguished by the future month becoming the 'cash' month. Price forecasts based on this approach have generally been more consistent than those based on other techniques. Since price information on futures is widely disseminated, the market participants are better informed, and can act more judiciously in order to reduce the random element in price movements.

The free and open distribution of information on price trends enables traders to compete on nearly equal terms. Insider information is at a minimum, and prices tend to reflect as accurately as possible the interplay of market forces. Futures prices are admittedly inaccurate at times, yet there is evidence to suggest that forecasts based on futures prices are not excelled by other forecasting techniques.[7] It is thus concluded that modern futures markets tend to be 'extremely price efficient. This means that their prices tend to reflect or discount known fundamentals very quickly, even before any formal analysis is conducted'.[8] Researchers have also found considerable support for the proposition that a change in cash prices frequently results in a similar change in futures prices. Although cash and futures prices do not always move together exactly, a material movement by them in opposite directions is quite unusual.[9] Recent studies have shown that futures tend to lead the cash markets in price changes, especially with regard to financial futures.

VI. Futures as Price Moderators

Futures trading tends to have a generally restraining effect on the cash price of commodities. The determination of futures prices takes into account the supply and demand prospects, storage costs, inflationary trends and seasonal factors, as well as political and international developments, national and climatic emergencies and so on. Many of these are, however, unpredictable and represent the random aspects of price fluctuation in both cash and futures prices. As far as the predictable factors are concerned, futures prices have a realistic influence on cash prices, which are generally on the conservative side and therefore averse to speculation and risk-taking. Futures prices for commodities that incur storage costs are, on the whole, lower than the cash market prices. Research findings are, in the main, consistent on this conclusion, which means that futures trading reduces the element of uncertainty and enhances stability in cash market prices. To illustrate this, suppose that there is currently a plentiful supply of wheat at relatively low prices, but forecasts for the coming season indicate that the crop will be small and that prices will rise. Speculators will take advantage of the current low prices and buy large amounts of wheat. By doing so, they will, in effect, be withholding wheat from current consumption in order to sell it in the future, thereby adding to the supply at that time. Such actions have a moderating effect on the price, because the purchase of the wheat at the present time tends to hold the price up, and the sale of wheat in the future tends to have a restraining effect on the price. Thus if the speculators and arbitrators are functioning properly, they will stabilise both the price and supply of commodities over a period of time.[10] Critics have often claimed that futures trading leads to abnormal price volatility, 'but the facts say otherwise. Numerous studies have supported the premise that liquid futures markets increase price stability'.[11] One of the most influential studies on the effects of futures in the United States was the 1984 'A Study of the Effects on the Economy of Trading in Futures and Options', which was jointly prepared by the Board of Governors of the Federal Reserve System, the Commodity Futures Trading Commission, and the Securities and Exchange Commission. This study concluded, *inter alia*, that 'financial futures and options markets serve a useful economic purpose, primarily by providing a means by which risks inherent in economic activity (such as market interest rates and exchange rate fluctuations) can be shifted from firms and individuals less willing to bear them to those more willing to do so'.[12]

To sum up, futures trading serves a beneficial purpose by providing marketing facilities and trading strategies which the cash markets do not provide. Futures trading enables better planning in the production and supply of basic commodities; it also serves as a minimum cost insurance which can protect commodity suppliers against unforeseeable risks. Similarly, futures trading enables traders to hedge against inflation, as the latter also tends to be an efficient indicator and moderator of prices. These are some of the benefits of futures trading which relate well to the needs and well-being of an agro-based economy, especially under conditions where the agricultural sector might be faced with disadvantages compared to the industrial sector of the economy. We often find that income levels of farmers and agricultural workers in developing Muslim countries do not compare well with those of other sectors. Futures trading is likely to enhance efficiency and better planning, and thereby realise the potential benefits for its participants. The *Sharīʿah* law concept of public benefit (*maṣlaḥah*) is, of course, an inherently relative one in which the possible benefits are weighed against the harm that might be involved. We also note, in this connection, that there is no such a thing as absolute *maṣlaḥah*. Prominent Muslim scholars, including al-Shāṭibī, have categorically stated and concluded that almost all *maṣāliḥ* (pl. of *maṣlaḥah*) involve some disadvantage or even harm, but may still be validated because of the preponderance of their likely benefits.[13] We are, of course, aware of the harmful aspects of futures trading, especially with regard to speculative risk-taking, which might resemble gambling, and the claim that it might have a destabilising effect on the cash market prices of commodities. We have already investigated this latter claim and concluded that it is not substantiated by research findings, much of which has, in fact, led to the opposite conclusion, namely, that futures trading has a moderating effect on prices. It remains for us to investigate the nature and scope of speculation in futures, and to ascertain whether the speculative aspect of futures should be equated with gambling or rather with commercial risk-taking of a questionable nature, whose benefits may nevertheless be seen to outweigh its possible harms.

NOTES

1. Ḥasan, *ʿAmal*, pp. 242-3.
2. Mūsā, *al-Bayʿ*, p. 150; Ḥasan, *ʿAmal*, p. 240.
3. Gitman, *Fundamentals*, pp. 516-17; Relly, *Investment Analysis*, p. 790.
4. Herbert B. Mayo, *Investments: an Introduction*, Chicago, Dryden Press, 1984, p. 515; Gup, *The Basics*, p. 482; Arthur L. Rebell *et al.*, *Financial Futures and Investment Strategy*, Homewood, Dow Jones-Irwin, 1984, p. 315; Teweles, *Commodity Futures*, p. 30; Wilson, 'Islamic Financial Instruments', p. 206; Shahabuddin, 'Future', *The Star*, November 27, 1991, p. 6.
5. NYIF, *Futures*, pp. 20 and 504; Teweles, *Commodity Futures*, p. 29; Relly, *Investment*, p. 789.

6. NYIF, *Futures*, p. 30; Courtney, *Investor's Guide*, p. 137.
7. Relly, *Investment*, p. 790; Kolb, *Understanding Futures*, pp. 55-8; NYIF, *Futures*, p. 30, Fink, *Futures*, p. 204.
8. NYIF, *Futures*, p. 95.
9. Teweles, *Commodity Futures*, p. 34. Bakken, 'Futures Trading', *Encyclopedia Americana*, XII, 208.
10. Cf. Gup, *The Basics* p. 482. Mayo, *Investments*, p. 509; NYIF, *Futures*, p. 30; Ḥasan, *ʿAmal*, pp. 241-2.
11. NYIF, *Futures*, p. 30.
12. Quoted in Fink, *Futures Trading*, p. 13.
13. Abū Isḥāq Ibrāhīm al-Shāṭībī, *Muwāfaqāt fī Uṣūl al-Aḥkām*, ed. Shaykh ʿAbd Allāh Dirāz, Cairo, Maṭbaʿah al-Tijāriyyah al-Kubrā, n.d., pp. 27ff.

CHAPTER THREE

Futures Contracts and Conventional Contracts

There is no parallel to futures contracts in the conventional Islamic law of transactions (*fiqh al-muʿāmalāt*). Although we may find that some of the provisions of the law of transaction do relate to certain aspects of the futures contract, the latter tends in many ways to depart from the basic framework of conventional contracts. In the light of the differences that I shall presently explain, to draw direct analogies between futures contracts and conventional contracts with a view to applying the rules of the one to the other would seem to be less than justified. The salient differences between futures and conventional contracts may be outlined as follows.

1. In a futures contract a person can sell a contract and undertake to deliver a specified commodity without actually owning the commodity in question. One can thus sell a commodity one has not previously bought. In futures, one who sells a contract is said to be 'short' precisely because he does not own the underlying commodity. Similarly, one who buys a contract is known as 'long' because he does not receive anything at the time of contract and nothing is delivered to him until the contract maturity date. The rules of law concerning the conventional contract of sale proscribe the sale of what the seller does not own and, in respect of certain foodstuffs, of what the seller does not possess at the time of contract. The position is different in futures, as there is no requirement of ownership or of having in one's possession the underlying commodity of the contract.

One of the essential requirements of sale, as Ibn Rushd explained, is that 'there must be two parties to the contract and they must both own the values they are exchanging, or else they must represent the authority of the owner'.[1] To this al-Kāsānī adds that if the seller can acquire ownership of the object he is selling only after the sale, the contract is invalid. An exception to this is the contract of forward or advance sale (*salam*), which is valid despite the fact that it is the sale of a non-existent object. The Prophet ﷺ has proscribed the sale of what is neither owned nor possessed. It is thus reported that one Ḥakim ibn Ḥizām used to sell things which he did not own. He accepted payment in advance and then purchased the object in the market and delivered it to the customer. The matter was brought to the attention of the Prophet ﷺ and he ruled that: 'You may not sell what is not with you.' Al-Kāsānī continues: this is so because selling an object entails the transfer of ownership, which is not possible unless the seller owns it prior to sale.[2] A more detailed analysis of this *ḥadīth* shall be attempted later; suffice it to note here that the *ḥadīth* is not explicit on the meaning al-Kāsānī has indicated. For the last three words, '*mā laysa ʿindak*'—'what is not with you', can be read as a reference to ownership or possession or the seller's ability to deliver. It should also be remembered that the Prophet ﷺ validated transactions such as *salam* in which the subject-matter of sale is neither owned nor possessed. The question that needs to be raised concerning this *ḥadīth* should surely be about its basic rationale and purpose, which was evidently to ensure fulfilment by the parties of their obligations, and to pre-empt the fear that the seller may be unable to make delivery, for one may own something which one cannot deliver, or possess something which one does not own. The point is therefore over fulfilment of contract and not necessarily over ownership or possession. This fear over non-fulfilment is, however, practically non-existent in the futures market and the question of fulfilment of contract, that is, delivery by the seller and payment of the price by the purchaser, is guaranteed in all cases. Hence we are looking at a different reality where the rationale of the prohibition does not seem to apply.

2. Another peculiarity of the futures contract, which represents a total departure from conventional contracts, is that either party can unilaterally terminate the contract at any time after the registration of the contract but prior to its maturity. Either the buyer or the seller may close out their position by offsetting and entering a reverse transaction which cancels their contractual liability altogether. A contract of sale is normally concluded, under the rules of law, by virtue of a valid offer and acceptance and, once concluded, neither of the parties may unilaterally terminate the contract. The conventional contract envisions two parties, one of whom makes the offer which the other accepts. In a futures contract, the transaction between two brokers/traders takes place on the floor of the exchange, following which each party reports the transaction to the clearing-house for registration and clearance. When this is done, the contracting parties have only to deal with the clearing-house and not with one another. The

former interposes itself between the parties and effectively terminates the link that was initially established when the buyer and seller concluded the contract. From that moment onwards, both parties must deal with the clearing-house, which stands as a fully qualified guarantor between them.

3. Futures contracts are highly standardised and are traded in standardised units, which are established and defined by the exchange. For example, a contract of grain (wheat, corn, soybean, oats etc.) calls for delivery of 5,000 bushels. In soybean oil, 60,000 pounds constitutes a contract. Futures contracts in three-month Treasury bills call for a delivery of $1 million T-bill. A gold futures contract is traded in 100 ounces. Standardised contracts also exist for foreign currency and financial instruments that are listed on the exchanges in the United States and Europe. The manner in which contract quantity and prices are standardised usually reflects the physical property of the underlying asset and commercial custom. Because of this high level of standardisation, there remains little room for negotiation between buyers and sellers. Standardisation is, in turn, only possible over fungible commodities which can easily be substitute by an equivalent. These includes goods that are storable for some time and goods in common demand, which means that they are regularly traded in the stock market. Futures contracts are concluded solely on the basis of a description of the type and quality of the underlying commodity, without any sampling or viewing. The contract information appears in the daily press and almost all the material information and contract specifications are predetermined by the exchange that offers the contract on its listing. Brokers who represent the contracting parties only select the type of contract and determine the quantity and price. Futures contracts are also standardised in respect of prices but, since the price that is quoted represents the closing price for the previous day, the bargain price is subject to the agreement of the parties. One of the main purposes of standardisation is to facilitate the interchangeability of similar contracts within the same or different delivery periods. Standardisation is also essential for the clearing-house operations, which are to match up and offset contracts of identical volume within the same delivery period. And lastly, standardisation facilitates liquidity and the daily flow of large volumes of trade on the floor of the exchange.

Although conventional forward contracts serve some of the functions of futures contracts, they tend to be inflexible and hard to transfer to a third party. Forward contracts lack the capacity to be matched with one another as they vary in important details that generally reflect the personal requirements of the parties. The parties are contractually bound to each other until the time of delivery. On the other hand, the anonymity of the parties in a futures contract, due in large measure to standardisation, has facilitated liquidity and the substitution of contractual obligations, which are not possible in forward contracts. Futures contracts give traders the opportunity to enter and exit futures obligations whenever it is beneficial for them to do so. Hedging, arbitrage and speculative strategies become possible and traders are enabled to take intermediate positions at any interval between the spot price and the futures delivery price, at nominal costs.[3]

Forward contracts are similar to futures contracts in that they are both agreements to buy or sell an asset at a certain time in the future for a certain price. Both can be used for hedging or speculative purposes, and yet they differ in a number of ways. Forward contracts are, as already noted, private arrangements between the parties, and there is generally a single delivery date rather than a range of dates such as is available in futures contracts. The delivery date and price in a forward contract are fixed. In a futures contract, on the other hand, the parties can close out their positions at any time prior to the maturity date at a price that may be different from the exercise price. Under the forward contract, the whole gain or loss is realised at the end of the life of the contract, but in a futures contract, the gain or loss is realised day by day because of the daily settlement procedures. Since forward contracts are not traded on exchanges, standardisation is not relevant to them, nor do they have to conform to the standards of a particular exchange.[4]

4. The nearest concept to a futures contract found in the scholastic expositions of *fiqh* is *ʿaqd al-muḍāf* (deferred contract), a contract in which both delivery and payment are specified but postponed to a future date. It is a contract which is concluded in the present but whose consequences are postponed to a specified time in the future.[5] A deferred contract of this type is valid in principle, but only with regard to cases which do not involve immediate transfer of ownership, such as agency (*wakālah*) and lease and hire (*ijārah*). A contract of sale (or gift), which under conventional law involves immediate transfer of ownership, may not be concluded by way of *ʿaqd al-muḍāf*, that is, with the delivery and payment of price both deferred to a future date. Conventional law does validate sales in which either the delivery or the payment of price is deferred to a future date—such as forward sale (*salam*) and delayed sale (*bayʿ al-mu'ajjad*) respectively—but not when both of these are postponed, apart from the contract of manufacture (*istiṣnāʿ*), which is exceptional. The reason for this, according to the majority of jurists, is that contracts which involve immediate transfer of ownership serve their purpose best when they are concluded on a prompt basis and 'there is no need for deferment. Besides, in deferring such contracts, there is the possibility of indulgence in gambling (*muqāmarah*)'.[6] It is thus stated that whenever transfer of ownership

of an object is possible at the present time, postponing it to a future date is not valid, except for certain contracts, such as bequests or the appointment of an executor (*wāṣīy*), which, by their nature, can only take effect in the future.[7] The contract of manufacture (*al-istiṣnāʿ*) is another case in point. Although this is a type of sale in which both delivery and payment are postponed to a future date, it has, nevertheless, been exceptionally validated by both customs and general consensus (*ijmāʿ*).

The main objection to *ʿaqd al-mudaf* is that it involves an element of risk-taking (*gharar*) and gambling (*muqāmarah*). This element is identified as the possibility that the price might fluctuate or alter during the interval between the time of contract (when the price is fixed) and the time of actual payment. A comparison of the *ʿaqd al-muḍāf* to the futures contracts shows that they tend to differ in certain respects: although a price is quoted and advertised in a futures contract, this is only a projected price, known as the 'exercise price'. The actual price in the futures contract is variable and is re-written, technically at least, every day. The real price in the futures contract, known as the 'settlement price', is always determined at the time of the execution of contract, that is, upon offset or delivery. Moreover, the marking-to-market procedure, which is explained below, generates daily cash flows, and this tends to interfere, technically at least, with the concept of fixed price. Furthermore, the juristic concept of *ʿaqd al-muḍāf* obviously contemplates conventional sales in the open market in which no guarantees are envisaged to ensure fulfilment of contractual obligations by the parties. This absence of guarantees and the fear that the parties may fail to fulfil their obligations apparently still exists in conventional sales, and the deferment of both the countervalues to a future date still involves risk-taking of the sort that may, or may not, be seen to be acceptable. The position is, however, totally different in futures contracts, where the fulfilment of contractual obligation is fully guaranteed by the clearing-house, there remaining no fear at all of failure in respect of either delivery or payment of the price by the seller and the buyer respectively. Thus the fear of risk-taking and gambling that prompted Muslim jurists to proscribed a deferred sale by way of *ʿaqd al-muḍāf* are seen to be eliminated in futures contracts. Finally, the point that there is no need or benefit in postponing both delivery and price—as the jurists maintained—is evidently no longer sustainable. This logic was good in its own time, but obviously cannot be extended to futures contracts.

5. Another feature of the futures contract, which sets it apart from conventional contracts, is that futures trading can only take place on organised exchanges. A futures contract is consequently a totally controlled contract and can, if necessary, be regulated and effectively controlled either by the house rules of the exchange or by legislation. The

vast majority of contracts are processed by professional staff and brokers, who only register contracts which fulfil the required formalities. The conventional contract of sale, on the other hand, is not susceptible to effective controls of this kind except perhaps in some sectors such as real property, but that too only up to a point. Beyond this, conventional contracts are not supervised and therefore deviation from the norm can only be dealt with *post facto*, often when one of the parties lodges a complaint. Consequently, for speculation, hoarding and profiteering, for example, to be checked in the open market and in respect of trade and transactions among individuals and traders is a much more difficult task than controlling excessive speculative risk-taking on the futures market.

6. Buying and selling on the commodity exchange takes place only on the basis of depositing a margin, which is a good faith deposit representing a fraction of the purchase price of the underlying commodity. The parties to a futures contract are required to pay an original margin of about ten percent of the purchase price. The commission rates that are payable to futures brokers are also lower compared, for example, to the stock market commission rates. Because of these low levels of cash requirements, traders can buy huge contracts for relatively small amounts of margin deposits. Moreover, there are no interest charges on the difference between the total value and the margin for a futures contract. This is because the futures contract is a deferred delivery contract, which means that the payment of the purchase price is deferred until the date when the contract is actually scheduled for delivery. Since no money changes hands and nothing is delivered at the point of entry in a futures trade, no interest is chargeable.[8] The trading volume is generally high, as is liquidity in commodity trading. It is often said that the high liquidity levels of futures trading encourage huge speculative risk-taking, which partakes in gambling. If this is proven to be the case, then quantitative restrictions on the volume of trade can be imposed, or it can to some extent be checked, perhaps through margin requirements and taxation, so that individual traders are discouraged from taking high speculation risks. In the United States, the Commodity Futures Trading Commission (CFTC) has, for some commodities, imposed maximum limits on the positions that an individual trader can control. This limitation is also intended to prevent possible 'corners' and 'squeezes'. Furthermore, the CFTC requires larger traders to file periodic reports on their trading activities in regulated commodities.[9] Another way of controlling the speculative side of futures trading may be to raise the margin requirements for traders who enter trading above a certain limit. There may indeed be other ways by which speculation can to some extent be checked. This will be discussed later, when the subject of speculation in futures is addressed in more detail.

7. Futures contracts are for limited periods. The holding period for agricultural contracts seldom exceeds ninety days, and generally cannot exceed a year, because the contracts are deliverable within that period. Financial futures such as treasury bond futures have delivery periods extending to almost three years, but the volume of trading in the distant delivery contracts is limited. In contrast, a conventional contract of sale does not envisage a limited holding period, although forward sales (i.e., *salam*) normally provide for a time frame for delivery; stock-market transactions are not time-bound and positions in stocks can be held almost indefinitely.

8. As stated earlier, performance on a futures contract—delivery as well as payment—is guaranteed by the clearing-house. In upholding this guarantee, the clearing-house marks a contract to market at the end of every trading day, thus ensuring that in the unusual event of default by a member broker and his customer, its obligations are limited by the maximum daily price change. If the futures price has moved in favour of the customer during the day, his account is credited with the amount of the price change. Any unfavourable price change is similarly debited to the customer's account. When the customer's margin falls to the level of the maintenance margin as a result of daily settlement, he may be required to top up the margin back to its original level. The performance guarantee that the clearing-house provides for futures contract and the detailed procedures which are geared towards that end, are peculiar to futures contracts. Neither the conventional contract of sale nor the stock-market transactions are protected in the same way. In regular stock trading, for example, there is no daily marking-to-market of the customer's positions.[10]

NOTES

1. Ibn Rushd al-Qurṭubī, *Bidāyah al-Mujtahid wa Nihāyah al-Muqtaṣid*, 5th edn, Cairo, Muṣṭafā al-Bābī al-Ḥalabī, 1401/1981, II, 172.
2. ʿAla'uddīn al-Kāsānī, *Badā'iʿ al-Ṣanā'iʿ fī Tartīb al-Shara'iʿ*, Cairo, Maṭbaʿah al-Jamaliyyah, 1328/1910, V, 146.
3. Cf. Courtney, *Investor's Guide*, p. 11ff; Fink, *Futures Trading*, pp. 28-9.
4. Hull, *Introduction to Futures*, pp. 38-43.
5. ʿAbd al-Nāṣir Tawfiq al-ʿAṭṭār, *Naẓariyyah al-Ajal fī al-Iltizam fi'l-Sharīʿah al-Islāmiyyah wa'l-Qawānīn al-ʿArabiyyah*, Cairo, Maṭbaʿah al-Saʿādah, 1978, p. 112; ʿAbd al-Ḥāmid Maḥmud al-Baʿlī, *Ḍawābiṭ al-ʿUqūd fi'l-Fiqh al-Islāmī*, vol. 1, Cairo: Matabiʿ al-Ittiḥād al-Duwali li'l Bunūk al-Islāmiyyah, n.d., p. 151; Ḥusayn, *al-Milkiyyah wa Naẓariyyah al-ʿAqd fi'l Sharīʿah al-Islāmiyyah*, Alexandria, Dār al-Jāmʿiyyah, 1986, pp. 283-4.
6. Ḥusayn, *al-Milkiyyah*, p. 290.

7. Muḥammad Amīn Ibn ʿĀbidīn, *Ḥāshiyat al-Radd al-Mukhtār ʿala'l-Durr al-Mukhtār*, ed. Taha ʿAbd al-Rawuf Saʿd, Cairo, Muṣṭafā al-Bābī al-Ḥalabī, 1386/1966, V, 361-2; ʿUthman ibn ʿAlī al-Zaylaʿī, *Tabyin al-Haqa'iq Sharḥ Kanz al-Daqa'iq*, Cairo, Bulaq, 1313 AH, V, 148; Muḥammad Madkūr, *al-Fiqh al-Islāmī: al-Madkhal wa'l-Amwal wa'l-Ḥuqūq wa'l-ʿUqūd*, 2nd edn, Cairo, Maṭbaʿah al-Fajalah, 1955, p. 396; al-ʿAṭṭār, *Naẓariyyah*, p. 114.

8. Relly, *Investment Analysis*, p. 762.

9. Ibid., p. 762.

10. Ibid., p. 766.

CHAPTER FOUR

The Futures Market

This chapter discusses the institutional structure of the market, that is, the exchange itself, the clearing-house, and the market participants, namely, the hedgers and speculators. Some of the more technical aspects of the market operations, such as the marking-to-market (or daily settlement) procedure, daily trading limits, spreading and disciplinary provisions are addressed in the next chapter.

I. The Futures Exchange

The commodity exchange is a venue where buyers and sellers (or their orders) meet to transact business. All futures contracts are traded on organised exchanges, and what the stock exchange is to listed securities, the commodity exchange is to a growing list of foods, metals, hides, wood, rubber etc. Until recently, traders could choose from a range of about eighty different commodities and assets, many of which were traded on more than one exchange. Commodity exchanges may perform many functions, such as supplying commodities for trading, handling and grading commodities, but basically they exist to provide their members with facilities for trading commodities for future delivery. Futures markets also serve a social purpose by helping people to form a better idea of what future prices will be, so that they can make judicious decisions on their consumption and investment requirements. It may appear strange to regard the provision of a speculative opportunity as beneficial to society. Without question, futures markets do provide opportunities for speculation. However, even if speculative activity is thought of as evil or immoral, there is strong evidence that the presence of speculators benefits the other users of futures markets by helping to provide liquidity.

This benefit extends to other sectors of society too: the individual interested in forecasts of future prices need not enter the futures market to benefit. These forecast are made available for the price of a daily newspaper.[1]

Trading in commodities has flourished in the United States and it is there that the most active exchanges are situated. The Chicago Board of Trade, which was formed in 1848, is the oldest and largest futures exchange in the world. It began as a spot market and started to trade futures in 1865. It is a voluntary, non-profit association of its members. Membership may only be held by individuals, and these memberships are traded in an active market like other assets. Members have a right to trade on the exchange and to have a voice in its operation.

Today there are eleven futures exchanges in the United States and one in Canada. Many others are located in major cities, including London, Hong Kong, Tokyo, Paris, Singapore, Kuala Lumpur, Sydney, Sao Paulo and Jakarta. New contracts are constantly being added while others are dropped for lack of activity. The volume of futures trading generally exceeds that of the cash market trading in commodities. In recent years, the trading volume of futures in the United States alone has exceeded 100 million contracts annually, with a total value of more then ten trillion dollars.[2] All the eleven futures exchanges that are currently active in the United States are separate and independent from one another. Although many individuals and organisations are members of more than one exchange, each exchange, nonetheless, has its own facilities, history and traditions.

Futures exchanges are generally required to be located near the terminals and cash markets of the commodities in which they trade. This allows for the easier standardisation of delivery terms, and enhances the relationship between the physical (cash) price of the underlying commodity and the futures contract prices. The exchanges have two essential features: their members and their 'pits'. The members are futures personnel and independent traders who are associated with the market and submit to its regulations in exchange for the privileges and protection it offers. Several of the newer exchanges are screen-based and computerised and consequently have neither pits nor floor traders.

The pits are those areas at the exchange, usually one for each commodity traded, in which the actual buying and selling of futures contracts takes place. Buying and selling on the floor generally follows a predictable course. Having received the necessary margin deposit from the customer, the broking member of the exchange gives the customer's order to a special broker, known as a 'floor broker', who makes a bid for the specified contract in the pit itself. All bids in the pit must be made by open outcry to ensure that the other brokers and traders have a chance to consider the bid and adjust their own prices accordingly, and also to ensure that the customer actually gets the contract at the market price. Except where screen-based, any trading which avoids open outcry is considered fraudulent and is illegal. This includes prearranged transactions such as 'offsetting' (matching buyers to sellers without putting each trade open to display) and 'cross-trading' (the broker becoming the buyer on the customer's sell order or vice versa). The commodity exchanges also trade option contracts which are discussed in Part Three below. No new contract markets were created to trade options; existing exchanges simply needed to register the options they wished to trade.[3]

As already stated, trading on the floor of the exchange is conducted mainly by certified members, known as Futures Commission Merchants (FCMs). Exchanges do not buy or sell commodities or contracts, nor do they establish prices; their main function is to provide an orderly market by enforcing rules and regulations in order to promote uniform practices among buyers and sellers. They also distribute price and market information and play a role in the adjustment of business disputes.

In contrast with the cash market, where commodities are physically bought and sold on a negotiated basis, in the futures market it is standardised contractual agreements that are bought and sold, rather than the actual commodities themselves. These agreements are predetermined contracts whose terms are defined by the exchange. The futures market also differs from the cash market in that all kinds of goods are traded in the latter, but only certain types of commodities are tradable in the former. Goods that are traded in the futures market must be storable over a period of time, a condition which precludes perishable goods from the purview of futures trading. The goods must also be fungible so that they can be substituted by goods with similar attributes. Furthermore, the goods must be saleable by number, measurement and weight. Items of unique character and value are therefore excluded. The goods must also be transferable from one place to another, and be available in large enough quantities to facilitate bulk trade in a busy market among a large number of traders.[4]

Most futures exchanges are structured as corporations that are owned and managed by their members. The board of directors and various committees are elected by exchange members; the former is often composed of exchange members and a few outsiders who bring balance and special expertise to the exchange management. The exchange rules and policies are set by the board and implemented by a network of committees and other support staff. Exchange members who serve on committees receive no compensation, but do enjoy membership privileges.

Every exchange has a fixed number of available memberships, although the number is occasionally adjusted by the exchange board. Determining the optimum number of memberships is a question largely of the balance needed between liquidity and dilution. If there are too few memberships, the volume of business is likely to be low. Too many membership positions will, on the other hand, decrease the value of an individual membership. As of March 1987, the authorised number of full memberships ranged from a low of 202 on the Kansas City Board of Trade to a high of 1,680 on the New York Futures Exchange.

The exchange authorities usually take into consideration the character and financial responsibility of applicants for membership. As a rule, applicants must be sponsored by two current members. Once an applicant's name is submitted, it is circulated to the membership for comment. The applicant must then appear before the admissions committee, which will make appropriate recommendations to the board of the exchange. Trading on the floor of the exchange is conducted exclusively by members. But the floor privilege is not automatically available, and the trader's badge is not given until the member demonstrates knowledge of the exchange's trading procedures. Although only individuals may be members of futures exchanges, every State exchange permits membership privileges to be conferred on corporations or partnerships by individual members. But the specific requirements for the conferring of membership privileges on a firm vary from exchange to exchange. Some specify that privileges can be conferred only by two or more individual memberships.[5]

The London Metal Exchange (LME) and the London International Financial Futures Exchange (LIFFE) are the largest futures exchanges outside the United States. The LME was founded in 1877 but it was not until 1987 that it became a futures exchange; until then, it was essentially an organised forward market. Contracts were strictly principal-to-principal with no clearing-house system as in the United States. In late 1985, the LME suffered a massive default. The International Tin Council (ITC), a cartel of tin-producing countries, ran out of cash and was unable to perform on contracts worth about $900 million. Because the LME was a principal-to-principal exchange, the losses, which totalled over $300 million, were absorbed by the LME members who held the opposite side of the ITC's long positions. Many observers believed that the problem could have been mitigated if the LME had been subject to the mark-to-market discipline of a clearing-house system. As a result, the LME decided, in mid-1987, to adopt a clearing system and this marked the end of its century old principal-to-principal approach to settlement.[6]

II. The Clearing-house

Although a separate entity, the clearing-house works in close association with the commodity exchange, and it is, like the exchange that it serves, a membership organisation. Membership of the exchange is a prerequisite for membership in its clearing-house, although not all exchange members are members of the relevant clearing-house. Members of the clearing-house are subject to strict financial and other criteria, which must be fulfilled before they can be admitted as certified members.

Anyone who buys a membership on the exchange and obtains a trader's badge is permitted to transact business on the floor of that exchange on behalf of himself and others. However, if that exchange member is not a clearing-house member, then all transactions must be cleared through a clearing member firm. What this means is that the non-clearing member maintains an account with the clearing member, and all trades of the non-clearing members are held in that account. The clearing member firm is responsible for the financial performance of these trades. If the non-clearing member fails to honour these trades, for whatever reason, it is the responsibility of the clearing member firm that carries his account to make good on these trades. Most major brokerage firms are clearing members of the major exchanges and, therefore, take responsibility for their own trades as well as for those of their customers.

Every clearing member firm that trades for its own account must maintain two accounts with the clearing-house: a customer account and a house account. Each account is margined separately, and positions in one cannot be netted against positions in the other. This practice is in keeping with regulations that relate to the segregation of customers' funds.[7]

The parties to a futures contract normally commit themselves to perform certain obligations, at some future date, for which they have not paid. There is thus a need for someone to guarantee the performance of contracts. This is done by the clearing-house, which guarantees full performance of all registered contracts. In the absence of a clearing-house, each party would be responsible to the other. If one party defaulted, the other would be left with a worthless claim. The clearing-house 'clears' all the transactions of one day's trading session before the start of the next, and it guarantees performance for each transaction that it clears. In other words, it guarantees proper and timely delivery to every buyer (if the buyer wishes to take delivery) and payment upon delivery to every seller (if the seller wishes to make delivery). Furthermore, it guarantees payment, whenever a net position warrants payment, on contracts that are to be closed out by offsetting transactions. The clearing-house nets out all the criss-crossing transactions of each day, offsetting contracts of one clearing member with those of others. The clearing-house guarantee enables parties to offset the contract at any time without having to obtain permission from the other party to 'break' the contract. The other party is, of course, the clearing-house itself, through which all trading is cleared and guaranteed. This function is similar to the clearing operation of banking firms, which consists of matching and settling transactions with a minimum of handling of cash transfers and actual deliveries.

Once the contracts are matched up by the clearing-house, the original parties to the contract no longer deal with one another. A contract is matched as soon as the clearing-house has determined that the following data are in agreement: contract commodity and month, quantity, price, contracting parties and clearing members. From the point that these data are verified onwards, the clearing-house assumes the role of the other party to the contract. It becomes the 'buyer' of all contracts that were sold and the 'seller' of all contracts that were bought. The seller has a contract with the clearing-house to sell his commodity and be paid for it, just as the buyer has a contract with the clearing-house to receive delivery. This enables the participants to trade freely in the market without having to concern themselves about the credit-worthiness of their counterparts. The matching of contracts increases the liquidity of the market and its ability to reflect the value and price behaviour of the traded commodities. Since traders are buying and selling identical contracts, the contracts are easily matchable and can therefore be substituted. Once the customer enters a reverse transaction, that is, by buying back the contract that was originally sold or selling one that was originally bought, he no longer has a contractual obligation.[8]

The clearing-house takes no active position in the market but interposes itself between all parties to every contract. In the futures market, the number of contracts bought must always equal the number of contracts sold. Thus if we were to add up all the outstanding long and short positions, the total would always be zero. This is because every transaction on the exchange floor involves a purchase and a sale. The number of purchases accepted by the clearing-house must always equal the number of sales that it accepts. As the intermediary to all transactions, the number of contracts it is long must equal the number of contracts it is short. No 'buy' order at a stated price will go through unless there is a 'sell' order at that price. Thus, trading on the exchange is really about price matching. This is also why screen-based trading, as opposed to open outcry, is possible. The computer simply matches the buy and sell orders. If a contract remains in the 'open' position until maturity, it must be settled, and it is at this point that the clearing-house administers the delivery and settlement of the contract. The seller is required to pass the documents which give title to the commodity (e.g., warehouse warrants) to the clearing-house; these will then be handed over to the buyer upon receipt of payment. The clearing-house then pays the seller.[9]

It is remarkable to note that in the history of futures trading, the clearing-house has always performed as promised. This is partly due to the fact that it maintains no futures market position of its own. Its prime concern is balancing out the transactions and guaranteeing performance. The clearing-house is able to eliminate the risk attached to contract performance, partly through its marking-to-market (or daily settlement) procedure, and also by ensuring that members provide sufficient collaterals to cover their potential liabilities. The clearing-house monitors the size of each member's position daily to ensure that they are not over-extending themselves by building-up large positions which they will have difficulty in fulfilling. It also evaluates each member's ability to make or take delivery when contracts approach their maturity month.[10]

As already noted, a contract can only be registered with the clearing-house by a clearing member. Just as an investor is required to maintain a margin account with his broker, a clearing-house member is required to maintain a margin account with the clearing-house. This is known as the 'clearing margin'. The margin accounts for the clearing-house members are adjusted for gains and losses at the end of each trading day, in the same way as the margin accounts of investors is adjusted. However, in the case of the clearing-house member, there is an original margin but no maintenance margin.[11] In addition to margin deposits, the clearing-house maintains a 'guarantee fund' to which each member is required to contribute as a condition of clearing membership. Throughout the period of membership, the deposit stands as a share in the financial stability and integrity of the organisation. The guarantee fund is usually held, not with the clearing-house itself but with an approved securities fund, and it can only be withdrawn by following a certain procedure. There is yet a third fund, namely, the 'surplus fund', which is accumulated from fees that are charged for clearing each contract. These clearing fees are usually small (about $0.25 per contract) but, even so, the total at the end of each year may be large enough to meet a major part of the operating expenses, and can also be used as a financial guarantee. Clearing member failures have occurred on rare occasions, but 'there has never been a clearing-house failure in the history of the United States futures trading'.[12]

To illustrate the clearing-house operation procedures, assume that on Day 1 a doctor in New York who has his account at FCM A places an order with his account executive to buy one contract of December comex gold. At the same time, a lawyer in Boston sells one contract of December comex gold through FCM B. The orders reach the trading floor at the same time and the floor broker who is acting for FCM A buys one contract from the floor broker who is acting for FCM B at a price of $410.

Because both FCMs are clearing members of the exchange, the traders are taken on their books. At FCM A, the doctor's account shows long one December gold at $410, while at FCM B the lawyer's account shows him short one December gold at the same price. Both the doctor and the lawyer have deposited $1,500 of original margin at their respective FCM. In turn the FCM have deposited original margin for their customers' positions at the clearing-house.

At the end of Day 1 December gold closes at $411, and the doctor has an unrealised profit of $100 and the lawyer an unrealised loss of $100.[13] On the morning of Day 2, after all business of the previous day has been settled, the following transfers and entries are made:

1. The clearing-house transfers $100 from FCMs B's account to FCM A's account. This leaves FCM A with a balance at the clearing-house of $1,600 and FCM B with a balance of $1,400.

2. FCM A credits the $100 to the doctor's account, which raises the doctor's total equity to $1,600.

3. FCM B debits the $100 from the lawyer's account thereby reducing his equity to $1,400.

Several aspects of this transaction merit attention. First, the actual identities of the parties to the transaction are not known by the clearing-house. The latter only knows the positions of its clearing member firms. Second, each clearing member is responsible for the maintenance of a balance at the clearing member firm that reflects his position at the firm. Thus the customer is financially responsible to his clearing member firm, and the latter to the clearing-house. Third, the accounts of all customers and clearing members are brought up to date each day. This process greatly simplifies record-keeping and the transfer of funds. The clearing-house need not know the original price of any transaction. In order to properly credit a member firm's account, all the clearing-house needs to know is the member firm's position and the amount that the market moved up or down that day. Likewise, this is all the FCM needs to know to properly credit or debit its customers each day.[14] This daily marking-to-market reduces the exchange's exposure since failure to respond to a margin call leads to the immediate closure of an account and this reduces the risk of potentially huge losses that could result if losses were allowed to accumulate.

The above examples may also be used to illustrate the offsetting procedure at the clearing-house. Assume that on Day 2 the lawyer decides to cut his losses short by buying back (covering) his short position. Without the clearing-house, he might have to locate the doctor and arrange to unwind the contract at a loss. With the clearing-house he simply enters an order to buy one December gold contract. When the order reaches the trading ring, a floor broker who has a sell order sells one contract at, say, $411.50 to the broker who is acting for FCM B. Thus the lawyer has covered his position, which has been transferred to a different customer, who may be establishing a new short or who may be liquidating a previously held long position. As far as the clearing-house is concerned, one short position at clearing FCM B has been transferred to another clearing FCM. The identity of the customer is not known. All that matters is that the new FCM now has responsibility for the transferred short. The settlement by offset greatly enhances market liquidity, which would not be possible without the central role played by the clearing-house.[15]

III. Market Participants: Hedgers and Speculators

Participants in futures trading, whether individuals or institutions, can be divided into three main groups: hedgers, speculators and arbitragists. The hedgers enter into a futures contract mainly to reduce the risk of loss from price fluctuations in a cash market position. Speculators, on the other hand, are only interested in futures in order to make a profit from the price movements of the underlying commodities. Hedging is the primary economic function of futures markets and the most common method of price-risk management. Arbitragists mainly occupy themselves with arbitrage between cash and futures/forwards and cash, or even inter-market and inter-commodity spreading activities. Arbitragists help to keep prices in different markets and commodities in line with one another, and speculators help to enhance market liquidity. The hedgers consist mainly of farmers and grain merchants with heavy inventories of unsold crops who could face disastrous losses in the event of a material drop in prices, for as long as the commodity is in their possession, tanner and dealers are exposed not only to risks such as fire and theft, but also to the vagaries of supply and demand, the weather conditions and unexpected political developments. They resort to hedging as a means of transferring the risk of loss to other participants in the market. These could be other hedgers who might be offsetting an opposite risk or liquidating another hedge, or simply need the commodity. But more often than not the opposite side of a hedging transaction is a speculator who is willing to assume the risk the hedger wants to shed.[16]

In commodities and financial futures, a natural opportunity is built into the relationship between the futures market and the cash market. Since the price in each tend to rise and fall more or less together, their parallel behaviour can be used by a dealer to decrease the risk in commodities. A loss in one market usually means a profit in the other as long as opposite positions are maintained, one in each market. Futures trading depends on hedging. Markets simply do not come into existence solely to furnish a speculative arena, nor do they persist if hedgers do not find it rewarding to continue to use those markets. Without hedgers there would be no economic justification for futures and options. Hedgers provide actual goods and services to the economy; futures and options enable them to provide these goods and services more efficiently. Hedging allows the risk of price changes to be shifted or shared; hence the costs of production, marketing and processing are reduced, and this is ultimately beneficial to the public.

In addition to transferring risk, hedging can also be used to make a profit, which is why it is difficult to draw a clear distinction between the hedger and the speculator, for hedging is also a form of speculation. Indeed, few trading activities are free of speculation. What the hedger does is to confine, rather than eliminate, risk, and he differs from the speculator in that the variation in his outcome is generally less. The hedger is insured against price risk only if cash and futures prices move in parallel, which is often, although not always, the case. The traditional risk transferral concept of hedging has in many ways evolved into a more dynamic concept of risk management, which aims not only at minimising risk but also at maximising the expected profit.[17]

The presence of speculators in the market enables the hedgers to hedge, since speculators assume the risk that the hedgers want to shed. Finding offsetting hedging trades would be very time-consuming, if not impossible, without speculators bridging the gap. When speculators enter the market, the number of ready buyers and sellers increases, and hedgers are no longer limited by the hedging needs of others. A small number of speculators operate from exchange floors, but the vast majority are non-member customers of futures brokerage firms. In most markets, some hedgers will be long and others short. To the extent that their (the hedgers') positions match, the speculators are not needed for the job of bearing risk. The long and the short hedger can balance each other out, otherwise for every short hedger there will have to be a long speculator and vice versa. Hedging may be a selling hedge, known as short hedge, or a buying, or long, hedge. To illustrate this, suppose that a farmer owns 100,000 bushels of wheat, and is therefore considered long, with the market price at $2 a bushel, but fears a decline in prices and decides to sell 100,000 bushels of futures contracts at $2, which means that he becomes short-hedged. If the feared decline occurs and wheat drops to $185 a bushel, the profit on the short sale of futures exactly offsets the loss on the inventory. An example of long hedge is a merchant who is committed to sell

80,000 bushels of wheat (or its equivalent of bread) at a specified price and time in the future, but who neither owns it, nor has contracted to buy it. He can protect himself by buying a futures position equal in amount to his forward sale and thereby fix the forward costs. Hedging, in this way, minimises the risk of price fluctuation, and offers protection against loss.[18]

Speculators are individuals who buy and sell commodity contracts without wanting to deal in the actual commodities. This differentiates them from the growers, processors, warehousers and other dealers who also buy and sell commodity futures but who really wish to buy or sell the actual commodity. While a hedger is one who assumes a futures position that is equal in quantity but opposite to his cash market position, a speculator, in contrast, is one who trades a futures contract without a corresponding position in the underlying cash asset.[19] A speculator enters the futures market in order to make a profit by taking the risk which the hedgers are not willing to take, although risk-taking is not the only factor that is accountable for making profit. Research findings indicate that speculators' profits are primarily due to their forecasting abilities rather than their risk-bearing function.[20] The speculator in futures is like the typical common stock investor who buys stock when he expects a price increase and sells stock short if he expects a price decline. Active speculation in futures markets tends to dampen extreme price movements. When prices are low, for example, speculators purchase futures in order to add to demand. The effect of rising demand is an increase in price. Similarly, by selling futures when prices are high, speculators decrease demand and therefore help to lower prices.

Speculators differ from one another in several ways. Some trade small positions and some large positions, even to the limits imposed by regulating authorities. The main difference between them is with regard to the length of time for which they are prepared to hold on to a position. A small number may prefer to wait for a full move, which could take months or a year, but most hold their positions for much shorter periods. The overwhelming majority of speculators are either scalpers, who hold a position for a fraction of one trading day, or day traders, who both acquire and dispose of a position within the space of one trading day. These two types of speculators either make a small profit or end up with a net loss.[21] On the other hand, professional speculators, known as position traders, can make consistent and substantial profits. The majority of such profits (up to seventy-five per cent, according to some commentators) are the result of the position traders' ability to forecast short-term price trends; the remaining profits arise from their ability to forecast long-term price trends. Small speculators (non-professionals) can experience substantial losses and higher transaction costs.[22]

Futures trading appeals to speculators because of the prospects of making large profits from relatively small amounts of investment. This is partly due to the fact that a commodity contract controls a substantial amount of the commodity, and the margin deposit required is relatively small compared to the contract value. This high leverage, and the inherent credit guarantee of a futures contract, allows a degree of speculative trading that is not available in the open market. It is also easier for speculators to take short positions in futures because no securities need be borrowed and no financing is required.[23] What is unique about futures is that a speculator can enter the market by either purchasing a futures contract or by selling a futures contract. The speculator's decision about whether he should buy or sell first depends on his markets expectations. Potential gains and losses are as great for the selling (short) speculators as for the buying (long) speculators.

Other market participants are floor traders, who are members of the exchange and make their transactions in the pit or around the ring on the exchange floor. In contrast with other members, who use the services of brokerage houses, floor traders can trade for their own accounts, and are known as locals. They may establish long-term positions or day-trade, or act as scalpers, trading many times each day.[24]

NOTES

1. Cf. Kolb, *Understanding Futures*, pp. 14-15.
2. Cf. Fink, *Futures Trading*, p. 11.
3. NYIF, *Futures*, pp. 4, 22; Teweles, *Commodity Futures*, pp. 26, 547; Courtney, *Investor's Guide*, pp. 38ff.
4. Teweles, *Commodity Futures*, pp. 17ff; NYIF, *Futures*, p. 16; Mayo, *Investment: An Introduction*, p. 513; Kolb, *Understanding Futures*, p. 86.
5. Fink, *Futures Trading*, pp. 86-90.
6. Ibid., pp. 89-97.
7. NYIF, *Futures*, p. 78; *SFC Finance Co. v. K. Masri*, p. 44; Fink, *Futures Trading*, p. 154.
8. R. J. Parker and S. Ramli, 'The Role and Organisation of the Clearing House', paper presented at the KLCE workshop, Johor Bahru, Malaysia, September 28, 1985, p. 3; NYIF, *Futures*, p. 79.
9. NYIF, *Futures*, p. 6; see also Kolb, *Understanding Futures*, p. 5.
10. NYIF, *Futures*, p. 76ff; Kolb, *Understanding Futures*, p. 6; R.J. Parker and S. Ramli, 'The Clearing House Procedures', paper presented at the KLCE workshop, Johor Bahru, Malaysia, September 28, 1985, pp. 6-17; *SFC Finance Co. v. Masri*, pp. 44ff; Relly, *Investment Analysis*, pp. 780ff.
11. Hull, *Introduction to Futures*, p. 26.
12. Fink, *Futures Trading*, p. 163.

13. The reason is that one gold contract equals 100 ounces and the profit is $1 per ounce.

14. Ibid., pp. 155-6.

15. Ibid., p. 159.

16. Kolb, *Understanding Futures*, p. 55; Fink, *Futures Trading*, pp. 63ff.

17. Teweles, *Commodity Futures*, pp. 32-4; NYIF, *Futures*, pp. 145ff; Gup, *Basics*, p. 483.

18. Teweles, *Commodity Futures*, p. 33; NYIF, *Futures*, p. 146.

19. Mayo, *Investments*, p. 505; Relly *Investment Analysis*, p. 786; Kolb, *Understanding Futures*, p. 79.

20. Relly, *Investment Analysis*, p. 776.

21. Teweles, *Commodity Futures*, pp. 29ff; Kolb, *Understanding Futures*, p. 61.

22. Relly, *Investment Analysis*, pp. 776-7.

23. Rebell, *Investment Strategy*, pp. 18-19.

24. Teweles, *Commodity Futures*, p.28.

CHAPTER FIVE

Risk Reduction Strategies

This chapter discusses some aspects of the operational procedures and rules of the market which are designed to contain speculative risk-taking and manipulation in market transactions. The discussion that follows addresses in particular the daily trading limits, marking-to-market, spreading and disciplinary regulations. Some of the specifics of these operations may vary from one exchange to another, but the broad outline offered here represents a fairly accurate picture of these operations.

I. Trading Limits

To prevent extreme price changes, all exchanges limit the amount by which the prices are allowed to move in any one day. There are two types of limits: the daily limit and the daily range, both of which are the key tools of the regulatory policy for preventing squeezes and corners. The daily limit determines the maximum permissible price increase or decrease to the settlement price of the preceding day. The daily range, on the other hand, determines the maximum permissible range in the commodity futures price for the day. These limits are set in order to prevent unreasonable price moves based on undue reactions to news. Securities markets deal with similar situations either by suspending trading until a fair and orderly market is possible again, or by allowing prices to move over a large and unlimited range.

Once the price of the futures contract rises by the permissible daily limit, further price increases are not allowed. Trading can still continue at the maximum price or below. The same applies to declining prices, which cannot fall below the established minimum limits, but trading may still take place at the lowest price and above. Although the daily limit and daily range leave plenty of room to turn a quick profit, traders are often anxious about the possibility of being 'frozen in' by an adverse limit move. It should be noted, however, that in nearly all markets the board of directors, or governors, has the power to change the limits in emergency situations. In some cases, an exchange may decide that the market can trade over the limits. Some exchanges allow greater than normal limits, or variable daily price limits, during periods of extended price volatility. It has been found that limits can prove to be an artificial restraint on a commodity that is advancing rapidly on its own merit and not as a result of temporary circumstances. These limits may be illustrated in the following example. Suppose that a commodity futures price is $4.00 and the daily limit is $0.10. The price could accordingly increase to $4.10 or fall to $3.90 in one day. However, if the maximum daily range is also $0.10, then the price could rise to $4.10 but then could not fall below $4.00, or the price could fall to $3.90 but then could not rise above $4.00 Thus the price could range from $4.10 to $3.90 only if the daily range were twice the daily limit (i.e., if the daily range is $0.20 in this example).

The daily limits on price fluctuations of certain commodities do not apply to trading in the current, or spot, delivery month after the first notice day. But the regular daily limits remain in effect for all other delivery months trading at that time. For example, on 31 December, the first notice day, the daily limit on the January delivery of soybean meal is removed until the contract expires at the end of January. However, the daily limit of $10.00 per ton for the March, May, July, August, September, October and December deliveries remains in effect.[1]

II. Marking-to-Market

Marking-to-market, also known as 'daily settlement', means that at the end of every trading day, all futures positions are balanced and rewritten by the clearing-house at the settlement price for that day. This is done by adjusting the margin account so as to reflect the investor's gain or loss at the close of the day's trading. If the price has moved upward since the previous day's cash market price, the price gain is credited to long futures positions and debited to short futures positions. The effect of the marking-to-market is that a futures contract is settled daily rather than at the end of its life. At the end of each day, the investor's gain or loss is added to or subtracted from the margin account. A futures contract is in effect closed out and rewritten at a new price each day.[2] If the upward trend in prices persists until the delivery date, the buyer of the contract (i.e. long) will accumulate daily cash flows but will face a higher settlement price than the initial futures price, called the exercise price. The net amount the buyer is obliged to pay at final settlement is equal to the initial exercise price. Clearly, the cash flows accruing to the seller of the futures contract are just the opposite of those accruing to the buyer.[3] Although the settlement price which is paid at the offset or delivery is different from the initial exercise price, the net amount remains the same as the exercise price. The technicality involved in calculating the settlement price of the contract is due to the marking-to-market operation, which the customer may find very confusing. One source of this confusion is the expectation that the price at which delivery is taken should be the same price as that of the initial price of the futures contract, which is usually not the case. How then is it possible that the price that the buyer must pay when taking delivery (the invoice price) is somewhat different from the initial price? For example, if a precious-metals dealer buys one contract of June comex gold on 1 April at $395.00 per ounce, should not he expect to pay $39,500 ($395 per ounce x 100 ounces) if he stands for delivery of this contract?

Not quite. In fact he will be asked to pay the price that prevails on the day the notice is issued. In this case, one may ask, what good the futures contract was? To pursue the example:

1 April: A precious-metals dealer buys one contract of June comex gold at $395.00 with the intuition of taking delivery.

1 June: A short issues a delivery notice to the clearing-house. The current June gold settlement price is $410.30.

2 June: The precious-metals dealer receives a delivery notice and is expected to take delivery of, and make payment for, a warehouse receipt that represents 100 ounces of gold.

3 June: The dealer receives delivery and makes payment of $41,030 ($410.30 per ounce x 100 ounces).

This is what actually happens, but it does not mean that the cost to the dealer was $410.30 instead of $395.00. This is because the dealer has accrued a profit of $15.30 per ounce in his futures account, which has been marked to the market daily up to the time that the notice was received. The dealer's net price will consequently be $395.00 after the $15.30 accrued profit is taken into consideration.[4]

III. Spreads

In order to limit exposure to risk, a trader may choose to follow a more conservative method known as spreading (also known as 'straddle'). This is to combine two or more different contracts into one investment position that might generate a modest amount of profit, while restricting exposure to loss. An investor can set up a spread by buying one contract and simultaneously selling another in the same commodity, but with a different delivery month. Alternatively, a spread may consist of the purchase of one commodity and the sale of another related commodity on the same or a different market. If one side of the transaction leads to a loss, the investor hopes that the profit earned from the other side will compensate for the loss. The terms 'spread positions' and 'hedge' are used interchangeably but incorrectly by some traders. A hedge refers to the concurrent holding of two opposite commodity positions, one in the cash market and the other in the futures market. A spread position also refers to two concurrent and opposite positions, but both are in the futures market. The essence of taking spread positions lies in the intelligent use of differences among the prices of various contract months. Position spreaders are less interested in the direction of price than in the difference between two prices. Instead of deciding that a given contract price is too high or too low, they are interested in taking advantage of price differences between contract periods, commodities and markets. One of the most popular spreads is that of any single commodity trading in two delivery months. Normally the futures price is at a premium to the cash market price, which reflects the cost of storage, insurance and finance over a given period. The longer the period for which these costs most be incurred, the greater the theoretical price difference. It is thus possible to look at commodity prices in varying delivery months from the perspective of the cash month and determine an approximate differential between the cash price and likely price in any month in the future. If after such an analysis the differential appears to be out of proportion, a position can be taken in the market to take advantage of the potential realignment of relative prices.[5]

IV. Disciplinary Regulations

In the United States, public interest is protected by the Commodity Futures Trading Commission (CFTC), which supervises commodity exchange operations in all the states. Under the CFTC Act of 1974, an independent authority similar to the Securities Exchange Commission (SEC) was created, and the CFTC replaced the regulatory authority previously vested in the Department of Agriculture. The Commission is composed of a chairman and four other commissioners. Each is appointed by the president with the advice and consent of the Senate, and holds office for a five-year term. The terms are staggered and, by law, no more than three commissioners can belong to the same political party. The Commission had a staff compliment of 496 at the end of 1986. The 1974 Act provides that the congress must re-authorise the powers of the CFTC every four years and, since 1986, every three years.[6]

The CFTC designates exchanges and regulates all commodities traded on the exchange. All newly introduced contracts require CFTC approval, and the Commission is required to regulate transaction activities on all contracts, to control speculation and, ultimately, to protect the investor. The Commission has authority to refer a violation of the provision of the Act to a United States District Court, and it has itself powers to impose penalties of up to $100,000 for each violation by an exchange or a participating trader. It has, likewise, the authority to limit the size of any speculative position, to suspend or terminate any individual's or corporation's participation in the futures market, to introduce changes in position limits or set price limits if it feels that the market is not sufficiently well ordered. The CFTC has in turn delegated some of its functions to the National Futures Association (NFA). Most of the regulations of the CFTC and NFA, such as those which relate to licensing, capital requirements and book-keeping, are of concern primarily to brokerage houses and their employees, but some regulations apply to individual traders too. Established in 1982, the NFA assumed, from the Commission, various regulatory responsibilities that are more effectively handled within the futures industry itself. The NFA is an organisation of individuals who participate in the futures industry; its objectives are to prevent fraud and ensure that the market operates in the best interests of the general public.[7]

The CFTC headquarters are in Washington DC, and it has regional offices in New York, Chicago, Kansas City and Los Angeles–near all the major futures exchanges. The control exercised by the CFTC on futures personnel through compulsory registration requirements is constant and rigorous. Every registered member is required to keep a record of all his transactions. Compulsory registration is obviously designed to keep undesirables out of the business. Registered members must also report daily on the positions of all large traders who exceed the quantitative limit requirements. The traders themselves are similarly required to report when they trade in excess of those limits.[8]

The CFTC prohibits broker firms or their employees from executing any transaction for a customer unless the customer has either specifically authorised it or given written authorisation to his account executive. This rule is designed to prevent, among other things, 'churning', which is the overly active trading of an account for the purpose of generating commissions. Similarly, a floor broker may not execute a trade for his own account while holding an executable customer order in the same futures. This rule is designed to prevent 'front-running' customer orders. An example of front-running would be to buy ten contracts for oneself before executing a 100 contract customer buy order on the assumption that the latter would move the market higher and create a profit on the broker's own trade. Floor brokers are similarly not permitted to tip off others in the ring so that they can front-run the order and later share the profits with them.[9]

Many of the regulations in futures trading in the United States target specific abuses, the most pervasive controls being those against fraud and price manipulation. The Commodity Exchange Act of 1974 highlighted fraudulent and unauthorised trading, misrepresentation (including omission and wilful deceit), churning and several types of 'fixed' sales including bucketing and cross-trading. Regulations against price manipulation prohibit all activities that cause or maintain an artificial price for commodity futures. In order to be actionable, a violation must be intentional, but intentions can be inferred from the market: holding a long position that is grossly in excess of deliverable stocks, or one that is dominant or monopolistic, may be taken as evidence of price manipulation. An undue spread between future months, a rise in futures prices with no corresponding rise in the spot price, or consecutive days of maximum price rises for questionable reasons, are also considered evidence of an artificial price. Price manipulation in the United States market is a criminal offence.[10] In Malaysia, attempts to manipulate the futures market is a punishable offence which carries a fine of up to RM100,000 and imprisonment for up to five years.[11]

NOTES

1. Cf. Fink, *Futures Trading*, pp. 41ff; Ḥasan, *ʿAmal*, pp. 232-3.
2. Hull, *Introduction to Futures*, p. 25.
3. Relly, *Investment Analysis*, p. 773.
4. Fink, *Futures Trading*, pp. 55-6.
5. Kolb, *Understanding Futures*, p. 61; Gitman, *Fundamentals*, p. 532; Gup, *The Basics*, p. 484; Courtney, *Investor's Guide*, p. 90; There are four basic types of spreads: interdelivery spreads, which involve buying and selling the same commodity in different delivery months; intermarket spreads (different markets involving the same or different delivery months); intercommodity spreads (different but related commodities); and commodity product spreads (purchase of raw material and sale of derived products). See for details NYIF, *Futures*, pp. 182ff; Teweles, *Commodity Futures*, pp. 195ff; Hull, *Introduction*, p. 26.
6. Fink, *Futures Trading*, pp. 127ff.
7. Gene Smith, 'Commodity Market', *Encyclopedia Americana*, vol. 7, p. 391; *SFC Co. v. K. Masri*, p. 45; Gup, *The Basics*, pp. 487ff; Teweles, *Commodity Futures*, p. 89; Hull, *Introduction to Futures*, p. 36.
8. Courtney, *Investor's Guide*, pp. 40-1; Fink, *Futures Trading*, p. 105.
9. Fink, *Futures Trading*, pp. 106 and 111.
10. Courtney, *Investor's Guide*, p. 44.
11. Megesvaran, 'Commodities Futures: a New Horizon', *Malaysian Business*, September 16, 1985, p. 7.

CHAPTER SIX

The Futures Markets of Alexandria and Kuala Lumpur

I. The Commodity Exchange of Alexandria

There are two stock markets in Egypt, located in Cairo and Alexandria respectively, but futures trading is almost entirely based in Alexandria. There are two markets for cotton in Alexandria, one of which is a futures contract market, and the other a centralised spot market for cotton in the Mīna al-Baṣal district. The futures market has had a chequered history in Egypt because of political changes which on several occasions led to the closure of the futures market in Alexandria. Before elaborating on this, a brief explanation as to why Egypt needed to introduce a futures contract in cotton is offered.

The need to introduce futures trading in cotton was generated by the uncertainties that prevailed over the production planning and pricing of cotton up to the mid-nineteenth century. The textiles plants were often unable to commit themselves to a specific price for delivery of cloth to cloth merchants until they had determined the price for cotton and had received assurance from cotton producers and suppliers for timely delivers. The cotton producers themselves could not respond to these needs as and when the demand was made because they needed to plan well in advance. Futures trading in cotton responded to these needs, as various parties in the chain were unable to make firm commitments in advance, and meet their production and marketing requirements. This also facilitated the determination of the sale and purchase prices of cotton for several months ahead, which in turn went a long way towards overcoming and removing uncertainties that hitherto had prevailed over pricing and production strategies.[1]

Trading in the Egyptian Futures Market, known as *burṣāt al-ʿuqūd* (lit., contracts' market), is mainly conducted in cotton. It is one of the oldest futures markets in the world, which began trading in 1861 (and preceded its counterparts in Chicago, New York and Liverpool, which date to 1865, 1870 and 1873 respectively), when a group of brokers in cotton and foodgrains joined together and opened business activity in Alexandria. They were, however, soon divided into two groups, and the split between them led to the formation of a second market for cotton only a short distance away from the first. The two bourses operated side by side until it became known that this duality in close quarters led to confusion in the prices of the commodities they were trading. This situation led, in 1889, to the setting up of the Commodity Brokers' Association (*Jamāᶜah Samāsirah al-Badā'iᶜ*), which consisted of twenty-five brokers and soon acquired control over forward and futures trading in cotton, foodgrains and pulses. For about half a century, the government of Egypt did not intervene in these activities, and it was not until 1909, when the Bourses Act (*Qānūn al-Burṣāh*) was introduced in Egypt for the first time, that trading in futures contracts was brought under the government supervision. The Ministry of Economic Affairs was entrusted with regulatory powers over the futures markets, and a manual of floor procedures was consequently enacted in 1916, which was later to be amended on several occasions—in 1927, 1931, 1948 and 1955.[2]

In 1882, a market for spot sales of cotton started operation in Mīna al-Baṣal, in the vicinity of the cotton futures market of Alexandria. It resembled a huge depot where the delivery of large quantities of commodities took place within specified periods. The Alexandria Cotton Company (*Shirkah al-Quṭn al-Iskandariyyah*), renamed in 1884 the Public Productivity Corporation of Alexandria (*Ittihād al-Iskandariyyah li'l-Maḥāṣīl al-ᶜĀmmah*), was subsequently formed to regulate the somewhat centralised cash market transactions, and it acquired control of the quality grading and classification as well as of delivery and export operations without government intervention. However, because of the hoarding and cornering activities of individual traders in the late 1920s, the government decided to supervise the cash market operations of Mīna al-Baṣal. This was at a time when the government had already acquired a supervisory role over the contracts market, and it was seen to be in the interests of uniformity that cash market activities in cotton and foodgrains should also be conducted under government supervision, for cash commodity markets logically complemented one another, and effective supervision was needed in order to increase the co-ordination and coherence between them. It was not until 1930 that the Egyptian government set up the Bourses Committee (*Lajnat al-Burṣāh*) to co-ordinate activities in both the cash and futures markets of Alexandria, and it comprised members and experts from both sides under the chairmanship of a government representative. The Bourses Committee was further expanded, as a result of legislation in 1955, to thirty-six members to comprise representatives from the government, farmers, textile merchants and the commodity exchange. There were five sub-committees that assisted the main committee on the specific matters of grading, prices, publication, arbitration and disciplinary regulations.[3]

For around three years between 1952 and 1955, the market experienced irregularities which were partly due to foreign factors such as tighter trade regulations, the closure of the Liverpool cotton exchange and the cessation of links with New York, as well as internal factors - especially currency restrictions and the consequent drop in the volume of trading. As a result, cotton prices in Egypt experienced serious setbacks. It was then decided, in 1952, to close the market until the necessary changes were made to restore normal trading conditions. At this stage the government decided to link Egyptian cotton prices to those of United States cotton, which had hitherto accounted for 50 per cent of world cotton produce. Furthermore, in order to stabilise the prices, the government established the Cotton Price Stabilisation Fund (*Sunduq Muwāzanah Asᶜār al-Quṭn*) in 1953, which was to moderate seasonal fluctuations in cotton prices. The Fund became a net buyer of cotton from farmers at a low price only to sell it back at a profit, and it was able to return 75 per cent of its net profit back to the farmers. The cotton exchange of Alexandria was re-opened in 1955 on the condition, stipulated by the government at that time, that only genuine traders were to be allowed to engage in cotton futures, thereby excluding speculators who had no interest in cotton other than making profit from its price movements. A clearing-house with a statutory and corporate status of its own was established on the exchange, and all market transactions were to be cleared and validated by it. A new daily clearance procedure was also instituted, and quantitative day limits were introduced in order to reduce volatility and speculative risk-taking in daily trading. The government and the Central Bank expanded their supervisory functions over market operations, and normal relations with foreign markets were resumed, and indeed continued for the next six years or so.[4]

The socialist overtones of the Egyptian government's ideology in the 1960s had a negative effect on both the shares and futures markets, and led, in July 1961, to the suspension of trading for an indefinite period in the futures market of Alexandria. This was partly as a result of new legislation issued in that year (Law no. 69) which established direct government supervision over the futures market activities. The role and powers of the Bourses Committee were drastically revised and the then powerful Committee was reduced to a nominal existence in Alexandria. Its functions were taken over by the Egyptian Cotton Committee (*Lajnah al-Quṭn al-Miṣriyah*), which exercised direct government control over the cotton trade. The government also acquired control over all the major sectors of commerce: it would buy agricultural produce from farmers and producers and offer them for sale in the international markets, there remaining no viable role for a futures market. This situation continued without significant change until 1973, when the Egyptian government announced its open-door economic policy, which was to encourage investment and market capitalisation, and this led, in turn, to the revival of trading activity in the bourses. New laws were introduced in 1974, 1977 and 1981 respectively in order to enhance the financial viability and role of private investment companies in trading and development activities. The result is seen to have been generally positive as trading volume has steadily increased both in the futures and share markets of Alexandria and Cairo.[5]

There are three types of members at the futures market of Alexandria: clearing members or brokers, floor traders or locals, and associate members. The clearing members (*al-aᶜḍā al-samāsirah*) are fully qualified brokers who must pass a qualifying examination, possess the necessary brokerage qualifications and have at least four years' work experience as a stock brokers; or have successfully undergone two years of attachment to a qualified broker at the futures market. Persons with a work experience of five years in banks and financial institutions can also apply and may be selected if they fulfil the necessary capital and financial requirements. The brokers are forbidden from trading in futures for their own accounts or those of their relatives up to four degrees of relationship. Only Egyptian citizens can be clearing members and brokers in futures.

Al-aᶜḍā' al-munḍammūn, or locals, as they are known, are traders and cotton merchants who are allowed to trade on their own behalf, but only through a clearing member. The locals too must fulfil certain requirements in terms of experience and financial qualification. The third category of membership, known as *al-aᶜḍā' al-murāsilūn*, or associate members, can be foreign broking firms and institutions that may be granted trading facility in futures, but they would need to be associated with a clearing member on the exchange who is prepared to clear their trades.[6]

Cotton contracts are the most active on the contracts market (*burṣāt al-ᶜuqūd*) in Alexandria, and they are traded in basically two varieties: the long fibre cotton contract (*ᶜaqd al-quṭn ṭawīl al-tīlah*) and the medium fibre cotton contract (*ᶜaqd al-quṭn mutawassiṭ al-tīlah*). About thirty-four per cent of all traded contracts are of the first type and the remainder fall into the second category. The long fibre cotton of Egypt is known to be the best in the world for its fibre length, ranging between 1⅜ to 1⅝ inches, while the medium fibre ranges from 1¼ to 1⅜ inches in length.

Each variety is then graded by criteria of purity, cleanliness, moisture level and colour quality into about half a dozen sub-categories respectively. The long fibre contracts are normally traded for delivery in January, March, May, July, September and November, whereas the medium fibre variety is traded for the six other months of the year. The contract specifications, market rules and clearing procedures are similar to those of the New York and Liverpool markets, and a great deal of Egyptian cotton is also exported to the United States and Britain.[7]

Commercial custom at the Egyptian futures market has approved of sale-at-the-market-price (*bayᶜ taḥt al-qaṭᶜ*) which, to the best of my knowledge, is not practised in exchanges outside Egypt. This formula permits the sale of cotton prior to harvesting on condition that the seller is entitled to specify the exact price within a stipulated period. The price is then determined on the basis of the prevailing futures price on the settlement date, albeit with some flexibility as to selecting the mid-point between the minimum and maximum for that particular day. This transaction is sometimes criticised because it causes the accumulation of a large number of contracts for roughly the same dates, which may cause price distortion. But it also has the advantage that the cotton farmer is enabled to raise cash for the time when he needs the money, without which facility he might need to borrow on interest. It is also noted that sales prior to the harvesting of expected crops may have a moderating effect on prices, yet the general advice is that this mode of sale should be kept down to the extent of its genuine utility to the farmers, and too much of it should not be encouraged.[8]

II. The Kuala Lumpur Commodity Exchange (KLCE)

The KLCE was established in July 1980 under the provisions of the Commodities Futures Trading Act 1980. Trading activity began in two contracts: crude palm oil (CPO) in October 1980 and rubber (RSS) in 1983. The tin futures contract was launched in 1987 and cocoa in 1988. This was followed in 1990 by the introduction of a second palm oil contract, RBD palm olein. The CPO and palm olein have proved to be active and have shown consistent increase in trading volume over the years. The CPO standard contract of 25 tonnes is the most successful to date, and it is traded up to twelve months forward for the current month, the next five succeeding months and alternative months thereafter. The trading volume per year was over six and a half million tonnes for 1989 and 1990. Rubber, tin and cocoa contracts, although available, often show a 'no activity' situation for various reasons, including a lack of involvement by the general public and the fact that rubber producers and suppliers still rely on conventional spot trading methods.[9]

The KLCE was restructured in 1985 and new rules and procedures were adopted in order to increase uniformity with other world markets, especially the United States. American experts, especially Dr. Mark Powers (known as the father of financial futures in the United States), participated in the planning and restructuring of the KLCE as well as determining the feasibility of introducing financial futures and options in Malaysia. The Commodity Trading Act 1985 was introduced to refine the market procedures and improve the government's supervision over its activities. Under this Act, the KLCE is to conduct its operation under the supervision of a cabinet Minister (the Minister of Primary Industries) and the Commodities Trading Commission. The Exchange Company and its clearing-house are in turn answerable to the Commission, and these organisations, together with dealers and commodity trading advisors, have all been assigned well-defined functions in the operation and management of the exchange. The Commodities Trading Commission consists of a chairman, who is appointed by the Minister in charge, and nine members, including a representative each from the Ministries of Finance and Primary Industries, the Governor of the Central Bank and six persons with appropriate experience and knowledge. Members hold office for a renewable period of two years. The Commission exercises effective supervision over the exchange and it is responsible for making changes to the constitution and rules of the exchange. It may also, if necessary, take action against the exchange company or clearing-house for failure to comply with the exchange regulations (ss. 3, 21, 28 of the Commodities Trading Act 1985). The employees of the exchange company and clearing-house are forbidden, on pain of fines of up to RM 10,000, or one year's imprisonment, or both, from engaging directly or indirectly in commodity futures trading and unauthorised disclosure of confidential information (s. 119). The Commodities Trading Act 1985 authorises only the registered dealers, or their representatives, to conduct trade in commodity futures and anyone who does so without completing the registration formalities is committing an offence that carries a fine of RM50,000 (s. 33). The registration certificate issued by the Commodities Trading Commission is non-transferable and must be renewed every twelve months. In order to qualify for registration as a dealer, the applicant must be 'a fit person with a clean record, be a member of the exchange company and have paid a minimum deposit of RM100,000' (ss. 37-40).

Membership of the Exchange is open to any Malaysian company of good standing that has a minimum paid-up capital of RM500,000. Each membership costs RM50,000, and a member is also required to contribute RM30,000 to the Compensation Fund set up by the Exchange to compensate clients who have suffered losses because of default by a member of the exchange. Exchange membership can be bought and sold, but a member wishing to sell his membership must notify the exchange of his intention and the offer price. The number of memberships at the KLCE is currently limited to 130 and all of them have been taken up. An exchange member must also be associated with the clearing-house to enable him to clear and guarantee all his trades.

Individual Malaysians may also apply for membership as 'locals' or floor traders on a restricted basis in order to trade on their own account, but they must be associated with a clearing member who can clear and guarantee their trades. Finally, any Malaysian or overseas company may apply for Trade Affiliate status by paying an entrance fee of RM10,000, but they would need to conduct trade through a clearing member.

The Exchange Management Company is under an obligation to establish a clearing-house. Thus the Malaysian Futures Clearing Corporation (MFCC) has been established and its main functions under the Commodities Trading Act 1985 are the 'registration and settlement of futures contracts and the day-to-day adjustment of the financial position of such contracts'. The Act also provides that 'futures contracts registered by the clearing-house shall be fulfilled in the event of default by either of the two parties to such contracts' (s. 19). The MFCC is a limited liability company with an authorised capital of RM50 million and issued capital of RM25 million. The Exchange and the clearing members own seventy per cent of the MFCC shares and the balance of thirty percent is held by a consortium of nineteen Malaysian banks.[10]

A corporate member of the KLCE becomes eligible for clearing membership by fulfilling the following:

a. Maintaining a minimum paid-up capital of RM1 million and net tangible assets (NTA) of RM2 million.

b. Owning at least two memberships of the exchange.

c. Purchasing 3 per cent shares in the MFCC.

d. Registering oneself as a corporate dealer with the Commodities Trading Commission.

e. Paying a 'security deposit' of RM50,000 upon admission to the MFCC.

The establishment and enforcing of minimum financial requirements on all member firms which deal with the public and hold customer funds is the joint responsibility of the exchange company and the clearing-house. They are similarly required to establish 'an early warning system for monitoring undesirable situations and practices in the market' (CTA, s. 23). The management board of the exchange and that of the clearing-house may also conduct surprise audits of their member firms, especially those which hold customer funds, to ensure propriety and prevent violations of the market rules.

Upon the execution of a client's order by the floor trader, the details of the transaction are recorded on a trade form which is time-stamped and signed by both parties to the transaction. Each party will then submit his copy of the trade form to his respective clearing member for registration with the clearing-house. The trade form identifies the contract bought or sold, the delivery month, the quantity and the price. The buying clearing member and selling clearing member each initial the trade form for confirmation and return the initialled copy to the clearing-house within fifteen minutes.

III. Trading Limits and Discipline

The Commodity Trading Act 1985 authorised the Commodities Trading Commission to establish, after consultation with the exchange company and clearing-house, fixed limits on the amount of trading that may take place, or positions that a person may hold, in respect of a specified commodity futures contract. The purpose of imposing such limits, which are to be published in the KLCE Gazette, would be to prevent excessive speculation in the futures market. The Commission has powers, however, to fix different trading limits from those that are printed in the Gazette in respect of different commodities or delivery months, or exempt certain transactions from such limits altogether (ss. 5, 66). The KLCE has determined the maximum daily range of price fluctuation for crude palm oil contract as follows: the maximum limit of price increase in any day is RM50 per tonne. If this level is reached at the end of the day, the second day's limit will be RM75 per tonne, and RM100 on the third day. There will be no limit on the fourth day but it will be back to RM50 on the fifth day. In practice, these limits are rarely, if ever, reached and they usually leave a wide margin of flexibility in trading. The Commission may also establish, for any traded commodity, a reportable level and whenever a trader's aggregate position reaches that level, 'such person shall each day that the level is equalled or exceeded' file a report of the position with the Commissioner. All the accounts of a person who might hold, or have financial interest in, several accounts, are to be considered as a single account for the calculation of his aggregate trading position (s. 68). Violators are liable, upon conviction, to a fine of up to RM20,000, or imprisonment for up to one year, or both (s. 78). The Commission may also forbid the clearing-house, whenever appropriate and necessary, from making a payment or refunding, or releasing any money or security pertaining to a contract which is in default of the rules of the exchange until the completion of investigation and the determination of default (s. 7).

The Commodities Trading Act 1985 turns the false trading, bucketing, wash sales, fictitious sales, cross trading, price manipulations and cornering, employment of fraudulent or deceptive devices, false statements and syndicate trading into criminal offences. Manipulation and cornering carry, upon conviction, a fine of up to RM1,000, or imprisonment for up to five years, or both, and the offender may also be prohibited from trading on the exchange (ss. 72, 73). Syndicate trading carries a punishment of a fine not exceeding RM15,000, or one year of imprisonment, or both (s. 76). Dealers are also prohibited from knowingly executing a transaction in commodity futures without a *bona fide* purchase or sale of such a commodity for the specified delivery date (s. 70). Similarly, members of the management board, the board of the clearing-house and committee members are prohibited, under the pain of fine up to RM10,000, one year's imprisonment, or both, from disclosing confidential information which might be expected to materially affect the movement of prices on the exchange (s. 120). Moreover, the Commission or the exchange company may file a suit in the High Court, and request an order to restrain a person from acquiring, disposing of or transferring any assets out of Malaysia, and may request the court to declare a futures contract to be null and void (s. 116). Finally, in emergency situations, the CTA authorise the Minister in charge to order suspension of trading on the exchange 'for a period not exceeding five days' in order to ensure regularity in market operations (s. 27).

IV. The Kuala Lumpur Options and Futures Exchange (KLOFFE)

The KLCE has in recent years been planning to introduce financial futures and much of the preparatory work has already been done to facilitate the launch of the new contracts. This is partly due to the rapid growth of the Malaysian economy in recent years and the increased demand for capital that creates, in turn, the need for risk-management facilities—which is what an efficient financial futures market can provide. Another factor that encourages the introduction of financial futures might be the rather sluggish performance of tin and rubber contracts in recent years. It is generally felt that the potential for success in financial futures is far better. Yet, even here, it is recommended that 'a core group of banks, pension funds, insurance companies and the like start the ball rolling because these institutions have the need to utilise financial futures in their business'.[11] Financial institutions have the most to gain from the use of financial futures since they are exposed to interest rate risks and foreign exchange fluctuations.

The Futures Industry Act (FIA) 1993 was specifically introduced to provide the necessary legal framework for trading in derivative instruments, or financial futures, which include interest rates, currency, stock index, metal and energy futures. It has entrusted the Minister of Finance and the Securities Commission with overall supervisory powers over the operation of financial futures, including the establishment of a management company to take charge of the operational affairs of the exchange, the appointment of officials, disciplinary action and temporary closure of the exchange in emergency situations (ss. 4-12).

Two exchanges are planning to introduce contracts in derivative instruments: the Kuala Lumpur Options and Financial Exchange (KLOFFE), which began operations in stock index futures in late 1995, and the Kuala Lumpur Futures Market (KLFM). The latter started trading its first financial futures contract, the three-month Kuala Lumpur Interbank Offered Rates (KLIBOR), in the third quarter of 1995. This was an interest rate-related contract that was followed by new contracts in Malaysian bonds and currency futures, in spite of delays. These exchanges determine the rules governing membership, exchange administration and member-customer relationships. The exchanges were required by law to establish a clearing-house to clear the contracts traded on the exchanges and guarantee performance on all contracts.

Membership of the exchange is drawn from investment houses, banks, brokerage firms and individual traders. The KLOFFE offers two membership categories: trading members and local members. The first is open to companies that are incorporated under the Companies Act 1965. Trading members can trade in futures and options both for themselves and on behalf of their clients. To conduct trade, trading members also need to obtain a futures broker licence from the licensing officer of the Ministry of Finance. The person who deals directly with the customers of a trading member is a futures broker representative, who also needs to be licensed by the licensing officer (FIA ss. 16, 18).

'Local' membership is open only to individuals intending to trade for themselves rather than a client. They can conclude transactions but cannot be clearing members and therefore need to clear their trades through a clearing member. Local membership is not governed by the FIA and local members therefore need not be licensed by the licensing officer. Trading permit holders may also conduct trading for themselves; they are like local members except that their trading permit allows them to trade in the KLOFFE for up to twelve months only.[12]

The FIA (s. 49) requires all brokers to make out and issue a contract note upon conclusion of every futures transaction, in which the following is clearly recorded:

a) the name and address of the customer and that of the futures broker;

b) where the futures broker is acting as principal, a statement that he is so acting;

c) the name of the futures exchange and the amount of commission payable;

d) the contract execution date and the date when the contract note is made out;

e) whether the contract is a new one or a contract for settlement, and whether it is by way of purchase, sale or exchange;

f) the name of the underlying instrument, its unit of trading and the price and number of trading units;

g) the date of the performance of the contract.

When the broker is acting as the principal, the contract note is to be made out 'not later than the end of the next trading day', but if the broker is acting as the agent, he must deliver the contract note to the customer 'not later than five days after the execution of transaction'. He must also provide the customer, on request, with a copy of any contract note relating to the trade, and a copy of the customer's account with the broker (s. 51). Failure to comply with these provisions is an offence which carries, upon conviction, a fine of up to RM1 million, or imprisonment for up to ten years, or both (s. 56).

The KLOFFE and the KLFM are, at the time of writing, planning to set up a common clearing-house. While the KLOFFE contract in stock index futures is designed to appeal to retailers and institutions, KLIBOR is expected to appeal mainly to banks and big corporations. The KLOFFE has recently installed a fully-automated trading and clearing system, called KLOFFE's Automated Trading System (KATS). This is designed to be cost-efficient, and also to ensure transparency in that all traders will have access to the same information.[13]

Trading in financial futures and options, under the Futures Industry Act 1993, may be subject to fixed or varying limits, and the exchange authorities are empowered to determine, as they deem necessary, the amount of trading which may be done, or the net positions which may be held, by any person under a futures contract. Failure to comply with such limits 'is an offence and shall be liable upon conviction to a fine not exceeding one million ringitt, or to imprisonment for a term not exceeding ten years, or both' (s. 55). In its sections on licensing, the Futures Industry Act 1993 (ss. 16-36) requires all futures brokers, futures trading advisors and their representatives to have a valid brokerage license which is renewable every twelve months. A futures broker license can only be granted to a corporation, whereas a license to conduct a business as a futures trading advisor may be granted to an individual or to a corporation. To qualify for a trading license, the applicant must possess the necessary skills and financial resources, and have a clean record free of conviction for an offence or bankruptcy. Anyone who engages in futures broking business without a license is liable to a fine of up to RM1 million, or imprisonment for up to ten years, or both. The licensing officer has powers to revoke a license, to suspend it temporarily, reprimand the license-holder or impose a fine of up to RM50,000 on grounds of improper conduct of business. In such an event, however, the aggrieved person may appeal to the Minister against the licensing officer's decision.

Futures brokers are required to segregate all assets into a separate trust account, including margin money, security or documents relating to property title received from the customer. The broker may not combine that money, security or property with his own asset, or use it to margin, guarantee or secure a futures contract, or the payment of debts, for anyone other than the person for whom it is held. Failure to comply with these provisions is liable, upon conviction, to a fine of RM1 million, or imprisonment for up to ten years, or both (ss. 51-57).

Part VII of the Malaysian Futures Industry Act 1993 (ss.79-89) penalises—with a fine of up to RM1 million, or imprisonment for up to ten years, or both—a variety of offences that include false trading, bucketing, the dissemination of information about false trading, the manipulation of prices of futures contracts and cornering, the employment of devices, schemes or artifices in order to defraud, false statements and the falsification of records by anyone, including the directors and employees of the exchange. False trading is described as 'anything that is calculated to create a false or misleading appearance of active trading', whereas bucketing means executing a trade order on the exchange 'without having effected a *bona fide* purchase or sale of the futures' in accordance with the business rules of the market. The law also forbids, under pain of the same penalties, all employees of the exchange company or clearing-house from directly or indirectly engaging in futures trading or making unauthorised disclosures of any confidential information.

NOTES

1. Cf. Sami Wahbah ʿAlī, *al-Burṣāt wa Taswiq al-Quṭn*, Cairo, Maṭbaʿah al-Risālah, 1966, pp. 7-8.

2. Cf. ʿAlī, *al-Burṣāt*, p.168; Murad Kāẓīm, *al-Burṣah, Jihazuha, Anwaʿuha, ʿAmaliyatuha*, Damascus, Maṭbaʿah al-Thubat, n.d., pp. 143ff.

3. Kāẓīm, *al-Burṣah*, pp. 136-7.

4. ʿAlī, *al-Burṣāt*, pp. 170-5.

5. Cf. al-Khaṭīb, *al-Siyāsah al-Māliyyah*; al-Jundī, *Muʿāmalāt al-Burṣāh fi'l-Sharīʿah al-Islāmiyyah*, Cairo: Dār al-Nahdah al-ʿArabiyyah 1409/1988, pp. 26ff; ʿAlī, *al-Burṣāt*, pp. 157-77.

6. Cf. Kāẓīm, *al-Burṣah*, pp. 145-50.

7. Ibid., pp. 130-3.

8. Ibid., pp. 160-1.

9. Mahidin, 'Still Far to Go', *Malaysian Business*, December 1-15, 1990, p.38; Bharathi's interview with Mark Powers, *Malaysian Business*, November 1, 1987, pp. 12ff; Muhammad Firdaus Jamaluddin *et al.*, 'The Kuala Lumpur Commodity Exchange', unpublished research paper prepared by a team of six LL.B students of the International Islamic University, Malaysia, 1994, pp. 49ff.

10. Jamaluddin *et al.*, 'The Kuala Lumpur Commodity Exchange', note 8, pp. 53ff.

11. Mahidin, 'Still Far to Go', *Malaysian Business*, December 1-15, 1990, pp. 10, 38.

12. 'KLOFFE's Role in Derivative Mart', *New Strait Times*, January 14, 1995, p. 20.

13. Ibid., p. 20.

PART TWO

FUTURES TRADING AND CONVENTIONAL SALES:
A Discourse in *Fiqh*

INTRODUCTORY REMARKS

The first part of this section of this study is devoted to a general characterisation of the *Sharīʿah*'s view of civil transactions, where attention is drawn to the definition of principles such as *ibāḥah* (permissibility) as a basic precept of *muʿāmalāt*. This is followed by an exposition of the Qur'ānic principles of *taysīr* (bringing facility and ease), *rafʿ al-ḥaraj* (removal of hardship) and the freedom of contract (*ḥurriyyah al-taʿāqud*), and also the respective roles of ratiocination (*taʿlīl*) and custom in commercial transactions. The discussion then turns, in the succeeding chapter, to a problem which is of central concern to this investigation. This is the issue of uncertainty or risk-taking (*gharar*), which seems to relate to almost every aspect of this area of research. In this section, I review the positions of the schools of law (*madhāhib*) on *gharar*, and my review here discusses the inherently relative nature of this concept.

The rest of this study is concerned with the rules of Islamic law pertaining to certain aspects of the conventional contract of sale and their relevance, or otherwise, to trading in futures. The latter part of this discussion relates mainly to the subject-matter of sale, and addresses the issue of the existence, or otherwise, of the subject-matter at the time of contract, the rule that the object of sale must be deliverable and the seller must be able to make delivery, the sale of the unseen (*bayʿ al-ghā'ib*), and sale at the market price, that is, sale in which the price is not specified at the time of contract. Other related themes that are addressed are the Islamic legal perspective on sales prior to taking possession, deferred sales (*bayʿ al-mu'ajjal*), an analysis of the *ḥadīth* 'sell not what is not with you', debt clearance sale (*bayʿ al-kali' bi'l-khali'*) and a review of the Qur'ānic evidence on deferred contracts of exchange. This is followed by a discussion of speculation and gambling, and a summary of modern opinion on futures trading. The last part of this volume offers an analysis of the options being traded in the market-place, and addresses the issue of their validity from an Islamic legal perspective.

CHAPTER SEVEN

The *Sharīᶜah* Perspective on Commercial Transactions (*Muᶜāmalāt*)

This chapter addresses a number of the important principles of the *Sharīᶜah* with regard to commercial transactions. Some of these, namely, *ibāḥah* (permissibility), bringing facility and ease (*al-taysīr*) and the removal of hardship (*rafᶜ al-ḥaraj*), are included among the salient legal maxims (*qawāᶜid kulliyyah*) of *fiqh*, whereas the freedom of contract (*ḥurriyah al-taᶜāqud*), ratiocination (*taᶜlīl*) and customs are substantive topics of *Sharīᶜah* each in their own right. Each of them merits attention as a specific aspect of the law of sale that I discuss in the succeeding chapters.

I. The Principle of Permissibility (*Ibāḥah*)

The *Sharīᶜah* norm regarding commercial transactions and contracts is that they are permissible unless there is a clear injunction to the contrary. Muslim jurists have held that the injunction which overrules the basic presumption of permissibility must be decisive both in meaning and transmission (*naṣṣ qatᶜī al-thubūt wa'l-dalālah*). Al-Qaradāwī has suggested, rightly perhaps, that it is sufficient if the text in question is authentic and conveys a clear meaning (*naṣṣ ṣaḥīḥ al-thubūt ṣarīḥ al-dalālah*), because a text of this kind is generally sufficient to establish a practical ruling of *Sharīᶜah*.[1] The position is precisely the opposite with regard to devotional matters (*ᶜibādāt*), because the basic presumption here, as Ibn Qayyim stated, is that they are forbidden unless there is a clear text to validate them. This is because God Most High may only be worshipped in the manner He has specified.[2] The presumption of *ibāḥah* is thus mainly concerned with those commercial transactions that are permissible, and 'nothing in them is forbidden', as Ibn Taymiyyah points out, 'unless God and His Messenger have decreed them to be forbidden. But God Most High never prohibited a contract in which there is benefit for Muslims and does not inflict any harm upon them'.[3] The Ḥanbalī school has adopted the principle of *ibāḥah* and applied it more extensively than the other schools. But minor differences apart, *ibāḥah* is generally upheld in commercial transactions by almost all the *madhāhib*. Thus, according to a legal maxim of *fiqh*, 'permissibility is the basic norm in regard to things (which are not otherwise regulated)—*al-aṣl fi'l-ashyā' al-ibāḥah*'.[4] The legal maxim here is, in turn, based on the authority of the Qur'ān, in which we read the following:

> We have subjugated to you all that is in the heavens and the earth (45:13).
>
> وسخر لكم ما في السماوات وما في الأرض جميعا .
>
> He it is who created for you all that is on the earth (2:29).
>
> هو الذى خلق لكم ما في الأرض جميعا .
>
> God has explained to you in detail what is forbidden to you unless you are compelled to it (6:119).
>
> وقد فصل لكم ما حرم عليكم إلا ما اضطررتم
>
> And God will not mislead a people after He has guided them, so that He makes clear to them what to fear [and what to avoid] (9:115).
>
> وما كان الله ليضل قوما بعد اذ هداهم حتى يتبين لهم ما يتقون

The Qur'ānic declaration that God has subjugated the heavens and the earth to the benefit of man implies that it is permissible for mankind to utilise the resources of the universe. The right to utilise takes for granted that all acts and transactions that are necessary to facilitate the legitimate use of these resources are permissible. To reinforce the general import of their proclamation, the Qur'ān further lays down the principle that God Most High has clearly explained His prohibitions. Hence a mere presumption is normally not enough to declare something unlawful. Prohibitions, in other words, need to be clear and specific. The position is precisely the reverse with regard to permissibility, which is presumed in the absence of a clear prohibitive text in all cases of *muʿāmalāt*, with one exception, namely, relations between members of the opposite sexes, which are forbidden unless validated by marriage. The Qur'ān also reaffirms, in the last passage quoted above, that all divine guidance to mankind has one feature in common, which is that it provides clear explanations with regard to prohibitions. These Qur'ānic proclamations have, in turn, been endorsed and elaborated by the *Sunnah*, which has, on more than one occasion, advised the believers that God Most High has determined the lawful (*ḥalāl*) and the unlawful (*ḥarām*), but then He has also chosen to remain silent over certain things. When this is the case and there is no clear ruling on a matter, this is a sign of its permissibility. Thus, according to a *ḥadīth*:

> God Most High has made certain things obligatory, so be sure not to neglect them; He has also laid down certain limits, which you must not exceed; and then He has prohibited certain things which you have to observe; and finally He has, out of mercy, but not forgetfulness, chosen to remain silent over certain matters, so try not to be [too] inquisitive about them.[5]

ان الله فرض فرائض فلا تضيعوها ، وحد حدودا فلا تعتدوها ، وحرم أشياء فلا تنتهكوها ، وسكت عن أشياء رحمة بكم من غير نسيان فلا تبحثوا عنها .

Islam does not encourage an over-regulated system of government which might impinge on the basic liberties of the individual. Similarly, we normally do not expect the textual rulings of the Qur'ān and the *Sunnah* to regulate the vast realm of permissibility. To illustrate this, I refer to the Qur'ānic verse on the prohibited degrees of relation in marriage where the text states: 'Forbidden to you are your mothers, your daughters, your sisters, your paternal and maternal aunts...' (4:23-24).

حرمت عليكم أمهاتكم وبناتكم وأخواتكم وعماتكم وخالاتكم

The Qur'ān continues to spell out all the close relatives with whom marriage is forbidden; it then goes on to declare: 'It is lawful for you to seek in marriage women other than these.' (4:24).

وأحل لكم ما وراء ذالكم ...

The Qur'ān has thus provided an almost exhaustive list of the prohibitions that must be observed in marriage, but it merely makes a general reference, without giving any detail, to those with whom marriage is lawful. On another subject, that is, the lawful and unlawful types of food, the Qur'ān similarly specifies the prohibited substances, namely, dead carcasses, blood that has been shed, the flesh of swine and meat slaughtered in the name of deities other than Allāh. As for the rest, the text merely states, in the same passage, that nothing is forbidden for consumption except what has been mentioned specifically (6:144-145). The Qur'ān does not attempt to elaborate on what is permissible in either of these instances. The *Sunnah* has elaborated on the Qur'ān and supplied further instructions as to what it states, for example, concerning food, that 'the dead of sea is clean'

البحر طهور ماءه وحل ميتته

and also declared two types of clotted blood, namely liver and spleen, to be permissible for consumption. The *Sunnah* has similarly added one other prohibition, known as unlawful conjunction, to the list of the Qur'ānic prohibitions on marriage. It is thus unlawful to simultaneously marry the maternal or paternal aunt of one's wife. The *Sunnah* has thus taken the same approach as that of the Qur'ān, which is to single out the prohibitions, or necessary additions and exceptions, as the case may be, to the general rulings of the Qur'ān; but neither the Qur'ān nor the *Sunnah* provide elaborate details on what is permissible. Permissibility and freedom thus become the basic presumptions that prevail in the absence of clear prohibitions.

There are other passages in the Qur'ān that tend to widen the scope of permissibility, and encourage openness in its application. Note, for example, the address 'O believers, do not forbid the good things which have been made lawful to you' (5:87)

يا أيها الذين أمنوا لا تحرموا طيبات ما أحل الله لكم

and 'Say: Who has forbidden the adornment of Allāh, which He has brought forth for His servants, and the good provisions? Say: these are for the believers' (7:32).

قل من حرم زينة الله التى اخرج لعباده والطيبات من الرزق ، قل هى للذين آمنوا .

The Qur'ān and *Sunnah* thus provide clear guidance on the normative validity of *ibāḥah*, which means that any attempt to declare something forbidden on merely speculative grounds, or to impose rigidity and hardship upon people, violates the spirit of freedom, permissibility and tolerance that the Qur'ān and *Sunnah* have consistently encouraged.

The scholars of Islam and commentators have drawn the following conclusions from the relevant evidence of the Qur'ān and *Sunnah* on the subject of *ibāḥah*:

1. In order to declare a transaction valid, there is no need to search for affirmative evidence in the sources. All that one needs to investigate is

whether a clear, self-explanatory prohibition exists, and if none is found, the transaction may be presumed to be valid. It is, therefore, incorrect to ask such questions as, 'Where is the evidence to prove that this or that transaction is permissible?' We may here refer, once again, to the Qur'ān, which advises caution in matters of declaring something as *ḥarām*. For this is the sole prerogative of the Lawgiver, and this is why the subject invokes a sharp denunciation in the Qur'ān, as the text provides:

> And say not any falsehood that your tongues may put forth that, 'This is lawful and this is forbidden', for this is tantamount to ascribing lies to Allāh (16:116).
>
> ولا تقولوا لما تصف ألسنتكم الكذب هذا حلال وهذا حرام لتفتروا على الله الكذب .

2. The forms of trading and transactions that the Qur'ān and *Sunnah* have explicitly validated are not exhaustive, and do not preclude new varieties on which the *Sharīʿah* might have remained silent.[6]

3. With regard to new transactions, there is in principle no need to search for supportive evidence in the views and precedents of the early jurists, for it is essentially incorrect to extend and apply a medieval juristic opinion to a form of trade that did not exist in medieval times. The correct approach in such instances would be to attempt independent *ijtihād* in light of the basic guidelines of the Qur'ān and *Sunnah*.

II. Bringing Ease (*Taysīr*) and the Removal of Hardship (*Rafʿ al-Ḥaraj*)

Making things easier for people and removing unnecessary hardship from them are among the cardinal objectives (*maqāsid*) of the *Sharīʿah*, and these principles tend, in many ways, to characterise Islam itself.[7] The subject is referred to in a number of Qur'ānic verses and also in many *ḥadīth*. *Taysīr* and *rafʿ al-ḥaraj* are complementary and often integral to one another, although they differ in some respects. Both are identified as objectives (*maqāsid*) rather than rules of specific application. This is because each is inherently dynamic and comprehensive, and tends to involve a process capable of continuous application and refinement. In this sense the two principles are as relevant to the conditions of society today as they were in the early days of Islam. The scholars have generally characterised the *Sharīʿah* as the legal system of pragmatism and convenience. While commenting on the Qur'ānic verse that 'Allāh has imposed no hardship (*ḥaraj*) in religion' (22:78), the renowned companion Ibn ʿAbbās regarded a concrete manifestation of this to be the fact that Islam validates expiation (*kaffārah*) and leaves the door open to repentance (*tawbah*).[8] Ibn ʿAbbās is reported to have said, concerning the meaning of *ḥaraj*, that it is when there is no way out of a difficult situation (*al-ḥaraj mā lā makhraja lahu*).[9] The scholars have pointed out three areas where *taysīr* is manifested in *Sharīʿah*. The first of these is that the *aḥkām* of the *Sharīʿah* are easy to comprehend because they consist mainly of practical rules concerning the conduct of individuals. Secondly, since the Qur'ān explicitly states that 'God does not burden a soul beyond its capacity' (2:286), the *Sharīʿah* is not difficult to follow, and it contains concessionary rules in almost all the areas that it seeks to regulate. Finally, the *Sharīʿah* instructs individuals, judges and rulers to opt for easy solutions.[10] Elsewhere, the Qur'ān proclaims the removal of hardship to be God's absolute intention, within or outside the scope of religion, for 'God desires not to inflict any hardship upon you' (5:6). In a commentary on this verse, al-Jassas stated that the jurist and *muftī* are not allowed to give an opinion that causes hardship when there is an easier alternative, for God Most High has not made His religion one of difficulty, and so the judge and the *muftī* should also avoid hard choices in matters which are open to differences of opinion and interpretation.[11]

Bearing in mind some of the conditions of modern society, such as the ever-rising tide of secularity, doubts, uncertainty and weakness in religious practice, as well as the ever-increasing temptation to sin, it can be argued that people today are in greater need of *taysīr*, and of a more liberal application of principles such as *ibāḥah*, than ever before. We need, therefore, a more effective utilisation of the concessions that the *Sharīʿah* offers in order to prevent hardship in the observance of its commands. Similarly, the Qur'ānic principle of necessity, which is embodied in many legal maxims, such as that 'necessity makes the unlawful lawful'

الضرورات تبيح المحظورات

'hardship attracts alleviation'

المشقة تجلب التيسير

and 'when rigidity sets in any matter, it should be opened up'.

اذا ضاق الأمر اتسع .

These are invoked, whenever appropriate and justified, in the interest of alleviating hardship and encouraging pragmatism in the implementation of the *Sharīʿah*. The legal scholars (*fuqahā*) should bear this in mind and try to opt for easier positions in subsidiary matters while at the same time stand firm on basic principles. If particular individuals wish to observe higher standards, so much the better but, when it comes to issuing legal rulings (*fatāwa*) on matters that concern the entire community, their motto should be flexibility and ease, not rigidity and stricture. This would be beneficial to people, and show Islam to be a practical proposition rather than a rigid system and a reason for fear.[12] To do otherwise would clearly contravene numerous Qur'ānic directives on the alleviation of hardship:

> Allāh wishes to lighten your difficulties, for man was created weak (4:28).
>
> يريد الله أن يخفف عنكم وخلق الانسان ضعيفا .
>
> Allāh intends every facility for you, and He does not want to put you into difficulty (2:185).
>
> يريد الله بكم اليسر ولا يريد بكم العسر .

A further affirmation of this is found elsewhere in the Qur'ān with reference to upright individuals:

> As for him who gives [generously], is pious and accepts what is good, We facilitate for him the way to ease (92: 5-7).
>
> فأما من أعطى واتقى وصدق بالحسنى فسنيسره لليسرى .

And then with regard to the solvent debtor, the Qur'ān directs that he should be given time until he has means to pay back:

> And if [the debtor] is in straitened circumstances, let there be postponement till [he is in] ease (2:280).
>
> وان كان ذو عسرة فنظرة الى ميسرة .

Taysīr is also manifested in a Qur'ānic passage which discourages the believers from indulgence in asking too many questions, for 'you may dislike the answer if it were revealed to you' (5:104). When the Qur'ān, in other words, remains silent on a matter, it is an indication that God Most High has not intended to make that matter the subject of an obligation.[13]

> يا أيها الذين آمنوا لا تسئلوا عن أشياء ان تبد لكم تسؤكم .

Furthermore, among the three principal objectives of the prophethood of Muḥammad ﷺ, which the Qur'ān expounds, one is 'to remove from them [the believers] their burden and the shackles that were on them before' (7:157).

ويضع عنهم اصرهم واغلال التى كانت عليهم .

The other two are to command good and forbid evil, and to prohibit the consumption of impure substances. The *Sunnah* is entirely supportive of the Qur'ānic directives on *taysīr*. Note, for example, the report in which the Prophet ﷺ instructed two of his leading Companions, Abū Mūsā al-Ashʿarī and Muʿādh ibn Jabal, upon their departure as judges to the Yemen, to do the following:

> Let the two of you bring ease, not hardship, and give good news, not gloom.[14]
>
> يسرا ولا تعسرا وبشرا ولا تنفرا .

According to another report, the Prophet ﷺ also said on that occasion:

> You have been sent in order to make things easy, not as ones who make them difficult.[15]
>
> انما بعثتم ميسرين ولم تبعثوا معسرين .
>
> The best of your religion is that which is easy.[16]
>
> ان خير دينكم أيسره .
>
> Leniency (*al-rifq*) does not fail to bring beauty and the opposite of it does not fail to bring ugliness.[17]
>
> الرفق لا يكون في شئ الا زانه ولا ينزع من شئ الا شانه .
>
> Whoever forbids leniency closes the door to goodness.[18]
>
> من يحرم الرفق يحرم الخير كله .

With regard to utilising the concessionary rules of the *Sharīʿah*, the *Sunnah* encourages them to be utilised, for 'Allāh loves His concessions to be utilised in the same way that He loves His commands to be observed'.[19]

ان الله يحب أن تؤتي رخصة كما يحب أن تؤتى عزائمه .

The leading *mujtahidūn* of the past have, on the whole, followed these directives and have leaned, in their legal reasoning (*ijtihād*) and rulings (*fatāwa*) on commercial transactions in particular, toward permissibility and ease, but instances to the contrary can be found in the works of imitators and *muqallidūn*.

Sufyān ibn Saʿīd al-Thawri, a prominent jurist (*faqīh*) and a most respected *imām* of his time, has aptly characterised the role of the *faqīh* in the development of the *Sharīʿah* when he said that '*fiqh* essentially consists of finding credible concessions. As for bringing rigidity and rigour, almost everyone can do it well'.[20]

It is therefore firmly established that prohibiting what God has made permissible is no less a sin than permitting what is prohibited. The main direction of the evidence of the Qur'ān and *Sunnah* is clearly to narrow down and minimise the scope of prohibition, and try in this way to lighten the burden on the people. To follow a trend in the opposite direction, that is, to expand the scope of prohibitions, is thus contrary to the Qur'ānic directives of *taysīr* and *rafʿ al-ḥaraj*.

III. The Freedom of Contract (*Ḥurriyyah al-Taʿāqud*)

Muslim jurists have differed as to whether the Islamic legal norm with regard to contracts is permissibility, prohibition, or an intermediate position between the two. The majority have taken the view that the parties create a contract by their mutual agreement, but that the legal effects of that contract, such as the transfer of ownership in the case of sale, or the permissibility of sexual relations in the case of marriage, are determined by the *Sharīʿah*. The legal consequences of contracts are not necessarily the natural corollary of those contracts, nor is the will of the parties alone, without affirmative enactment by the Lawgiver, enough to determine those consequences. It is thus stated that if all of this were a matter for the parties alone to determine, there would be the risk of some people taking advantage of others, and a greater likelihood, therefore, of fraudulent manipulation (*ghabn*) and risk (*gharar*) in transactions. The *Sharīʿah* has thus validated the contract as a cause (*sabab*) which creates a legal effect (*musabbab* or *ḥukm*) often consisting of rights and obligations. But the actual relationship between the cause and the legal consequence that it generates is determined by the Lawgiver. Thus according to Ibn Taymiyyah, 'We create the means or causes (*asbāb*) towards certain legal consequences (*aḥkām*) by our conduct, but the Lawgiver establishes the nature of the relationship between them.'[21] The *Sharīʿah* nevertheless entitles the contracting parties to stipulate the terms of their agreement, and insert conditions in contracts in order to fulfil their legitimate needs. But even so, stipulations of this kind are valid in so far as they do not violate the essence and lawful purpose of the contract in question. The *madhāhib* have differed regarding the scope of the parties' liberty with respect to such stipulations. The Ḥanbalīs have given it the widest scope, and their contribution to the freedom of stipulation in contracts is widely acknowledge to be the most outstanding of the rich legacy of the juristic scholarship of the *madhāhib*.

As for the other schools of Islamic jurisprudence, on the one extreme there are the Ẓāhirīs, who maintain that the norm of *Sharīʿah* in regards to contract is prohibition (*ḥaẓar*), which means that every contract is unlawful unless the *Sharīʿah* has specifically declared otherwise. This basic presumption can only be overruled by the clear textual authority of the Qur'ān and *Sunnah* and not merely by the will of the parties. Hence a contract, or even a stipulation for that matter, which the *Sharīʿah* has not validated is of no legal consequence. The parties to transactions and contracts are thus expected to conform to the given terms of the (nominate) contracts which the *Sharīʿah* has validated and thereby avoid innovating and creating new forms of transactions and contracts. In Muḥammad Salām Madkūr's assessment, the Ẓāhirī jurists have been 'exceedingly restrictive' in insisting that business activity among people should remain as they were at the time of the advent of Islam. They have thus 'totally ignored the change of time and circumstances and their effects on the commercial life and activities of the people'.[22]

The proponents of this view have quoted in its support the Qur'ānic verse to the effect that 'to Allāh belongs the kingdom of the heavens and the earth' (45:27). From this, the conclusion is drawn that only with God's permission may people conclude transactions and contracts among themselves.[23]

The following two *ḥadīth* have also been quoted in support of the Ẓāhirī argument, but I should perhaps add that many scholars, including al-Shawkānī, have disputed their authenticity:

> Whoever takes action on a matter which we have not authorised, it shall be rendered void.
>
> من عمل عملا ليس عليه أمرنا فهو رد .
>
> Stipulations which are not indicated in the Book of God shall be void–even if they be a hundred stipulations. The Book of God and His stipulations are the most credible of all.
>
> ما كان من شرط ليس في كتاب الله فهو باطل ولو كان مأته شرط ،
> كتاب الله أحق وشرط الله أوثق .

It is then argued that if a mere stipulation which is not authorised by the text is void, then contracts for which there is no authorisation in the sources are also void.

The opposite stance is taken by Imām Aḥmad ibn Ḥanbal, who maintained that the norm in regards to contracts and stipulations (*ʿuqūd wa shurūṭ*) is permissibility, or *ibāḥah*. People are therefore at liberty to enter into any contract or engage in any trade that they wish to, whether this is in conformity with an existing precedent or not. The parties to a contract are likewise free to stipulate and add conditions to nominate contracts as they see fit for their needs, provided that this does not violate the clear prohibitions of the *Sharīʿah*.[24] Ibn Taymiyyah has categorically stated that the Qur'ānic address to the people to 'fulfil [their] contracts' (5:1) is evidently broad and comprehensive, and thus naturally comprises every contract that the Lawgiver has not specifically forbidden. The only basic requirement is the mutual consent of the parties, which, by the explicit authority of the Qur'ān (4:29), constitutes the essence of all contracts.[25] It is thus permissible to add conditions and stipulations to contracts when this proves to be beneficial, and does not seek to validate what God and His Messenger have prohibited, for everything that secures benefit for the people and involves no violation of the *Sharīʿah* is permissible, and no one has the authority to proscribe it.[26]

The Ḥanafī and Shāfiʿī schools have taken an intermediate position on the subject, but both seem closer to the Ẓāhirī stance than to the Ḥanbalī regarding the freedom of contract. They have departed from some of the rigidities of the Ẓāhirī school by recourse to analogical reasoning, juristic preference, the consideration of public interest and custom. Consequently, they have validated certain types of stipulations and additions to nominate contracts on these grounds. But the Ḥanafīs and Shāfiʿīs nevertheless remain fairly distant from the considerably more liberal position taken by their Ḥanbalī counterparts on the freedom of contract.[27]

Although the Mālikī school has not embraced the Ḥanbalī view of the freedom of contract, in comparison with the other *madhāhib*, they are closer to the Ḥanbalī position. The Mālikīs have achieved this mainly through the application of their doctrine of unrestricted public interest (*maṣlaḥah mursalah*).[28]

The Ḥanafīs divide contractual stipulations into the three types: valid (*ṣaḥīḥ*), irregular (*fāsid*) and void (*bāṭil*). A valid stipulation is one which either reiterates and endorses the substance of the contract, or does not seek to change its requirements. In a contract of sale, for example, when the vendor stipulates that he will retain the object of sale until he receives payment for it, or when the buyer in a deferred sale stipulates the provision of a guarantor, the stipulations in both cases are in harmony with the requirements of the contract (*muqtaḍā al-ʿaqd*). The Ḥanafīs generally validate stipulations of this kind because they do not seek to introduce any changes of substance to the contract. There are, on the other hand, stipulations which do not correspond with the requirements of a given contract, and yet the Lawgiver may have validated it by a specific decree, in which case there remains no doubt as to their validity. An example of this is the option of cancellation (*khiyār al-sharṭ*), that is, when the buyer or the seller of a contract of sale stipulates that he or she will confirm or cancel the bargain in two or three days. This kind of stipulation is anomalous since it is essentially not in harmony with the contract of sale but, since *khiyār al-sharṭ* has been validated by the *Sunnah* of the Prophet ﷺ, the anomaly in it is ignored and it is still valid. This is also the case with regard to postponing the delivery of the subject-matter of a sale to a future date, such as in the forward sale of *salam*, which is said to be anomalous because it fails to effect an immediate transfer of ownership of the countervalues to the buyer and seller respectively. But, since *salam* has been explicitly validated by the *Sunnah*, it is permissible despite its anomalous content.

A stipulation is sometimes validated by the prevailing custom (*ʿurf*) of the community, in which case it is upheld unless there is evidence to the contrary. The general custom with regard to the sale of houses, for example, may determine whether certain items (such as light fittings) are included in the sale, even if the contract is silent on this point. If the prevailing custom so requires, it represents a customary stipulation to the sale. A voidable stipulation (*al-sharṭ al-fāsid*) is one which, although advantageous to one or other of the parties, is not validated by the law. An example of this would be to sell a house on condition that the seller continues living in it. The sale in this case is voidable, and a condition of this nature is not admissible in pecuniary contracts (*ʿuqūd māliyyah*) such as sale, but it is valid in contracts that do not involve the exchange of assets, such as gift and divorce. The reason why the Ḥanafīs have distinguished the two classes of contracts for this purpose is that there is a basic equivalence between the countervalues in the pecuniary contracts, which is then disturbed by stipulations that violate the requirements of such contracts. This is why they are voidable. Stipulations which fall under neither of the two categories of valid and voidable are deemed to be wholly null and void (*bāṭil*) and are therefore completely ignored. An example of this would be to sell a book on condition that it is not read. The contract is upheld, but the condition is totally ignored.[29]

IV. Ratiocination (*taʿlīl*) in Commercial Transactions

The position of the *Sharīʿah* in the area of *muʿāmalāt*, especially with regard to illicit gain (*riba'*), hoarding and risk-taking (*gharar*), are predicated on the prevention of conflicts, exploitation and injustice among people. These are not, in other words, founded on devotional (*ta*ʿ*abbudī*) principles but on rational causes. This is an important *Sharī*ʿ*ah* principle that is sometimes neglected by those who maintain that the intellect and human reason have no place in the *Sharī*ʿ*ah*. Many problems in the fields of Islamic economics, banking and finance arise from this inability to understand the proper role of reason in the *Sharī*ʿ*ah*. When the effective causes of *mu*ʿ*āmalāt*-related prohibitions are properly ascertained, they serve as basic indicators of the continuing validity of the transaction in question, which means that the prohibition in each case stands or falls, as the case may be, in accordance with its effective cause. This is what al-Shāṭibī has pointed out in his discussion on the differences between ʿ*ibādāt* and *mu*ʿ*āmalāt,* where he states that the basic norm in the former is submission and devotion without expatiation in effective causes, but that the law concerning *mu*ʿ*āmalāt* is generally founded on their rationale, effective cause and benefit. This means that the law in this area is open to rational analysis, enquiry and evaluation.[30] This is illustrated by the fact that the jurists of the *tābi*ʿ*ūn* period (i.e., the generation after the Companions) validated price control (*tas*ʿ*īr*) despite the fact that the Prophet ﷺ refused to authorise it during his lifetime. They were able to validate *tas*ʿ*īr* by paying attention to the effective cause and rationale behind the original ruling, and the conclusion that circumstances had undergone such a radical change that the benefit (*maṣlaḥah*) of the community could be better served by the legalisation of *tas*ʿ*īr*. We also note that the *fuqahā'* have occasionally validated transactions which involved a measure of tolerable risk-taking (*gharar*) because they did not lead to conflict, and were beneficial at that time. An example of this is the manufacturing contract of *istiṣnā*ʿ, which is validated despite the fact that it involves the sale of non-existent objects (*bay*ʿ *al-ma*ʿ*dūm*). *Istiṣnā*ʿ was validated because it responded to legitimate needs, and it was commonly practised without actually leading to inordinate conflicts.

This analysis also explains why contemporary jurists do not see it to be improper to enquire into the effective cause and rationale (ʿ*illah wa ḥikmah*) of the *ḥadīth* 'sell not what is not with you—*lā tabi*ʿ *mā laysa* ʿ*indak*'. Many have observed that the basic purpose of this *ḥadīth* was to prevent conflict, for a person who sold goods which were not in his possession risked the possibility of those goods not being available in the market and, therefore, of failure to make delivery. This was a particular cause of concern in the market-place of Medina, which was very small, and where uncertainty prevailed over regularity in the supply of commodities.[31] When we compare this market-place to the market conditions of today, we are faced with a set of totally different conditions.

Given modern means of transport and communication, it may well be possible for a merchant to obtain the goods he needs to deliver without excessive difficulty or costs. Here we note that the basic purpose and rationale of the original prohibition no longer relates to the modern market reality (especially in the area of futures trading), because the fear of failure to deliver, or of disputes arising from this, are no longer major causes for concern.

Furthermore, even with reference to *ʿibādāt*, the effective *ʿillah* and rationale of a given ruling of *Sharīʿah* may present a persuasive case for a certain change. To illustrate this, we note that the Prophet ﷺ forbade taking the Qur'ān on a journey to non-Muslim territories. But today people travel and take the Qur'ān with them everywhere, which is obviously due to a change in the rationale of the original prohibition, namely, to prevent contempt of and disrespect to the Holy Book. When this is no longer the case, that is, when the effective cause of the prohibition no longer applies, then the prohibition itself ceases to operate. The same analysis may be extended to the initial ruling of Imām Abū Ḥanīfah that, as an act of piety, teaching the Qur'ān was to be free of charge. But with the change of circumstances, Ḥanafī jurists reversed this ruling and validated remuneration for teaching the Qur'ān simply because not enough people were coming forth to disseminate the knowledge of the Qur'ān without a financial incentive.[32]

Ijtihād is the main vehicle by which the *Sharīʿah* can be adjusted so as to accommodate social change, and it relies, to a large extent, on the proper understanding and application of *taʿlīl*. Ascertaining the effective cause and rationale of a given law is necessarily the first step in the application of *taʿlīl*, and it consists almost entirely of rational enquiry into the rules of the *Sharīʿah*. The scholars within and without the leading *madhāhib* have differed on their understanding of *taʿlīl* and the scope within which it can validly operate. While no one has refuted the basic validity of *taʿlīl*, the rationalists (*ahl al-ra'y*), and their supporters in the Ḥanafī in Mālikī schools, have applied it more extensively than their counterparts in the other schools, with the Ẓāhirīs being the most restrictive of them all.

V. The Role of Custom (*ʿUrf*)

Custom is recognised as a source of law in almost all legal systems, including the *Sharīʿah* of Islam. The changing needs of a society are often reflected in its customs, which are in many ways the vehicle of society's adjustment to new conditions. Custom is also an indicator at once of the people's needs, and their acceptance or resistance to change. It is inherently dynamic and open-ended, and always remains susceptible to further refinement. The role that custom has played in the development of the *Sharīʿah* is manifested in the acknowledgement that a great deal of what is known in the name of *ijmāʿ* (general consensus), *maṣlaḥah* (public good) and *fatwa* (juristic opinion) often originates in the customs and living experience of the community.[33]

Custom is also utilised as an aid to the textual interpretation of the Qur'ān and *ḥadīth*. The general (*ʿāmm*) and the absolute (*muṭlaq*) of the text may thus be specified and qualified in the light of custom. For example, when it is stated in the Qur'ān, on the subject of maintenance (*nafaqah*), that 'let those who possess the means provide in accordance with their means' (65:7),

لينفق ذو سعة من سعته

the court of the *Sharīʿah* determines the precise portion of maintenance by reference to social custom and what people consider to be suitable and fair. Similarly, when the Qur'ān requires witnesses to be upright and just (65:2), or when it declares, with reference to victuals, that 'God permits to them [the believers] what is good and forbids them what is evil' (7:157),

ويحل لهم الطيبات ويحرم عليهم الخبائث

the precise meaning of these qualifications is in each case determined by reference to prevailing custom and the general guidance of the *Sharīʿah*.

Custom is upheld and declared authoritative in many legal maxims of *fiqh*, such as 'what is stipulated by *ʿurf* is like that which is stipulated by the text'[34]

المعروف عرفا كالمشروط شرطا

and also that 'what is proven by *ʿurf* is like that which is proven by a *sharʿī* proof',[35]

ان الثابت بالمعروف ثابت بدليل شرعي

that 'custom is authoritative'[36]

العادة محكمة

and that 'the usage of people is a proof that must be acted upon'[37].

استعمال الناس حجة يجب العمل بها .

The essence of all this is reflected in the saying of the renowned Companion ʿAbd Allāh ibn Masʿūd (sometimes designated as a *ḥadīth*) that 'what the Muslims deem to be good, is good in the eyes of Allāh'.[38]

ما رآه المسلمون حسنا فهو عند الله حسن .

There is thus unequivocal recognition of the authority of custom as a proof and basis for an adjudication, especially in civil transactions and commerce. In order to be valid, *ʿurf* must fulfil certain conditions, namely, that it must be a dominant practice and that it does not violate the injunctions of the *Sharīʿah* or the clear stipulations of a contractual agreement. When *ʿurf* fulfils all the necessary requirements, it is authoritative.[39]

The leading Imām of *fiqh*, especially Abū Ḥanīfah, Mālik and al-Shāfiʿī, not only relied on custom but also changed their own *fatāwa* and *ijtihād* in the light of changes in popular customs. This is particularly noted in the life and works of Imām al-Shāfiʿī, who developed a new school after he left Iraq and took residence in Egypt. He consequently revised and changed many of his earlier rulings in the light of the mores and customs of Egyptian society.[40] One also finds in the works of the *fuqahā'* numerous instances where they formulated the rules of *fiqh* by reference to the prevailing custom. One example of this is the division of the dower (*mahr*) into two parts: prompt and deferred; if the portion of either of these is not specified in the contract of marriage, this will be done by reference to custom. Similarly, what is considered a defect (*ʿayb*) in an object of sale, which may or not warrant revocation of a sale that is already concluded, is to be determined by reference to custom. So also the question of who might be entitled to remuneration in industries—the apprentice or the instructor—is to be determined by reference to the prevailing custom. A ruling of *fiqh*, a *fatwa* or *ijtihād* which originates in *ʿurf* is particularly liable to change when there is a change in its underlying *ʿurf*, and hence the legal maxim of *fiqh* that the 'change of rules is undeniable with the change of time'.[41]

Conclusion

Muslim scholars across the centuries have understood the *Sharīʿah* to be inherently rational since it is founded, both in principle and in practice, on the realisation of benefits. This conclusion is drawn from the affirmative stance that the Qur'ān takes towards rational enquiry and investigation. The Qur'ān refers, on numerous occasions, to the causes, objectives and benefits of its laws, and speaks approvingly of those who think, enquire into the world around them and possess knowledge, those who refuse to be overwhelmed by the demands of meaningless imitation and those who exercise their own faculty of reason in the understanding of God's law. The Qur'ān thus clearly encourages a broad, rational and comprehensive approach to the understanding of its laws, as opposed to a literalist and mechanical approach (such as that of the Ẓāhirīs) which has hardly ever commanded general acceptance. Thus according to al-Shāṭibī, the rules of the *Sharīʿah* concerning civil transactions and customary matters (*muʿāmalāt wa ʿādāt*) fully pursue the benefits (*maṣāliḥ*) that they aim for. The *Sharīʿah* may thus forbid something because it is devoid of benefit, but permits the same when it serves a beneficial purpose. Fresh dates may not, for instance, be sold in exchange for dry dates for fear of usury and *gharar*, but the Prophet ﷺ permitted this very transaction, known as *ʿarayā*, because of the people's need and *maṣlaḥah*.[42] Ratiocination in the Qur'ān means that the laws of *Sharīʿah* outside *ʿibādāt* are not imposed for their own sake but in order to realise certain benefits. From this we learn, as Amīr Bādshāh has also stated, that when a particular ruling no longer attains its underlying purpose and rationale, it should be changed and substituted with a suitable alternative. To do otherwise would mean neglecting the objective of the Lawgiver (*maqṣūd al-sharīʿ*) and the purpose of His law.[43] To make *fiqh* accommodate with the realities of society is at once the essence and principal task of *ijtihād*. It is a collective duty (*farḍ kafāʾī*), on all of those qualified to make a contribution, to initiate the necessary changes to *fiqh* and thereby help to keep the *Sharīʿah* a relevant and viable force for the Muslim community.

NOTES

1. Yūsuf al-Qaradāwī, *Bayʿ al-Murābaḥah li'l-Amir bi'l-Shira'*, 2nd edn, Cairo, Maktabah Wahbah, 1407/1987, p. 13.
2. Cf. Ibn Qayyim al-Jawziyyah, *Iʿlām al-Muwaqqiʿīn ʿan Rabb al-ʿĀlamīn*, Cairo, Maktabah al-Kulliyyat al-Azhariyyah, 1968, I, 344.
3. Taqī al-Dīn ibn Taymiyyah, *Naẓariyyah al-ʿAqd*, Beirut: Dār al-Maʿrifah, 1317 AH, p. 226.
4. Madkūr, *al-Fiqh*, p. 133.
5. Recorded by al-Nawawī in his *Arbaʿīn Ḥadīth* (Forty Select *Ḥadīth*). For this and similar other *ḥadīth*, see also al-Qaradāwī, *Bayʿ al-Murābaḥah*, p. 13ff.
6. Cf. al-Qaradāwī, *Bayʿ al-Murābaḥah*, p. 125.
7. Cf. Wizārat al-Awqāf wa'l-Shu'ūn al-Islāmiyyah, *al-Mawsūʿah al-Fiqhiyyah*, Kuwait, 1408/1987, article on *Taysīr*, XIV, 213.
8. Ibid., p. 213.
9. Al-Shāṭibī, *Muwāfaqāt*, II, 159.
10. See for details *al-Mawsūʿah al-Fiqhiyyah*, XIV, 214-45.
11. Al-Jassas, *Aḥkām al-Qur'ān*, ed. Muḥammad al-Sadiq Qamhani, Beirut, Dār Iḥyā' al-Turath al-ʿArabī, 1985, II, p. 391; also quoted in *al-Mawsūʿah al-Fiqhiyyah* (Kuwait) XIV, p. 245.
12. Cf. al-Qaradāwī, *Bayʿ al-Murābaḥah*, p. 22.
13. Cf. Madkūr, *al-Fiqh*, p. 37.
14. Muslim, *Mukhtaṣar Saḥīḥ Muslim*, p. 294, *ḥadīth* no. 1112.

15 Abū ʿĪsā al-Tirmidhī, *Sunan al-Tirmidhī*, Istanbul, Cagri Yayinlari, 1981, *ḥadīth* no. 147; also quoted in *al-Mawsūʿah al-Fiqhiyyah*, XIV, 245.

16. Aḥmad ibn Ḥanbal, *Fihris Aḥādīth Musnad al-Imām Aḥmad b. Ḥanbal*, compiled by Abū Ḥajir Zaghlul, Beirut, Dār al-Kutub, 1405/1985, IV, 338; Shams al-Dīn al-Sarakhṣī, *al-Mabsūṭ*, 30 vols., Beirut, Dār al-Maʿrifah, 1408/1986, X, 145; in *al-Mawsūʿah al-Fiqhiyyah*, XIV, 214.

17. Muslim, *Mukhtaḍar Saḥīḥ Muslim*, p. 474, *ḥadīth* no. 1784.

18. Ibid. p. 474, *ḥadīth* no. 1783.

19. Ibn Qayyim, II, 242.

20. Quoted in *al-Mawsūʿah al-Fiqhiyyah*, XIV, 245, and by al-Qaraḍāwī, *Bayʿ al-Murābaḥah*, p. 23.

21. Taqī al-Dīn ibn Taymiyyah, *Majmūʿah Fatāwā Shaykh al-Islām Ibn Taymiyyah*, compiled by ʿAbd al-Raḥmān b. al-Qāsim, Beirut, Muʿassasah al-Risālah 1398 AH, III, 335. See also Madkūr, *al-Fiqh*, p. 418.

22. Madkūr, *al-Fiqh*, p. 421.

23. See for details Yaḥyā ibn ʿAlī al-Shawkānī, *Irshād al-Fuḥūl min Taḥqīq al-Haqqilā ilā ʿIlm al-Uṣūl*, Cairo, Dār al-Fikr, n.d., p. 251; Sayf al-Dīn al-Āmidī, *al-Iḥkām fī Uṣūl al-Aḥkām*, ed. ʿAbd al-Razzāq ʿAfīfī, Beirut: Maktab al-Islām, 1402/1982, V, 32.

24. Ibn Qayyim, *Iʿlām*, I, 344.

25. Ibn Taymiyyah, *Majmūʿah Fatāwa*, III, 239.

26. Idem, *Naẓariyyah al-ʿAqd*, p. 227.

27. Al-Qaraḍāwī, *Bayʿ al-Murābaḥah*, p. 18.

28. Ibid., p. 19; Muḥammad Abū Zahrah, *Uṣūl al-Fiqh*, Cairo, Dār al-Fikhr al-ʿArabī 1377/1958, p. 219; ʿAbd al-Raḥmān al-Sābūnī, *al-Madkhal al-Fiqhī wa'l-Tārīkh al-Tashrīʿ al-Islāmī*, Cairo, Maktabah Wahbah 1402/1982, p. 145.

29. Al-Shāṭibī, *Muwāfaqāt*, II, 305.

30. Amīr Bādshāh, *al-Taysīr Sharḥ al-Taḥrir*, Beirut: Dār al-Kutub al-ʿIlmiyyah, 1983, I, 360.

31. Yūsuf Mūsā, *al-Buyūʿ*, p. 193.

32. Abū Zahrah, *Uṣūl*, p. 219.

33. Cf. Muṣṭafā Shalabī, *al-Fiqh al-Islāmī bayn al-Mithāliyyah wa'l-Wāqiʿiyyah*, Cairo, Dār al-Jāmiʿiyyah, 1982, p. 8.

34. *Mujallah al-Aḥkām al-ʿAdliyyah* (known as the Mejelle), Eng. trans. C. R. Tyser, Lahore, Law Publishing Co., 1967, (Art.43).

35. Al-Sarakhṣī, *al-Mubsūṭ*, XIII, 14.

36. The Mejelle (Art.36).

37. The Mejelle (Art.37).

38. Al-Shāṭibī, *al-Iʿtiṣām*, II, 319; al-Āmidī, *Iḥkām*, I, 124.

39. For more details on *ʿurf* see Mohammad Hashim Kamali, *Principles of Islamic Jurisprudence*, 2nd revised edn, Cambridge, The Islamic Texts Society, 1991, pp. 364ff.

40. Abū Zahrah, *Uṣūl*, p. 217.

41. Cf. Muṣṭafā Aḥmad al-Zarqa, *al-Madkhal al-Fiqhī al-ʿAm*, Damascus, Dār al-Fikhr, 1387/1968, I, 136-7.

42. Ibid., p. 205.

43. Amīr Bādshāh, *al-Taysīr*, I, 360.

CHAPTER EIGHT

Uncertainty and Risk-Taking (*Gharar*) in Islamic Law

The initial part of this chapter expounds the concept of *gharar* and the juristic debate as to whether it consists mainly of uncertainty about the existence of the subject matter of a contract or of ignorance of a contract's material attributes. Some scholars have also suggested that the basic concern in all discussions of *gharar* is with elements of risk-taking, gambling and the unlawful appropriation of the property of others. This discussion continues to look into the conditions and typology of *gharar*, and the related issues of sale of the unseen (*bayᶜ al-ghā'ib*), sale of the non-existent (*bayᶜ al-maᶜdūm*), sale at the market price (*bayᶜ bi siᶜr al-sūq*) and the relevance of *gharar* to Islamic insurance (*takāful*), and futures trading in commodities.

I. Definition and Concept

The literal meaning of the word *gharar* is fraud (*al-khidaᶜ*), but in transactions the word has often been used to mean risk, uncertainty and hazard. In a contract of sale the word *gharar* often refers to uncertainty, and the ignorance of one or both parties of the substance or attributes of the object of sale, or of doubt over this object's existence at the time of contract. *Gharar* is, however, a broad concept and may carry different shades of meanings in different kinds of transactions. Muslim jurists have differed widely on the definition of *gharar*. Many have related it to doubt about the existence of the subject-matter of contract. Thus, according to Ibn ᶜĀbidīn, *gharar* in reference to a sale consists of doubt about the existence of its subject-matter.[1] According to the Ẓāhiris, *gharar* is basically concerned with ignorance of the material attributes of the subject matter rather than doubt about its availability and existence.

Gharar is thus present in a contract of sale where the buyer does not know what he is buying nor the seller what he is selling.[2] But the Ẓāhiris seem to be alone in this. The third view on *gharar*, which is adopted by the majority, tends to combine the two above views. *Gharar* thus includes both ignorance of the material attributes of the subject-matter of a sale, and also uncertainty regarding its availability and existence. Al-Sarakhsī has stated that *gharar* in a contract or transaction exists when its consequences are hidden and unknown to the contracting parties (*al-gharar mā yakūnu mastūr al-ʿaqībah*).[3]

Whereas much of the juristic discourse on *gharar* is focused on the contract of sale, and more specifically on the subject-matter of sale, it is by no means confined to this, for *gharar* can also consist of uncertainty regarding the terms of offer and acceptance, or determination of the price and other material elements of a contract of sale. *Gharar* can also affect other contracts, such as those of lease and hire (*ijārah*) and contracts of exchange generally. But *gharar* does not, in principle, apply to charitable contracts, or *tabarruʿāt*, such as gifts and bequests, although there is some disagreement on the latter point.

For *gharar* to have legal consequences, it must fulfil four conditions. The first of these is that it must be excessive, not trivial. A slight *gharar*, such as *gharar* in the sale of similar items that are not identical at one and the same price, is held to be negligible. Second, it must occur in the context of cumulative contracts (*ʿuqūd al-muʿāwaḍāt al-māliyyah*), thus precluding *tabarruʿāt*. Third, *gharar* must affect the subject-matter of contract directly, as opposed to what may be attached to it (i.e., in a cow, it is the animal itself that is the object, not its unborn calf). Fourth, the people concerned should not be in need of the contract in question. Should there be a public need (*ḥājjat al-nās*) for it, *gharar*, even if excessive, will be ignored. This is because satisfying the people's need takes priority by virtue of the Qur'ānic principle of removal of hardship (*rafʿ al-ḥaraj*). The *Sharīʿah* thus validates *salam* (advance purchase) and *istiṣnāʿ* (manufacture contract) regardless of the *gharar* elements therein, simply because of the people's need for them.[4]

Depending on its scale and magnitude, *gharar* may render a contract totally null and void, or it may constitute a cause for indemnity and compensation. A slight *gharar* may, on the other hand, be deemed to be tolerable, in which case its presence does not affect the basic validity of a contract, except for certain types of fiduciary contracts, such as the *murābaḥah* (cost plus profit) sale, where a slight *gharar* is enough to vitiate the contract altogether.[5] *Gharar* in a contract, according to Ibn Ḥazm, originates in ignorance of the quantity or attributes of the subject-matter of the sale at the time of contracting.[6] Al-Kāsānī has defined *gharar* as consisting essentially of the sort of uncertainty where the prospects of the existence and non-existence of something are about equal. *Gharar* in a contract of sale may consist of doubt about the attributes of an object, matters related to timing and other specifications of its delivery, and payment.[7]

Gharar is prevented when the contracting parties have adequate knowledge of the countervalues they intend to exchange; when the object is known to exist; when it is obtainable and its quantity, quality and attributes are then identified; when it can then be duly delivered. In the case of a deferred sale (*bayᶜ al-mu'ajjal*), it is important that the terms of delivery and payment, and the relevant time-frame, are clearly stated and that all necessary precautions are taken to ensure that the parties are able to fulfil their obligations.

It is reported in a *ḥadīth* simply that 'the Prophet ﷺ prohibited the sale of *gharar*'. While commenting on this *ḥadīth*, Ibn Taymiyyah wrote that '*gharar* sale is a sale which partakes in risk-taking (*mukhāṭarah*) and in unlawful devouring the property of others'.[8] Whenever there is uncertainty in a sale, whether the goods can be delivered to the purchaser or not, the sale *ipso facto* participates in *gharar*. The main issue here is the availability (*ḥuṣūl*) and deliverability of the subject matter of the sale. Ibn Taymiyyah adds further that some writers have classed ignorance of the quantity and attributes of this subject-matter as *gharar*, but the authority for this position is weak and a distinction between this kind of ignorance and *gharar* is therefore warranted.[9]

The jurists have drawn three different conclusions from the phrase '*naha an-nabiyyu*' ('the Prophet ﷺ prohibited') in the above *ḥadīth*. While some have held that the phrase here conveys a total ban (*taḥrīm*), the majority have interpreted it to mean corruption (*fasād*) and deficiency in the contract or transaction concerned. This would render the contract deficient in respect of the legal consequences it could generate. According to yet another view, the text here can mean both prohibition (*taḥrīm*) or deficiency (*fasād*) due to general (*ᶜāmm*) manner of its wording. A general text, in other words, can convey all its possible meanings, which may, however, be specified according to the rules of specification (*takhṣīs*). Moreover, the *ḥadīth* clearly singles out sale, which might suggest that *gharar* does not affect other contracts. This is, however, not the case as the jurists have, by analogy, extended the ruling of this *ḥadīth* to other contracts of exchange where *gharar* can generate similar consequences to those it does in regard to sale.[10]

II. Excessive and Minor *Gharar*

There is general agreement about the fact that excessive *gharar*, termed *al-gharar al-kathīr*, concerning the object of sale renders the transaction invalid. Jurists are equally in agreement that minor *gharar* (*al-gharar al-yasīr*) is tolerable and permitted.[11] Ibn Juzay has stated that *gharar* is prohibited by the *Sunnah*, and must be avoided unless it is very minor, in which case it can be tolerated.[12] It is thus evident that the basic issue in this classification of *gharar* is one of degree, since most commercial transactions may be said to involve some element of uncertainty, but this, alone, does not necessarily render them invalid. From the point of view of magnitude, *gharar* has been divided into three types, namely, excessive *gharar*, which vitiates the transaction, minor *gharar*, which is tolerated, and moderate *gharar* (*al-gharar al-mutawassit*), which falls between the other two categories. It is this third type which is most susceptible to being evaluated differently and wrongly placed in the category of one or the other of the two extremes.[13] Sales that are definitely forbidden because of excessive *gharar*, as Ibn Juzay points out, includes sales in which delivery is not attainable, such as, the sale of a runaway camel; a sale in which the price, or the object of the sale, are unknown; deferred sale in which the deferment period is unknown, such as when so and so arrives or dies; the sale of what is not expected to survive, such as a diseased animal; and a number of types of other sales, described below, that were practised in pre-Islamic Arabia.[14]

Excessive *gharar* may originate, as Ibn Rushd has explained, in ignorance and a lack of information about the nature and attributes of an object, in a doubt about its availability and existence, in doubt about its quantity, or in a lack of exact information concerning the price or the unit of currency in which the price is paid, or the terms of its payment. *Gharar* may also relate to the time of payment, especially in sales where payment or delivery is postponed to a future date. In addition, excessive *gharar* may arise regarding the prospects of delivery and the vendor's ability to make a delivery according to contract, or on the question of whether the object can be delivered intact and can remain, in the case of deferment, in a fit condition until the time of delivery. Ibn Rushd has further added that certain types of sale which partake in excessive *gharar* have been expressly forbidden on the authority of *ḥadīth*. These include the sale of the offspring of an unborn animal (*ḥabal al-ḥabalah*), the sale of fruit prior to its ripening, those sales termed *mulāmasah*, *munābadhah* and *al-ḥaṣṣāt* (sales, mainly of clothes, that were concluded, in pre-Islamic Arabia, when the buyer touched the object or when the parties threw the exchange objects to one another, and sale in which the object was identified by throwing pebbles in the dark); two bargains in one (*al-bayʿatayn fī bayʿah*), that is, sale in which two different prices are quoted, one prompt, one deferred; sale of what is in the loins and wombs (*al-maḍāmin wa'l-malāqiḥ*), and so forth. These were forbidden by the express authority of *ḥadīth* because of the ignorance of the parties regarding the existence or the attributes, or both, of the object of sale, and there is general agreement among the jurists concerning these prohibitions.[15]

There are other types of sale for which no explicit authority is found in the sources, and this is why they have become the subject of juristic opinion and *ijtihād*. In their evaluation of *gharar*, whether excessive or minor, the jurists have been influenced by prevailing circumstances, popular custom and their own vision and interpretation of public good or *maṣlaḥah*. As a result, certain types of *gharar* have been judged to be excessive by some jurists but trivial and negligible by others. There are also some types of transactions, such as *bayʿ al-ʿaynah* (a kind of deferred sale in which the sale is used as a means of obtaining a questionable gain), which some jurists have classified as *gharar*, while others have regarded them to be illicit gain (*ribā'*) or both.

Some types of sale that are deemed to consist of *gharar* of the average type are the sale of what is hidden in soil, lump sum sale, or *bayʿ al-juzāf*, sale at the market price (*bayʿ bi siʿr al-sūq*), in which the actual price is not specified, sale prior to taking possession (*bayʿ qabl al-qabḍ*), sale of consecutive produce in advance, sale of the absent (*bayʿ al-gha'ib*), and so forth. The jurists have differed in their evaluation of *gharar* in these situations, which is why they have reached different conclusions about their validity or otherwise. Some of these will be discussed separately in the following pages.

Abū'l-Walīd al-Bāji has advanced the view that minor *gharar* is that which is found in nearly all contracts but does not feature prominently therein, whereas excessive *gharar* is that which overwhelms and dominates a contract or transaction to the extent that it becomes a salient feature thereof. Ṣiddīq al-Ḍarīr has understood this to mean effective *gharar* (*al-gharar al-mu'aththir*) as opposed to that which is negligible and ineffective (*ghayr mu'aththir*). To this al-Ḍarīr adds the remark that it is otherwise not feasible to give precise definitions of what is excessive as opposed to what may be said to be minor *gharar*. This is particularly due to the circumstantial aspect of *gharar*, which may be seen as excessive and unacceptable in a certain setting but judged differently under different circumstances.[16]

Al-Kasānī thus elaborates that if ignorance of the object of sale or its price is such that it can lead to a dispute between the parties, the sale becomes void, but if it is unlikely to give rise to a dispute, the sale is not vitiated. When the expected dispute over a material aspect of the countervalues is such that it is likely to hinder delivery and completion, this renders the sale invalid since it frustrates the basic purpose of sale. But if the ignorance is of an aspect of the sale that is not likely to obstruct completion and delivery, the basic purpose of the sale is fulfilled and it remains valid. Knowledge of the specifics in a sale is necessary because it is a prerequisite for consent, which cannot exist without precise information. The question then arises as to whether the existence of such knowledge is a requirement for the validity (*ṣiḥḥah*) of a sale, or whether it signifies a deficiency that does not affect the basic validity of sale but may act as a delaying factor in its enforcement, known as condition of enforceability (*sharṭ al-luzūm*).

It is generally agreed that sufficient knowledge of the substance of an object of sale to an extent that precludes the possibility of disputes between the parties, is essential for the validity of a sale. As for the knowledge of attributes, the Ḥanafīs maintain that this is not a prerequisite for validity but for enforceability (*luzūm*). Hence, the sale of a thing which the buyer has not seen (*bayʿ al-gha'ib*) is valid but it is not enforceable, according to the Ḥanafīs, unless the buyer views and ratifies the bargain. The Shāfiʿīs, on the other hand, maintain that knowledge of both the essence and attributes of the countervalues is a precondition for validity, and a sale in which the buyer has not seen the object is therefore invalid because of excessive *gharar*.[17]

The Mālikī jurist, al-Qarāfī, has drawn a certain distinction between *gharar* and that which is unknown (*al-majhūl*), and commented that the scholars have often used these concepts interchangeably, even though they are not always the same thing. The essence of *gharar* is uncertainty regarding the availability of something, such as that of a bird in the sky or of fish in water. But when something is certain to be available, and doubt remains regarding its quality and attributes, this is a sale of the unknown (*bayʿ al-majhūl*). An example of this is the sale of what may be hidden in a bag or in one's sleeve, which is clearly available but not known. *Gharar* and *majhūl* thus converge and overlap, so that one may be predominant and subsume the other; at other times, one of the two may be more specific and does not extend to the other. The two can be present at the same time but they can also be found separately from one another. A sale which involves *gharar* but not ignorance of its substance, is like selling a stone which is suspected to be a ruby. The fact that it is present and available eliminates *gharar* of its accessibility but not the ignorance of its substance and attributes. In the sale, on the other hand, of a runaway camel that has been seen prior to its escape, ignorance regarding the subject-matter and material qualities of the sale is eliminated, but *gharar* over its availability remains. But *gharar* and ignorance would both be present in the sale, for examples, of a runaway animal which is unseen, or the sale of a commodity which is not named or identified.[18]

III. Sale of the Unseen (*Gha'ib*) and the Non-Existent (*Maᶜdūm*)

With regard to the sale of the unseen, or the sale of what is not visible (*bayᶜ al-gha'ib*), such as sale of nuts in their shells, or that of crops not yet grown to maturity, or the sale of fish in a pond, the schools of law have held different views on the subject, on the ground of their respective perception of *gharar*. Whereas Imām al-Shāfiᶜī considered *gharar* in *bayᶜ al-gha'ib* to be excessive, Imām Mālik viewed it to be negligible. Abū Ḥanīfah, on the other hand, held that there is no problem regarding *gharar* so long as the buyer is granted the option of viewing (*khiyār al-ru'yah*).[19] The schools have also differed on the determination of price. While the Ḥanbalīs permit the determination of price by reference to the market price, or even by the intervention of a third party, the majority of scholars consider such ambiguities to constitute excessive *gharar* that vitiates the sale. Price determination (*maᶜlūmiyyah al-thaman*) for the majority of scholars has meant an exact monetary value, in a normal sale, or exact quantities on both sides, in the case of a barter exchange. The Ḥanbalīs, on the other hand, have maintained that the price may be determined either in exact figures or in any manner which the parties find agreeable and which is clear enough to preclude the likelihood of a dispute arising between them.[20] The barometer of *gharar* to Ibn Taymiyyah is whether or not the transaction involves gambling and unlawful devouring of the property of others (*akl māl al-ghayr bi'l bāṭil*). *Gharar* thus occurs in a contract when one of the parties takes what is due to him but the other does not receive his entitlement. If his right continues to be unfulfilled, the first becomes guilty of the wrongful devouring of the property of his counterpart in the transaction, and a *gharar* sale of this kind engages in gambling and punting (*al-qimār wa'l-maysir*), which the *Sharīᶜah* has forbidden.[21] Ibn Taymiyyah is thus critical of those who consider the 'touch and throw' sales (*al-mulāmasah wa'l munabādh*) to be *gharar* sales on grounds of ignorance. This is not accurate. These kind of sales, such as that of the offspring of an unborn animal (*ḥabal al-ḥabalah*) or the sale of fruit prior to its ripening, are forbidden because of the presence of an element of risk-taking (*mukhāṭarah*) that involves devouring the property of others.[22] The same is true, Ibn Taymiyyah adds, of the sale of the unseen, of that which is unknown (*bayᶜ al-maᶜdūm wa'l-majhūl*) and sales in which the vendor cannot deliver.

Should any of these take part in unlawful devouring, they are unlawful; otherwise, they are lawful. If they participate in gambling, this amounts to the same thing. When one of the parties takes what is due to him but the other is faced with the risk of losing his, the former is a gambler.[23]

There is also some difference of opinion, as noted above, regarding the validity of sale of the non-existent (*bayᶜ al-maᶜdūm*). Although many scholars have stated that there is a general consensus (*ijmāᶜ*) among the leading schools of law on the prohibition of this sale, we note that Ibn Qayyim al-Jawziyyah and al-Sanhūrī, among others, have departed from the original verdict and maintained that there is no evidence in the sources to proscribe the sale of a non-existent object; that the *Sharīᶜah* prohibits *gharar* but that the jurists have somehow equated non-existence with *gharar*, even though this is not always the case.[24] Al-Sanhūrī concurs with Ibn Qayyim and elaborates that the conventional *fiqh* is somewhat too restrictive on this issue, and a re-evaluation is therefore warranted. Al-Sanhūrī is particularly critical of the prohibition of that variety of *bayᶜ al-maᶜdūm* in which the object of sale is non-existent at the time of contract, but it is certain to come into being in the future. Al-Sanhūrī thus divides *bayᶜ al-maᶜdūm*, *inter alia*, into four categories as follows: firstly, when the object exists in essence but comes into completion thereafter; secondly, when the object, although non-existent at the time of contract, is certain to exist in the future; thirdly, when the object is non-existent at the time of contract, or exists in essence, but whose existence in the future is uncertain; and finally, when the object is non-existent at the time of contract and cannot be expected to exist in the future. Of these four types, only the last two present situations in which *gharar* is deemed to be excessive and would, therefore, invalidate the contract. As for the first two, Ibn Qayyim and al-Sanhūrī have both concluded that *gharar* in them is negligible and the sale in both cases is therefore valid.[25] Ṣiddīq al-Ḍarīr has held a similar view in saying that the sale of the non-existent is unlawful if its future prospects are totally unknown, but that 'the sale is valid of every non-existent object which is certain, according to common knowledge and custom, to come into being in the future'.[26] Some types of *bayᶜ al-maᶜdūm* that were prohibited by clear *ḥadīth* included the sale of the unborn animal, or *ḥabal al-ḥabalah*. But there is disagreement about other kinds of *bayᶜ al-maᶜdūm*, such as the sale of unripe fruit, and that which is hidden in the soil, or in a shell.

The presence or absence of *gharar* in *bayᶜ al-maᶜdūm* has thus been judged and evaluated differently by the scholars, and a clear departure from the earlier assessment has been developed in the subsequent evolution of juristic *ijtihād*. In an attempt to ascertain the application of these views to futures trading in commodities, one would naturally need to know the technicalities of futures trading, especially the clearance procedures that are applied by the clearing-house. Here we note that market realities and the clearing-house procedures tend to preclude any serious doubt or uncertainty regarding the existence and delivery prospects of the subject matter of sale. One may justly conclude, then, that in the event of futures contracts leading to delivery, *gharar* over the existence of the underlying commodity in the future is not an issue. Nor do the prospects of delivery or of the fulfilment of all the material aspects of the contract—relating, for example, to grade/quality, the time of delivery and payment of price—involve the issues of *gharar*. In all cases where the buyer wishes to take delivery, the clearing-house guarantees to deliver.

A straight application of the concept of *bayᶜ al-maᶜdūm* to futures trading in commodities is likely to lead to passing a prohibitive judgement on futures, which is what many commentators have attempted, including Ṣiddīq al-Ḍarīr. But he then adds that modern legislation in Muslim countries has generally validated contracts that incur future obligations, and also the sale of non-existent objects. The *gharar* that is involved in futures contracts and the sale on non-existent objects has been ignored by the modern law that is currently in force in Muslim countries. Modern law thus validates the definite and binding sale of as yet uncultivated produce by farmers and landowners for a price determined in advance or determined by the prevailing market price at the time of delivery. This would be invalid under the formula of *bayᶜ al-maᶜdūn*. Al-Ḍarīr advances the same analysis concerning the sale of objects that are not owned by the seller at the tim of contract, for this too involves *gharar* on account uncertainty about the prospects of delivery. Thus uncertainty, al-Ḍarīr adds, is also the case with regard to futures trading in commodities, for the seller often does not own what he sells in the futures market. Al-Ḍarīr goes on to argue that this matter is open to fresh and, preferably, collective *ijtihād*, for when there is a time lag between the signing of a contract and delivery of its subject matter, the owner may be able to acquire ownership during the interval. Thus if someone sell a commodity that he does not own at the time of the contract but which he is certain to be able to own and deliver later, this may be considered lawful. The *gharar* in question, which consists of inability to deliver, may not present a problem and the sale may be declared valid. But al-Ḍarīr ends by saying: 'I believe the best platform to issue a collective verdict on this is probably the Fiqh Academy of Jeddah.'[27] I shall comment on this point in a moment, but suffice it here to note that the *gharar* content of futures trading in commodities has been evaluated variously by commentators and, although many have considered this *gharar* to be excessive and unacceptable, many have also expressed reservations about a total prohibition and considered the *gharar* aspect of futures trading to be less than substantive. Ṣiddīq al-Ḍarīr appears to have expressed a reservation of this kind.

IV. A Four-Part Classification of *Gharar*

Gharar can be summarised as occurring in four main ways. These are on account of uncertainty and risk pertaining to the existence of the subject matter of a sale, or its availability, uncertainty about the quantities involved and, lastly, uncertainty about time of completion and delivery. First, should uncertainty about the actual existence of something at the time of contract exist, this vitiates the contract according to the majority of jurists but not according to the Ḥanbalīs—that is, if the future existence of something is not in doubt. Modern scholars like al-Sanhūrī, Muḥammad Yūsuf Mūsā and others have supported the Ḥanbalī position on this issue. The second variety of *gharar* concerns a situation where a thing may exist, such as fish in a lake, but uncertainty surrounds its availability at the time of contract. If there is only a slight doubt about availability, for instance that of a fish in a small pond or of birds in a confined space, *gharar* arising from this kind of doubt is tolerated, but excessive *gharar* over availability vitiates the sale. Availability itself can also be actual or potential in that the object of sale, although not available at the time of contract, could become available later. The third of the four varieties of *gharar* mentioned above is concerned with uncertainty over the quantity either of the subject matter or its price, or both. The theory of contracts requires the precise determination of quantity, quality and number, but the Ḥanbalīs and some other jurists have taken a somewhat flexible stance on this by maintaining that this determination need only be specific enough to prevent a dispute arising between the parties. If the parties find a mere reference to 'the market price', for example, a good enough basis on which to operate them, then this is acceptable.

Lastly, *gharar* consisting of uncertainty about the time of completion and delivery of an object of sale is largely addressed under the theoretical category of *ajal*, or deferment in contracts. Deferment is valid if it involves one, but not both, of the countervalues in a sale. The jurists have not specified any minimum or maximum limits for deferment in payment or delivery, and there is some flexibility in the manner in which the time-frame can be determined. Delivery may thus be on a specific date in the future, or according to such other terms as would introduce some flexibility. A period like 'next month', for example, signifies the beginning of the month, and 'three months' the end of the period, and 'harvesting time' would most likely be an acceptable term for specific crops. Some questions pertaining to *gharar* that tend to arise in the context of futures trading are firstly that of whether the deferment of both of the countervalues to a future date can validly take place and whether the conventional theory of contracts should be adjusted so as to accommodate this eventuality. This question calls for consideration, especially with reference to futures trading, mainly because the operational methods of futures are such that they virtually eliminate the prospects of non-delivery, or of failure of the parties to fulfil their obligations. Futures contracts in commodities are virtually all deferred contracts since deferment to a future date is the *raison d'être* of futures. Futures contracts in commodities are thus bought and sold in standardised deferment periods ranging from three months to eighteen months or even three years. Both of the countervalues are deferred to a future date and nothing actually changes hands at the time of contract beyond a margin deposit of about ten per cent of the price, which the buyer pays at the point of entry. Deferment of this kind encompasses both sides of the bargain, that is, the price and the subject-matter, and the degree of risk-related *gharar* involved here would normally be judged to be unacceptable and excessive under the rules of *fiqh* pertaining to conventional sale. There is, however, one aspect of futures trading which represents an entirely new development and which is not covered by the Islamic law of transactions. This is the guarantee function of the clearing-house. Since futures contracts basically consist of nothing more than an exchange of offer and acceptance often involving huge amounts of money payable after a period of several months, trading in them could simply not proceed without an indisputable guarantee system, as it would involve exorbitant risk and *gharar* pertaining to deferment and delivery. It is precisely this need which is addressed by the clearing-house, for it provides the necessary guarantee to ensure that the parties to the contract will honour their obligations. It is due to this novel feature of futures trading, which is not available in conventional sales, namely, the system of guaranteeing payment and delivery, that the risk-related *gharar* in futures trading in commodities has been virtually eliminated.

Muslim scholars have generally considered *gharar* in conventional insurance to be excessive on account of uncertainty and ignorance of its outcome as well as element of gambling (*maysir*) therein. *Takāful* insurance provides an alternative that is not free of uncertainty or *gharar*. Yet, since it involves a paradigm shift from one of competing interests among the contracting parties to a form of contract that is based on co-operation and mutual support in order to combat calamity and loss, the *gharar* in *takāful* loses much of its meaning and may be said to have been reduced to minor *gharar*.

V. Sale at the Market Price (*Bay*ᶜ *bi-Sir*ᶜ *al-Sūq*)

Sale is, by definition, the exchange of values between two parties by mutual consent. Muslim jurists have generally held that mutual consent can only materialise if the parties know the price of the object of the sale. There is unanimity among the scholars of the *madhāhib* that the price must be determined at the time of contract, but there is disagreement about the exact nature of this requirement. While some have understood the 'determination of price' (*ma*ᶜ*lūmiyyah al-thaman*) to mean an exact figure in monetary terms, or an exact quantity on both sides in the case of a barter exchange, others have held this to mean a price on which the parties have agreed, and which is clear enough to preclude conflict even without naming a precise figure.

Al-Sarakhṣī has stated that absence or ignorance of an exact price invalidates a sale. If, for example, a person sells something 'for the same amount that so and so received from so and so'— if this is an amount that is known to both parties, the sale is valid, but not otherwise, for a contract of sale requires the consent of both parties and this cannot materialise over an unspecified amount.[28] This is also the basic view of the Shāfiᶜī and Mālikī, and also the Ẓāhirī, schools, as they all maintain that ambiguity and ignorance of the price vitiate a sale, and that uncertainty or *gharar* is prevented only by assigning a specific price (*al-thaman al-musamma*).[29] Al-Kāsānī seems to have departed from the idea of an exact figure when he wrote that a sale is valid when 'the object of a sale and its price are known and the knowledge is such that it prevents disputes arising between the parties'. In the absence of such knowledge, the parties cannot know their obligations and this can hinder delivery and frustrate the basic purpose of a sale.[30]

The Ḥanbalī scholars Ibn Taymiyyah and Ibn Qayyim al-Jawziyyah have taken a broader view of the manner in which a price can be determined at the time of contract. They state that a price may be determined in exact figures or it may be *thaman al-mithl*, that is, the price which other people pay; or the market price, provided that only one price prevails; or it may be determined in any manner that the parties find agreeable and is clear enough to eliminate disputes. It is thus perfectly valid for the parties to conclude a sale by reference to the prevailing market price. To substantiate his position on this point, Ibn Tayimyyah has referred to the general consensus (*ijmā*ᶜ) of the scholars on the validity of assigning a proper dower (*mahr al-mithl*) in a contract of marriage. The idea of a proper price (*thaman al-mithl*) is analogous to that of a proper dower. Ibn Taymiyyah adds that there is nothing in the Qur'ān and the *Sunnah* against the concept, and general custom has validated it. Indeed, Imām

Aḥmad Ibn Ḥanbal has issued an affirmative *fatwā* on it.[31]

Muḥammad Yūsuf Mūsā has gone on record to speak in support of the Ḥanbalī position by observing that specification of the exact figure for a price is not a *Sharīʿah* requirement. It is sufficient, for example, for the parties to conclude the valid sale of a quantity of cotton 'at the prevailing market price on such and such a date'. This is clear enough, Mūsā adds, to preclude the likelihood of a dispute arising between them concerning the price.[32] With reference to futures trading, Mūsā has further observed that 'the futures contract (in the contracts market of Alexandria, for example), wherein price is determined by reference to the prevailing market price on a specified date, does not leave room for disagreement and dispute; it is determined by the mutual agreement of the parties and it is valid.'[33] This view has also found support in both Aḥmad Yūsuf Sulaymān and Aḥmad Ḥasan, who have spoken in support of the validity of a sale on the basis of the 'prevailing market price'.[34]

I believe that in view of the considerable progress that has been made in market techniques for price determination and forecasting, more refined and reliable methods are now available to inject a certain degree of objectivity and professionalism in the determination of market prices. The concern that market prices may be liable to manipulation and distortion is no longer prominent. If the parties wish to agree on the prevailing market price within a particular time-frame, there is no fear of excessive uncertainty or *gharar*, and the agreement should be seen as a manifestation of the individual freedom of contract of the parties to determine the terms of their contractual agreement.

Conclusion

Gharar is evidently a pervasive concept that permeates the whole spectrum of contracts and transactions in Islamic law. It is also a broad concept in that it comprises uncertainty and risk-taking as well as excessive speculation, gambling and ignorance of the material aspects of contracts. This is how the majority of jurists have understood the term. Hence, the attempt on the part of some to isolate some of these meanings and narrow down the concept of *gharar* is less than warranted. This enquiry has shown that *gharar* is ubiquitous in that hardly any contract is totally free of *gharar* and the salient question is often that of whether the *gharar* in question is exorbitant or not. Another feature of *gharar* that the present enquiry has underscored is its relativity and relevance to the prevailing conditions of society and custom. A certain degree of risk and ambiguity that was deemed unacceptable in earlier times may not be seen in the same light in contemporary market realities. There is a strong element of subjectivity and value judgement in *gharar* which has led to differences of opinion among jurists. The relative and circumstantial dimensions of *gharar* are not likely to change with advanced computerisation, information technology and science, simply because modern methods also bring with them uncertainties of a different order, which may be a cause of *gharar* no less serious than that which exists without them. Having said this, it is quite obvious that uncertainties about pricing, delivery and deferment have often been reduced to acceptable levels by the availability of modern means. Yet the complexities that are generated by the introduction of new products and modes of transactions in banking and finance, stock markets and futures markets have brought with them new and equally complex levels of *gharar* that often require careful assessment and analysis. The basic tools of evaluation and analysis that Islamic law has provided are comprehensive enough to relate to all these concerns and especially to the overriding one, namely, to ensure fairness and prevent excessive uncertainty and abuse in commercial transactions and contracts. These are the valid concerns of the *Sharīʿah* that must guide the evaluation of *gharar* in all its manifestations.

NOTES

1. Ibn ʿĀbidīn, *Ḥāshiyah*, IV, 147.
2. Muḥammad ʿAlī b. Aḥmad ibn Ḥazm, *al-Muḥallā*, ed. A. G. Sulaymān al-Bandarī, Beirut, Dār al-Kutub al-ʿIlmiyyah, 1408/1988, VII, 343.
3. Al-Sarakhṣī, *al-Mabsūṭ*, XIII, 149; Shaykh Ṣiddīq al-Ḍarīr, *al-Gharar wa Atharūh fi'l-ʿUqūd fi'l Fiqh al-Islāmī*, Dār al-Nashr al-Thaqāfah, 1386/1967, p. 11.
4. Cf. Ibn ʿĀbidīn, *Ḥāshiyah*, IV, 140; al-Ḍarīr, *al-Gharar fi'l-ʿUqūd*, pp. 39ff.
5. Ṣubḥī Mahmassānī, *al-Mawjibāt*, pp. 425-7; Liaquat Ali Khan Niazi, *The Islamic Law of Contract*, Lahore, Research Cell, 1990, p. 124.
6. Ibn Ḥazm, *al-Muḥallā*, IX, 363.
7. Al-Kāsānī, *Badā'iʿ*, V, 163.
8. Ibn Taymiyyah, *Naẓariyyah al-ʿAqd*, p. 225.
9. Ibid., p. 224.
10. al-Ḍarīr, *al-Gharar fi'l-ʿUqūd*, p. 10.
11. Ibn Taymiyyah, *Naẓariyyah al-ʿAqd*, p. 224.
12. Ibn Juzay, *Qawānīn al-Aḥkam al-Sharʿiyyah*, Cairo, ʿAlam al-Fikhr, 1975, p. 268.
13. Ibn Rushd, *Bidāyah*, II, 148; ʿAbd al-Razzāq al-Sanhuri, *Maṣādir al-Ḥaqq fi'l-Fiqh al-Islāmī*, Cairo: Maʿhad al-Dīrāsāt al-ʿArabiyyah al-ʿĀliyyah, 1956, III, 51; al-Baʿlī, *Ḍawābiṭ*, pp. 113-14.
14. Ibn Juzay, *Qawānīn*, pp. 268-9.
15. Ibn Rushd al-Qurṭubī, *Bidāyah*, II, 148-9.
16. Abū al-Wālid Sulaymān al-Bāji, *al-Muntaqā Sharḥal-Muwaṭṭā*, Beirut, Dār al-Kitāb al-ʿArabī, 1332 AH, I, 41; al-Ḍarīr, *al-Gharar fi'l-ʿUqūd*, p. 41.
17. Al-Kāsānī, *Badā'iʿ*, V, 163.
18. Al-Qarāfī, *Kitāb al-Furūq*, Cairo, Maṭbaʿah Dār Iḥyā' al-Kutub al-ʿArabiyyah, 1346 AH, III, 265; al-Sanḥūrī, *Maṣādir*, III, 50; al-Baʿlī, *Ḍawābiṭ*, pp. 113-14.

19. Ibn Rushd al-Qurṭubī, *Bidāyah*, II, 150.
20. Ibn Taymiyyah, *Naẓariyyah al-ᶜAqd*, p. 221; Nabil A. Saleh, 'Financial Transactions and Islamic Theory of Obligation and Contracts' in C. Mallat (ed.), *Islamic Law and Finance*, London, Graham & Trotman, 1988, p. 19.
21. Ibn Taymiyyah, *Naẓariyyah al-ᶜAqd*, p. 228.
22. Ibid., p.227.
23. Al-Kāsānī, *Badā'iᶜ*, V, 163.
24. Ibn Qayyim, *Iᶜlām*, I, 357.
25. Al-Sanhūrī, *Maṣādir*, III, 15.
26. Al-Ḍarīr, *al-Gharar fi'l-ᶜUqūd*, p. 29.
27. Ibid., pp. 53-6.
28. Al-Sarakhsi, *Mabsūṭ*, XIII, 6-7.
29. See for a summary of the views of the *madhāhib* see Ḥasan, *ᶜAmal*, pp. 313ff.
30. Al-Kāsānī, *Badā'iᶜ*, V, 106.
31. Ibn Taymiyyah, *Naẓariyyah al-ᶜAqd*, pp. 220-1.
32. Mūsā, *al-Buyūᶜ*, p. 185.
33. Mūsā, 'al-Islām wa Mushkilatuna al-Ḥādirah', in *al-Thaqāfah al-Islāmiyyah*, p. 51. Mūsā's article (not available to me) has been quoted by Aḥmad Yūsuf Sulaymān in *Mawsūᶜah al-ᶜIlmiyyah wa'l-ᶜAmaliyyah li'l-Bunūk al-Islamiyyah*, vol. V, pp. 406 and 418.
34. Sulaymān, 'Ra'y al-Tashrīᶜ', p. 420; Ḥasan, *ᶜAmal*, p. 316.

CHAPTER NINE

The Subject-Matter of a Sale

This chapter addresses the following three themes: the existence of the subject-matter of a sale; the sale of the unseen; and the deliverability of the object of a sale.

I. The Existence of the Subject-Matter

One of the requirements of a valid contract of sale upheld by Muslim jurists is that the subject-matter of a contract must exist at the time of contract. The sale of a non-existent object (*bayᶜ al-maᶜdūm*) is therefore null and void, and it matters little whether the non-existence is temporary or permanent. The sale of something whose existence is doubtful is also invalid, such as that of the milk in the udders of a cow, or the sale of fruit on a tree prior to its actual appearance.[1] To justify this position, it has been stated that the effect of a sale, which is the transfer of ownership, is basically abstract and invisible. It is therefore deemed necessary that the effect of sale should be attached to something that exists at the time of its conclusion.[2] This requirement is generally maintained with regard to the sale of tangible objects, but when the subject-matter of a sale is something that can only come about in the future, such as usufruct and labour, which is the case in *istiṣnāᶜ* (manufacturing order), the requirement is omitted, according to the majority of scholars, on an exceptional basis. Thus when one hires a lawyer or an architect, the service that they render cannot be in existence at the time of contract. This is also the case in the conventional forward sale of *salam* and of manufacturing contract (*istiṣnaᶜ*). The jurists have held these to be anomalous, yet they have nevertheless validated them by way of exception to the norm, that is, on grounds of juristic preference (*istiḥsān*), and subsequently of *ijmāᶜ*. The Ḥanbalī scholars Ibn

Taymiyyah and his disciple, Ibn Qayyim al-Jawziyyah, and also the Shāfiʿī jurist ʿIzz al-Dīn ʿAbd al-Salām, have, on the other hand, held that *salam* and *istiṣnāʿ* are normal (*muwāfiq al-qiyās*). This they were able to say because they maintained—once again, contrary to the majority opinion—that the existence of the subject-matter is not a prerequisite for a valid contract. It has consequently been held that the sale of an object which is non-existent at the time of contract, but whose attributes are known and can be described accurately enough to eliminate conflict, uncertainty and *gharar*, is generally valid.[3]

Imām Mālik has drawn a distinction between contracts of exchange (*ʿuqūd al-muʿāwadah*) and charitable contracts (*ʿuqūd al-tabarruʿ*), the latter being contracts which do not involve the exchange of countervalues, such as gifts or bequests. The Imām has thus maintained that the existence of the subject-matter is a requirement in the former but not in the latter. It is therefore valid, according to Mālikī law, to make a gift, for example, of what is in the womb of an animal, but not valid to sell the same for a price.[4]

To Ibn Taymiyyah, the sale of a non-existent object is unlawful only if it involves gambling and the misappropriation of the property of others (*muqāmarah wa akl al-māl bi'l bāṭil*), but it is otherwise lawful. As for the claim that the sale of a non-existent object is generally forbidden, Ibn Taymiyyah points out that there is neither textual ruling nor general consensus to support this view. On the contrary, the *Sharīʿah* has validated such sales, for example lease and hire, and also the sale of unripe fruit after it has emerged. It is thus not the existence or non-existence of something which determines the legality or otherwise of its sale, but whether or not the sale in question involves misappropriation and gambling.[5]

Ibn Qayyim has also elaborated that the *Sharīʿah* prohibits *gharar*, and also, therefore, all those types of sale that involve *gharar*, such as sales in which an inability is feared, on the part of one or both of the parties, to fulfil their obligations. A sale is therefore unlawful if it involves *gharar* and the possibility of a dispute arising between the parties, regardless of the existence or non-existence of its subject-matter. To quote Ibn Qayyim:

> There is nothing in the Book of God nor in the teaching of the Prophet ﷺ nor in the saying of any of his Companions to the effect that the sale of something non-existent is unlawful, neither by specific nor general reference. The *Sunnah* admittedly bans the sale of some things which do not exist, just as there is a ban on some things which do exist. Hence the effective cause (*ʿillah*) of prohibition is not existence or non-existence but uncertainty and *gharar*. This is when a thing cannot be delivered, whether existent or not ... The

> essential element of a sale is delivery of the thing sold, and if the seller is unable to deliver, this is *gharar*, gambling and risk.[6]

Ibn Qayyim has highlighted the confusion that has arisen among the scholars between two different things, namely, non-existence of the subject-matter and *gharar*, on account of uncertainty over its delivery. What the *Sharīʿah* forbids is not the sale of a non-existent object *per se*, but the sale in which there is a risk that the parties are unable to meet their obligations.

With reference to the future availability or otherwise of its subject-matter, the sale of the non-existent (*bayʿ al-maʿdūm*) is envisaged as one of the following three types.

The first model is where the subject-matter exists in essence, and then comes to completion thereafter. This category includes the sale of crops and fruits prior to their ripening, or of produce which ripen in consecutive waves. Despite the element of uncertainty and *gharar* in the sale of these objects, the sale is basically valid provided that the produce in question has emerged to the extent that it has become beneficial. The jurists have, however, disagreed as to whether such sales are absolutely valid, or valid only if the crop is plucked and removed. While some have stipulated that the produce should be left *in situ* until it ripens and that this should naturally be with the permission of the seller, others have differed.[7] The Mālikīs, who permit the sale of consecutive yield, have justified their position by stating that *gharar* in this instance is not excessive, and it is permitted because of the people's need for it. The majority of Shāfiʿīs and Ḥanbalīs permit the sale only of the yield that has already emerged but not of the expected yield that does not yet exist. The Ḥanafīs basically hold the same view, but there is a minority view in the Ḥanafī school that validates the sale of consecutive waves of yield absolutely on the grounds of necessity and custom.[8] The *Mejelle* ruling on this issue, which is stated in Article (206), validates consecutive waves of yield, and this is based on the Mālikī *ijtihād*.

In the second type, the subject-matter does not exist at the time of contract, but is certain to exist in the future. In this connection, al-Sanhūrī has discussed the views of the majority on this issue, which he finds to be unnecessarily restrictive. Having referred to several works of authority in the established *madhāhib*, al-Sanhūrī concludes that there is a consensus among the *madhāhib* that the sale of something which does not exist at the time of contract is null and void, even if it is certain to exist in the future. Al-Sanhūrī continues:

> We find the *fiqh* which was developed during the era of imitation (*taqlīd*) to be restrictive, for there is in it a departure from the basic

> norm ... sale of the non-existent object was forbidden because of *gharar*, not because of it being non-existent. Yet the jurists began to adopt non-existence of the subject-matter as the cause of prohibition in its own right. This is so even if the object is certain to exist in the future.[9]

Al-Sanhūrī is critical of the majority position because it has 'moved the *fiqh* of Islam away from the realities of transactions and commerce', and he states that public welfare requires a move away from this rigidity. To support this, he then refers to the views of Ibn Taymiyyah and Ibn Qayyim who have, as discussed above, clearly validated the sale of non-existent objects which do not involve *gharar*.[10]

Assuming that futures trading in agricultural commodities consists of the sale of goods that are non-existent at the time of contract, their availability in the future, that is, at the end of the contract period, is guaranteed. Although delivery does not occur in most cases, the rules of the clearing-house entitle the buyer to take delivery, if he wishes to do so, during the delivery month. The subject-matter of the contract is, in other words, certain to become available in the future. Futures trading thus fulfils the criteria as articulated by Ibn Taymiyyah, Ibn Qayyim and al-Sanhūrī in that the parties' ability to meet their obligations in the future is not in question. Futures trading is highly regulated, so much so that it virtually precludes the possibility of *gharar* or of disputes arising between the parties. These fears admittedly still exist in conventional contracts of sale, but not in futures. The operational techniques of futures are so designed that they virtually eliminate the problems of *gharar*, uncertainty over delivery and the inability of the parties to meet their responsibilities.

With the third model, the subject-matter exists neither in its entirety nor in essence, and it is not established that it will exist in the future. This is the third eventuality discussed by both Ibn Qayyim and al-Sanhūrī in the context of *bayʿ al-maʿdūm*. Both authors have held that when the subject- matter of a contract is non-existent at the time of contract and its existence in the future is also doubtful, the sale involves *gharar*, excessive uncertainty and risk. Thus the sale of 'milk in the udders', or that of the unborn animal, is unlawful because it entails unacceptable *gharar*. Apart from the fact that milk is not a valuable commodity prior to extraction, its quantity constantly increases and blends with the part that might have already been sold. The sale of the unborn animal takes part in *gharar* because of uncertainty about its birth, its monetary value at that time and the seller's ability to make delivery.[11]

It may thus be concluded that the *gharar* which the *Sharīʿah* has forbidden relates to uncertainty about the existence of the subject-matter of a sale at the time when the seller is due to make delivery, and not necessarily to its existence at the time of contracting.

II. The Sale of the Unseen (*Bay*ᶜ *al-Ghā'ib*)

One of the essential requirements of a conventional contract in Islamic law is that its subject-matter must be defined precisely in terms of its essence, quantity and value, and the parties' knowledge of these at the time of contract must be such that it precludes material ignorance (*al-jahālah al-fāḥishah*) that could lead to a dispute.[12] The subject-matter of the sale may be an object which is seen by the parties, or it may be an object which is not seen but identified by a description of its material properties. There is no question of the validity of the former, but doubt has arisen as to the legality in Islamic law of sales in which the object is not seen. This distinction is relevant to futures trading because futures contracts are normally concluded on the basis of a description of the underlying commodity. Contracts in foodstuffs that are listed on commodity exchanges largely concern fungible agricultural commodities that are sold by measurement and weight, and they are generally standardised on the basis of quality, grade and delivery terms. The standardisation of contracts is an essential feature of futures trading, and compliance with the stated description is particularly emphasised for the smooth running of exchange operations. There are also provisions, as discussed earlier, which compensate the buyer, in the event that the latter accepts delivery, for any material variation in the stated quality and grade. The seller is granted some flexibility to deliver a different grade but, when this is the case, the buyer can ask for compensation and may consequently pay a lower price.

Muslim jurists have disagreed about the validity of a sale in which the subject-matter is absent and cannot be seen at the time of contract. The basic issue is once again one of *gharar* arising from ignorance of the material properties of the object of sale. There seems to be general agreement that a sale by description alone involves a certain measure of uncertainty and *gharar*, but the jurist have differed as to whether the *gharar* in question is trivial (*gharar al-yasīr*) or exorbitant (*gharar al-kathīr*). Imām al-Shāfiᶜī has held the *gharar* here to be exorbitant, whereas Imām Mālik has considered it to be slight and negligible. Imām Abū Ḥanīfah, on the other hand, has held that there is no issue at stake here regarding *gharar*, because the buyer is normally granted the option of viewing (*khiyār al-ru'yah*) and the contract is not effective until the buyer exercises his option. The Ḥanafī school has thus validated *bay*ᶜ *al-ghā'ib* generally, that is, even without the description of the object of sale, because in a sale of this kind, the buyer automatically reserves the right to view the object. The sale is finalised when it is confirmed, but otherwise collapses, and the buyer is not bound by it until he views the object.[13]

When the subject-matter of a sale can be known by a description of its genus, type and quantity, etc., these must be clearly stated and identified. The Ḥanafīs, as already noted, stipulate the option of viewing. This is in contrast with the Mālikī position, which does not admit that there is an overlap between the option of viewing and the acquisition of knowledge by description. Thus when something is bought on the basis of its description, the option of viewing has not been established. Conversely, when something is bought, and its sale is contingent upon the option of viewing, there remains no need for a description.

The Mālikīs have validated *bay*ᶜ *al-ghā'ib* on the condition that the type and quality of the goods are described and clearly identified in a manner that eliminates uncertainty and *gharar*. The buyer is also entitled to the option of cancellation in the event that the goods turn out to be different from how they were described. The Mālikī author Ibn Juzay further points out that the object sold *in absentia* should not be too remote or too near that viewing the object can only be achieved with difficulty; and that the description comprises all the material qualities. The Mālikīs have further stipulated that the object in question should not be liable to any change before the buyer takes it into possession. In the event where a substantial change is feared during the interval, the *gharar* may become excessive, and this consequently invalidates the transaction.[14] To Imām al-Shāfiᶜī, the necessary knowledge that eliminates *gharar* in all cases cannot be acquired by anything less than direct observation. Description alone, in other words, is not enough to eliminate *gharar*, which is why al-Shāfiᶜī considers *bay*ᶜ *al-ma*ᶜ*dūm* to be generally invalid, regardless of the nature of the description, whether it specifies only the genus, or both the genus and the type of the object of a sale. Al-Shirāzī, however, has recorded the additional detail that if both the genus and type of the subject-matter are identified (such as when A says to B 'I sell you a tonne of Indian wheat' as opposed to just saying a tonne of wheat), then the sale is valid according to the older ruling of the Shāfiᶜī school, and the buyer is entitled to the option of viewing. The 'new ruling' of the Shāfiᶜī school, however, declares this to be invalid because of the *ḥadīth* which simply proclaims, as Abū Hurayrah transmits, that 'the Prophet ﷺ, prohibited *bay*ᶜ *al-gharar*', and also on account of the *ḥadīth* 'sell not what is not with you'. Al-Shirāzī's commentator, al-Nawawī, has stated, however, that the correct view of the Shāfiᶜī school is that of invalidity (*buṭlān*).[15] Another Shāfiᶜī jurist, al-Sharbīnī, has gone against the ruling of his *madhhab* and agreed with the majority in saying that the sale of the unseen is valid if both the genus and type of the subject-matter are clearly identified.[16] This is, in fact, in line with al-Shāfiʿī's own ruling in the *Kitāb al-ʿUmm*, where he validates not just *bayʿ al-ghā'ib*, but also the deferred payment of the price in *bayʿ al-ghā'ib* to a future date. The Imām also entitles the buyer to the option of cancellation in the event that the goods do not correspond with the stipulated description.[17] Yet the majority of Shāfiʿī jurists have held the opposite opinion to this, and proscribed *bayʿ al-ghā'ib* on the basis of the analysis that this was what al-Shāfiʿī concluded in his 'new ruling'.[18]

The Ḥanbalī school validates *bayʿ al-ghā'ib* on the condition that the subject-matter of the sale is one in which forward sale (*salam*) would be valid, and this is limited to fungible commodities that are sold by measurement and weight. The qualities by which the goods are described must also be firm and predictable, and the seller should be able to make delivery according to the agreement, regardless of the distance or time it might take to view the goods. And lastly, like the Mālikīs, the Ḥanbalīs also entitle the buyer to the option of cancellation in the event of variations in the stated quality. Yet the Ḥanbalī scholar Ibn Taymiyyah is generally critical of those who have passed prohibitive judgements on the sale of the unseen, stating that the Prophet ﷺ only prohibited the sale containing *gharar* which involved devouring the property of others. There is also evidence that the Companions bought and sold unseen objects, and none of them declared such sales to be unlawful.[19]

The majority of scholars have thus validated *bayʿ al-ghā'ib*, and the basic evidence on which they rely is the Qur'ānic proclamation of the legality of sales (2:275). The text here is conveyed in the form of a general provision (*ʿāmm*), which validates all types of sale unless they are otherwise forbidden by *Sunnah* and/or *ijmāʿ*. There is also the *ḥadīth*, reported on the authority of Abū Hurayrah, in which the Prophet ﷺ is reported to have said that the 'one who buys something he has not seen shall have the option of [cancellation] when he sees it'.

من اشترى شيئًا لم يره فهو بالخيار اذا رآه .

Some have regarded this to be a disconnected (*mursal*) *ḥadīth*, but others have stated that the chain of its transmission is unbroken (i.e., *musnad*). The Ḥanafī jurist al-Sarakhsī states that the Ḥanafī have followed it even though it is a *mursal*, because its transmitters include Ibn ʿAbbās and Ḥasan al-Baḍrī, and also because prominent scholars like Imām Mālik and Aḥmad Ibn Ḥanbal have followed it.[20] This position is further substantiated by the legal maxim that the norm in respect of trade and transactions is permissibility (*ibāḥah*). In validating *bayʿ al-ghā'ib* in principle, the scholars have also given due consideration to public interest (*maṣlaḥah*), and the smooth running of business transactions in the community. The conditions that the *madhāhib* have stipulated in this connection, especially that which entitles the buyer to the option of viewing and cancellation, tend on the whole to ensure propriety in this type of sale, and to prevent the possibility of its being used as an instrument of *gharar*.

III. The Object Must Be Deliverable (*Maqdūr al-Taslīm*)

Another requirement for a valid contract of sale, one on which the jurists are generally in agreement, is that the subject-matter of the contract must be deliverable at the time of contract. This is a basic requirement, according to the majority of all contracts. Imām Mālik, however, has made an exception to the general application of this rule with regard to charitable contracts (*ᶜuqūd al-tabarruᶜ*), where he maintains that the ability to deliver is not a requirement in charitable contracts such as gifts and bequests. Thus when a person makes a gift of his runaway camel to another, this is valid, because there is no exchange of values and, therefore, no likelihood of a dispute or *gharar* arising over delivery.[21] But there is general agreement that a contract of sale is invalid when the seller is unable to deliver the goods that are sold at the time of contract. Some typical examples of this type of sale that occur in the works of *fiqh* include the sale of fish in a river or of birds in the sky, which are invalid, as al-Kāsānī has stated, because a contract is not concluded unless its basic utility (*al-fa'idah*) is served, and this cannot be the case if the object of the sale cannot be delivered. But the sale is in both cases valid if the fish or the birds in question are in a confined space and can easily be caught. The seller's inability to deliver the object of sale at the time of contract renders the sale null and void (*bāṭil*); if the inability comes to exist only after the conclusion of contract, the contract is voidable (*fāsid*), but not void *per se*. The object may be deliverable physically by the seller, or it may be deliverable only by the force of law, in which case the sale is valid but suspended (*mawqūf*) until it leads to actual delivery. An example of this is the sale of an usurped object (*bayᶜ al-maghṣūb*) by its lawful owner, which is valid but *mawqūf* because it is deliverable only through judicial intervention. A sale is voidable (*fāsid*) in the event where delivery is possible only by incurring a harm, such as the sale of a fixed object in a building which could not be extracted without causing structural damage.[22]

The authority for this is the *ḥadīth* which states that 'harm may neither be inflicted nor reciprocated'.[23] Thus a contract may not be used as a means of inflicting manifest harm to the seller. If the seller agrees to accept the harm that may be incurred by delivery, the sale is valid and he delivers at his own peril. But sale of an object which the seller is absolutely incapable of delivering is null and void (*bāṭil*). The jurists have also ruled that the sale of a debt (*bay*ᶜ *al-dayn*) to a third party is not valid, but that its sale to the debtor himself is valid. This is because of the seller's inability to deliver the object of sale, which in the case of a debt is a charge on the person of the debtor. An example of this would be for A to sell the two tonnes of wheat which he gave on credit to B, to a third party C, which is invalid because of A's inability to guarantee delivery; but the debt here may be sold to B himself, since the question of delivery does not arise in this case.[24]

The majority of scholars have maintained that, except for such sales as *salam* and *istiṭnā*ᶜ, sale must lead to the immediate transfer of ownership and delivery, and if the seller is unable to do this, the basic purpose of the sale is frustrated.[25] Here we note once again that Ibn Taymiyyah and his disciple Ibn Qayyim have differed from the majority ruling. To quote Ibn Qayyim:

> In response to the assertion that the effect of contract materialises by immediate delivery, it must be stated that the effect of a contract is either specified by the Lawgiver, or by the contracting parties, neither of which is proven in this assertion. The Lawgiver has nowhere stipulated that the subject matter of sale must in all cases be delivered immediately after contract, nor would the contracting parties always want immediate delivery.[26]

Ibn Qayyim goes on to point out that the parties may wish to postpone either the payment of the price, or the delivery of the object of sale, to a later occasion. This was the case, for example, in the event when Jābir sold his camel to the Prophet ﷺ, and then asked if he could postpone delivery until he (Jābir) reached Medina, and the Prophet ﷺ granted Jābir's request. Having quoted this *ḥadīth*, Ibn Qayyim then adds that, 'supposing there were no authority in the *Sunnah*, rational evidence and analogy alone would be enough to validate [our] position'. He adds further that Imām Aḥmad ibn Ḥanbal and his followers have unanimously held that delivery may be delayed when the prevailing custom of society requires this. Thus when a large quantity of goods are sold, and they cannot be transferred in one day or a few days, delayed delivery is acceptable. The *Sharī*ᶜ*ah* has not made the provision, Ibn Qayyim adds, 'that all the beasts of the town should be hired to carry and deliver the goods at once'. In response to the majority ruling, which maintains that the prevailing custom here represents an exceptional case, Ibn Qayyim argues that 'we say that this is not an exception at all, but strong evidence against your [the majority's] position'. If the contracting parties are allowed to stipulate for delayed delivery, and the general custom of society agrees with that, then delayed delivery is permitted by *Sharīʿah* as a matter of principle and not, as it were, by way of exception.[27]

With reference to futures trading, the clearing-house guarantee in respect of the delivery of open contracts in the delivery month means that delivery is assured, and that all outstanding contracts are deliverable at maturity. As discussed earlier, the mechanics of futures trading with regard to delivery entail procedures which make delivery a guaranteed prospect whenever the buyer wishes to take delivery. Needless to say, the rules of *fiqh* on the subject of delivery, from beginning to end, focus on the conventional contract of sale. Delivery in such contracts is, of course, not always guaranteed and the rules of *fiqh* still remain applicable in this area. But with regard to futures, the near certainty of delivery, and the fulfilment of contract as guaranteed by the clearing-house, mark a departure from the legitimate concern of the *fuqahā'* over *gharar* and uncertainty in contract delivery and fulfilment. There may be other aspects of futures trading operations which need to be addressed, indeed new issues which are not yet covered by the rules of *fiqh* pertaining to conventional sales. But the rules of *fiqh* on the subject of delivery have become redundant and cannot be meaningfully applied to delivery processes in the context of futures. Since all possible avenues of failure to deliver have been practically foreclosed, the issue is no longer relevant. The fact that the buyer normally does not wish to take delivery and can offset his position by entering into a reverse transaction is, of course, another matter which will be discussed later. It is basically the buyer's privilege, not his obligation, to accept delivery. Since this is the buyer's right, he is at liberty to exercise it or not; but whenever he chooses to take delivery, the clearing-house procedures ensure that delivery takes place. The seller who wishes to deliver gives notice of delivery to the clearing-house, and the rest of the delivery procedure takes its course within days. Here we note once again that the seller's obligation to make delivery in a conventional sale is no longer the same in a futures contract. It is due to the availability of offsetting procedures in futures that the seller has the choice of whether to make delivery or to enter a reverse transaction which would cancel his obligation. The clearing-house guarantee, and the availability of offsetting procedures, have essentially rendered the juristic debate over deliverability redundant, and the seller's ability to deliver is therefore not an issue in futures.

NOTES

1. Kamal al-Dīn ibn al-Humam, *Fatḥ al-Qadīr*, Cairo, Muṣṭafā al-Bābī al-Ḥalabī, 1389/1970, VI, 400; Ibn Qudāmah, *al-Mughnī*, Riyadh, Maktabah al-Riyāḍ al-Ḥadīthah, 1401/1981, IV, 156.
2. Madkūr, *al-Fiqh*, p. 427; Mahmassānī, *al-Mawjibāt wa'l-ᶜUqūd*, p. 326.
3. Ibn Qayyim, *Iᶜlam*, I, 357; ᶜIzz al-Dīn ᶜAbd al-Salām, *Qawāᶜid al-Aḥkām fī Masalih al-Anam*, Taha ᶜAbd al-Rawuf Saᶜd ed., Cairo: Makhtabah al-Kulliyyah al-Azhariyyah, 1968, II, 111-112; Madkūr, *al-Fiqh*, p. 427.
4. Al-Baᶜlī, *Ḍawābiṭ*, p. 110; Madkūr, *al-Fiqh*, p. 429.
5. Ibn Taymiyyah, *Naẓariyyah al-ᶜAqd*, p. 231.
6. Ibn Qayyim, *Iᶜlām*, I, 357.
7. For details see Ibn Qayyim, *Iᶜlām*, II, 28ff; al-Sanḥūri, *Maṣādir*, III, 15ff; al-Baᶜlī, *Ḍawābiṭ*, pp. 111ff.
8. For details see al-Kāsānī, *Badā'iᶜ*, v, 138ff; *Mawsūᶜah al-ᶜIlmiyyah*, V, 404ff.
9. Al-Sanḥūri, *Maṣādir*, III, 33.
10. Ibid., III, 44-5.
11. Ibid., III, 46; see also al-Sarakhsī, *al-Mabsūṭ*, XII, 194; al-Baᶜlī, *Ḍawābiṭ*, p. 112.
12. Al-Kāsānī, *Badā'iᶜ*, V, 147; al-Baᶜlī, *Ḍawābiṭ*, p. 116.
13. Ibn Rushd al-Qurṭubī, *Bidāyah*, II, 155-8; al-Kāsānī, *Badā'iᶜ*, V, 163.
14. Ibn Juzay, *Qawānīn*, p. 268; al-Jazīrī, *al-Fiqh* (al-Maktabah al-Tijāriyyah al-Kubrā edition) p. 214; al-Baᶜlī, *Ḍawābiṭ*, p. 116; al-Sanḥūri, *Maṣādir*, III, 69-70.
15. Al-Shirāzī, *al-Muhadhdhab fi'l Madhhab*, Cairo, Muṣṭafā al-Bābī al-Ḥalabī, 1396/1976, I, 263; al-Nawawī, *al-Majmūᶜ*, IX, 318.
16. Al-Sharbīnī, *Mughnī al-Muḥtāj*, Cairo, Muṣṭafā al-Bābī al-Ḥalabī, 1377/1958, II, 18.
17. Muḥammad ibn al-Shāfiᶜī, *al-ᶜUmm*, Bulaq, Maṭbaᶜah al-Kubrā, 1321/1901, III, 40.
18. Cf. Abū Sulaymān, *ᶜAqd al-Tawrīd*, pp. 38-40.
19. Ibn Qudāmah, *al-Mughnī*, III, 582; Ibn Taymiyyah, *Naẓariyyah al-ᶜAqd*, p. 225. Manṣur b. Idris al-Buhūtī, *Kashshaf al-Qannaᶜ*, Muṣṭafā Hilal ed., Riyadh, Maktbah al-Ḥadīthah, n.d., III, 164.
20. Al-Sarakhsī, *al-Mabsūṭ*, XII, 69.
21. Al-Sarakhsī, *al- Mabsūṭ*, XIII, 6-7.
22. Madkūr, *al-Fiqh*, p. 435.
23. Muḥammad b. Yazīd al-Qawzīnī ibn Mājah, *Sunan Ibn Mājah*, Istanbul, Cagri Yayinlari, 1401/1981, II, 784, *ḥadīth* no. 2340; al-Kāsānī, *Badā'iᶜ*, V, 147, 168; al-Sarakhsī, *al-Mabsūṭ*, XII, 194; al-Baᶜlī, *Ḍawābiṭ*, p. 116.
24. Cf. Ḥasan, *ᶜAmal*, p. 283.
25. Cf. al-Kāsānī, *Badā'iᶜ*, V, 147; al-Sanḥūri, *Maṣādir*, III, 60.
26. Ibn Qayyim, *Iᶜlām*, I, 359.
27. Ibid. See also al-Sanhūri, *Maṣādir*, III, 54-5.

CHAPTER TEN

'Sell Not What Is Not With You'

The title here is a direct translation of a well-known *ḥadīth* which the scholars of the established *madhāhib* have quoted as a standard authority for many of their rulings on the subject-matter of sale. It is thus stated that the subject-matter must not only exist, but also be owned by the seller at the time of contract. Futures trading consist of short selling in which the seller does not own the subject-matter and normally sells a commodity prior to purchasing it, which is why futures sales are often said to be contrary to the requirements of this *ḥadīth*. However, the juristic conclusions that the scholars have drawn from this *ḥadīth*, as we shall presently elaborate, consist mainly of their different interpretations, and these fall short of unanimity and consensus. The rulings that we have may therefore be seen as manifestations of juristic *ijtihād* which command no finality, and the matter may thus be said to remain open to further interpretation. Our attempt to ascertain the position in *Sharīʿah* on futures trading necessitates an analysis of this *ḥadīth*, initially with reference to conventional sales, since this is the main context in which the scholars have discussed the matter. We shall then be in a position to ascertain the relevance of the juristic discourse of established *fiqh* to futures trading. This, in turn, enables us to ascertain the points, if any, where a departure from conventional *fiqh* might be warranted in light of the operative procedures of futures trading while still remaining within the general framework and rationale of the said *ḥadīth*.

Several issues have been raised concerning the text before us, one of which is a certain weakness in its authenticity and transmission. Neither al-Bukhārī nor Muslim have recorded this *ḥadīth* in their collections, but it does appear in other collections, including those of Abū Dāwūd and al-Tirmidhī.[1] Among those who have recorded this *ḥadīth*, there is a discrepancy in its chain of transmission. Whereas Abū Dāwūd, Aḥmad ibn Ḥanbal and Ibn Ḥabbān have stated the *ḥadīth* to have been narrated by Jaʿfar ibn Abī Wahshiyah, from Yūsuf ibn Mahak from Ḥākim ibn Ḥizām, a fourth name, that of ʿAbd Allāh ibn ʿIsmah, occurs in other *ḥadīth* collections between Yūsuf and Ḥākim. Al-Dhahabī has stated in *Al-Mīzān* that this intermediate name is totally unknown (*lā yuʿraf*). Even the principal narrator of this *ḥadīth*, that is Ḥākim ibn Ḥizām, is said to be 'obscure' (*majhūl al-ḥāl*). No one, except Ibn Ḥabbān, has included him among reliable narrators (*al-thiqqāt*). Al-Nasā'ī has recorded one *ḥadīth* narrated by him, but others have described him as 'obscure'.

There is another Ḥadīth recorded by Abū Dāwūd and al-Tirmidhī, narrated by ʿAmr ibn Shuʿayb, from his father, from his grandfather, and it states the following:

> It is not permissible to combine *salam* with a sale, nor two transactions in the same sale, nor to gain a profit over something which is not guaranteed [in terms of liability for loss] nor a sale of what is not with you.
>
> لا يحل سلف وبيع ولا شرطان في بيع ولا ربح ما يضمن ولا بيع ما ليس عندك .

However, disagreement over the authenticity of this *ḥadīth* and its chain of transmission has persisted from early times. Al-Qaradāwī has discussed both this and the earlier *ḥadīth*, and concluded that the doubt in the authenticity of both must have a bearing on their authority as a basis of legislation. Although some have spoken of these two traditions as though they were decisive injunctions (*nuṣūṣ qatʿiyyah*), they are not. Having said this, we do note that the two *ḥadīth* support one another; they may not reach the rank of *ṣaḥīḥ* (authentic) *ḥadīth*, but they may perhaps be classified as the lower rank of *ḥassan* (good) *ḥadīth*, acting upon which is both valid and meritorious.

There is also room for interpretation regarding the precise legal value of the *ḥadīth* under discussion. We need to ascertain whether it conveys a total ban (*taḥrīm*), or abomination (*karāhiyyah*), or even mere guidance and advice of no legal import. For the phrase '*lā tabiʿ*' (sell not) could sustain any of these interpretations. The scholars of the principles of *fiqh* admit all of these meanings within the purview of a prohibition (*nahy*). Only when a prohibition is fused with a warning (*waʿẓ*) is its meaning reinforced in order to convey a total ban (*taḥrīm*).[2] Since there is a weakness in the transmission of this *ḥadīth*, and it is not accompanied by a warning, or words that would imply special emphasis, and also because it is open to interpretation as discussed above, it seems likely and reasonable that it conveys abomination and moral opprobrium (*karāhiyyah*) rather than a total prohibition (*taḥrīm*). A contemporary writer, ʿAbd al-Karīm al-Khaṭīb, has in fact recorded the view that this *ḥadīth* conveys moral guidance (*irshād*) rather than a prohibition *per se*[3]. Now we may turn to the *ḥadīth* itself. The full version of it reads as follows: 'Jaʿfar ibn Abī Waḥ shiyah reported from Yūsuf ibn Māhil, from Ḥākim ibn Ḥizām [who said]: I asked the Prophet ﷺ: O Messenger of Allāh! A man comes to me and asks me to sell him what is not with me, so I sell him [what he wants] and then buy the goods for him in the market [and deliver]. And the Prophet said: sell not what is not with you.'[4]

روى جعفر بن ابى وحشية عن يوسف بن ماهل عن حكيم بن خزام ،
سألت رسول الله ﷺ فقلت : يارسول الله يأتينى الرجل يسألنى البيع
ليس عندى ، أبيعه منه ثم ابتاعه له من السوق ، قال لا تبع ما ليس
عندك .

In an attempt to ascertain the precise meaning of this *ḥadīth*, the jurists have advanced various interpretations, which may be summarised as follows:

1. 'Sell not what is not with you' means not to sell what you do not own (*yaʿnī mā laysa fī milkik*) at the time of sale. One of the basic requirements of sale, as al-Kāsānī has stated, is that the seller owns the object of sale when he sells it, failing which the sale is not concluded, even if the seller acquires ownership afterwards. The only exception, in this context, is the forward sale of *salam*, where ownership is not a prerequisite. This is confirmed, al-Kāsānī adds, by the text of the *ḥadīth* in which Ḥākim ibn Ḥizām reported that he would sell what he did not have, which means that which he did not own. He would take the price of the object from the prospective buyer, buy the goods in the market and then deliver them but, when the Prophet ﷺ learned of this, he discouraged it. When Ḥākim ibn Ḥizām sold the goods to his customers, he attempted to transfer the ownership of those goods at the time when he received the price, which was unfeasible, since he could not transfer the ownership of what he himself was not the owner of.[5] Al-Sanʿānī has concurred with this interpretation and stated that 'sell not what is not with you' implies that it is not permissible to sell something before owning it.[6] Ibn al-Humam and Ibn Qudāmah have similarly concluded that the sale of something which the seller does not own is not permissible, even if he buys and delivers it afterwards.[7]

The Ḥanafīs have elaborated, however, that the seller's ownership of the object of sale is not a condition of the validity (*sharṭ al-ṣiḥḥah*), but of the effectiveness (*nifadh*) of the sale. Thus they validate the *bona fide* sale by an unauthorised person (*al-fuḍūlī*) who does not own the object but nevertheless sells it (for a good reason), because in this case the sale is valid but not effective, and it becomes effective upon obtaining the consent of the owner.[8]

2. Some jurists and scholars have generally held that the *ḥadīth* under discussion applies only to the sale of specified and unique objects (*al-aʿyān*) but not to fungible goods since these can easily be substituted and replaced. This is the view of al-Baghāwī, his commentator Mullā ʿAlī Qārī, al-Khaṭṭābī and many others, who have stated that the prohibition in question is confined to the sale of special objects (*buyūʿ al-aʿyān*) and does not apply to the sale of goods by description (*buyūʿ al-ṣifāt*). Thus when the forward sale of *salam* is concluded over fungible goods that are commonly found in the locality, it is valid even if the seller does not own the object of the sale at the time of contract.[9] Imām al-Shāfiʿī has also held that one may sell what is not with one provided that it is not a specific object, for the delivery of a specific object cannot be guaranteed if the seller does not own it.[10] A similar view has been recorded by al-Khaṭṭābī, who stated that the *ḥadīth* in question refers to the sale of specific objects, because the Prophet ﷺ permitted deferred sales of various kinds in which the seller did not have the object of sale at the time of contracting. The prohibition here is essentially designed to prevent *gharar* in sales such as that of a runaway camel, sales in which delivery is uncertain, such as sale prior to taking possession, and the sale of someone else's property without his permission.[11]

The commentator of *Sunan Abū Dāwūd*, Ibn Qayyim al-Jawziyyah, and the commentator of *Jāmiʿ al-Tirmidhī*, al-Mubārakfūrī, have, in their respective commentaries on this *ḥadīth*, both subscribed to the view that it is concerned with the sale of specified objects, and not the sale by description of goods that are commonly available in the market, for if we were to include fungible goods within the purport of this *ḥadīth*, as Ibn Qayyim wrote, then it would mean that *salam* is forbidden, which is evidently not the case. *Salam* is valid precisely because it deals with fungible goods that are commonly available in the appointed place and time, despite the fact that the subject-matter thereof is non-existent at the time of the contract.[12] This would effectively take futures trading out of the purview of this *ḥadīth* simply because futures trading only takes place in respect of fungible commodities, and cannot be expected to apply to specific objects with unique qualities.

3. The third position taken by some scholars on the interpretation of this *ḥadīth* is that the sale of 'what is not with you' means the sale of what is not present and which the seller is unable to deliver. This is the view of Ibn

Taymiyyah and his disciple Ibn Qayyim al-Jawziyyah, who state that the emphasis in the prohibition is on the seller's inability to deliver, which gives rise to risk-taking and uncertainty (*mukhāṭarah wa gharar*). Al-Shāfiʿī wrote, concerning this *ḥadīth*, that the seller was accordingly not permitted to make any transaction if he was not sure of being able to deliver the goods, because such a sale involves *gharar* and is hazardous. Nevertheless, if the sale is clear of doubt, such as a guaranteed sale, and it is certain that the vendor will be able to fulfil his obligation in time, then it is valid, since it resembles *salam*. Al-Shāfiʿī has quoted ʿAbd Allāh ibn ʿUmar, concerning *salam*, that there is no harm caused if a person enters into a transaction with another over foodstuffs of a set description and price with a set date of delivery, provided it is not a matter of concern whether the seller has the foodstuffs with him or not. Ibn Taymiyyah and Ibn Qayyim have also observed that if the *ḥadīth* were to be taken at face value, it would proscribe *salam* and a variety of other sales, but this is obviously not intended. The Prophet ﷺ forbade Ḥākim ibn Ḥizām the sale of particular objects, either because he did not own them, in which case he would be selling other people's property before buying it, or because the seller was uncertain of obtaining the object and was therefore unable to deliver it, and the latter is the more likely reason of the prohibition.[13] The Mālikī jurist al-Bājī has recorded a similar view, and stated that '"what is not with you" means a specific object which is not in your ownership and your power to deliver'.[14] It is possible that a seller could own an object and yet be unable to deliver it, or that he possesses the object but does not own it—in either case he would fall within the purview of this *ḥadīth*. The emphasis in the *ḥadīth* is therefore not on ownership nor on possession but on the seller's effective control and ability to deliver. Thus the effective cause (*ʿillah*) of the prohibition is *gharar* on account of inability to deliver. Ibn Qayyim al-Jawziyyah has confirmed that the underlying intention of this *ḥadīth* is the same as the *ḥadīth* in which the Prophet ﷺ has forbidden *gharar*. This is because when 'a person sells what is not with him, he is not certain as to whether he could or could not obtain the goods in order to make delivery'. Ibn Qayyim adds further that the sale of what is not with one is forbidden partly because the subject-matter of it is not guaranteed (*ghayr maḍmūn*), and partly because the buyer who is selling without first acquiring possession of the object has neither effective control over the objects, nor is it a charge on his person (*dhimmah*).[15]

This analysis is premised on the understanding that liability for loss (*ḍ aman*) in the subject-matter of a sale is only acquired upon taking possession thereof. I may hasten to add that in futures trading the question of liability is determined by reference to the contract and not the taking of possession.

Among modern writers, Yūsuf Mūsā, ʿAlī ʿAbd al-Qādir and Yūsuf al-Qaradāwī have drawn attention to the fact that the market place of Medina during the Prophet's time was so small that it did not offer the assurance of regular supplies at any given time. The *ḥadīth* therefore prohibits the sale of objects that are not available at the time of sale. This is perhaps indicated, as Mūsā adds, in the *ḥadīth* where Ḥākim ibn Ḥizām said that people would come to him asking to sell them what he did not have. The purchasers were, in other words, eager to secure the goods they could not find in the market because of uncertainty in supply. In contrast, modern markets are better equipped, regular and extensive, which means that the seller can find the goods at almost any time and make delivery as may be required. With reference to futures trading, Mūsā observes that the futures contract normally operates on a deferred basis, which gives the seller a fair amount of time to buy what is required in order to make delivery, if necessary, within the contract period.[16] When we compare the Medinan market with today's market, we are faced with a different reality. Given the means and facilities that are available today, the fear of failure to find the goods and make delivery, which was the basic rationale of the original prohibition, is no longer present in the way that it was in the early days of Islam.[17] Al-Ḍarīr has observed that this *ḥadīth* is relevant to the spot sales of specific objects, which involve no deferment to a future date, since the *ḥadīth* only deals with this latter eventuality. But when a sale is concluded on a deferred-delivery basis, it is governed by a different set of rules, namely, those which apply to *salam* and deferred sales.[18]

The short selling of commodities that are not owned by the seller takes place, in the futures market, with the assurance that identical contracts dealing with the underlying commodity can be bought and sold on an almost instantaneous basis. There is normally no fear of the seller's inability to find an equivalent contract with which to offset his position, or to find and deliver the underlying commodity in the event that he wishes to make delivery. The seller is, in other words, not faced with the prospect of searching for the underlying commodity in the open market, or of making detailed preparation for delivery. The clearing-house guarantee function, in this context, means precisely that delivery of the exact quantity and grade (or of the nearest grade) is guaranteed. The short seller admittedly does not own the underlying commodity at the time he sells a futures contract, but his ability to make delivery is nevertheless assured beyond any doubt. This is a peculiarity of futures trading which provides systematic guarantees regarding delivery and payment, something that the open market does not provide.

NOTES

1. There is a title in al-Bukhārī's 'Book of Sales' which reads: 'Sale of foodstuffs prior to taking possession and sale of what is not with you.' Al-Bukhārī's commentator, Ibn Ḥajar al-ʿAsqalānī, has observed: 'It looks as if the *ḥadīth* at issue did not fulfil al-Bukhārī's conditions, so he merely joined its meaning to the *ḥadīth* on the "prohibition of sale prior to taking possession".' Al-Bukhārī has probably added the latter part of the title by way of inference (*istinbāt*) from the *ḥadīth* on the requirement of *qabḍ*. See Muḥammad b. Ismāʿīl al-Bukhārī, *Ṣaḥīḥ al-Bukhārī*, tr. Muḥsin Khān, 6th edn, Lahore, Kazi Publications, 1986, III, 195; Aḥmad b.ʿAlī ibn Ḥajar al-ʿAsqalānī, *Fath al-Bārī bi Sharḥ Ṣaḥīh al-Bukhārī*, ed. Taha ʿAbd al-Rawuf Saʿd, Cairo, Maktabah al-Kulliyyah al-Azhariyyah, 1978, V, 525; al-Qaradāwī, *Bayʿ al-Murābaḥah*, p. 54.

2. For further detail on commands and prohibitions see Kamali, *Jurisprudence*, pp. 139-49.

3. Al-Khaṭīb, *al-Siyāsah al-Māliyyah*, p. 176.

4. Abū Dāwūd, *Sunan Abū Dāwūd*, Eng. trans. Aḥmad Ḥasan, 3 vols., Lahore, Ashraf Press, 1984, vol. III, *Kitāb al-Buyūʿ*, *Bāb fī Bayʿ al-Rajul Mā Laysa ʿIndah*.

5. Al-Kāsānī, *Badāʾiʿ*, V, 146.

6. Al-Sanʿānī, *Subul al-Salām Sharḥ Bulugh al-Maram*, Cairo, Maktabah al-Tijāriyyah al-Kubrā, 1353 AH, III, 17.

7. Ibn Qudāmah, *al-Mughnī*, IV, 155; Ibn al-Humam, *Fatḥ al-Qādir*, VI, 336.

8. Al-Kāsānī, *Badāʾiʿ*, V, 146.

9. Abū Muḥammad al-Ḥusayn al-Baghāwī, *Sharḥ al-Sunnah*, Damascus, Maktab al-Islāmī, 1974, VIII, 140-41; Abū Sulaymān al-Khaṭṭābī, *Maʿālim al-Sunan*, ed. M. Ḥ. al-Faqi, Cairo: Maṭbaʿah al-Sunnah al-Muḥammadiyyah 1368/1949, V, 143.

10. Muḥammad b. Idris al-Shāfiʿī, *al-Risālah*, ed. Aḥmad Muḥammad Shakir, Cairo, Muṣṭafā al-Bābī al-Ḥalabī, 1940, p. 337.

11. Al-Khaṭṭābī, *Maʿālim al-Sunan*, V, 143; see also al-Qaradāwī, *Bayʿ al-Murābaḥah*, p. 56.

12. Ibn Qayyim al-Jawziyyah, *ʿAwn al-Maʿbūd Sharḥ Sunan Abī Dāwūd*, ed. A. R. M. ʿUthman, 3rd edn, Cairo, Dār al-Fikr, 1399/1979 IX, 401; Muḥammad al-Mubārakfūrī, *Tuḥfah al-Ahwazi bi-Sharḥ Jamiʿ al-Tirmidhī*, 2nd edn, Cairo, al-Maktabah al-Salafiyyah, 1965, IV, 430.

13. Al-Shāfiʿī, *al-ʿUmm*, III, 94, 95; Ibn Taymiyyah, *Majmūʿah Fatāwa*, XX, 529; Ibn Qayyim, *Iʿlām*, I, 399.

14. Al-Bājī, *al-Muntaqa*, IV, 286.

15. Ibn Qayyim, *Iʿlām*, I, 399; see also Nūr al-Dīn ʿAtr, *al-Muʿāmalāt al-Maṣrafiyyah wa'l-Ribawiyyah wa ʿIlajuha fi'l-Islām*, Beirut, Mu'assasah al-Risālah, 1406/1986, pp. 88-9.

16. Yūsuf Mūsā, *al-Buyūʿ*, p. 193; ʿAlī ʿAbd al-Qādir 'Taʿqīb ʿalā Ra'y al-Tashrīʿ', in *al-Mawsūʿah al-ʿIlmiyyah*, V, 439.

17. Al-Qaradāwī, *Bayʿ al-Murābaḥah*, p. 19.

18. Al-Ḍarīr, *al-Gharar*, p. 320.

CHAPTER ELEVEN

Sale Prior to Taking Possession (*Qabḍ*)

One of the requirements of a valid conventional sale in the *fiqh* of *muʿāmalāt* is that the purchaser may not sell the goods he has bought until they are in his possession. In support of this ruling, the jurists have referred to the authority of *ḥadīth*, which we shall once again review in the following pages, not only in relationship to conventional sales, the principal way in which the scholars have discussed it, but also in relationship to futures trading. The main purpose of this enquiry is to ascertain whether futures trading can be validated within the given terms of the *ḥadīth* and whether the concerns that the scholars have expressed in connection with the conventional contract of sale are equally relevant to futures contracts.

The key concept we need to discuss here is *qabḍ*, which literally means taking and holding something in one's hands. In its juristic sense, *qabḍ* is used to suggest legal custody and possession in a proprietary capacity, even if it does not involve the physical act of holding. In reference to the contract of sale, *qabḍ* and *taqābuḍ* mean that each of the parties receive the countervalues, namely, the object of the sale and the price. Delivery (*taslīm*) and taking possession (*qabḍ*) are corresponding concepts: the seller is under duty to deliver the goods sold, and it is for the buyer to take possession. This is also true of *takhliyah* (lit., evacuation) and *qabḍ* in that the seller evacuates the object of the sale, and only then is the buyer enabled to take possession. The seller is under an obligation to deliver the object of the sale and the buyer is under a similar duty to pay the price. The buyer is not, however, under an obligation to receive the goods, or to take possession; this is a privilege which he may or may not choose to exercise.[1]

With reference to futures trading, delivery and taking possession are for the most part theoretical propositions which actually occur in only about two per cent of the bulk of transactions in any one of the commodity exchanges. The only exception to be noted is trading in stock index and financial futures, which do not involve any physical exchange of assets and are therefore free of the complications of delivery. Delivery and taking possession in financial futures occur in the form of merely the debiting and crediting of accounts.[2]

Notwithstanding the fact that the vast majority of contracts are offset prior to delivery, the prospect of delivery nevertheless remains the most important factor in futures trading. What is deliverable and when it can be delivered influences the price relationships between cash and futures, and between different contract months. Delivery is also an important factor in distinguishing various futures contracts from one another. The trader who holds his position into the delivery month must be aware of the last day of futures trading after which offset is impossible and delivery is the only route open. Delivery thus remains a legal commitment and the seller must deliver unless he or she closes his or her position by entering into a reverse transaction.[3]

The following three *ḥadīth* need to be reviewed on the subject of *qabḍ*. ʿAbd Allāh ibn ʿUmar has reported that the Prophet ﷺ said:

> He who buys foodstuffs should not sell it till he has received it.[4]
>
> من ابتاع طعاما فلا يبعه حتى يقبضه .

According to another report transmitted by ʿAbd Allāh ibn ʿUmar, the Prophet ﷺ said:

> He who buys foodstuffs should not sell it unless he is satisfied with the measure with which he bought it.[5]
>
> من ابتاع طعاما فلا يبعه حتى يستوفيه .

Ibn ʿAbbās has also reported the following *ḥadīth* from the Prophet ﷺ:

> He who buys foodstuffs should not sell it until he has taken possession of it. Ibn ʿAbbās said: I think it applies to all other things as well.[6]
>
> من ابتاع طعاما فلا يبعه حتى يستوفيه ، قال ابن عباس واحسب كل شئ مثله .

All three reports are substantially concurrent. The only variation between them is concerned with the use of words that may be said to be synonymous: the word '*yaqbiḍahu*' (takes possession) in the first *ḥadīth* is substituted by '*yastawfihī*' (obtains full measure). This variation in words does not seem to change the substance of the message that is conveyed in all the three reports. The third *ḥadīth* has an added element which is clearly not a part of the original *ḥadīth* and represents an addition by Ibn ʿAbbās himself. The word *taʿām* (foodstuffs), according to the generally accepted version, occurs in precisely the same way in all three reports and constitutes the only subject-matter of the prohibition therein.

The juristic discourse that has ensued is mainly concerned with the proper understanding of *qabḍ* in relationship to various commodities and transactions on the one hand, and with the prevailing custom and commercial practice of society on the other. The jurists have discussed the requirements of *qabḍ* in relationship to certain specified commodities, including precious metals and foodgrains, which are particularly relevant to the subject of usury (*ribā'*). Also discussed is the actual value of *qabḍ*, and its role in the validity or otherwise of a sale, and the consequences that might accrue from failure to comply with the requirement of *qabḍ*.

As for the basic rationale of the *ḥadīth*, it is stated in the *Hidāya* that the Prophet ﷺ prohibited the sale of commodities, especially perishable ones, which the seller did not possess, because of uncertainty and doubt about their delivery to the buyer. There was an equal chance that delivery could not be accomplished due to many unforeseeable circumstances. The *ḥadīth* obviously sought to protect the buyer against harm in the event that the object of sale was lost or destroyed before delivery. Based on this analysis and the prohibitive language of the *ḥadīth*, all the leading Imāms of *fiqh* have held that it is not right for the seller to sell foodstuffs before taking possession of them. According to Imām al-Shāfiʿī, it is not right to sell anything, foodstuffs, land or gardens, before taking possession. Imām Aḥmad ibn Ḥanbal is of the view, however, that possession is not a requirement in the sale of real property, on the grounds that the fear of destruction and loss, which is the basic rationale of the prohibition, is absent in this case.[7]

Qabḍ in the sale of foodgrains that are sold by measurement and weight takes place upon measurement (note that during the Prophet's lifetime wheat and barley were sold by measurement; their sale by weight is a latent practice). When foodgrains are bought in lump sum (*juzāfan*), they are taken into possession, according to Imām al-Shāfiʿī, when they are physically removed. The requirement of taking possession is omitted, in the sale of both foodstuffs and real property, in the event where the goods in question were owned other than by purchase, such as through a gift or inheritance. They may be sold prior to taking possession, because gifts and bequests involve no financial exchange and the seller is not committed to the payment of a price to someone else.[8]

Qabḍ in moveables is accomplished by carrying the object, and with regard to immovable objects, it is customarily accomplished when the seller evacuates the property. Thus if one buys a house, it may not be sold until it is evacuated by its previous owner.[9] This ruling of the Shāfiʿī school is basically upheld by all the leading scholars. There is also general support for the view that the manner in which *qabḍ* is accomplished is determined by reference to the prevailing custom.

Qabḍ was the subject of a recent resolution by the Fiqh Academy, where it was stated, with reference to the basic rationale of the rulings of *ḥadīth* on this subject, that 'the effective cause (*ʿillah*) of the prohibition of sale prior to taking possession is *gharar*, which consists of a possible failure in respect of delivery. The buyer stands the risk of not receiving the goods as it is possible that the seller may delay the delivery or wish to revoke the contract'. The resolution further states that while *gharar* of this kind tends to be of general application, there is an additional element of *gharar* in the sale of foodgrains and agricultural crops, which is that they may be perished or destroyed due to *jā'iḥah*, that is, climatic disasters and disease.[10]

Qabḍ, according to the Ḥanafī school, is not an essential requirement (*rukn*) of sale, but a subsidiary condition, namely, that of effectiveness (*sharṭ al-nafādh*). Thus a valid sale can even be concluded, as al-Kāsānī points out, prior to the seller's taking possession, but it will remain in abeyance until *qabḍ* has taken place.[11] To this al-Sarakhsī has added that *qabḍ* signifies the effect or outcome of the contract that materialises after its conclusion. *Qabḍ* is not, therefore, a prerequisite of a valid contract, and it is perfectly lawful to postpone delivery and *qabḍ* to a subsequent occasion. Only in the case of sale of currency for currency (*al-ṣarf*) is *qabḍ* elevated to the status of a prerequisite for a valid contract.[12]

While maintaining the basic prohibition in the *ḥadīth* concerning *qabḍ*, the Mālikī school has further relaxed the strict application of its terms and has instead laid emphasis on the rationale of its ruling. It is thus stated that foodstuffs may not be sold prior to taking possession, but that this requirement only applies to transactions that involve exchange of values, but not to loans and gifts. Thus a person who buys food may give it away as a gift or loan even prior to possessing it. Imām Mālik has also confined the application of the *ḥadīth* being discussed to foodgrains only. This means that commodities other than foodgrains, such as cotton, palm-oil, etc., may be sold prior to taking possession.[13] Ibn Rushd has confirmed this and stated that 'there is no disagreement in the Mālikī school on the permissibility of such sales. Only usurable foodgrains (mainly wheat and barley) may not be sold prior to *qabḍ*.' Imām Mālik has also validated the sale of foodstuffs in lump sum (*juzāfan*), that is, without weighing and measuring, in which case the buyer may sell them prior to taking possession.[14] This is because the liability for loss and destruction (*al-ḍaman*) in this case transfers to the buyer as of the moment of contract, and not upon taking possession.

The Ḥanbalī school is not as strict as the Shāfiʿī on the issue of *qabḍ*. The renowned Ḥanbalī scholar Ibn Taymiyyah has departed from the majority position by opening the concept of *qabḍ* up to the consideration of prevailing custom. He thus criticises the majority position that confines the meaning of *qabḍ* to holding and retention (*ḥabs*), or evacuation (*takhliyah*) and the like, and states that no specific meaning has been given to *qabḍ* in either the Arabic language or in *Sharīʿah*. *Takhliyah* also varies from object to object, and the manner in which *takhliyah* occurs is not always the same. The precise meaning of *qabḍ* is therefore to be determined by reference to prevailing custom.[15] Ibn Qudāmah has also stated that *qabḍ* in all things refers to the appropriate manner of taking possession. The *Sharīʿah*, he adds, does stipulate *qabḍ*, but the manner in which it is to be accomplished is determined by custom. It may consist of holding and retention, taking into custody (*al-ḥirz*), evacuation (*takhliyah*) and separation (*al-tafarruq*). *Qabḍ* is required for all fungible goods that are sold by weight, measurement or number. For responsibility on account of loss (*ḍaman*) in such commodities is transferred to the buyer after *qabḍ*, and *qabḍ*, in respect of such goods, takes place when they are weighed and measured. As for goods that are not sold by measurement and weight, such as clothes and livestock, they may be sold even prior to *qabḍ*. The reason for this is that responsibility for loss in such items devolves upon the buyer prior to *qabḍ*, that is, upon conclusion of the contract.[16]

It is interesting to note that the Ẓāhirī school has confined the application of this *ḥadīth* to one item only, namely, wheat. Ibn Ḥazm has thus reached the conclusion that the sale of anything prior to taking possession is lawful, except wheat. The reason for this interpretation, according to Ibn Ḥazm, is that the word '*taʿām*' which occurs in the *ḥadīth* means wheat and nothing else, because '*taʿām*' during the lifetime of the Prophet ﷺ was used in this sense alone. It matters little, according to this ruling, whether the ownership of the wheat in question has been acquired through purchase, charity, gift, or inheritance. Anyone who sells wheat must take it into possession first, and this must be in the literal sense of receiving delivery, holding and retention.[17]

Qabḍ has been understood as a relatively open concept that is amenable to the changing influences of commercial reality and custom. *Qabḍ* has thus meant evacuation, taking into custody, separation, measurement, identification (*taʿyin*, or *tamyīz*) and viewing (*mushāhadah*). While the

Ẓāhirīs understood *qabḍ* in its literal sense of holding and retention, their literalist position is probably the most liberal of all the schools in that they confine the requirement of *qabḍ* to sales in a single commodity (i.e., wheat). There is perhaps a point of general interest to be found in the Ẓāhirī approach to the understanding of the textual rulings of *Sharīʿah*: the prohibitive rulings of the Qur'ān and *Sunnah* ought to be read as narrowly as possible and should not be generalised and extended by analogy beyond their original intention and context.

With the exception perhaps of the Shāfiʿīs, none of the other schools require *qabḍ* prior to sale in immovable objects. The Mālikīs have confined *qabḍ* to foodgrains only. *Qabḍ* in fungible commodities takes place, as already noted, when they are weighed and measured for the purpose of delivery.

We note further that the requirement of measurement and weight for fungible foodgrains is reflected in the rulings of the *madhāhib* mainly for reasons of conformity to the *ḥadīth*. This conformity has a devotional (*taʿabbudī*) aspect which is not rationally comprehensible. To say that *qabḍ* in the sale of foodgrains takes place upon weighing and measuring is to confine delivery to only one method, which is not reasonable but, since this is expressly recommended in the *ḥadīth*, it has been upheld by scholastic jurisprudence in order to maintain conformity to the text.[18] The evidence on this point is more specific in at least two other *ḥadīth* as follows:

> The Prophet ﷺ prohibited the sale of foodstuffs prior to weighing and measuring.[19]
>
> المروى عن النبى ﷺ انه نهى عن بيع الطعام حتى يكال .

The second *ḥadīth* on this theme simply proclaims:

> Measure your foodstuffs and it will be blessed for you.[20]
>
> كيلوا طعامكم يبارك لكم .

In at least two varieties of sale, namely the forward sale of *salam* and the manufacturing contract (*istiṣnāʿ*), the requirement of *qabḍ* has been totally omitted, and the exemption here extends to all goods and commodities including foodgrains. *Salam* and *istiṣnāʿ* are validated on grounds of their utility to and convenience for the people.

We can perhaps readily say that *qabḍ* is not a requirement in futures trading in cotton, rubber and tin, which are not foodstuffs, according to the explicit text of the *ḥadīth* quoted above, and the majority ruling of the *madhāhib*. According to the Ẓāhirī interpretation the ruling also applies to palm oil. We may further add that measurement and weighing, which are the recommend modes of *qabḍ* in the sale of foodstuffs, may be said to be a requirement, with regard, for example, to the bulk sale of commodities or consecutive sales of the same commodity, only in the first transaction in the series. Futures contract in foodgrains are bought and sold in standardised quantities and packages that are weighed and measured once; the packages are sealed and labelled accordingly, there remaining no need for weighing each time they are sold. The warehouse receipts provide the documentary evidence of the total weight and measurement of the underlying commodity. The prevailing commercial custom, in futures trading at least, has thus evolved into a new phase which has made the personal supervision of weight and measurement unnecessary and unfeasible. It would appear that *qabḍ* in such commodities takes place in subsequent transactions, following the initial packaging, by obtaining the official warehouse receipt, rather than weighing and measuring of foodgrains at the time of contracting.

We have shown that customary practice has a role in determining the manner in which the legal requirements of *qabḍ* and delivery may be fulfilled. Provided that the process that is adopted for these purposes is free of uncertainty, unwarranted *gharar*, and the likelihood of giving rise to dispute, it may be acceptable even if it transforms the initial concept of physical delivery and *qabḍ* into an altogether different procedure. In banking transactions, whether involving money or other trading activity, account records (*al-qayd al-ḥisābī*) in both Islamic and conventional banks are accepted as proof of liability and credit, and they are deemed to be equivalent to actual *qabḍ* (*al-qabḍ al-haqīqī*).[21] It is quite conceivable that modern technology and computerisation may bring further changes to the conventional concept of *qabḍ* that may gain popularity and customary approval. These are acceptable from the point of view of the *Sharīʿah* if they fulfill the basic rationale of *qabḍ*, which is to prevent uncertainty and *gharar*.

Bearing in mind the fact that only about two per cent of the futures contracts in commodities lead to actual delivery, it may be said that the main issue in futures trading is not over *qabḍ* or the manner in which it occurs. Although delivery (*taslīm*) and receiving delivery (*qabḍ*) remain an important aspect of futures trading, it is not widely invoked and has therefore been marginalised in practice. This analysis of the position of *qabḍ* in Islamic law naturally applies to that part of futures trading in which the contracts are held to maturity and delivery takes place. As for the bulk of futures contracts in which the contracting parties close out their position by entering into a reverse transaction, this is an issue which need to be addressed separately. Since the *Sharīʿah* validates in principle the sale of a physical objects (*bay*ᶜ *al-*ᶜ*ayn*) as well as the sale (involving exchange) of debts (*bay*ᶜ *al-dayn*) which become a charge on the person (*dhimmah*) of the debtor, and because offsetting in futures contract tend to fall in the category of *bay*ᶜ *al-dayn*, we need to address this subject in further detail. Delivery and *qabḍ* in *bay*ᶜ *al-dayn* are no longer a matter of physical delivery or retention of an actual asset, but of appointment (*ta*ᶜ*yīn*) and computation of a debt that is established on the person (*dhimmah*) of the bearer of that debt. This is the subject to which we turn next.

NOTES

1. 'Taqābuḍ', *al-Mawsu*ᶜ*ah al-Fiqhiyyah*, XIII, 116.
2. See for detail Rebell, *Financial Futures*, p. 10.
3. Ibid., p. 26.
4. Al-Bukhārī, *Ṣaḥīh*, III, 194.
5. Ibid., III, 191.
6. Ibid., III, 195.
7. Burḥān al-Dīn al-Marghinānī, *The Hidāya*, Eng. tr. C. Hamilton, Lahore, Premier Book House, 1975, p. 275
8. Al-Shāfiᶜī, *al-*ᶜ*Umm*, III, 60; al-Jundī, *Mu*ᶜ*āmalāt*, p. 122.
9. Al-Shirāzī, *al-Muhadhdhab*, I, 349-50; al-Sharbīnī, *Mughnī*, II, 262.
10. The Fiqh Academy Resolution No. 7, 1989, p. 36.
11. Al-Kāsānī, *Badā'i*ᶜ, V, 156.
12. Al-Sarakhsī, *al-Mabsūṭ*, XII, 198.
13. Ibn Juzay, *Qawānīn*, pp. 221-2.
14. Ibn Rushd al-Qurṭubī, *Bidāyah*, II, 144; *al-Mawsu*ᶜ*ah al-*ᶜ*Ilmiyyah*, V, 440.
15. Ibn Taymiyyah, *Majmū*ᶜ*ah al-Fatāwa*, X, 375.
16. Ibn Qudāmah, *al-Mughnī*, IV, 124ff.
17. Ibn Ḥazm, *al-Muḥallā*, VIII, 518; al-Jundī, *Mu*ᶜ*āmalāt*, p. 124.
18. Cf. al-Qādir, 'Taᶜqīb', in *Mawsū*ᶜ*ah* ᶜ*Ilmiyyah*, V, 440.
19. *Mawsū*ᶜ*ah* ᶜ*Ilmiyyah*, V, 440.
20. Al-Bukhārī, *Ṣaḥīh*, III, 192.
21. Cf. Samī Ḥassan Ḥamoud, *Taṭwīr al-A*ᶜ*māl al-Maṣrafiyyah bima Yattafiq wa al-Sharīᶜah al-Islāmiyyah*, 2nd edn, Oman, Maṭbaᶜah al-Sharq, 1402/1982, p. 346.

CHAPTER TWELVE

Debt Clearance Sale (*Bay*ᶜ *al-Dayn bi'l-Dayn*)

An offsetting transaction in futures trading essentially consists of a sale in which two parties transact over a debt that one owes to the other, and settle their debts through the modality of sales and purchases. The subject here is somewhat technical, and juristic writings are not consistent about the nature of this transaction or its validity in *Sharī*ᶜ*ah*. A large variety of sales have been included under *bay*ᶜ *al-duyūn* (lit., sale of debts, also known as *bay*ᶜ *al-kāli' bi'l-kāli'*), and many of them have been disputed as to whether they do in fact qualify as 'sale of debts'. Some instances of this transaction may be illustrated as follows:

1. A man buys a certain commodity from another on credit, for a fixed period. When the period of payment comes and the debtor finds that he is unable to pay, he asks the seller, 'Sell it to me on credit for a further period, for something additional.' The seller agrees and sells on credit what was already credit. It is stated in *al-Muwaṭṭa'* that Imām Mālik considered this transaction to be unlawful. I may hasten to add, however, that an offsetting sale in the futures market is not always for 'something additional', since it is possible that the seller will make a profit, sell at cost price, or make a loss—which means that *ribā'* is not involved, and the case is not analogous to the one which invoked a prohibitive opinion from Imām Mālik.[1]

2. A has borrowed two tonnes of wheat for his personal needs from a farmer B, returnable in six months. Prior to expiry of this period, B sells the wheat, which is a debt on A, to C in exchange for a ploughing machine to be delivered in one month. The sale here consists of an exchange of debts, which is considered unlawful because of the uncertainty that it involves over delivery, and the likelihood, therefore, of

gharar. The proper way for the parties to transact would be for each party to take possession of what is due to them first, before proceeding on to another transaction over the same assets.[2]

3. A has borrowed $2,000 from B for a period of one year but, before the repayment is due, B suggests to A that he (B) can rent A's house in exchange for the sum owed to him. This is also held to be unlawful because the transaction here consists of the sale of one debt for another, there being no delivery on either side, and if the proposed exchange is advantageous to one of the parties, it will also involve unlawful gain amounting to *ribā'*.[3]

4. A is indebted to B for ,say, 20 ounces of gold, and B owes C 150 ounces of silver. A and C may not settle their debts directly between themselves because this would amount to the sale of one debt for another. The reason for this is that A is personally indebted to B (and the latter to C), and his *dhimmah*, which is occupied in that order, can only be released by repaying his creditor directly. The Ḥanbalīs only forbid such a clearance of debts if the two commodities are different, whereas the Shāfiʿīs forbid it even if they are identical in genus and quantity, in which case it would actually amount to a simple clearance of mutual debts (*al-maqāsah*).[4] Futures sales are not in the nature of simple *maqāsah* of mutual debts because of the likelihood of differences in the respective prices of the sale and purchase of the same contract, and the consequent profit or loss that may be made.

5. A sells a garment to B for 100 dinars, payable in one month, and then buys from B the same or a similar garment for 120 dinars, payable after two months. This transaction, known as *al-ʿinah*, although validated by the Shāfiʿīs, is invalid according to the other leading schools. Another example of the same transaction would be that A sells the garment to B for 100 dinars, payable in six months and then B, who may or may not take delivery, sells it back immediately to A for a prompt price of 80 dinars. This could be just another way of B borrowing 100 dinars from A for a fixed interest of 20 dinars, payable in six months. Some jurists say this is invalid because it involves *ribā'*, while others include it under the debt clearance sale.[5] It is stated in *Mughnī al-Muḥtāj* that the sale of a debt to a third party (that is, a person other than the debtor) is null and void, but there is a second opinion on this which validates the sale of a debt to a third party on condition that the debtor acknowledges his debt and is willing to repay it, that the debt is due to be repaid, and that both parties take into possession what is due to them before they part each others' company.[6] We also read in the Mālikī text *al-Mudawwanah* that the sale of a debt to a third party is valid if the following conditions are met: a) that the debtor is present and acknowledges the debt; b) that the

object is not foodstuffs; c) that the buyer is not hostile to the debtor and does not intend to annoy him; d) that the price is not of the same genus as the object of sale, as it may otherwise amount to *ribā'*; and e) that the price is paid promptly. Some of these conditions are evidently concerned with the barter rather than the monetary sale. Be as it may, the Mālikī school also validates the sale of a debt in the absence of the debtor in what is known as the reverse mortgage (*qahl al-rahn*). This is when the person who has the mortgaged item in his possession needs his money prior to maturity. He may sell it for the price himself paid for it and let the buyer step into his shoes, provided that the substitution here is recorded in the mortgage document.[7] We may note further that the debt transfer (i.e., *ḥawālah*), which is validated by all the leading schools of *fiqh*, consists, in fact, of the exchange of credits (*bay*ᶜ *al-dayn bi'l-dayn*) and this confirms, once again, the basic validity of the transaction at issue. The cautious stance that the jurists have generally taken is thus to prevent uncertainty, *gharar* and the possible conflict that may arise from it.

6. Ibn Qudāmah has stated that if a person borrows a quantity of foodstuffs from another, the creditor may not sell it to a third party without receiving what is owed to him first.[8] There is also an opinion that the transaction here is like selling the debt that is involved in the forward sale of *salam*, which may not be sold prior to *qabḍ*. It is further stated that a sale of this kind falls under the explicit terms of the *ḥadīth* which prohibits the sale of foodstuffs prior to taking possession. Ibn Rushd has stated that it is one of the conditions of a valid *salam* that the price of the commodity to be delivered later is not deferred for a long time, since otherwise this would turn *salam* into *bay*ᶜ *al-kāli' bi'l-kāli'* (a debt for debt sale).[9] As for the question of whether the buyer may sell the subject-matter of *salam*, Ibn Taymiyyah has stated that Imām Aḥmad ibn Ḥanbal validated the sale of the debt in *salam* prior to maturity. This is because the prohibition of selling foodstuffs prior to taking possession is confined to spot sales in specified tangible foodstuffs (*al-ta*ᶜ*ām al-mu*ᶜ*ayyan*). As for transacting over a debt which is proven on the *dhimmah*, it is in the nature of repaying the debt to discharge one's obligation over it.[10]

A general consensus (*ijmā*ᶜ) is said to have materialised on the prohibition of *bay*ᶜ *al-kāli' bi'l-kāli'*. Imām Aḥmad ibn Ḥanbal has gone on record to say that common consensus (*ijmā al-nās*) has forbidden it. But evidence shows that such an *ijmā*ᶜ would not be unfeasible bearing in mind the fact that the scholars are not in agreement about the definition of this transaction, or the various forms that it can take. The *madhāhib* have also recorded divergent rulings on this issue, which would suggest that the claim of an *ijmā*ᶜ having materialised is clearly unfounded.[11]

Then there remains the evidence in the *Sunnah*: Mūsā ibn ᶜUbaydah reported from ᶜAbd Allāh ibn ᶜUmar that 'the Prophet ﷺ prohibited *bay*ᶜ *al-kāli' bi'l-kāli*'' [12]

عن ابن عمر رض أن النبى ﷺ نهى عن بيع الكالئ بالكالئ .

This *ḥadīth* appears in only some collections, such as that of al-Daraqutnī, and al-Shawkānī has reproduced Daraqutnī's version in *Nayl al-Awṭār* only to say that many prominent scholars have considered it to be less than reliable. There is some doubt in the precise meaning of this *ḥadīth* since the word *kāli'* is somewhat unfamiliar even to the native Arabs, but is generally understood to mean the sale of one debt for another. Al-Shawkānī has stated: 'Only Mūsā ibn ᶜUbaydah al-Radbhī has reported it, and its authenticity is weak. Imām Aḥmad ibn Ḥanbal has said: "I do not know of any other *ḥadīth* transmitted by him (Ibn ᶜUbaydah) nor has anyone else transmitted this *ḥadīth*."[13] Imām al-Shāfiᶜī has also said that the scholars of *ḥadīth* have considered this *ḥadīth* to be weak.' Ibn Qudāmah and Ibn Taymiyyah have concurred with this conclusion and stated that no *ḥadīth* on the prohibition of the transaction at issue has been verified. Ibn Taymiyyah has stated that no words or statements prohibiting the 'sale of one debt for another' have been transmitted from the Prophet ﷺ and that the *ḥadīth* on the *bay*ᶜ *al-kāli' bi'l-kāli'* is a broken one (*munqati*ᶜ). Imām Aḥmad ibn Ḥanbal has also said that no *ḥadīth* on this subject can be verified.[14] Majd al-Dīn ᶜAzzām's recent enquiry into this *ḥadīth* has led to the conclusion that the evidential basis of this *ḥadīth* is too weak for it to constitute a binding rule of *Sharī*ᶜ*ah*. [15]

Some jurists have validated the sale of one debt for another if it is to the debtor himself but not, as noted above, if it is to a third party, since uncertainty over delivery is greater when a third party is involved. Other scholars have, on the other hand, held that *bay*ᶜ *al-dayn* is not only permissible to the debtor himself, but also to a third party. Many Ḥanafī and Mālikī jurists, as well as Ibn Taymiyyah, have generally validated this transaction on the grounds that a debt in the charge (*dhimmah*) of a debtor who does not dispute or deny it, is as good as a tangible asset (*al-*ᶜ*ayn al-ḥāḍirah*), and there is no issue at stake over its validity. Thus, according to Ibn Taymiyyah, 'this form of transaction, which involves sale of what is clearly proven to be the *dhimmah* of a person, may be cancelled out for a similar debt which is also proven upon another person; and there is no text, or general consensus or analogy on its prohibition'.[16] While reviewing the evidence on this issue Siddīq al-Ḍarīr has categorically stated that '*bay*ᶜ *al-dayn* is absolutely lawful, whether the sale is to the debtor or to a third party, for cash or for credit, provided that the sale is clear of *ribā'* and no textual injunction has declared it forbidden'. Al-Ḍarīr has added that the claim about uncertainty over delivery is unwarranted if the debt is not disputed by the debtor who clearly admits his obligation and shows readiness to discharge it.[17]

In light of the foregoing evidence, and the absence of a clear prohibition on *bayᶜ al-dayn*, what remains for us is to bring in the original principle of permissibility (*ibāḥah*) and conclude that this type of sale is permissible provided that it is devoid of *ribā'* and *gharar*.

We need now to ascertain the relevance of *bayᶜ al-dayn bi'l-dayn* to futures trading. I began the discussion in this section with the premise that the offsetting transaction, which enables traders in the commodity exchange to close out their positions, resembles that which is involved in a debt clearance sale. This may be illustrated as follows: I sell to the clearing-house what I had earlier purchased from the clearing-house; I do not need a specific agreement on this each time, because the reverse transaction and offsetting are basic functions of the clearing-house and an integral term of our mutual agreement. Both parties acknowledge their obligations and there is no question of denial or any kind of uncertainty in that regard. The terms of our agreement have all been recorded and verified, there remaining no likelihood of uncertainty and *gharar*, nor indeed of any unwarranted gain or advantage for one party at the expense of the other. The purchase price that had remained a debt on my *dhimmah* has now been cleared because I sold an equivalent asset to my creditor (the clearing-house), which means that the debts we owed one another have consequently been cleared. The assets involved in the debt were, in other words, sold back to the creditor and there is no third party involvement in this transaction that might introduce uncertainty over clearance and delivery. The reverse of this would be when I buy from the clearing-house what I had previously sold to it and not having then received the full price. The price had, in other words, remained a debt on the clearing-house, which is the principal party in the transaction and, even if it acts on behalf of another customer, it acts in the capacity of a fully committed guarantor (*kafīl*). It would be more accurate, however, to regard the clearing-house as the principal party in this bilateral transaction. It is admittedly true that the initial sale or purchase that I transacted is normally with a party other than the clearing-house, who may be an individual trader or his broker/agent. But this is only a temporary arrangement and to all intents and purposes does not affect the liability and standing of the clearing-house in respect of the material consequences of the sale, namely, delivery and price. The moment that the clearing-house has registered and matched up the facts of the transaction, which is usually on the same day (due to the daily settlement procedure), it becomes a principal party to the transaction. From that moment onwards, the identity of the original parties, and the question of who buys from whom, is basically immaterial, as is the question of their creditworthiness or ability to deliver. All of this, that is, the identity of the parties, their creditworthiness etc., although vital elements of a conventional sale, become almost totally insignificant in futures in the light of the fact that these tasks are being assumed by the clearing-house. There is no uncertainty and risk-taking (*gharar*) in this transaction because of the clearing-house guarantee in respect of delivery and payment of price. The transaction is also free of unlawful gain (*ribā'*) as it does not involve any payment of interest that might have been fixed in advance. The traders may make a profit or incur a loss, there being no question of gaining profit without commitment and liability for loss in the event where this becomes the case.

We may therefore conclude that the *bayᶜ al-dayn* which is incurred in futures transactions is in the nature of the fulfilment of an obligation and the repayment of a debt by the debtor. This is in line with the basic Qur'ānic norm (5:1) in respect of the fulfilment of contracts.

NOTES

1. Mālik ibn Anas, *al-Muwaṭṭa'*, ed. ᶜAbd al-Wahhāb ᶜAbd al-Latīf, Beirut, Dār al-Maᶜrifah, 1399/1979, p.550; see also Abdullah Alwi Haji Hassan, *Sales and Contracts in Early Islamic Commercial Law*, Islamabad: Islamic Research Institute, 1994, p. 65.
2. Cf. al-Ḍarīr, *al-Gharar*, p. 312; Ḥasan, *ᶜAmal*, p. 293.
3. Cf. Ḥasan, *ᶜAmal*, p. 290.
4. Ibid., p. 291.
5. Cf. al-Qaradāwī, *Bayᶜ al-Murābaḥah*, p. 45; Ḥasan, *ᶜAmal*, p. 289.
6. Al-Sharbīnī, *Mughnī*, II, 71.
7. ᶜAbd al-Salām Sahnun, *al-Mudawwanah al-Kubrā li'l-Imām Mālik ibn Anas*, Beirut: Dār al-Maᶜrifah, n.d., 15, 126-7; see also Mahmassānī, *al-Mawjibāt*, p. 159.
8. Ibn Qudāmah, *al-Mughni*, IV, 91.
9. Ibn Rushd al-Qurṭubī, *Bidāyah*, II, 152.
10. Ibn Taymiyyah, *Majmūᶜah Fatāwa*, XXIX, 512; Ḥasan, *ᶜAmal*, p. 282.
11. Yaḥyā ibn ᶜAlī al-Shawkānī, *Nayl al-Awṭār Sharḥ Muntaqā al-Akhbār*, Cairo, Muṣṭafā al-Bābī al-Ḥalābī, n.d., V, 176; Ḥasan, *ᶜAmal*, p. 292.
12. Al-Shawkānī, *Nayl al-Awṭār*, V, 176.
13. Ibid., V, 176-7.
14. Ibn Qudāmah, *al-Mughnī*, IV, 46; Ibn Taymiyyah, *Naẓariyyah al-ᶜAqd*, p. 235.
15. For further details of ᶜAzzām's views see the chapter below, entitled 'A Summary of Modern Opinion'.
16. Ibn Taymiyyah, *Naẓariyyah al-ᶜAqd*, p. 235.
17. Al-Ḍarīr, *al-Gharar*, p. 316.

CHAPTER THIRTEEN

Deferred Sale (*Bay*ᶜ *al-Mu'ajjal*)

One of the basic features of the Islamic law of contract, according to Muslim jurists, is that contracts are immediately effective and engender their proper consequences without delay, unless the parties have stipulated otherwise.[1] Consequently, the jurists have visualised sale as a contract that must generate immediate results, chief among these being the transfer of ownership to the buyer and the seller's liability to deliver the object of sale without delay. Although the contracting parties generally enjoy considerable liberty to stipulate terms and conditions into nominate contracts, there are nevertheless limitations that vary from contract to contract. One of these limitations, which extends to almost all contracts, is that any stipulation by the contracting parties should not frustrate the basic nature and purpose of the contract in question.

The jurists have defined sale from two different angles, namely, the general and the specific. Sale has been generally defined as 'a contract of exchange which is binding on the parties'. More specifically, sale is defined as the 'exchange of a tangible object (ᶜ*ayn ḥāḍirah*) that is present for a price that is assigned to the person (*dhimmah*) of the buyer'.[2] In this general sense, sale comprises, in addition to normal sale, barter exchange, in which both of the countervalues are tangible objects, and the sale of currencies, in which both sides of the transaction consist of money. Delivery in both cases is immediate, involving no deferment that might be regarded as a debt on the other side. Sale in its general sense also comprises forward sale (*salam*) in which one of the countervalues, namely, the price, is paid at the time of contract but delivery of the object of *salam* is postponed to a later date. Many jurists have somehow regarded *salam* to be an anomaly to the norm of immediacy of exchange and the tangible presence of the object of sale at the time of contract. 'The norm in the contract of sale', as Ibn ᶜĀbidīn has stated, 'is immediate exchange of the countervalues, but deferred sale is permitted if the deferment is for a specified period in such a way as to eliminate the possible grounds of conflict.'[3] The Mālikīs have voiced the same reservations but validate deferred sale when it is devoid of the possibility of *gharar*. The Mālikīs are, however, somewhat restrictive in their stance on deferred sales (*buyūᶜ al-ajal*) and have proscribed many varieties of them on precautionary grounds. This is to some extent due to their liberal application of the doctrine of *sadd al-dharā'iᶜ* (blocking the means) and the fear of indulgence in *ribā'*. Al-Qaradāwī has criticised the Mālikī position and observed that the inclusion of these sales under the prohibited varieties of sale is not founded on the authority of the Qur'ān or *Sunnah*, but is rather based on juristic *ijtihād*, and this is why many different views have been recorded on the subject.[4]

The Shāfiᶜīs are the most liberal in validating deferred sale as a matter of principle, provided that the deferment period is clearly defined so as to preclude *gharar*. In validating deferred sale, Imām al-Shāfiᶜī has relied on the Qur'ānic text on the permissibility of deferred liability contracts (2:282), which is discussed below. Imām al-Shāfiᶜī has on the same basis validated the sale of *ᶜinah* which many others have considered unlawful. *ᶜInah* may take a variety of forms of which the following is a typical one: A sells an object to B on a deferred payment basis, and buys it back from B for a lower price which is paid immediately, or deferred for a lesser period.[5]

The Ḥanbalīs, too, validate deferred sale provided that it is devoid of usury and *gharar*. Ibn Taymiyyah and his disciple Ibn Qayyim al-Jawziyyah, as discussed earlier, have not only considered deferred sales to be valid in principle, but they have also criticised the majority ruling which declares immediate delivery to be the basic norm and requirement of sale. It thus appears that the scholars have generally considered deferred sale to be valid, but they have done so with reservations. Ibn Qayyim has in turn criticised these reservations and stated that the idea of deferment in transactions should be accepted as a matter of principle. I shall return to this theme in my discussion of the relevant Qur'ānic text below; here I turn briefly to some of the varieties of deferred sale which the *Sharīᶜah* has expressly validated.

As noted above, the *Sharīᶜah* validates both the forward sale of *salam* and the manufacturing contract of *istiṣnāᶜ*, notwithstanding the fact that delivery in both of these is postponed to the future. In *salam* the vendor's right of ownership is promptly established in the price, which is payable at the time of contract. The vendor in *salam* has no title over the object of sale, which may be agricultural produce, but undertakes to deliver it in the future. The subject-matter of *salam*, in other words, is a promise given against payment, but not a real object. The goods that the vendor promises to deliver do not exist, but the law requires that their quantity, quality and delivery date should be precisely determined at the time of the bargain. *Salam* is normally valid for fungible items, although some have extended the validity of *salam* to all commodities except gold and silver, in which case deferment is unacceptable for fear of *ribā'*.[6] The scholastic *fiqh* has regulated *salam* and *istiṣnā*ᶜ in considerable detail, and various safeguards have been provided lest the deferment therein lead to unwarranted risk taking or unlawful gain (i.e., *gharar* and *ribā'*). The Ḥanafī *ijtihād* has led the scholars to the conclusion that the goods stipulated in *salam* must exist continuously from the time of the contract until delivery, and the date of delivery must be specified at the time of contract. The Shāfiᶜīs, on the other hand, have relaxed some of these requirements by ruling, for example, that the date of delivery in *salam* need not be fixed. These are some of the different conclusions in the *ijtihādī* rulings of the *madhāhib* on *salam*, whose validity or otherwise can perhaps be readily debated merely by looking at the textual rulings of the Qur'ān and *Sunnah* relating to the subject. Be that as it may, our purpose is to illustrate the point, as noted above, that many of the *ijtihādī* rulings of *fiqh* are influenced by the requirements of public interest and the prevailing conditions of the time in which they are formulated.

Briefly, the manufacturing contract (*istiṣnā*ᶜ) consists of an agreement made in advance to pay a definite price for something that is to be made and delivered at a future date. Unlike the contract of *salam*, which has been validated on the explicit authority of *ḥadīth*, *istiṣnā*ᶜ has been validated by general consensus (*ijmā*ᶜ), custom (ᶜ*urf*) and 'the necessities of business'.[7] Notwithstanding the fact that nothing changes hands immediately, and that the subject-matter is also non-existent at the time of contract, *istiṣnā*ᶜ has been validated by all the leading schools. The contract is concluded by an offer and acceptance between the parties, and it creates an obligation on the contractor to manufacture the goods and a corresponding obligation on the customer to pay the price once the goods are manufactured according to the contract. A minority opinion, held by some scholars, including Imām Abū Ḥanīfah, has it that *istiṣnā*ᶜ is not a binding contract, but an exchange of promises (*tawā*ᶜ*ud*); however, the majority of scholars, including Abū Ḥanīfah's disciple Abū Yūsuf, are in agreement that *istiṣnā*ᶜ is a binding contract.[8]

Notwithstanding the validity in *Sharī*ᶜ*ah* of *salam* and *istiṣnā*ᶜ, as well as the clear authority in the Qur'ān for the validity of deferred liability transactions, the ᶜ*ulamā'* have expressed reservations about those deferred sales and future sales that they have considered to be anomalous on the grounds that the very purpose of sale is the immediate transfer of ownership of the object of sale and that deferment tends to hinder this purpose. It is thus stated in many scholarly sources that deferment is valid if it involves only one, but not both, of the countervalues in a contract of sale. Either the payment of price, or delivery of the subject-matter may be postponed to a future date, but a sale in which both of the counter values are deferred to a future date is invalid.

It is further stated that a sale in which the parties do not aim for the immediate transfer of ownership in at least one of the countervalues at the time of contract, is not really a sale but an agreement which amounts to no more than a promise. Unless deferment is specified and carefully regulated, it tends in all sales to give rise to the possibility of uncertainty and *gharar*, as well as to unlawful gain (*ribā'*). The *gharar* that is apprehended here relates to price changes over the course of time, changes that might affect the subject-matter of sale, and the question of whether the parties might consequently dispute the terms of their agreement.[9]

Despite these reservations, deferred sale has been validated if it fulfils two conditions, one of which is that the countervalues must not include usurable items wherein deferment could lead to usury: the schools of law tend to apply differential reasoning and *ʿillah* in regulating this. If the countervalues in a barter exchange are of the same genus and both are sold by measurement and weight, the Ḥanafīs consider this a usurable transaction, whereas the *ʿillah* of usury in such an exchange, according to the Shāfiʿīs, is commonality in genus and edibility. The Mālikīs, on the other hand, consider the *ʿillah* of prohibition here to be unity of genus, plus edibility and storability. A barter exchange is thus valid for items that fall outside these combinations. The second condition that a valid deferred sale must fulfil is that the countervalues should be clearly identified and described to the extent that there remains no ambiguity about the delivery period or other material aspects of the transaction.[10]

A deferment period (*ajal*) is clearly determined if it is for specific dates, counted either by the number of days and months, or specified by other indicators such as the New Year Day. But *ajal* is void if its beginning is either undetermined or uncertain, for instance, if it is designated 'whenever the rain falls'. If deferment is somewhat vague, such as 'the month of Ramaḍān' or 'the harvesting time', it pertains to the first of that month or period and, if it stipulates a terms such as 'three months', this signifies the end of that period. Although Imām Mālik has validated deferred sales for very long periods, such as ten or even twenty years and longer, many jurists have held that the period should not be excessively long for fear of indulgence in *gharar*.

The question of whether deferment can be reciprocated by an increase in price, or the performance of a task or service, has drawn different responses from commentators. Although many are inclined to regard such increases as usury, there is authority in the *Sunnah* in support of its validation. The evidence quoted in this connection is a *ḥadīth*, reported by Ibn ᶜAbbās, concerning a discount granted on a loan that is paid back prior to maturity (*da*ᶜ*wa ta*ᶜ*ajjal*). It is thus reported that the Prophet ﷺ granted permission for period loans to be recovered ahead of their stipulated periods, and the debtors were allowed to pay less because of early repayment. The conclusion has thus been drawn, by means of analogy, that if early repayment can engender a discount in a period loan, a deferred payment of price can similarly bring about an increase in the price because of the deferment.[11]

Deferment is, however, not of the essence of an obligation, but an extraneous and subsidiary factor which does not play a role in the essential validity of a contract. According to al-Sarakhsī, 'option and deferment (*khiyār wa ajal*) fall under the attributes of a contract ... Their presence or absence is subsidiary to the essence of contract'. Thus when deferment is attached to a debt, it does not affect the substance of the obligation concerning the payment of that debt.[12]

From the point of view of the time in which a contract may come into effect, the jurists have classified contracts into three types, namely, prompt (*al-*ᶜ*aqd al-munajjaz*), contingent (*al-*ᶜ*aqd al-mu*ᶜ*allaq*) and deferred (*al-*ᶜ*aqd al-muḍāf*). A contract may thus be effective immediately, it may be contingent upon the fulfilment of a condition, or deferred to a future date. These terms are normally understood from the words and sentences that are used in the contract. The first of these, namely, the prompt contract, is concluded in words that are neither contingent nor deferred, and its consequences immediately follow the conclusion. This is the most typical of the three forms under discussion; all contracts can be concluded in this way and be immediately effective, except for two, namely, bequest and executorship (*īṣā'*), both of which come into effect only after the death of the testator and not before.[13]

Briefly, a contingent contract (*al-*ᶜ*aqd al-mu*ᶜ*allaq*), as the term implies, is dependent for its conclusion upon the occurrence of some other event. An example of this would be when A tells B: if you give a loan to my brother, I will be his guarantor (*kafīl*); or: you can be my representative in the sale of my house if you travel to Egypt. If the stipulated condition has already materialised, the contingent contract automatically converts to a prompt one, but no contract will exist until the occurrence of the stipulated event. In order to be valid, a contingent contract must meet two requirements, one of which is that the condition relates to the future, for otherwise it would be a prompt contract, and the other one being that the condition is one which is possible and can become effective.[14]

A deferred contract (*al-ʿaqd al-muḍāf*), which can conceptually apply to a futures contract, is one which is concluded in the present but whose consequences are postponed to a future date. The deferred contract is thus valid, according to the Ḥanafīs and Mālikīs, as of the moment of conclusion, but it becomes effective only at a specified time in the future which is normally stipulated in the contract. The Shāfiʿīs do not recognise the division between the contingent and deferred contracts, since they maintain that both are concluded in the present but become effective in the future. The Ḥanafī-Mālikī rationale, on the other hand, in distinguishing the contingent and the deferred contract from one another, is related to a parallel distinction between the cause (*sabab*) and consequence (*ḥukm*) of the contract respectively. It is thus stated that in the case of deferred contracts, the stipulation as to time affects only the consequence of the contract but not its cause. The position is different in a contingent contract, where the stipulated condition affects the essence or cause of the contract, and the contract does not come into being unless the stipulated condition materialises.[15]

The jurists have then added that a deferred contract is valid when the contract in question does not involve a transfer of ownership. Sale, as a contract for the transfer of ownership, is consequently precluded, as explained below, and it may not be concluded in the manner of *ʿaqd al-muḍāf*. This would effectively mean that a contract of sale cannot be concluded on a deferred basis such that would postpone both the delivery and payment of price to a future date.

From the point of view of the amenability and openness to deferment (*ta'jīl*), contracts have been further classified into three types, which may be summarised as follows. Firstly, contracts that can only become effective in the future, such as executorship and bequests. Secondly, contracts that are capable of being either prompt or deferred. The jurists have listed about fourteen nominate contracts under this classification, chief among which are usufructuary contracts, such as lease and hire, agency (*wakālah*), commenda or *muḍārabah*, charitable endowment (*waqf*) and divorce. Thirdly, contracts that do not admit deferment to a future date. Included in this category are contracts which involve a transfer of ownership, such as sale, gift, partnership (*shirkah*), release of debt (*ibrā' al-dayn*) and mutual reconciliation (*ṣulḥ*). It is thus stated that contracts of this type may not be deferred to a future date since they do transfer ownership and are best concluded on a prompt basis, and there is besides 'no need for deferment, for deferment in such contracts is also likely to lead to indulgence in gambling (*muqāmarah*)'.[16]

The above three types are, however, based on juristic *ijtihād* that deals with the prevailing conditions of a particular time. The different categories were evidently designed to foreclose the avenues leading to *gharar* and uncertainty that imperilled the integrity of contracts. But the evidence in the sources that I have reviewed in the following pages is confined to an exposition of the basic guidelines, and does not speak of any particular categories of contracts as such.

I. A Glance at Modern Law

Modern legislation on contracts and transactions in the Muslim countries of the Middle East and beyond has generally been guided by the Qur'ānic principle that validates commercial transactions and contracts on the basis of mutual consent. The text thus states, in an address to the believers, 'Devour not each other's property in vain, but let there be lawful trade by your mutual consent.' (4:29).

Since the Qur'ānic proclamation here is absolute, every contract is consequently deemed to be valid unless there is a clear prohibition to the contrary. Many Arab states have introduced legislation which does not restrict the basic freedom of the parties to conclude a contract and has consequently overlooked some of the restrictions of the conventional *fiqh* on this subject. Modern law has thus validated transactions in things that are non-existent at the time of transaction, provided that they can exist in the future.

The Egyptian Civil Law 1948 (arts. 131-5) regulates the subject-matter of contracts, and provides in art. 131 that 'the subject-matter of an obligation may be a future thing'. Article 132, on the other hand, declares that a contract is null and void (*bāṭil*) when its subject-matter does not exist. Articles 133-4 provide that the subject-matter of a contract must be lawful and clearly identified. Recourse may be had to custom in the event of ambiguity, or when the parties disagree over the grade or quality of the subject-matter of the contract. Commenting on these provisions, Madkūr has observed that in validating a contract dealing with a non-existing object which is clearly described and identified, the Egyptian law has followed the views of the Ḥanbalī scholars Ibn Taymiyyah and Ibn Qayyim al-Jawziyyah.[17]

The Civil Code of Iraq 1951 (art. 129.1) has also provided that 'the subject-matter of an obligation may be non-existent at the time of contracting, provided its future existence is possible and provided it is determined in a way which dispels the want of knowledge (*jahl*) and risk (*gharar*)'. The one exception to this that has been singled out is that a transaction over the estate of a person while the person is still alive is null and void.

The Qatar Civil and Commercial Law of 1971 (art. 33) maintains the same position as that of Iraqi law. Jordan's Civil Code of 1976 has similarly stated that the subject-matter of a contract may be a thing in the future provided that *gharar* is averted (art. 160.1). The succeeding article 161 equates *gharar* with an exorbitant want of knowledge.

Kuwait's Commercial Code (Law No. 68 of 1980) permits the sale of property not yet in existence (art. 130). It also permits a contract that does not specify a price, if the intention is to use the market price or a price fixed by a third party (arts. 124, 125). The Civil Code of Kuwait (Law No. 67 of 1980) allows contracts for the sale of something not yet in existence (Art. 168). Dubai and Sharja (Dubai Law of Contract 1971) also allow contracts which are conditional upon future events (arts. 36, 37).

Article 126 of the United Arab Emirates Federal Civil Code of 1985 permits the parties to stipulate any provision in a contract which is not prohibited by law, and is not contrary to public order and morality. This has been taken a step further by the Commercial Code of Bahrain (Law No. 7 of 1987), which provides that 'commercial matters are regulated by the agreement of the contracting parties provided that such agreement does not conflict with mandatory legislative provisions' (art. 2). The Qatar Civil and Commercial Law (art. 2) has similarly upheld the parties' freedom of contract and their liberty to stipulate what they will, provided that no principles of law and morality are violated thereby.

It will be noted that whenever the law permits contract over a non-existing object, it does not require that the object in question must be deliverable at the time of contracting, for once a contract over a future thing is permitted its presence or deliverability at the time of contract is no longer a requirement.

II. A Review of the Qur'ānic *Āyah al-Mudāyanah*

The Qur'ān validates deferred transactions involving future obligations as follows:

> O you who believe! When you deal with each other in transactions involving future obligations for a fixed period (*idhā tadāyantum bi-daynin ilā ajalin musamman*), reduce them into writing. Let a scribe write down faithfully as between the parties. (2:282)

The subsequent verses further accentuate the importance of accurate documentation in future transactions. Transactions of this kind, whether large or small, must be for a fixed period and all the material facts as well as the rights and obligations of the parties therein must be certain, reduced into writing and witnessed. The text thus leaves no doubt about the validity of future transactions in which the parties' rights and liabilities and the time in which they become due are clearly defined and documented. The question is whether 'transactions involving future obligations for a fixed period' should also include futures trading.

The words *dayn* and *tadāyantum*, being the key terms in this text, call for some elaboration. Firstly, *dayn* in this context means the deferred liability that arises from a contract involving the exchange of values. Typical among these is the contract of sale which requires either an immediate exchange of values, e.g. in a spot sale, or that one of the counter values, such as either the payment of price or delivery of the subject-matter, is deferred to a future date. The liability that arises from this deferment is thus referred to as *dayn*. This is different from a liability that arises from a straight loan or *qarḍ*, which is also a deferred liability, but one arising from a contract in which there is no exchange of values. Since the *Sharīᶜah* prohibits *ribā'* (interest) on loans, *qarḍ* becomes a loan which is given as an act of goodwill and co-operation (*taᶜāwun*) without interest, and nothing is given in exchange.

Our information of the commercial practices of the Arabs indicates that deferred transactions that took into account the seasonal patterns of agriculture were commonly practised. Some well-known varieties of contract of exchange that were in vogue at the time of the advent of Islam included deferred sale (i.e., *bayᶜ al-mu'ajjal* or *bayᶜ bi-thaman al-ājil*), *bayᶜ al-murābaḥah* (cost plus profit sale), *al-ijārah* (leasing), *al-salam* (forward sale), and *al-istiṣnāᶜ* (manufacturing order).[18] All of these were contracts of exchange in which the delivery of one of the countervalues was deferred to a future date. The deferred liability that arose from these transactions was generally known as *dayn*. The following *ḥadīth* is also reflective of some of the realities of the Arab commercial life in the early days of Islam:

> Ibn ᶜAbbās narrated that when the Prophet ﷺ arrived in Medina, he found that the people had been practising forward sales [i.e., *salam*] in fruits for one or two years [the sub-narrator is in doubt whether it was one or two years or two to three years]. The Prophet said: Anyone who pays money in advance for dates (to be delivered later) should pay it for a specified measure and a specified weight and a specified period.[19]

The verb *tadāyantum*, being a derivative of *dayn* (that is, the present tense in the plural and reciprocal mood) indicates that the subject at issue was a recurrent social phenomenon. The linguistic usage here suggests reciprocity and exchange of goods and services on a deferred liability basis. The fact that *tadāyantum* in the text before us is immediately followed by the expression *bi-dayn* (i.e., with a future obligation) implies an emphasis that reinforces the preceding segment of the text, and demonstrates the centrality of this theme (i.e., *dayn*) to the whole of the *āyah* (verse), which is why it is known as *āyah al-mudāyanah*. Ibn Kathīr has confirmed this by saying that the *āyah* is exclusively concerned with the deferred transactions (*muʿāmalāt mu'ajjalah*) that were practised by people, and the Qur'ān regulated the manner in which they were to be concluded.[20]

It is also useful to distinguish the two concepts of *dayn* and *ʿayn* from one another. *ʿAyn* refers, in the linguistic usage of the Arabs, to an object or commodity that is present at the time of transaction, such as the sale of an object in a spot sale. *Dayn,* on the other hand, refers to an asset which has no tangible existence but represents a charge, or a personal commitment, on the *dhimmah* (legal personality) of its bearer. This juristic distinction between *ʿayn* and *dayn* is important in the sense that only a *dayn*, but not an *ʿayn*, is capable of deferment. Future transactions are therefore transactions that are exclusively concerned with personal liabilities. Transactions which involve the exchange of tangible objects can be either in the present and on the spot, in which case the bargain would consist of exchanging one *ʿayn* for another, such as in barter, or of an object for its monetary value, such as in a normal cash sale. The exchange of values here does not involve a transaction over *dayn*. But when there is a deferment either in the payment of price, or in the delivery of an object, a deferred liability or *dayn* is created, and it is only with such transactions that the *āyah* under discussion is concerned.

In contradistinction to 'the future transactions for a fixed period' (*bi-daynin ilā ajalin musamman*) the subsequent portion of the same verse reads 'unless it be a spot trade which you carry among yourselves' (*illa an takūna tijāratan ḥāḍiratan tudīrūnaha baynakum*), which is exempted from the requirement of precise documentation and witnessing. *Tijāratan ḥāḍiratan* here means a contract of exchange which is concluded and completed on the spot, both of the countervalues of which are delivered upon conclusion without involving any deferred liability to a future date.

Having reviewed the principal Qur'ānic evidence on deferred transactions, it is interesting to note that the jurists have confined the general concept of a deferred sale basically to sales in which the payment of price is postponed, by mutual agreement of the parties, to a future date.[21] The attempt to confine the wider scope of the Qur'ānic verse to transactions in which only one but not both of the countervalues is deferred to a future date has probably originated in a report, attributed to Ibn ʿAbbās, to the effect that this verse was revealed concerning the contract of *salam* and that it did not apply to other varieties of deferred sales.[22] Fakhr al-Rāzī has commented that the text under consideration applies to normal sales (i.e., *bay^c al-^cayn bi'l-dayn*) in which the price of the object sold becomes, upon the conclusion of contract, a debt on the purchaser; it also applies to *salam*, which is the sale of what becomes a debt on the person of the vendor (i.e., *bay^c al-dayn*): the buyer in the *salam* sale pays in cash for what becomes a debt on the *dhimmah* of the vendor. As for barter sale (*al-muqāyadah*), this is the sale of one object for another, and although commonly practised at the time, it did not fall within the purview of the verse. This is because the barter sale requires immediate give and take (*taqābuḍ*), whereas the text under discussion is concerned with deferred transactions. This analysis is also extended to the sale of currencies, which consists of the sale of one object for another (*bay^c al-^cayn bi'l-^cayn*) and is therefore precluded from the scope of this *āyah*.[23]

Conventional *fiqh* has, however, taken this analysis to the extreme to the extent that the theory of deferment in contracts (*naẓariyyah al-ajal*) is held to virtually precludes from its scope all real and tangible objects (*al-a^cyān*). Thus it is invalid in an ordinary spot sale of, say, a house or a car, to defer their delivery to a future date. A sale of this kind, that is, when the subject-matter is a real object or *^cayn*, is said to effect an immediate transfer of ownership from the seller to the buyer as of the moment of contract, which means that the countervalues must change hands at that time, without any deferment on either side. The buyer in such a transaction may be allowed to pay the price at a later date and, if the seller agrees with that, the price becomes a deferred liability, or *dayn*, on the person (*dhimmah*) of the buyer. But the deferment facility in this case may not be extended to the *^cayn*, which must be transferred immediately to its new owner.[24] This legal position tends to incline towards rigidity and may call for a fresh review and *ijtihād*. The juristic conclusion here runs counter to the explicit authority of the *Sunnah* in which one of the Companions, Jābir, is reported to have sold his camel to the Prophet ﷺ and then asked if he could deliver it later in Medina, to which the Prophet ﷺ is said to have agreed. Having quoted this report, Ibn Qayyim adds that Imām Aḥmad ibn Ḥanbāl and his disciples have held that delivery may be delayed when the parties agree to it, or even by reference to the prevailing custom of the community.[25]

As for the sale of one debt for another (*bay^c al-dayn bi'l-dayn*), which is the basic model for futures trading, Fakhr al-Rāzī has commented that although it is in the nature of *mudāyanah*, that is, a deferred contract of exchange, it is not valid in *Sharī^cah*. For when the text states that *idhā tadāyantum bi-daynin* (when you deal with each other in transactions involving future obligations), it is implied that there is one *dayn*, not more, in which case debt clearance sale would be excluded. So the verse, according to this interpretation, applies to two types of sales, one being a deferred sale in which the price is paid at a later date, and the other being *salam*, each consisting of a debt on one side of the transaction only.[26]

Imām al-Shāfiʿī has, on the other hand, held the view that the Qur'ānic text under discussion is general, and can include all varieties of *dayn*. This would mean that the deferment of any debt is valid, just as it is valid in the case of *salam*. Ibn ʿAbbās has admittedly specified the meaning of *dayn* to *salam*, but by *salam* or *salaf*, he probably meant any period loan, or else we could, by analogy, extend the Qur'ānic ruling to all debts which fall within its purpose (*qulnā bihī fī kull dayn qiyāsan ʿalayh li-annahū fī maʿnah*).[27] Ibn Kathīr has basically upheld the same view and commented that the Qur'ānic text here permits the believers to enter into 'deferred transactions' (*muʿāmalāt mu'ajjalah*) with one another, and when they do so they should put them into writing.[28] It thus appears that the scholars have held different views on the interpretation of the word *dayn*. While some have confined *dayn* to certain types of debts, others have applied it generally to all deferred liability transactions that could fall within its broad meaning. The Qur'ān has evidently not specified the general meaning of '*dayn*' or '*mudayanah*' and there is no compelling evidence to warrant a departure from this position. Our analysis here also concurs with the conclusion that al-ʿAṭṭar has drawn in his book on the *Naẓariyyah al-Ajal* (Theory of Deferment) in *Sharīʿah*.[29] The preferred view would thus appear to be that the general language of the text should convey its general and unqualified meaning, and even if we admit Ibn ʿAbbās's interpretation, that interpretation, it may be said, was based on the occasion of revelation (*sha'n al-nuzūl*) of the verse of *mudāyanah*. According to the general rules of *uṣūl al-fiqh*, the *sha'n al-nuzūl* of a text may be specific, but this does not necessarily restrict the general purport and ruling of the text. It may thus be concluded that even if the text was revealed concerning *salam* alone, the language of the text is general and applies to all debts, which suggests the basic legality of deferred transactions in all of its varieties in *Sharīʿah*, provided, of course, that none of the principles of the Qur'ān and *Sunnah* on such other themes as usury, gambling and *gharar* are violated.

There is, on the other hand, clear evidence in the Qur'ān of the legality of sale and the prohibition on usury. The text simply proclaims that 'Allāh permitted sale and prohibited usury' (2:275). The proclamation here is general, and this is borne out by the fact that the word '*bayʿ*', being a singular noun, is prefixed by the article '*al*'. The general (*ʿāmm*) here must therefore apply to all varieties of sale, unless the general is specified in some way. When this is the case, the specified portion is seen as an exception of the general application of the *ᶜāmm*.[30] The general provision of the Qur'ān here includes all sales, be it the sale of one object for another, such as in barter (*al-muqāyadah*), or of one currency for another (*al-ṣarf*), a spot sale which involves the exchange of goods for their monetary value, or the forward sale of *salam*. It also includes other types of sale, such as sale at cost price (*al-tawliyah*), sale at cost plus profit (*al-murābaḥah*) and sale at lower than cost price (*al-waḍīᶜah*), absolute sale in which no reference is made to the cost price (*al-musāwamah*) and sale by auction (*al-muzāyadah*) and so forth.[31] All of these are lawful, as indeed is any sale, including a future sale, which is clear of *ribā'* and *gharar*, and sales which have not been specifically forbidden in the *Sunnah* are permissible by virtue of this general proclamation. The rule concerning prohibitions is that there must be a clear injunction on them; a *ḥarām*, in other words, cannot be established by anything less than an explicit injunction. In the absence of a prohibition or an obligatory command, the normal state of permissibility (*ibāḥah*) should therefore prevail.[32] The Prophet ﷺ, has specified the general provisions of the Qur'ān in respect of the certain types of sale which he has declared forbidden. But he has done so within the general understanding of the Qur'ān. The Prophet ﷺ has only forbidden questionable sales which were in vogue among pre-Islamic Arabs, but has not explained the lawful varieties of sale, which were presumed to be lawful, and there was no need for these to be declared such.[33] Since the Qur'ān validates sale and commerce generally, as well as deferred liability transactions, and there is no specific prohibition in the Qur'ān or *Sunnah* on future sales, then these may be said to be lawful provided, as already noted, that they are clear of *gharar*, usury and gambling. We have already discussed the issue of *gharar* in conjunction with futures and drawn the conclusion that futures trading is generally clear of *gharar* in almost all of its varieties, including, that is, *gharar* over the knowledge of material details that would prevent uncertainty and unwarranted risk and *gharar* which involve the parties ability to obtain and deliver the subject matter of their agreement.

Broadly speaking, futures trading in commodities is also clear of *ribā'*. This is because futures do not operate on the basis of a fixed and predetermined profit without the possibility of incurring a loss. All futures trading involves the possibility of both making a profit or incurring a loss. The sums of money that are deposited, such as the margin money, do not earn interest as they are a good faith money deposited with one's own broker and agent, and are returnable to the depositor should the transaction conclude without a loss that might exhaust the margin money. There is also no unwarranted gain involved in futures, for either of the parties, that might partake of usury. This is because in a futures sale, nothing changes hand at the time of contract: the buyer does not pay the price nor does the seller deliver the goods at the time of the bargain. Hence no interest is earned by either party between the moment of contract and the final conclusion of the round turn transaction.

There now remain the questions of speculation and gambling and it is to these issues that we turn next.

NOTES

1. Madkūr, *al-Fiqh*, p. 517; al-Baʿlī, *Ḍawābiṭ*, p. 151.
2. Al-Kāsānī, *Badā'iʿ*, V, 133; al-ʿAṭṭār, *Naẓariyyah*, p. 172; Muḥammad Yūnus al-Ghiyātī, *Bayʿ Milk al-Ghayr fī'l-Qānūn al-Madani wa'l-Fiqh al-Islāmī*, Tanta, Maktabah Jāmiʿah Tanta, 1986, pp. 6-7.
3. Ibn ʿĀbidīn, *Hāshiyah*, IV, 531.
4. Ibn Rushd al-Qurṭubī, *Bidāyah*, II, 130; al-Jundī, *Muʿāmalāt*, p. 136; al-Qaradāwī, *Bayʿ al-Murābaḥah* pp. 40-41.
5. Al-Shāfiʿī, *al-ʿUmm*, II, 201.
6. See for details Abur Rahim P*rinciples of Muhammadan Jurisprudence*, Lahore, All Pakistan Legal Decisions, 1977, p. 292; Anwar Ahamd Qadri, *Islamic Jurisprudence in the Modern World*, 2nd edn, Lahore, Shah Muhammad Ashraf, 1981, p. 325; Nabil A. Saleh, 'Definition and Formation of Contract under Islamic and Arab Law', *Arab Law Quarterly* 5 (1990), p. 101.
7. Abdur Rahim, *Jurisprudence*, p. 293.
8. Al-Qaradāwī, *Bayʿ al-Murābaḥah*, pp. 80-81; Niazi, *Islamic Law of Contract*, p. 218; Qadri, *Islamic Jurisprudence*, p. 326; Saleh, 'Definition and Formation of Contract', p. 102.
9. Cf. al-ʿAṭṭār, *Naẓariyyah*, pp. 112ff; Ḥusayn, *al-Milkiyyah*, pp. 283-4.
10. Ibn ʿĀbidīn, *Hāshiyah*, IV, 531; al-ʿAttar, *Naẓariyyah* p. 133; Muḥammad Aḥmad Sirāj, *Niẓām al-Maṣrafī al-Islāmī*, Cairo, Dār al-Trhaqāfah li'l-Nashr wa'l-Tawziʿ, 1410/1989, p. 315.
11. Ibn Rushd al-Qurṭubī, *Bidāyah*, II, 108.
12. Al-Sarakhsī, *al-Mabsūṭ*, XIII, 24; see also Ibn ʿĀbidīn, *Hāshiyah*, IV, 62.
13. Cf. Madkūr, *al-Fiqh*, p. 517.
14. Ibid., p. 521; al-Baʿlī, *Ḍawābiṭ*, p. 152; Ḥusayn, *al-Milkiyyah*, p. 284.
15. Madkūr, *al-Fiqh*, p. 525; Mahmassānī, *al-Mawjibāt*, p. 475; *Mejelle* (art. 440).
16. Ḥusayn, *al-Milkiyyah*, p. 290, see also al-ʿAṭṭār, *Naẓariyyah*, p. 112.
17. Madkūr, *al-Fiqh*, p. 436.
18. For details see Abdul Halim Ismail, 'The Deferred Contracts of Exchange in al-Qur'an', in Ghazali *et al.*, *Islamic Finance*, Kuala Lumpur, Quill Publishers, 1992, pp. 288ff.
19. Bukhārī, *Ṣaḥīḥ*, III, 243-44, *ḥadīth* nos. 441 and 443.
20. Abū'l-Fidā'ī Ismāʿīl ibn Kathīr, *Tafsīr al-Qur'ān al-ʿAẓīm*, Cairo, Dār al-Kitāb al-Miṣrī, 1408/1988, I, 316.
21. Sirāj, *al-Niẓām al-Maṣrafī*, p. 313.
22. Cf. al-ʿAṭṭār, *Naẓariyyah*, p. 129.
23. Fakhr al-Dīn Muḥammad b. ʿUmar al-Rāzī, *Tafsīr al-Kabīr*, Beirut, Dār al-Fikr, 1398/1978, II, 364; al-ʿAṭṭār, *Naẓariyyah*, p. 126.

24. Al-ᶜAṭṭār, *Naẓariyyah*, p. 130.
25. Ibn Qayyim, *I*ᶜ*lam*, I, 359.
26. Al-Rāzī, *Tafsīr*, II, 364.
27. Al-Shāfiᶜī, *al-*ᶜ*Umm*, III, 81.
28. Ibn Kathīr, *Tafsīr*, I, 316.
29. Al-ᶜAṭṭār, *Naẓariyyah*, p. 127.
30. Ibn Rushd, *al-Muqaddimāt*, p. 539.
31. Cf. al-Qaradāwī, *Bay*ᶜ *al-Murābaḥah*, p. 15.
32. Ibid., p. 16.
33. Cf. al-Shāfiᶜī, *al-*ᶜ*Umm*, III, 2.

CHAPTER FOURTEEN

Speculation or Gambling

Risk-taking is an inalienable aspect of human life, so much so that even the most mundane of human activities in day-to-day life involve a measure of uncertainty and risk. This is partly because the future prospects of human activity and conduct cannot be meaningfully separated from what is being done in the present. Although all human activity takes place in the present, a great deal of it bears fruit only in the future, and the manner in which the present is related to the future is influenced by the surrounding reality, past experience and custom. Indeed our activities are often motivated by the desire to realise some future interest, or to safeguard against something perceived to be harmful. Our knowledge of the past and understanding of the present enable us to calculate the expected results of our conduct with a certain degree of confidence. The future course and consequences of a certain activity may often become predictable with greater certainty in the light of scientific advances and experimental techniques in various fields. A medieval farmer of foodgrains naturally experienced greater anxiety about the prospects of a good harvest than his twentieth-century counterpart. This is due not only to advances in irrigation techniques and safeguards against plant disease, but also to the availability of superior storage facilities and insurance. Even so, it would be less than true to say that we now live in an era of risk-free agriculture. Far from it. There are no water-tight formulas against risk, either in farming or in the fast-developing field of contemporary commerce. New modes and techniques of trading often bring new problems and hazards that are known and discovered only through experiment. Certain risks cannot even be anticipated, but are discovered as a result of subsequent development and interaction with other market conditions over a period of time. Since the resources of human inventiveness are virtually endless and largely unpredictable, it follows that the risks that are generated by them are also a part of the continuous human quest for self-development and growth. Indeed, a risk-free existence, however comforting an idea, has hardly held a great appeal for the imaginative side of the human intellect, nor has it ever been realistically attainable. It is only natural, therefore, that any law that seeks to regulate commercial transactions should not only be amenable to the idea of development and change, but that it should function as a vehicle for the accommodation of changing commercial realities and custom.

I. A Market Analysis of Speculation

Many observers have regarded 'speculation' and 'gambling' as synonymous terms. One hears of 'investing in securities' and 'gambling in futures'. Others regard speculation and gambling as wholly distinct activities. The main difference between them relates to the issue of risk versus potential contribution to the social good. Gambling involves the creation of a risk for the sake of risk. Horse racing and poker games, for example, create risks that would not be present without them. The gambler wilfully seeks out, through betting and wagering, a risk that was not there before, and even if it was, it would not personally concern him. The risk of financial loss could have been avoided if the gambler had chosen to do so. The avoidance of gambling is also required because no social good is accomplished by it.

Investing, on the other hand, consists of the commitment of capital to an enterprise in the hope of earning a profit. The difference between investment and speculation is largely semantic, but most would agree that commitments with time-horizons that are longer than several months qualify as investment, regardless of whether the commitment is in securities, real estate or commodities.[1]

Defining speculation or identifying the speculator is always difficult and many have stated that no clear definition can be arrived at. Speculation has, nevertheless, been defined as 'the purchase and sale of an asset in the expectation of a gain from changes in the price of that asset'.[2] The difficulty of providing a comprehensive definition is partly due to the fact that the distinguishing lines between investment, speculation and gambling are not always clear and the grey areas between them tend to persist regardless of particular definitions. Consider the following examples:

1. If A buys a corn futures contract from a farmer and B sells a corn futures contract to a flour mill, then A and B are both speculating in corn futures. However, if the farmer sells a futures contract directly to the

miller and A and B make a bet with one another on the direction of the corn prices, then they are gambling. They have not invested any capital labour or skill, but engage in a bet rather than a commercially beneficial endeavour or enterprise.

2. A is a football enthusiast. He meets a young player and decides that with some expert training, he could become a champion. He offers to contribute $50,000 toward one year's training and promotional expenses in return for thirty per cent of the player's earnings, which he believes could be $1 million. Is A a gambler, a speculator or an investor? What if instead he gave the player $50,000 per year job as a part-time chauffeur and bet on each of his prize-winning games? What if the player became an incorporated company and A bought thirty per cent of the stock for $50,000?

Examples like these can make it tempting to conclude that the distinctions between gambling, speculation and investment are wholly artificial. But this does not alter the fact that there are profound economic differences between betting on a football match and financing a promising new technology, or between playing roulette and trading palm oil futures. The fact that precise distinctions are difficult to make does not mean that they do not exist, or do not matter. When it comes to futures trading it is important to distinguish between motives and economic effects because economic effects are what really matter.[3]

Speculation deals in risks that are necessarily present in the process of marketing goods and services in a free market economy. As a wheat crop grows and is harvested, concentrated and dispersed, the obvious risk of price change must be taken by those who own the wheat or have made a commitment to buy it. These risks would be present whether futures markets existed or not. If the speculators were unwilling to take them on, someone else would have to do so. The issue that arises is whether the winners and the losers are going to be the producers and consumers of wheat, or whether the price risks can be shifted to the speculators, to the government, or diffused and absorbed through market mechanisms and modes of trading.

The motivation of many individual speculators could well be identical with that of gamblers, that is, they are willing to take relatively large risks in return for the chance to gain large profits. The main difference is that futures speculation really does reallocate risk from those who do not want it to those who do. Futures speculation, in other words, directs the appetite for risk-taking into an economically productive channel. Futures markets are basically risk transfer mechanisms that redistribute price risk, and speculators are the ones who assume it—without them there would be no one to whom hedgers could shift their risks. Speculation in the positive sense is intelligent and rational forecasting of the future trend of prices on the basis of evidence and knowledge of the past and present conditions.[4] The speculator is an observer and theorist who is willing to support the accuracy of his observations and theories with risk capital. Speculators in commodities are not simply gamblers. In commodities, the risks are real commercial risks, and therefore quite a different matter from the activity of a gambler, who does not assume any risk other than what is created by the rules of the game.[5]

A common criticism of futures speculation is that it causes violent price moves that bring considerable hardship to those engaged in more productive pursuits. Wide publicity is given to the relatively rare but highly dramatic manipulations that cause many to conclude that speculation is just another word for gambling. Speculators can point to equally scandalous events in all types of business at all times and in all countries. Some early instances of manipulation in America by men such as Hutchinson, Leiter and Patten in the years just before the turn of the century, and more recently by Bunker Hunt in 1980, resulted in damaging price distortions. Since then, however, balance has returned to the market and this, aided by the introduction of regulatory and punitive legislation, has diminished the threat of such manipulation.[6] Furthermore, the evidence does not confirm the suspicion that futures trading is dominated by large speculators. Data may vary from market to market but for all markets, the holdings of the large speculators' total long and short positions are less than twenty per cent of the total holdings of the small traders. The large speculators probably constitute less than two per cent of the total futures trading population.[7] Major price movements are usually caused by basic changes in supply or demand, or both, for a given product and only rarely by a group of speculators successfully creating self-fulfilling prophecies. The weight of the evidence obtained from the considerable research carried out in this area suggests that 'speculation probably does more to smooth price fluctuation than to increase it'.[8] However high the speculative activity may be, speculators are generally not in a position to 'dictate prices or set artificial trading levels'.[9] It is further suggested that commodity prices are less volatile than stock market prices, which may be due to the fact that there are two limitations in place, namely the 'daily limit' and the 'daily range', which effectively confine the scope of fluctuation in futures.[10] Empirical evidence is inconclusive on the question of whether or not futures trading encourages excessive speculation and thereby destabilises commodity prices in the cash market. This is because the behaviour of spot prices is influenced by many other factors. Research work carried into the pattern of behaviour of certain commodities such as onion and live beef cattle, before and after the institution of futures markets have on the whole supported the conclusion that futures trading has not increased fluctuation in cash market prices.[11] Statistical analysis shows that the volatility of futures prices is approximately the same as that of equity prices.[12] What makes futures trading more prone to speculative risk-taking is the high degree of leverage that comes from the low margin requirements. This low margin facility is not available in the stock market and this is the main factor that accounts for the high volume of speculative trading in futures.

Certain areas of speculation, aside from futures trading, have been popular for many decades. Speculative trade in land, precious stones and metals, oils, stocks and bonds, and rare items such as stamps and paintings have required different trading skills because they have special characteristics. But the common attraction in all of these is the potential for profit. Futures speculators who prefer to make their own decisions may be attracted to the market by the relative ease of securing information on the price trends of commodities. Important political and economic information is readily available in the mass media and commercial newspapers. Vital supply and demand information concerning specific futures in the United States are published by various government departments, and are available at frequent intervals. The various futures exchanges also provide publications on specific futures markets which are available on request, most of them at no charge. The Chicago Board of Trade, for example, has published an annual bibliography of publications on the futures markets since 1977 and a cumulative bibliography through 1976. Other exchanges also provide valuable sources of information. An adequate amount of accurate information about the handful of futures that are actively traded is considerably easier to obtain than information about the tens of thousands of stocks, bonds and mutual funds that are available. The futures speculator must in the long run be primarily concerned with the real forces of supply and demand, whereas speculators in stocks must know about both the markets of the companies in whose stocks they are speculating and the market for the stocks themselves. Notwithstanding these differences between stocks and futures, no model clearly superior to a random walk has been developed to describe the behaviour of either stocks or futures prices. Access to information is one factor, but the principal feature that attracts speculators to futures trading is still the low margin requirements that enable them to trade futures without a large capital outlay. High market liquidity and the assurance that positions can be liquidated almost instantaneously, especially through offsetting, adds stimulus to speculation in futures.[13]

II. *Qimār* and *Maysir*

Gambling and games of chance are as old and as widespread as humanity itself. The human desires for gain and excitement, and the instinct for combativeness, are among the three main causes of gambling. The first two are self-evident; the element of combativeness is also evident in all games of pure chance. Gambling or *qimār* is defined as 'a combative relationship between two contracting parties, each of whom undertakes the risk of loss and the loss of one means gain for the other'.[14] It is a violation of the law of equivalence, a kind of robbery by mutual agreement, like duelling, which is murder by mutual agreement. Gambling also consists of an appeal to chance, and making chance the arbiter of one's conduct is to subvert the moral order and stability of life. It focuses attention on material gain and unwarranted reward in a way that is usually impulsive and can be so overwhelming as to divert attention from the pursuit of worthier activities in life.[15] Gambling is neither useful to civilisation nor could it be made the basis of co-operation in business activities and commerce. In an already-existent atmosphere of co-operation and brotherhood, gambling has no place. On the contrary, gambling destroys co-operation and fraternity in favour of combativeness and the desire to win, and it has no harmony with the normal processes that are important to civilisation.[16]

The Qur'ān is explicit on the prohibition of *maysir* (the game of chance) which is described, along with other activities like wine-drinking, sacrificing to stones (*al-ansab*) and divination by arrows (*al-azlām*), as the devil's work. It is characterised as a morally unclean activity which sows the seeds of enmity and hatred among fellow human beings, as well as creating a barrier to piety, spiritual awareness and the remembrance of God (5:90-91). To Ibn Taymiyyah the evil of gambling is greater than *ribā'*, for gambling combines two evils: the unlawful acquisition of property and the playing of an unlawful game, both of which are *ḥarām*.[17] The word *maysir*, being a derivative of *yasira*, to be easy, and *yassara*, to succeed, means lucky chance or easy success at getting something of value without earning it. The law recognises only three ways in which property can be legitimately acquired—by gift, inheritance, and an exchange of values. Gambling stands outside all of these, and does not aim for the legitimate objective of the fair distribution of wealth that is pursued by these methods. Ibn Qayyim al-Jawziyyah has stated in unequivocal terms that the *maysir* which the Qur'ān has forbidden is identical with gambling as it is commonly understood, and it consists of two players who engage in a combative game that involves loss and gain where the gain of one is equivalent to the loss of the other. They are two competing parties, somewhat resembling two horse riders who race one another with the agreement that the winner will be paid by the loser if he wins, or pay his opponent if he loses.[18] Gambling is called *maysir* because the gambler seeks to amass wealth without effort. It is synonymous with *qimār* and defined by Abū Ḥabīb as 'every game over property which the winner then takes from the loser'.[19] This is almost identical to al-Jurjānī's definition of *qimār,* which is 'taking one thing after another from one's partner in a game', or 'a game with the condition that the winner (*ghālib*) of two contestants gets something from the loser (*maghlūb*)'.[20] More accurate is perhaps Ibn al-ʿArabī's definition: 'Each one of two contestants seeks to defeat his partner in an action or statement in order to take over property that is set aside for the winner.'[21] The common elements among these definitions thus include playing a game which is created by the contesting parties, each aiming at winning the game and defeating the opponent in order to take over his property. To Rosenthal *qimār* is 'a contract among two or more persons involving the exchange of money or other valuables depending upon the uncertain outcome of a staged event'.[22] The Qur'ānic prohibition of *maysir* is based on the premise that an apparent agreement between the two parties is in actuality the result of unclean and immoral inducement which is driven by the hope of making a profit at the expense of the other party to the agreement. In his discussion of insurance in juxtaposition with *maysir,* Siddiqi has concluded that our definition of gambling completely fits the description of *maysir* in pre-Islamic Arabia. The gambling parties thus court a risk which is of their own creation and which involves both the hope of gain as well as the fear of loss in a way that is not a necessary part of any of the normal activities of life. The main distinction between risk-taking in insurance and gambling is that the risk involved in the former is associated with the normal activities of life, and that insurance serves a useful purpose in that context.[23]

There is a difference of opinion about whether *maysir* in the Qur'ān is a designation for a particular kind of gambling, or whether it is used in reference to all kinds of gambling. It seems that *maysir* has been used in the *ḥadīth* to refer to any gambling activity depending on the throw of arrows or other gambling devices. Casting lots by arrows was the custom of the Arabs before Islam. It was a method by which a head of cattle was divided. A group of ten Arabs would buy a young camel, which was cut into ten portions, and the *yāsir* who presided distributed the portions among his companions by means of arrows on which he had written their names and which he drew at random out of a bag. The game was considered a pagan practice and the Qur'ān forbade it along with wine and idols as a major sin. Throwing dice was another gambling device which was commonly known to the Persians and then also to the Arabs. According to a *ḥadīth* of the Prophet ﷺ, *maysir* is applied also to dice: 'These accursed dice are the *maysir* of Persia (*maysir al-ʿajam*).'[24] Rosenthal has commented that all through Islamic times, the dice (*faṣṣ*, *kaʿb*, *kaʿbah*) used in games were usually two in number and that the word *qimār* is specifically applied to their case.[25]

Horse racing was a favourite pastime in pre-Islamic Arabia and the Prophet ﷺ himself and early Muslims encouraged it for military reasons. The Prophet ﷺ is reported to have given prizes to the winners of horse races. It was a highly organised activity and in certain places horse races were held on regular schedules. The evidence further suggests that in later times, during the rule of Abbasids and Buyids, non-participatory betting on horse races was also practised.[26]

Rihān (betting) is a term related to that of *maysir* and it occurs in the Qur'ān (2:283) in a different sense, namely, that of security, or safety deposit. However, it is used in the *ḥadīth* and also in the sayings of the Companions in the sense of betting. *Rihān* is co-extensive with *qimār* and *maysir* and all are forbidden; yet they differ technically in that the betting parties are usually not direct participants but bet as outsiders on the outcome of a certain activity or game. The activity may be a sporting activity such as running, wrestling, or a horse race, or it may be an anticipated event, such as the bet that is recorded by the Qur'ān commentators between Abū Bakr and the pagans of Mecca on the eventual victory of the Romans over the Persians (the subject of the Qur'ānic chapter 22). Betting thus involves two parties, the actual players and the betters and, unlike the typical form of gambling, betting need not be a zero sum game, in the sense that the gain of one party in betting may or may not be the same as the loss of the other party. Another technical difference here is that unlike *qimār*, betting is usually not a staged event in that the betters may not have a hand in creating the game or activity on which they bet. Thus a person who buys a lottery ticket, or the one who speculates on the price movement of goods, does not have any control over the activity that is the subject of the betting. Having said this, however, *rihān* partakes in the essence of *qimār* since it is a game played between two parties in which the winner takes the property of the loser, and there is, from the juristic point of view, no difference between them.[27] Certain incidents of both *qimār* and *rihān* are clearly tolerated in Islam and these are mainly related to military purposes, as is the throwing of lots (*al-qurʿah*) in certain legal situations where no better alternative can be found to determine the position. To these instances modern law in many Muslim countries has added a lottery for national charitable purposes.[28]

In an attempt to ascertain the relationship between gambling and *gharar* and their bearing on the contract of sale, Ibn Taymiyyah points out that if a sale which partakes in *gharar* also involves 'devouring the property of others—*akl al-māl bi'l-bāṭil*', then it becomes indistinguishable from *qimār* and *maysir*, which are clearly forbidden. If in a contract of sale one party receives what was due to him but the other does not and the latter's side of the bargain is open to risk-taking (*mukhāṭarah*) of a kind that frustrates and nullifies his right, then the sale partakes both in *gharar* and gambling at the same time.[29] Ibn Taymiyyah then adds: 'The *gharar* sale which the Prophet ﷺ has forbidden is one which participates in the meaning of gambling. God Most High has forbidden the unlawful devouring of the property of others, and it occurs in two ways, namely, usury and gambling (*ribā'* and *maysir*), and the Book of God is explicit in respect of both. The *Sunnah* of the Prophet ﷺ on these subjects has only explained and elaborated on the Qur'ān.'[30] Ibn Taymiyyah has thus attempted to establish a common denominator between *gharar* and gambling, and that is the misappropriation of the property of others. This being the hallmark of both, it is clear that gambling in a commercial transaction does not arise unless the appropriation of the property of another person is involved.

Ibn Taymiyyah relates his analysis to a Qur'ānic passage where an address to the believers states: 'Devour not each others' properties unlawfully unless it be through trading by your mutual consent' (al-Nisa, 4:29). 'Unlawful devouring' is a broad Qur'ānic concept, which includes gambling, fraud, usurpation, bribery and profit gained from unlawful transactions. The Qur'ānic text here was revealed in reference to some varieties of sale that were in vogue among pre-Islamic Arabs, namely *bay*ᶜ *al-mulāmasah wa'l-munābadhah*, the sales, typically of cloth, in which the deal was completed when the buyer touched the material, or when it was thrown in his direction, and sale of an unborn animal (*ḥabal al-ḥabālah*). Ibn Taymiyyah then comments that if the sale in these cases is finalised prior to the buyer's viewing the object, then it participates in risk-taking and gambling (*mukhāṭarah wa qimār*) because the object may be good and to the buyer's liking or it may not be so. If the buyer is bound by the sale without actually knowing about the object, this is gambling and none of the leading scholars have permitted it. But if the parties have seen the cloth and one tells the other that the deal is done 'if I throw it to you' or 'when you take it' or the like, then this is a conditional sale which is in the nature of *bay*ᶜ *al-mu*ᶜ*atat* (give and take sale) and there is no gambling involved. Ibn Taymiyyah then extends the same analysis to the sale of the unseen, that of the unknown (*bay*ᶜ *al-ma*ᶜ*dum wa'l-majhūl*) and the sale in which delivery is not possible. The question to be asked in all of these is whether they involve unlawful appropriation (*akl al-māl bi'l-bāṭil*) and, if so, the sale is invalid and partakes of gambling. If one of the parties takes what is due to him or her and the other is liable to risk whereby he or she may or may not get what is due to him or her, then this is gambling.[31]

It thus appears that risk-taking which involves *akl al-māl bi'l-bāṭil* and the unlawful gain of one party at the expense of another is central to Ibn Taymiyyah's understanding of the Qur'ānic concept of *maysir*. When this is applied to futures trading, the question that needs to be addressed is whether the risk-taking element and speculation in futures sales are such that leave the other party to the sale exposed to risk, and if so whether there is unlawful gain and misappropriation involved. There is evidently no dishonest appropriation of the property of others in futures trading in the sense that the buyer in a futures contract is engaged in a transaction which is aimed at making profit through trading but not at any dishonest devouring of the property of others. We can safely say that the only forbidden variety of risk-taking (*al-mukhāṭarah*) in trade is that which partakes of *qimār* and *maysir*. For even the beneficial varieties of commercial activity are not devoid of commercial risk-taking. The participant in such activities basically speculates over an uncertain prospect, whether of profit or loss, which is not known in advance. Speculative risk-taking in commerce that involves the investment of assets, labour and expertise is not forbidden; what is forbidden is excessive *gharar* and *qimār*. Risk-taking is likely to involve gambling if it is done, staged or created for its own sake, but not if it is incidental to a beneficial economic activity or trade.[32] Speculation is a mental activity in which a person formulates his judgement about the future course of the market. Speculation in this sense is not objectionable and there is nothing against it in the *Sharīʿah*. As to the question of whether speculation can be effectively controlled by legislation, it is suggested that no law can be enforced against speculators who might be involved in the lawful activities of buying and selling. It is only the intent of the speculator, which becomes manifest later, that may distinguish dubious speculation from genuine investment. The holding of an investment for a certain length of time is yet another factor that differentiates speculation from investment.[33]

The hallmark of both *maysir* and *qimār* thus appears to be involvement of two or more opponents in a combative game which each plays with the sole purpose of winning at the expense of the other. The gain of one party is equivalent to the loss of the other. The gain accruing from this game is unlawful, as is the act of playing a game which diverts the player's attention from productive occupation and virtuous conduct. If we apply this description to speculation in commercial activity, such as trading in stocks or in futures, we might be able to identify some common ground between commercial speculation and gambling, but only in the broadest of terms. Speculation in futures does not necessarily involve a combative game played for the sole purpose of beating the opponent and acquiring his property. The speculative risk that is undertaken in futures would seem to have greater affinity with commercial risk-taking than with *maysir* and *qimār*.

A trader who buys or sells a futures contract may make a profit or a loss and in the normal course of events does not even know his counterpart on the other side of the transaction. Nor is there any question of defeating another person in a combative game. The gain or loss in the transaction is not realised at the time of contract but at offset or maturity, which may be several months later. Then again, the loss and gain here are a function not of gambling as a staged event, but of fluctuations in the market price of the underlying commodity. If I buy a commodity contract with a view either to hedge against a possible loss or to make a profit in the months ahead, I take a certain risk, which is different from gambling in the sense that I do not create the risk; it is already there. It is a commercial risk and although it is possible that my gain, if I make one, might mean someone else's loss, making a profit through trading by mutual consent is lawful. My transaction is more likely to fit this description of trade than that of gambling, which involves the devouring of the property of others.

No business activity can be said to be devoid of speculation. This is simply because people do business in order to make a profit and profit-making necessitates speculation. However prudent or conservative one may wish to be, speculation and risk-taking are facts of modern commerce. When we compare the Islamic *muʿāmalah* to the interest-bearing transaction, the former is more inclined towards speculation than the latter, a point that I have further elaborated in my concluding chapter. Some trading activities are admittedly less speculative than others, but speculation is lawful in principle if only because without it, profitable commerce and risk-involving entrepreneurship cannot be expected to develop. It is equally true that speculation is susceptible to abuse, and that the dividing line between commercial speculation and gambling can easily fade into insignificance. There needs, of course, to be vigilance at all times that commercial speculation does not turn into gambling, and it is the proper role and function of government and the exchange authorities to ensure that commercial speculation is genuinely reflective of the natural flow of market forces. Imposing quantitative restrictions on daily trading volume and position limits is one way of containing speculation within acceptable boundaries. But speculation is a matter that can best be regulated through policy measures and operative floor procedures by the exchange authorities, so that they can easily be adjusted when the situation so requires. Legislative guidelines should, on the other hand, aim at regulating contractual relations between the parties, brokerage activities, and disciplinary procedures for serious violations.

Developing adequate safeguards is also a question, to some extent, of experimentation and gradual refinement, especially when one bears in mind the fact that new modes of commerce are being invented all the time. One can therefore only expect to know some of the undesirable, and excessively speculative, features of a new product after some experimentation and assessment. We know, of course, that many of these involve speculation, yet we allow them in the hope that their potential benefits will be greater than the harmful speculation they might stimulate. The containment of speculation in futures is, therefore, an evolving process that is always likely to be affected by the effort to balance the potential benefits and harms of every mode of transaction, and the formulation of policies in the light of their relative merits.

NOTES

1. Teweles, *Commodity Futures*, pp. 4-6; Fink, *Futures Trading*, p. 320; Muhammad Nejatullah Siddiqi, *Insurance in an Islamic Ecomomy*, Leicester, The Islamic Foundation, 1985, p. 27.
2. Cootner, 'Speculation, hedging and arbitrage', *Modern Encyclopedia of Social Sciences*, 1968.
3. Fink, *Futures Trading*, p. 321.
4. Ibid., p. 74; Abdul Jabbar Shahabudin, *Malaysian Business*, September 5, 1985, p. 13.
5. Courtney, *Investor's Guide*, p. 53.
6. Teweles, *Commodity Futures*, p. 43.
7. Ibid., p. 31; Courtney, *Investor's Guide*, p. 53.
8. Teweles, *Commodity Futures*, p. 13; Courtney, *Investor's Guide*, p. 52.
9. Courtney, *Investor's Guide*, p. 51.
10. Gup, *The Basics*, p. 490.
11. For details of these studies see Relly, *Investment Analysis*, pp. 792-3.
12. NYIF, *Futures*, p. 19; Gup, *The Basics*, p. 490.
13. Teweles, *Commodity Futures*, pp. 15-16 and 366.
14. Rafiq Yūnus al-Miṣrī, *al-Maysir wa'l-Qimār al-Musabaqat wa'l-Jawa'iz*, Damascus, Dār al-Qalam, 1413/1993, p. 31.
15. 'Gambling', *The Encyclopedia of Religion and Ethics*, VI, 166.
16. Shāh Waliyyullāh Dihlawī, *Hujjat Allāh al-Bālighah*, Cairo, Dār al-Turath, II, 106;
17. Ibn Taymiyyah, *Majmūʿah Fatāwa*, XXXII, 237.
18. Ibn Qayyim al-Jawziyyah, *al-Furusiyyah*, ed. Muḥammad Niẓām al-Fatih, Madīnah Munawarah, Maktabah Dār al-Turath, 1410/1990, p. 123.
19. Saʿdī Abū Ḥabīb, *al-Qāmūs al-Fiqhī Lughatan wa Istilahan*, Damascus, Dār al-Fikr, 1402/1982, p. 309.
20. Sayyid Sharīf al-Jurjānī, *Taʿrifāt*, Istanbul, al-Astanah, 1327 AH, p. 187.
21. Ibn al-ʿArabi, *ʿAradat al-Ahwadhi*, VII, 18; also quoted by Franz Rosenthal, *Gambling in Islam*, Leiden, E.J. Brill, 1975, p. 3.
22. Rosenthal, *Gambling in Islam*, p. 2.
23. Siddiqi, *Insurance in an Islamic Economy*, Leicester, p. 34 and *passim*; see also S. E. Reyner, *The Theory of Contracts in Islamic Law*, London, Graham & Trotman, 1991, p. 291; Niazi, *Islamic Law of Contract*, p. 117.

24. *The Encyclopedia of Islam*, 2nd edn, Leiden, E.J. Brill, 1965, III, 156.
25. Rosenthal, *Gambling in Islam*, p. 35.
26. Al-Miṣrī, *al-Maysir*, p. 71; Rosenthal, *Gambling in Islam*, pp. 48-50.
27. Ibid, pp. 32, 71.
28. Ibid, pp. 62-3.
29. Ibn Taymiyyah, *Naẓariyyah al-ʿAqd*, p. 228.
30. Ibid, p. 229.
31. Ibid, pp. 228-9.
32. Cf. al-Miṣrī, *al-Maysir*, p. 35.
33. Cf. Khan, 'Commodity Exchange', p. 101.

CHAPTER FIFTEEN

A Summary of Modern Opinion

Speculation and short selling are the two inter-related aspects of futures trading that have come under criticism in the recent writings of Muslim commentators. Although there is general agreement that speculation is essential to all trading, especially to stocks and futures, and that the futures market simply cannot function without it, commentators have expressed fears that the extent of speculative risk-taking that is involved in futures might bring them closer to gambling, and in this case the legal verdict on their permissibility or otherwise must reflect that assessment. From the discussion that follows, it becomes clear that speculation in futures is not a clear case of gambling; and inevitably, therefore, the analysis contains at least some element of value judgement.

Yūsuf Sulāyman has described speculation (*al-muḍārabah*) in futures as sheer risk-taking (*al-mukhāṭarah*) on the movement of prices that may anticipate either an upward movement in the prices or a downtrend. The speculators go long when they expect the prices to move upwards, and they short-sell when they expect the opposite, both of course in the expectation of making a profit. The transaction in either case occurs over goods that the seller neither owns nor possesses, nor is the buyer expected (or even able) to pay the price of what he buys at the time of contracting. Delivery is not expected to take place unless the buyer wishes to take delivery, in which case it will take place at maturity, and this is in practice only true of about one in ten cases—predominantly in the Egyptian markets and cotton futures of Alexandria—all the rest being paper transactions aimed at making a profit from the price differentials. Sulaymān then observes that 'this manner of speculation is unlawful (*ḥarām*) since it consists of the sale of what is not owned by the seller and then the buyer sells again prior to taking possession, both of which are impermissible from the viewpoint of *Sharīʿah*'.[1] In support of his view, the author refers to the *ḥadīth* of Ḥākim ibn Ḥizām which simply proclaims 'sell not what is not with you', the effective cause (*ʿillah*) of the prohibition here being the prevention of *gharar*. The author goes on to quote another *ḥadīth* in which sale prior to taking possession of its subject-matter is forbidden.[2] Having stated the grounds of his prohibitive verdict, Sulaymān then adds: 'The *Sharīʿah* of Islam does not proscribe the sale of what is not owned or possessed, unless this serves the valid purpose of realising a benefit for the people, and this is why *salam* (forward sale) has been explicitly validated.'[3] Sulaymān has thus merely touched on the subject of *gharar* and quoted the two *ḥadīth* directly but, like many others who have passed similar prohibitive judgements, he fails to explore the meaning of the evidence he has relied on and its relevance to the operating procedures of the futures market. If the avoidance of *gharar* is the basic rationale behind the prohibition in question, then surely one would need to ascertain whether this is still the issue in futures transactions. In a similar vein, there is a certain logic in the *ḥadīth* that Sulaymān has quoted that needs to be explained, but this has not been done. In my own discussion of these *ḥadīth* in a separate section above, I have developed a perspective over their basic rationale, and their application to futures trading.

In a follow-up to Yūsuf Sulaymān's article, Professor (al-Ustādh al-Kabīr) ʿAlī ʿAbd al-Qādir has published a commentary, which appeared in the same volume as that of Sulaymān's article, where the author has criticised Sulaymān's prohibitive judgement on futures trading. ʿAbd al-Qādir begins his critique by stating that Yūsuf Sulaymān has 'evaluated the conformity or otherwise of futures trading to *Sharīʿah* on the basis of what the jurists of the various schools have recorded in the well-known works of *fiqh*.'[4] A question arises, however, as to the wisdom and validity of this manner of application, as it tends to overlook the nature of futures trading. ʿAbd al-Qādir proceeds to discuss in some detail the issue of the sale in which the seller does not own, and also the sale in which the object of sale is non-existent. There is no doubt, ʿAbd al-Qādir tells us, that the jurists of various schools have proscribed the sale of the non-existent object for fear of indulgence in *gharar*, but then he adds, in much the same way, that we have known of Ibn Taymiyyah and his disciple Ibn Qayyim argue that the Lawgiver has nowhere declared such a sale to be unlawful. The Prophet ﷺ has forbidden the sale of non-existent objects just as he has forbidden certain varieties of sale in which the object may be present. The material factor in all of this was not the existence or non-existence of the subject-matter but the prevention of *gharar*. ʿAbd al-Qādir has also discussed *gharar* in some detail and quoted the views of al-Kāsānī, Ibn Ḥazm and Ibn Taymiyyah and then observed that *gharar* is not the issue in futures trading. This is because futures contracts are concluded on the basis of a description of the subject-matter in which there is no uncertainty or *gharar* that might give rise to disputes among the contracting parties. The detailed procedures of futures contracts are carefully regulated and virtually every contract is concluded by experts who are knowledgeable in commodity trading. Futures contracts are concluded under firm supervision and safeguards that are reinforced by a structure of guarantees (*ḥirāsah muḥkamah qawiyyah bi'l-ḍamānāt*) that tend to minimise or even eliminate the possibility of *gharar* over their fulfilment. ʿAbd al-Qādir adds that both the *Sharīʿah* and prevailing custom validate the sale of a non-existent object on the open market, and when this sale is concluded in the carefully regulated and supervised conditions of the commodity exchange, it is more reliable and inspires confidence in respect of performance. The futures market regulations are such that leave no cause for concern about the existence or otherwise of the subject-matter, or indeed about the prospects of disputes arising between the contracting parties. The fact that conventional *fiqh* equates the sale of the non-existent object with *gharar* is probably because the markets were very small in the early days of Islam, and this is no longer the case. The contemporary futures market operates on a regular, extensive and permanent basis, which enables the seller to obtain with complete confidence the goods he might need to deliver at any given time, and this virtually precludes *gharar* pertaining to the availability and supply of the underlying commodity.[5]

To further substantiate his argument, ʿAbd al-Qādir refers to the fact that the *Sharīʿah* has validated credit partnership (*shirkāt al-wujūh*), a partnership contract which involves no assets or even workmanship but is established merely on credible guarantees. The theory of partnership and contracts in Islam thus envisages not only tangible assets but also credibility (*thiqqah*) and guarantee (*al-ḍaman*) that are entirely based on the creditworthiness of the parties involved, without any pooling of tangible assets:

> The deferred sales (*buyūʿ al-ajal*) that take place in the contracts market (*bursah al-ʿuqūd*) are therefore lawful because they are devoid of *gharar* and there is nothing in the *Sharīʿah* to forbid contracts over non-existent objects. On the contrary, the fact that the *Sharīʿah* validates the manufacturing contract of *istiṣnāʿ* and leasing (*al-ijārah*) is evidence to show that the existence of subject-matter is not a requirement of a valid contract. Moreover, futures contracts are not instruments of risk-taking (*al-mukhāṭarah*) or of causing hostility and conflict between the contracting parties.[6]

ʿAlī ʿAbd al-Qādir then draws attention to the historicity of *fiqh* and the influence of the prevailing conditions and social customs on the formulation of its rules. Not only has the development of *fiqh* been influenced by the climate and custom of different localities, but so also have the *ḥadīth* materials on whose authority many of these rules were formulated in the first place. The local and circumstantial factors that have influenced the *ḥadīth* are indicated by the fact that some of them are labelled as Kūfī, others as Bāsrī and still others as Madīnī after these respective cities. In their attempt to verify the *ḥadīth*, the scholars were unquestionably influenced by local factors in the collection of *ḥadīth*, just as they were able to quote a certain *ḥadīth* in support of their views within a local or customary context. Juristic disagreement (*ikhtilāf*) that has been a part of the development and history of *fiqh* is due to a large extent to local particularities, as well as to a certain degree of selection and preference that the scholars have exercised in their juristic endeavours. It is therefore important to bear in mind that some juristic rulings, which were in all probability premised on the prevailing conditions and environment of a certain time, should not be considered as absolutely binding. We ought to look at them, respect and accept their credibility, but we should still attach greater priority and weight to the basic principles of the *Sharīʿah*, the public interest and the legitimate needs of the people and by this means try to arrive at a conclusion that is most suitable to the conditions of the present time.[7]

The Mecca-based Fiqh Academy has taken a somewhat ambivalent view of futures as it speaks in one paragraph of the benefits of futures to farmers, traders and manufacturers and then passes a negative judgement on it in the next. As for the benefits, it states that futures markets provide a permanent venue for traders in commercial instruments and commodities where prices are determined on the basis of the genuine market forces of supply and demand. In the absence of this facility, potential buyers and sellers would be unable to find the necessary outlet for their needs. This is a positive and, indeed, beneficial economic function. It is then added that 'this clear *maṣlaḥah* that is served by futures trading is accompanied by transactions which are forbidden in *Sharīʿah* as they partake in gambling, exploitation and the unlawful devouring of the property of others'. It is partly due to this combination of sorts that 'it is not possible to ascertain a single ruling of the *Sharīʿah* that would apply to all of the transactions concerned. What is needed instead is to explain the various market transactions and ascertain the ruling that applies individually to each'.[8] It is further added that the futures market also provides the opportunity for industrial, commercial and governmental institutions to finance their projects through the issuance and sale of stocks, bounds and promissory notes. A secondary market is thus provided for trading in these instruments on a guaranteed credit basis, which means that the issuing institutions can finance their projects without having to lay down advance deposits for immediate clearance. Trading in these instruments may also generate profits for the parties involved.[9]

While recounting the disadvantages of futures, the Fiqh Academy resolution notes the following:

1. Deferred (or future) contracts that are traded in the futures markets are by and large paper transactions, not genuine purchases and sales, because they do not involve delivery or taking into possession of their underlying commodities. A valid sale in *Sharīʿah*, in certain commodities at least, must involve a transfer of ownership and possession of both, or at least one, of the countervalues involved.

2. The sellers of futures contracts are involved, on the whole, in the sale of what they do not own. Whether they sell currency, stocks, bonds or commodities, the sellers conclude the sale in the hope of being able to buy the assets involved in the market at a later date, in order to make delivery upon maturity without actually receiving any payment at the time of contract - as would be required in the forward sale of *salam*.

3. The futures buyer is also involved, for the most part, in selling what he has bought to a third party prior to taking possession of the underlying assets, and then the next party in this chain also sells prior to taking possession of the assets involved. In this way, an asset is being sold and purchased several times without any physical transfer or delivery. The last link in this chain of transactions may be a buyer who wishes to take delivery from the first seller who has, in all probability, sold what he did not own in the first place. With the exception of the buyer and seller who actually take and make delivery, all the other sales in the chain are settled merely on the basis of price differentials at the time of maturity, which may consist of a profit or a loss for the parties concerned, and this is entirely similar to what happens between gamblers.

4. Futures also entail oppressive practices on the part of those who engage in profiteering by making large sales and purchases of contracts in stocks, bonds and commodities only to force smaller traders to take a loss and suffer hardship as a result.

5. Futures trading tends to bring about price distortion in that the determination of prices is not entirely a function of the market forces of supply and demand, or genuine sales and purchases by parties who need to conclude a certain transaction. A variety of other factors are known to cause unnatural price fluctuations and these include not only cornering and profiteering by the market participants, but also false rumours and the like, which are detrimental to economic life and unacceptable from the

point of view of *Sharīʿah*. To give an example, suppose that a group of financiers collaborate in offering for sale a large quantity of a certain asset with a view to lowering its price, and when this happens the small holders of the same asset rush to cut their losses and sell their holding for fear of further price falls. The increased supply is now likely to lower the prices even further, at which point the big players move in and buy at a low price; but now because of the fresh demand the price begins to move upward and the big players realise large profits, whereas the small player stand to suffer losses as a result of manipulation, and this can happen in both commodities and in commercial instruments.

It is for these reasons, the Fiqh Academy adds, that futures trading has aroused a major controversy among economists, which is, in turn, due to a number of historical events and crises that wreaked havoc with the world economy and inflicted devastating losses on market participants at short notice. Having highlighted the disadvantages of futures trading, the Academy states that in view of these considerations, and in the light of the relevant information on the nature of futures market transactions in commercial instruments and commodities from the Islamic perspective, attention is drawn to the following:

1. The benefits of futures in providing a market and stimulating commercial activity are accompanied by moral disadvantages that include gambling activity, unlawful exploitation and appropriation of the property of others.

2. That part of futures transactions in which delivery takes place and the seller sells a commodity that he owns and exists at the time of contract is clearly valid from the point of view of *Sharīʿah*, provided that the transaction does not proceed over unlawful substances. But when the seller does not own the object he sells, 'the sale in this case must fulfil the conditions of the sale of *salam*, which means that the buyer is not permitted to sell again prior to taking possession [of the underlying asset]'.

3. Prompt contracts (*al ʿuqūd al-ʿajilah*) over stocks and securities that the sellers own at the time of sale are lawful provided that the companies or institutions concerned are not engaged in usurious transactions, or trading in unlawful substances such as alcohol. But if they are so engaged, then trading in their stocks and securities is forbidden from the point of view of *Sharīʿah*.

4. All prompt and deferred contracts over interest-bearing instruments of whatever type and description are usurious transactions and, therefore, not permissible from the point of view of *Sharīʿah*.

5. Deferred contracts that are concluded on the basis of a description of assets and commodities that the seller does not own, are unlawful from the point of view of *Sharīʿah*. For these involve the sale of what a per-

son does not own, but which he concludes in the hope of subsequently purchasing the subject-matter of the contract in order to make delivery later. This is forbidden in *Sharīʿah* on the authority of a *ḥadīth* in which the Prophet ﷺ said, 'Sell not what is not with you.' There is a *ḥadīth* that Imām Aḥmad ibn Ḥanbal and Abū Dāwūd have both recorded on the authority of Zayd ibn Thābit which states: 'The Prophet ﷺ prohibited the sale of a commodity where it is bought, unless the traders take it into their possession and carry it.'

6. Deferred contracts that are concluded in the contracts market do not qualify as *salam* (forward) sales, which the *Sharīʿah* has validated. There are two reasons to support this: (a) the futures contract does not involve the payment of the price by the buyer at the time of contract, which is a requirement of *salam*. The buyer in *salam*, in other words, pays the agreed price at the time of contract and accepts delivery later. (b) Futures contracts involve sales of assets that have become personal obligations on the parties involved. The first buyer in the chain does not receive the underlying commodity, and this is also the case with every other sale that follows suit. They all tend to entail the giving or taking of price differentials, whether profits or losses, between the parties involved, who are in effect like gamblers undertaking risk in a zero sum game in order to procure profit. In a *salam* sale, on the other hand, the buyer is not permitted to sell prior to taking possession of the underlying commodity.[10]

Having drawn a full analogy with *salam* and used this as the sole basis for its prohibitive verdict, the Fiqh Academy then goes on to recommend 'to responsible officials in Islamic countries not to leave the futures markets in their countries at total liberty to act as they wish in respect of contracts and transactions, regardless of whether they are permissible or prohibited [in *Sharīʿah*]. They must not allow prices to become an arena for games only by those who play the game but ensure that the limits of permissibility in market transactions are observed'. It is then further recommended that transactions that the *Sharīʿah* has forbidden should be banned, 'for they destroy the public economy and inflict ruin on many. Benefit, indeed all benefit in all matters, is to be sought in following the path that is charted by the *Sharīʿah* of Islam'.[11] The resolution is signed by the Academy President, ʿAbd al-ʿAzīz ibn Bāz, its Deputy President, ʿAbd Allāh ʿUmar Nasīf, and the names of seventeen members are given of whom twelve have signed and five are shown to have been absent.[12] The resolution seems to be somewhat ambiguous towards the end when it recommends responsible officials not to leave the futures markets 'at total liberty to act as they wish'. One might ask: is there any such futures market in the world? The facts are that these markets are the most well-regulated and closely supervised. Besides, the Academy request evidently takes for granted the continuity of these markets, something that is, again, indicative of hesitation and ambivalence.

My critique here is precisely the same as I have voiced in discussing Yūsuf Sulaymān's position on the subject of futures. It is indeed remarkable that an international forum on *fiqh* should hand out a prohibitive judgment on an issue of immense significance to the economic well-being of the Muslim community (*ummah*) without making any attempt to offer a different perspective other than direct resort to *taqlīd,* or imitation of the rulings of the *madhāhib*. For this is all the Fiqh Academy has offered us in regard to the issues of the existence of the subject-matter of a sale, taking this into possession at the time of contract, and its conformity to the requirements of *salam*. There is no attempt in this approach to either advance a fresh perspective or to undertake *ijtihād* on new issues, and no questions are raised about the suitability of applying the rules of conventional sale to futures trading. The crucial issue is that of whether we are faced with a different reality when dealing with futures and if so, whether the occasion requires recourse to *ijtihād* in the light of that reality. If a ruling in *ḥadīth* exists, then surely we need to ascertain its proper application to a new situation, and establish whether the effective cause of that ruling, which is to prevent *gharar*, is also present in the issue before us. If the issue is no longer about *gharar*, and the facts of futures trading warrant a departure from the established positions of *fiqh* in favour of an easier alternative that would still be in harmony with the *ḥadīth* and secure the public interest, than that alternative must surely be explored.

In an attempt to determine the validity or otherwise of futures sales, Shahat al-Jundī has also addressed the issue of the sale of the non-existent, and has reviewed the position of the various schools of *fiqh*, which are generally prohibitive of such sales. He then turns to the views of the Ḥanbalī jurists Ibn Taymiyyah and Ibn Qayyim al-Jawziyyah, who affirm the validity of such sales. Al-Jundī then speaks in support of this latter position and says that the issue involved here is not the existence or non-existence of the subject-matter, but that of how to prevent *gharar*. A sale may well be invalid on grounds of *gharar,* even if the subject-matter therein exists at the time of contract. Provided that the sale is free of *gharar*, gambling and material ignorance of the parties about its subject-matter, the sale of the non-existent object is valid. Thus, by applying Ibn Taymiyyah and Ibn Qayyim's opinion, al-Jundī considers future sales to be valid. But he rightly draws attention to the point that futures sales are not exactly the sale of objects that are non-existent. This is because the futures market operates on a permanent basis, and the underlying commodities that are being traded are also expected to be available in the open market. Hence it cannot be categorically said that the subject-matter of a futures contract is non-existent. Having said this, however, al-Jundī still invokes Ibn Taymiyyah and Ibn Qayyim's views on the issue at hand. Al-Jundī expresses some reservation about the question of whether futures sales are devoid of *gharar*, since *gharar* is a wider issue and it is not confined to the existence or non-existence of the subject-matter of a sale. Notwithstanding the fact that futures transactions are carefully regulated and enjoy a network of financial guarantees that preclude uncertainty about the fulfilment of contracts, the risk-taking element of financial speculation is an aspect of *gharar* which still remains a cause for concern. 'Provided that the futures are devoid of *gharar,* or that the *gharar* is reduced to the level of what may be regarded as slight and tolerable, and provided that there is no element of gambling or material ignorance that could lead to disputes between the parties, then futures trading which involve sale of the non-existent is valid in principle ... but if *gharar* penetrates the transaction and affects its essence ... then the contract will be invalid.'[13] Notwithstanding the generally affirmative perspective that al-Jundī has developed on the validity of futures trading, his conclusions are so heavily stipulated that they tell us little more than what we find in the views of the early *fuqahā'*. Al-Jundī takes a similarly ambivalent stance elsewhere, where he elaborates on the subject of speculation. The essence of speculation in futures is stated by him to be the unreality of the transaction and the absence of intention on the part of buyers and sellers to make or take delivery. They enter the transaction with the sole purpose of making a profit from the movement of prices. Al-Jundī then draws a distinction between commercially valid speculation, which is not prohibited in Islam, and that which is tantamount to gambling and transgression. He denounces the one and praises the other, but does not tell us clearly which of these two he associates most closely with futures transactions.[14] Al-Jundī does take a more positive stance, however, when he discusses the issue of *qabḍ*, that is, the taking into possession of an object prior to selling it, as well as sale by description without actually viewing the object. Both of these requirements are laid down in *fiqh* with the purpose mainly of preventing uncertainty, risk taking and *gharar,* al-Jundī points out. When we look at futures market transactions, there is no risk of failure to make delivery as and when the buyer wishes to take it. Market transactions are also conducted by experts in the trade and the detailed procedures that govern the sales contract actually preclude *gharar*. The fact that there is a permanent market in operation with extensive participation and regularity in business means that there is no fear of *gharar* affecting the validity of transactions. We also know that the *Sharīʿah* aims to bring benefits and prevent hardship and harm. 'Based on this analysis, the futures market transactions in which commodities are sold prior to being taken into possession are permissible; there is no *gharar* therein, nor are they harmful in any way.'[15]

ʿAbd al-Karīm al-Khaṭīb has highlighted two issues concerning futures, one of which is deferred sale (*al-bayʿ al-mu'ajjal*) and the other speculation (*al-muḍārabah*). Futures contracts basically consist of deferred sales in which the contract is concluded but actual delivery, in case there is delivery, as well as the payment of price, are deferred to a future date, which may be several months later. As for the question of whether the *Sharīʿah* validates deferred sales, al-Khaṭīb gives a straightforward affirmative answer: 'From the point of view of *Sharīʿah*, deferred sale is valid without any question; in the language of *fiqh*, it is known as *salam*, which the *Sharīʿah* has explicitly validated, and *salam* takes for granted deferred delivery of the subject-matter to a future date, although the price in *salam* is paid in advance.'[16] Al-Khaṭīb then takes up the issue of the sale of the non-existent (*bayʿ ghayr al-mawjūd*), and the *ḥadīth* 'sell not what is not with you', which is the textual basis of the prohibitive ruling of *fiqh* on such sales. The basic purpose of that *ḥadīth*, as al-Khaṭīb observes, was to prevent future disputes between the parties, that is, when the buyer demanded delivery but the seller was unable to meet his liability because of the time interval, and the possibility that the seller might have changed his mind. The ruling of this *ḥadīth* naturally took into account the market conditions that prevailed at the time. But those conditions no longer exist, and no dispute is expected to be caused in futures trading merely on account of the non-existence of the subject-matter of a sale.[17]

With regard to commercial speculation, al-Khaṭīb has rightly emphasised the fact that speculation is essential to providing liquidity in the market. Without the presence of speculators, futures market transactions, both sales and purchases, are likely to move in roughly the same direction, but with the presence of speculators, there is always someone ready to buy as soon as prices decline and sell when they move upwards. It is also due to speculation, al-Khaṭīb adds, that drastic price movements are averted since the speculator entry at a time when the price begins to move up or down tends to have a moderating effect on the movement of prices. Speculation is therefore absolutely necessary to keep the market functioning; its efficiency and success rate are directly related to the number of speculators who engage in trading activity, and this activity generates liquidity and volume.[18] But despite its beneficial effects, al-Khaṭīb warns that speculation can become an instrument of abuse that can easily compromise the integrity of the market when it is employed for improper purposes. Speculation can turn the market into a gambling den and lead people to financial ruin if it is by self-seeking exploiters. When that is the case, speculation in the futures market can only be denounced as a mode of corruption and evil, in which case society at large is well within its rights to protect itself against unregulated speculation and take all necessary precautions to fight its pernicious influences. To prevent financial speculation being turned into gambling activity, we must ensure that speculation over price differentials takes place in line with market activity and the natural patterns of supply and demand.[19] At this point, al-Khaṭīb draws attention to the fact that, initially, the Egyptian government did not regulate speculative activity in cotton futures at all and did not do so until November 1909, when art. 79 of the Commercial Law was amended so as to subject all futures trading activities in the country to the rule of law and regulatory procedures of the exchange authorities. According to al-Khaṭīb, the Egyptian government not only validated but also encouraged financial speculation, including theoretical sales and purchases for the purpose solely of making profit. Yet Egyptian legislation has in the meantime taken measures to curb excessive speculation by enacting maximum and minimum limits on the price movement of commodities in any single day, and this means that speculation is effectively turned into commercial activity. The futures speculator, whether a buyer or a seller is thus engaged in trading (as opposed to gambling), and it can be said with confidence that speculation about the price differentials follows, on the whole, the natural trends of supply and demand, which means that futures speculation is a commercial activity based on genuine market forces.[20]

Al-Khaṭīb then draws attention to the brokers and the role they play in the propriety of market transactions. He stresses that brokers must not buy or sell for their own accounts, nor must they engage themselves in non-brokerage activities, for example by becoming the opposite side to transactions they conclude for their customers. When brokers begin to act on insider information and add an unnatural twist to commercial speculation, one can only expect irregularity and distortion. Having said this, al-Khaṭīb adds that trading in commodity futures in Egypt is well regulated and supervised by the government, and it is on the whole beneficial to the national economy. Brokerage activity is lawful under the *Sharīʿah*, and the broker performs a service in the capacity of an agent (*wakīl*), for which he receives certain remuneration.[21] The sales and purchases that occur in the futures market are binding transactions since they fulfil all the material requirements of a valid sale in *Sharīʿah*: they specify with complete clarity the parties' liability in respect of delivery and payment in a manner that precludes the possibility of disputes arising between them. Market activity as a whole, the parties' contractual liabilities and brokerage activity are all carefully regulated and supervised, and there are adequate precautionary measures which guarantee full performance on all sides. Since these transactions do not involve oppression (*ẓulm*) or the devouring of the property of others, and careful provisions are made to prevent disputes among the participants, even if some formal requirements of a sale are not complied with, the basic criteria that the *Sharīʿah* has laid down for a valid sale are fulfilled.[22]

A Review of Two *Fatwās*: ʿAzzām and ʿAbd al-Bāsiṭ

The remainder of this chapter is devoted mainly to a *fatwā* given by Majd al-Dīn ʿAzzām, in his capacity as Advisor to the International Union of Islamic Banks, which consists of a review and refutation of another *fatwa* given earlier by Badr al-Mutawalli ʿAbd al-Bāsiṭ, *Sharīʿah* Counsel to the Finance House of Kuwait. The *fatwā* given by ʿAzzām addresses four separate issues related to futures in almost all of which ʿAẓzām is critical of the somewhat conformist and prohibitive view that ʿAbd al-Bāsiṭ has taken of futures trading. The four issues addressed are as follows (for the sake of brevity I shall not quote ʿAbd al-Bāsiṭ in detail but try to give the gist of his *fatwā* in my discussion of ʿAzzām's views).

1. A representative (*wakīl*) concludes the sale of a non-existent commodity to be delivered in the near or distant future. The buyer in this transaction pays a part of the price at the time of contract and the remainder upon expiry of the stipulated time. What should this transaction be called (i.e., is there a term in the existing law by which it should be known)?

2. Is it permissible in *Sharīʿah* for me to sell the subject- matter of *salam* (i.e., *muslam fīh*) to a third party before it is delivered to me, and for the third party in question to replace me in taking delivery? Could the same object be sold to more than one purchaser (in a chain of transactions)?

3. Is it lawful to appoint an agent to represent both the buyer and seller simultaneously, and is it then lawful for this representative to conclude a purchase or sale at his or her own initiative without taking instruction from the buyer or the seller as the case may be? Is it a prerequisite for one or both of the principal parties to specify the price in advance? May the parties concerned stipulate the manner in which they wish to be represented in advance?

4. What is the position in *Sharīʿah* on taking possession (*al-taqābuḍ*) of assets in the customary manner known of commercial banks? Is the sale of a commodity before the buyer actually acquires possession of it lawful?[23]

In response to the first question, ʿAzzām wrote that ʿAbd al-Bāsiṭ's attempt to subsume futures sales under the conventional *salam* (forward) sale and then to declare it forbidden because it did not meet all the conditions of *salam* was unjustified. ʿAzzām added that ʿAbd al-Bāsiṭ's *fatwā* was premised, from beginning to end, on the rulings of the *madhāhib*, and did not venture out of the imitative tradition of *taqlīd*. This was not necessarily objectionable as far as it went, but that his own (ʿAzzām's) *fatwā* was an attempt, from the perspective of *ijtihād*, and so was not necessarily bound by the rulings of the jurists of the past. ʿAzzām elaborated his response to the first question under two headings as follows.

Firstly, scholars of Islamic jurisprudence (*uṣūl al-fiqh*) are in agreement that the norm in regards to devotional matters (*ʿibādāt*) is prohibition, in the sense that they are forbidden unless validated by the clear rulings of textual sources, but the norm concerning civil transactions (*muʿāmalāt*) is permissibility, which means that they are generally allowed unless clearly prohibited. The prohibition in this case, may be either definitive (*qaṭʿī*), which leaves no room for doubt, or it may be speculative (*ẓannī*), such as prohibition conveyed in a solitary (*āḥād*) *ḥadīth*. ʿAzzām then adds that he fully accepts and relies on the first part of this principle, but wishes to say, concerning its second limb, that the prohibitive evidence pertaining to civil and commercial transactions must be nothing less than decisive. This is because the basic permissibility of such transactions is based on decisive evidence, that is, the principle of *ibāḥah*, and this should prevail unless there is decisive evidence to warrant a departure in the opposite direction.

Secondly, the pace of development and change in international relations, economics and commerce has in many ways been unprecedented and has brought about completely new situations that did not exist in earlier times, nor were they even known to jurists of the past. But then to issue a prohibitive judgement on modern commercial transactions that have gained international recognition by reference to the rulings of those jurists, without decisive evidence, is bound to prove detrimental to the Muslim community and retard their development efforts, and such a judgement is therefore contrary to the basic objectives of the *Sharīʿah*. The basic purpose of *Sharīʿah* in the area of civil and customary transactions is bringing benefit to the people. The benefit in question may be essential (*ḍarūrī*), complementary (*ḥājjī*) or desirable (*taḥsīnī*), but none of these can be hindered on the basis of merely doubtful juristic speculation.

The attempt at juristic *ijtihād* is therefore inevitable and it is necessary that we see new developments in economics and commerce from new perspectives, even if such attempts do not correspond with the rulings of the early jurists. If some of those early jurists rose from the dead and saw the realities of modern life and the total contrast to what they had known, they would surely change their earlier rulings, attempt new *ijtihād* in line with contemporary conditions, and see for themselves that their earlier *fatwās* do not apply. With these introductory premises, ʿAzzām goes on to add that we may accept and validate a particular contract or transaction, even if it fails to fulfil a certain condition of the conventional contract, or adds something new to it, provided that it fulfils the following three conditions: that the transaction in question is not contrary to a decisive injunction; that it does not partake of genuine *ribā'* (usury); and that it is not predominantly harmful. When these three conditions are met, the transaction in question is valid from the point of view of *Sharīʿah* and may be practised regardless of whether or not it fulfils the *fiqhī* requirements of a conventional contract.[24]

In response to ʿAbd al-Bāsiṭ's question about what the transaction at hand should be called, ʿAzzām comments that if one wishes to give a futures contract a name, one may call it *shibh al-salam* (a *salam* look-alike), but one may also consider it a new contract, to be added to the varieties already known. There is no compelling need to subsume this type of contract under *salam* in any capacity whatsoever; rather, one should see it as it is and then determine its validity not by reference to the works of *fiqh*, but to the basic evidence of *Sharīʿah*.[25]

In response to the questions of whether the buyer in *salam* sale may sell the subject-matter to a third party prior to the stipulated delivery date, or before maturity, and whether this could be repeated and consecutive sales be concluded on the same basis, ʿAzzām's response is that these transactions are lawful.[26] This is because the sale is free of *ribā'*, is not harmful, and does not conflict with the decisive evidence in *Sharīʿah*, even though it does not correspond with the types of sale that the jurists have specifically ruled on through their juridical endeavour and *ijtihād*. The forms of sale that were specified as lawful were those which secured the benefit (*maṣlaḥah*) as perceived at the time, according to the prevailing custom and the commercial realities of society. But the *maṣlaḥah* in our own time can be secured by the transactions indicated above, as these have now become an accepted commercial custom world-wide, and it would be untenable to argue that Islam rejects what is deemed to be a commercial *maṣlaḥah* by prevailing international custom, for the *Sharīʿah* is premised, from beginning to end, on the realisation of *maṣlaḥah* and the prevention of harm and corruption. The arguments that have been advanced against this accepted form of *maṣlaḥah* consist entirely of speculative opinion, there being no decisive evidence to support the prohibitive position. We, on the other hand, maintain that international commercial custom has accepted futures trading to be lawful, and this by itself is clear evidence of its permissibility.

At this point, ʿAzzām refers to three main points raised by ʿAbd al-Bāsiṭ and then refutes them one by one. The first reference is to al-Bāsiṭ's *fatwā* where it is stated that, 'as for the sale of the subject-matter of *salam* prior to possession (*qabḍ*), we do not know of any disagreement in its prohibition'. This is the view, according to al-Bāsiṭ, of the author of *al-Mughnī*, which is founded on the rationale that the transaction at issue merely adds to the burden on consumers. For when a series of sales are concluded without the commodity changing hands, it carries the accumulated profits of all the sellers and it ends up with the consumer who has to absorb it to his own detriment. ʿAzzām disagrees with this reasoning and elaborates as follows: suppose a person buys a certain commodity from another for a specified price or by reference to the market price and then sells the same prior to taking delivery to a second buyer, while the commodity still remains with the first seller, at an agreed price or at market price, and another sale of a similar kind occurs to a third and fourth buyer while the commodity still remains with the first seller. Then, if we suppose, for the sake of argument, that each buyer in the series actually does take delivery and possession of the underlying commodity, we still maintain that in neither of these eventualities is there a consistent and cumulative increase of profit which, as al-Bāsiṭ assumes, is to the detriment of the consumer. ʿAzzām maintains that the question of *qabḍ* has no bearing on the size of the profit or its cumulative transfer to the consumer.[27] ʿAzzām's analysis is correct, in my view, because it is merely presumptuous to say that every seller in the series makes a profit, and even if this were so, the settlement price that is paid upon delivery, assuming that delivery does occur, is normally a predetermined price that has been agreed between the buyer and seller in the first link. If delivery takes place upon maturity, it is basically this price, subject to daily settlement (or marking-to-market) procedure, as I have explained earlier, that applies at the delivery stage. Our analysis has also shown that futures prices are often lower than cash market prices and end up, upon maturity of contract, the same as those of the cash market prices. The buyers and sellers between the first and last transactions may make profit or incur losses; and there is no certainty that there will in fact be a cumulative profit at the end. The question of delivery and taking into possession is a relevant one, but if anything, actual delivery is likely to have an adverse effect on prices: transportation and storage are costly and if we were to require that each buyer in the chain take physical possession of the commodity, this would push the price up and the position of the last buyer would be likely to be the opposite of what al-Bāsiṭ anticipated.

Al-Bāsiṭ claims that the sale of the subject-matter of *salam* prior to *qabḍ* is prohibited, and quotes Ibn Qudāmah's view to that effect. ʿAzzām's response to this assertion is that we are not bound by that opinion, especially in view of the fact that the scholars are in disagreement about this issue. Al-Shawkānī, for example, has discussed the matter in his *Nayl al-*

Awṭār and has recorded different opinions on it, including that of ʿUthmān al-Batti who held that sale prior to *qabḍ* is generally lawful in everything. Al-Shawkānī has also recorded the views of Imām Mālik and al-Awzāʿī regarding the sale of commodities in lump sum, which is held to be lawful prior to *qabḍ*. It is therefore incorrect to say that no disagreement is known to exist over the prohibition of the transaction under discussion. There may well be a legitimate need, ʿAzzām adds, for sale to be prior to *qabḍ*: imagine a person who buys agricultural machinery to set up a business for his son while the father and son live in distant localities. Then circumstances change and his son decides to join the diplomatic service, while the seller of machinery refuses to cancel the deal; in this case, there is no harm for this machinery to be sold to a third party prior to *qabḍ*. The likes of this example can be seen in relation to many commodities and services, especially when one bears in mind the ever-increasing range and diversity of choice and opportunity in the market place. When there is a legitimate benefit in a transaction and no manifest harm is expected as a result, the norm is that it is lawful.[28]

In another part of his *fatwā*, al-Bāsiṭ has also stated that the transaction in question partakes of *ribā'*, for it amounts to the sale of cash for cash with a discrepancy: the first buyer in the series pays cash, according to the rules of *salam*, and then he sells the commodity at a profit before taking possession of it. All the subsequent sales are in effect sales of money for money plus a profit, and this is *ribā'*, as was understood by Ibn ʿAbbās concerning the prohibition of sale prior to *qabḍ*.

ʿAzzām has responded by saying that labelling the sale of the subject-matter of *salam* prior to *qabḍ* as *ribā'* is an error because it does not fit the definition of *ribā'*. For we are not talking of a simple exchange of money with an addition on one side of the exchange (which would be *ribā'*), but of an exchange of money for money based on the sale of a commodity of which the buyer becomes the owner once he assumes liability for the payment of its price. Note, for example, that Imām al-Shāfiʿī has excluded the sale of *ʿinah* from the purview of *ribā'* precisely because the money exchange that is involved is incidental to the sale of a commodity, and not, as it were, the main purpose of the transaction. As for the reference to Ibn ʿAbbās, al-Bāsiṭ has actually quoted al-Shawkānī's report in *Nayl al-Awṭār* on the matter and it fails to prove al-Bāsiṭ's claim. Even if we accept Ibn ʿAbbās's version of the issue, the saying or *fatwā* of Companion is not, as per al-Shāfiʿī, a proof, which is where ʿAzzām stands.[29]

Another aspect of al-Bāsiṭ's *fatwa* that is of interest to us, ʿAzzām adds, is that he equates futures trading with *salam*, but then says that 'a *salam* in which the payment of price, whether wholly or in part, is postponed to a future date is invalid, for it is then turned into an exchange of debts (or debt clearance sale), known as *bayᶜ al-kālī' bi'l-kālī'*, which is prohibited on the authority of *ḥadīth*, although Imām Mālik has held that the price of *salam* may be postponed to a future date if the contract does not stipulate otherwise'.[30] ᶜAzzām writes in response that the *ḥadīth*, quoted in some collections such as that of al-Dāraqutnī on the authority of Ibn ᶜUmar, to the effect that 'the Prophet ﷺ prohibited sale of *al-kālī' bi'l-kālī'*" is controversial. Al-Shawkānī has discussed it in *Nayl al-Awṭār*, where he writes that al-Dāraqutnī states that there is a point in its chain of transmission where only one person, Mūsā ibn ᶜUbaydah al-Rabdhī, reports, and Imām Aḥmad ibn Ḥanbal has regarded this transmitter as unreliable. No one else has reported it either. Even so, Imām Ibn Ḥanbal has said that 'according to popular consensus (*ijmāᶜ al-nās*), the sale of one debt (*dayn*) for another is not permissible'. Imām al-Shāfiᶜī has said that the scholars of *ḥadīth* have classified this *ḥadīth* as unreliable, despite the fact that the jurists have frequently discussed it in their works. As for Imām Ibn Ḥanbal's reference to popular consensus (*ijmāᶜ al-nās*), the phrase he uses is somewhat ambiguous and doubtful. *Ijmāᶜ* is decisive evidence when: it is verbal *ijmāᶜ* as opposed to tacit *ijmāᶜ*; or it is transmitted through continuous reporting or *tawātur*; or it builds up definitive knowledge. The *ijmāᶜ* that Imām ibn Ḥanbal has mentioned fails to fulfil these conditions, and the most that can be said of it is that it is a speculative *ijmāᶜ* (*ijmāᶜ an ẓanniyan*) which is in the nature of *ijtihād*, and we are therefore at liberty to oppose it. For the issue before us is a new transaction which was not known before, and the alleged *ijmāᶜ* of an early period could not provide a conclusive proof for or against it.[31]

As for the assertion that the *ijmāᶜ* here corresponds with the afore mentioned *ḥadīth* and that the two pieces of evidences reinforce one another, ᶜAzzām points out that the wording of the *ḥadīth* is prohibitive on the sale of one debt for another when the two sides of the transaction consist of a *dayn* each *per se*, but the issue before us is one of deferred sale of the unseen, in which delivery is postponed to a future date and the price is also payable, either wholly or in part, in the future, and this does not qualify for what is specified in the *ḥadīth*. For one thing, not every deferred sale in which the delivery of the subject-matter is postponed to a future date can qualify either as *salam* or *bayᶜ al-kālī' bi'l-kālī'* (debt clearance sale). The-subject matter of a deferred delivery sale may be a specific object, as opposed to a fungible commodity, and the mere fact that delivery, in the sale of such an object, is postponed to a future date does not turn it into a *salam*, and it would be lawful to defer the payment of its price, wholly or in part, to the time of the delivery of the subject-matter or indeed to a different date. This is because a specific object (*ᶜayn*) is different from a debt (*dayn*) in that an *ᶜayn* cannot become a charge on the personal liability, or *dhimmah*, of a person. But if the subject-matter of *salam* is specified by its genus, type and quality, such as a fungible commodity, and the price is also postponed to a future date, then it may fall within the meaning of the *ḥadīth* and may become *bayᶜ al-kāli' bi'l-kāli'* but, as already stated, there still remains some doubt as to the precise meaning and authenticity of the *ḥadīth*.[32]

ᶜAzzām and Bāsiṭ seem to be in agreement on only one of the four issues, and this is concerning representation (*wakālah*) in a type of sale in which one person may act on behalf of both parties to a contract. Some jurists have stated clearly that there is no objection to this and that the parties are at liberty to appoint anyone, even the same person, as their representative. Furthermore, the agent handling a purchase or sale is not required to notify the principal about the identity of the contracting party, for it is possible that the agent may not know the other party to the transaction. It is also not necessary for the principal to specify the price in a sale or purchase to his agent, and if this is the case, the agent should observe the prevailing market price (*siᶜr al-mithl*).[33]

ᶜAzzām has evidently told us that in addressing new issues, one need not necessarily refer to the opinions of the jurists of early Islam by trying to read into them an awareness of what they could not possibly have known about. If we find in their contributions a precedent that relates to the issues of concern to us, we may utilise it to our advantage, but we should otherwise address their rulings as they are. Futures trading is a new development, an unprecedented variety of sale, and the best approach is to begin by acknowledging it as such. Provided that it fulfils the three afore mentioned conditions, it may be brought under the general principle of *ibāḥah* (permissibility) and declared to be lawful. The rest of this chapter elaborates on the subject of representation (*wakālah*) discussed by ᶜAzzām, and I propose to take this discussion a little further.

Representation (*Wakālah*)

There is no problem in *Sharīᶜah*, with the charging of brokerage commission, or the taking of a margin deposit in futures trading. When a person appoints another as his attorney or *wakīl*, it may be with remuneration or without. Normally, the *wakīl* is entitled to remuneration for his effort. At the same time, voluntary or unpaid representation is also valid and it falls into the category of co-operation (*taᶜāwun*) between people. However, if the agency is on a paid basis, the transaction falls into the category of lease and hire (*al-ijārāt*) and the rules of *ijārah* consequently apply to it. The specific terms of a contract, whether of representation (*wakālah*), or of lease and hire, may be determined by the mutual agreement of the parties provided that they are lawful and do not violate the dictates of public policy and *maṣlaḥah*. Representation may be specific or it may be general. In its specific (*khāṣṣ*) form, the *wakīl* is appointed to carry out a particular task, such as the purchase of a particular commodity. In this case, the principal party specifies the price and attributes of the object(s) he wishes to buy. If the agent then violates the stipulated terms of his agency and concludes a contract beyond the scope of his authority, then it will be a suspended (*mawqūf*) contract, which becomes effective (*nāfidh*) when the principal approves of it, or will otherwise lapse. A general representative (*wakīl ʿāmm*) is, on the other hand, granted wide-ranging authority that entitles him to exercise his own best judgement and *ijtihād* regarding the subject-matter of the agency. If the latter is the purchase of a house, for example, the general *wakīl* may pay a price either below or above the market price and the transaction will still be valid. But since the *wakīl* is, from the *Sharīʿah* perspective, a trustee (*amīn*) on behalf of the principal party he must exercise his best judgement. The leading schools of law are in agreement that *wakālah* in its general form is on the whole subject to the prevailing custom of society. In the case of futures trading, the trader appoints the broker as his agent by means of signing a document of attorney when he opens the account. The broker is a special agent since his terms of agency are limited in accordance with the information and specific order that the principal party normally places in the contract. The brokerage commission represents the remuneration that the principal party pays him for the service.

Since the margin deposit is a good faith deposit and is in any case deposited in the trader's own account, there is basically no issue of unlawful gain. The immediate purpose of depositing margin money is to ensure the integrity of the transaction by protecting the rights of the seller or buyer, as the case may be, against excessive price fluctuation. Appointing an agent, paying commission fees and depositing a margin are all valid in Islamic law, and the provisions of established *fiqh,* as they stand, can accommodate current practices of brokerage and representation in futures contracts.

NOTES

1. Yūsuf Sulaymān, 'Ra'y al-Tashriʿ', in *al-Mawsuʿah al-ʿIlmiyyah*, v, 427.
2. Ibid.
3. Ibid., v, 430.
4. Al-Qādir, 'Taʿqib ʿalā Ra'y al-Tashriʿ', in *al-Mawsuʿah al-ʿIlmiyyah,* v, 438.
5. Ibid., v, 439.
6. Ibid., v, 439-40.

7. Ibid., V, 442.
8. Majlis al-Majma' al-Fiqhī al-Islāmī, 'Suq al-Bada'i' (al-Burṣah)', p. 122.
9. Ibid., p. 120.
10. Ibid., pp. 122-4.
11. Ibid., p. 124.
12. Ibid., pp. 124-5.
13. Al-Jundī, *Mu'āmalāt*, pp. 99-100.
14. Ibid., pp. 50-4.
15. Ibid., p. 127.
16. Al-Khaṭīb, *al-Siyāsah al-Māliyyah*, p. 175.
17. Ibid., pp. 175-6.
18. Ibid., pp. 184-5.
19. Ibid., pp. 188, 190.
20. Ibid, pp. 189-90.
21. Ibid., p. 191.
22. Ibid., pp. 181-2.
23. Majd al-Din 'Azzām, in Bayt al-Tamwil al-Kuwaitī, *al-Fatawa al-Shar'iyyah*, p. 113.
24. Ibid., pp. 114-16.
25. Ibid., pp. 118, 124.
26. Ibid., p. 121.
27. Ibid., p. 122.
28. Ibid, p. 123.
29. Ibid., p. 33.
30. Ibid., pp. 129-30.
31. Ibid., pp. 104, 129.
32. Ibid., pp. 34, 107.
33. Ibn Juzay, *Qawānīn*, p. 281; Ibn Taymiyyah, *Naẓariyyah al-'Aqd*, p. 222; al-Jundī, *Mu'āmalāt*, p. 37.

PART THREE

OPTIONS

INTRODUCTORY REMARKS

Options trading is discussed below in two sections. The first is devoted to a market analysis of options and the second to the *Sharīʿah* perspective on options trading. There is no real shortage of information on the operational procedure of options and the various ways in which options are utilised as trading vehicles as well as hedging and risk-reduction devices. On the other hand, we are faced with a totally different picture when it comes to analysing options trading from a *Sharīʿah* perspective. There is a distinct lack of in-depth information in this area, and the analysis I have presented in the second part of this chapter is tentative because certain aspects of this issue are still in need of further development and research. The literature I have consulted on the subject seems to be in its early stages of development and does not appear to have reached a point where any consensus about the issues can be identified. At present, opinion on the question of validity or otherwise of options from the Islamic legal perspective is wholly divided. I shall review two opposing currents of opinion in due course, but suffice it to note here that this presentation does not seek to advocate the validity of those types of options that proceed, either directly or indirectly, by charging fixed interest to accounts. This latter qualification may be said to be one of the distinctive features of the *Sharīʿah* perspective on options, which applies equally to all types of commercial transaction in Islamic law. If a case can be made for interest rate options that are solely utilised for hedging purposes, it may perhaps be attempted under the rule of necessity (*ḍarūrah*), as I elaborate in my concluding chapter below. The review of the mechanics of options trading in the first section of this chapter broadly indicates that options trading does not proceed by charging fixed interest, nor does it involve unwarranted risk-taking, uncertainty or *gharar*. Options trading has a logic of its own, dominated by the idea of risk-reduction and hedging against taking excessively large positions in its underlying assets. This aspect of options is essentially attractive from the perspective of Islamic law, and it is from the latter perspective that we make out a case for the legality of options. I may also add here in passing that options trading cannot be equated with gambling or over-indulgence in financial speculation since it is basically designed to minimise speculative risk-taking, and for the most part operates as an antidote to gambling.

Although the basic logic of options as a risk-management tool extends to all areas of options trading, and there is support for the view that options in financial instruments and interest rates tend to have a limiting effect on the latter, the research findings on this aspect of options are not presented here, and I propose to exclude interest rate options from the scope of this presentation.

CHAPTER SIXTEEN

A Market Analysis of Options

Trading in futures emerged in the early 1970s and in options in the early 1980s, each in response to the growth of international trade and to the increased volatility in financial markets. Futures and options are ways of managing and reducing risk by means of hedging. Futures markets for agricultural produce developed as a result of substantial price fluctuations that were faced by the buyers and sellers of that produce. Agricultural futures allowed farmers to guarantee selling prices and merchants to guarantee buying prices so that both could avoid making losses. Financial futures emerged in the early 1970s in response to fluctuations in currency prices following the breakdown of the Bretton Woods fixed exchange rate system. These developments in the financial markets were followed by innovations in options markets.

Options are versatile and can be used in a large number of ways. Strategies that can be applied to options are virtually limitless and new products are being continually introduced in the market. Options are largely sold (or written) by companies and institutions, such as banks, which hold inventories of commodities or financial instruments. By writing options against these inventories, profits can be realised with little assumption of risk. For most individuals, on the other hand, option writing is much less attractive than option purchasing, not least because the potential profit to the option writer is limited to the amount of the premium. The price in the options contract is known as the 'exercise price' or the 'strike price', and the date in the contract is known as the 'expiration date', the 'exercise date', or simply the 'maturity'.

Trading in options has become popular for a variety of reasons. Options can be bought for a fraction of the money required to buy the underlying assets. Investors who do not have enough funds or who do not want to tie up large sums of money in futures contracts can, by buying options, acquire control over large quantities of commodities and their related contracts. If market prices move in their favour, they can exercise the options and buy the underlying assets and then sell them on at a profit. In the event of an unfavourable move in the market prices, the option holder simply does not exercise it and forfeits the premium. Options are also used by speculators as a hedging device against open positions both in the stock and futures markets.[1]

Although options are traded on a variety of underlying assets—stocks, currencies, treasury bills, and futures—one can explain the rudiments of options trading by reference to conventional stocks and securities, since trading strategies in other sectors are fundamentally the same as in conventional stocks. We may note at the outset that options are not securities in the true sense. Securities are issued by corporations, municipalities and government treasuries, whereas options on a security, such as the IBM stock, are issued not by IBM, but rather by an individual or a firm known as a writer (or grantor). An option may be issued or written by anyone. An option is simply a contract entered into by two parties. The buyer of the contract is granted the privilege of buying or selling a security at a specific price, while the seller (writer) of the contract assumes an obligation to accommodate the buyer should the buyer exercise his privilege. As the value of the underlying security can fluctuate sharply during the life of the contract, the buyer pays the seller a fee for granting the privilege. This fee is called the premium.

The logic of options can be applied to things other than securities. Suppose you own a valuable oil painting valued at RM1 million. You enter into a contract with another party allowing him to purchase the painting for RM1 million at any time during the next 12 months. Since the painting could be worth RM1,100,000 within a year, you demand a fee of RM10,000 for granting the option. If the value of the artefact does rise to RM1,100,000 within the year, the owner of the contract will exercise the option and purchase it for RM1 million. You will have lost the picture but would have received a total of RM1,010,000. If, on the other hand, the value of the painting falls to RM900,000, the contract would not be exercised. You would keep the RM10,000 fee and still own the painting.

Options on equity securities have been traded for many decades, but until 1973 the market was very informal. Someone who wished to purchase an option on IBM stocks would contact one of a handful of option dealers, generally small firms that specialised in the product. The option dealer would seek out another party willing to sell (write) the option. All of the terms of the contract, including the premium, were subject to negotiation and agreement.

A major change in the trading of equity options occurred in 1973, when the Chicago Board of Trade (CBT), which dealt in commodities, set up the Chicago Board of Options Exchange (CBOE) and for the first time equity options began to trade on an exchange. This centralisation of the market led to an increased interest in options, and many other bourses in the US followed suit and established similar facilities for options trading.[2]

The listing of equity options eliminated the uncertainties of the earlier markets. Before 1973, the parties to an option contract would have to agree on three important aspects of the contract: a) the exercise price. The buyer might have wanted the contract exercised, say, at $4.00 per share but the seller at $4.50 a share; b) the length of the contract. The buyer might have wanted the option to extend to nine months, the seller only six months; c) the premium. All three aspects were subject to negotiation and agreement. But with the listing and centralisation of equity options, the need to negotiate the first two, namely, the exercise price and the contract period, was eliminated since they were now determined by the exchange on which the contract was traded. Only the premium was left for the parties to decide. Another important development was the creation of a clearing-house, the Options Clearing Corporation, which clears all listed options transactions. One of the tangible advantages of this was that transactions were henceforth cleared through electronic computation and the debiting and crediting of accounts, thus marking a departure from the cumbersome practice of physically transferring securities. There are now no physical securities to deliver or receive and all accounts are cleared on the next business day after the trade. On that day the buyer is credited with the option and debited the amount of premium. The seller is debited the option and credited the premium.

An option may be defined as the right, but not the obligation, to buy (in the case of a call option) a particular item at a predetermined price on or before a specific date.[3] It is basically a forward or futures contract that may be cancelled prior to maturity if one of the two parties involved chooses to do so. The party with the cancellation privilege is the buyer of the option. Whereas a futures contract involves an obligation for both the buyer and seller to perform on the contract, in options the traders mainly buy a right to buy or a right to sell the underlying asset without the need to make or accept delivery. An option is a suitable tool for the currency manager who has a view as to future exchange rate movements but is not absolutely certain that the direction of change will be as he or she anticipates, and wishes to reduce the losses that would arise in the event of his forecast being incorrect. Options are of three types: calls, puts and doubles.

A call option is a contract that confers on the buyer of the option the right to buy a specified asset from the clearing-house at a predetermined price (exercise price) during a specified period of time. The clearing-house is consequently under obligation to sell the underlying asset to the option buyer.

A put option confers on the option buyer the right to sell the underlying asset to the clearing-house at a fixed price during a specified period of time. The buyer of the option pays the price of option, or the premium, to the seller, which entitles the buyer to buy or to sell, but the seller has an obligation to perform when the buyer exercises the option. The option buyer is not obliged to buy or sell the underlying commodity or the futures contract; he may let the option lapse, in which case he only loses the premium he paid. The option premium resembles the insurance premium that is paid as protection money against misfortune, such as fire or flood.[4]

A distinction needs to be drawn here between 'European-type' and 'American-type' options. The former can be exercised on one date only: the expiry date. The latter may be exercised on any business day up to the expiry date. American-type options provide greater flexibility, and the choice of date increases the likelihood of a profit being made. Accordingly, it is to be expected that an American-type option will involve a higher premium than that of the European-type option.[5]

The call option resembles a futures contract as both involve the future delivery of an item at an agreed-upon price. This obvious similarity occasionally leads people to make the mistake of considering a futures contract an option. But while the seller in a futures contract is allowed some flexibility concerning the delivery date and grade, both parties are nevertheless obliged to complete the transaction either by a reversing trade or actual delivery. In the case of an option, there is no obligation of any kind on the part of the holder, but only a right to buy or to sell a specified amount of a real or financial asset at a specified price during a specified period. Whereas it costs nothing (except for margin requirements) to enter into a forward or futures contract, the purchase of an option requires an up front payment.[6]

In addition to the two types of options outlined above, there is also a third variety known as a double option, which provides the taker with the right either to buy from, or sell to, the grantor a specified quantity of commodity or a specified futures contract during a fixed period at a predetermined price. In essence, the double option is no more than a put and call option combined. The expiration date in all options is predetermined and varies from anything between one day and two years. By this date, the purchaser of the option must declare his or her intention to exercise the option and take physical position, sell the option, or let the option lapse.

An option can be 'in the money', 'out of the money' or 'at the money'. An option is 'in the money' if exercising the option would result in a profit (disregarding premium). A call option is 'in the money' if the market price of the underlying stock is higher than the strike price of the option. An option is 'out of the money' if exercising the option will result in a loss (disregarding premium). A call option on a certain stock is 'out of the money' if the market price of the stock is lower than the strike price of the option. An option is 'at the money' when the market price of the stock and the option's strike price are the same. The option is neither in nor out of the money.[7]

Long and short sales in options are similar to those in other securities. Someone who has purchased a put or a call three weeks ago and sells it today, is selling long. He owns the option. If someone does not own the option and sells (or writes) one, he is selling short. If the option is exercised, the short seller will have to make arrangements to live up to the contract. The option writer thus writes (or sells) an option in one of two ways: 'covered' and 'uncovered'. A covered writer has access to the underlying security, whereas an uncovered writer has nothing but an open contract. Obviously, uncovered writing poses a greater risk than covered writing.[8]

Options on Futures

Trading options on futures is similar to trading options on other underlying assets. Just as there are options on actual commodities, there are options on the futures contracts concerning those commodities. There are a number of goods, besides stocks and currencies, for which options are traded; for many of these goods there are also futures contracts and options on the future contracts. The only difference to note here is that options on futures are a three-tiered instrument. The primary trading vehicle (the options contract) is a derivative instrument whose underlying interest is another derivative contract (the futures contract), whose value, in turn, can depend on anything from stocks or bonds to currencies and indices.[9]

The evolution that began with listed stock options and financial futures eventually led to the merger of options and futures, and to the creation of options on futures contracts. Known as futures options, they represent listed puts and calls on a select but growing number of standardised futures contracts. They give the buyer the right to buy (calls) or sell (puts) a single standardised futures contract for a specified period of time at a predetermined strike price. They have the same standardised striking prices, expiration dates and quotation system as other listed options.

Futures options are, in other words, valued like any other listed puts and calls by reference to the differences in the option's striking price and the market price of the underlying futures contract. Traded options are particularly attractive instruments because they not only provide all the same rights to buy or sell the underlying commodity futures contract, they are also instruments which may be traded in their own right.

The prime rationale for the existence of options on futures is a function of their different price performance characteristics in comparison with futures contracts. Taking a position in the futures market means that one is immediately exposed to a theoretically unlimited risk of loss. This is not the case for the buyer of an option. Another reason for preferring options on futures to options on the physical commodity itself is the economy and ease of exercise. To exercise an option on the commodity itself, one must have the entire cash value of the striking price. To exercise an option over a futures contract, the amount of money involved is basically limited to the option premium. Another difference between futures and options is that futures attract margin requirements, whereas buying options require no margin deposits.[10] Futures are symmetrical, that is, the seller (short) and the buyer (long) are subject to symmetrical gains and losses: the buyer gains by the amount that the seller loses and vice versa; their rights and obligations regarding delivery and payment are also symmetrical. Options are asymmetrical in that the buyers and sellers of options have unequal rights and obligations. The option buyer has the right to initiate the delivery process at any time, while the seller is under obligation to comply. Thus the long is in a superior position because the long has the right and the short has the obligation. The long's potential losses are confined to the size of the purchase premium, while profits are potentially unlimited. This asymmetry also enables contingencies and unforeseen events to be hedged more effectively with options than with futures or forward contracts.[11]

The Option Clearance Corporation (OCC) performs much the same sort of function for options markets as the clearing-house does for futures markets. It guarantees that the option writer will fulfil his or her obligations under the terms of the option contract, and keeps a record of all long and short positions. All option trades must be cleared through a member. Members are required to have a certain minimum amount of capital and to contribute to a special fund that can be used if any member defaults on an option obligation.[12] Moreover, both the exchanges and the OCC, as well as federal and state authorities, have rules which regulate the behaviour of traders. In general, options markets have demonstrated a willingness to regulate themselves. 'There have been no major scandals or defaults by OCC members. Investors can have a high level of confidence in the way the market is run.'[13]

Not all options are traded on exchanges. Some interest rate and foreign exchange options are traded over the counter between two financial institutions or between a financial institution and one of its corporate clients. Over the counter options have the advantage that their expiration dates and strike prices do not have to correspond with the standards of an exchange.[14]

Trading futures is similar to trading futures options in that both devices are bought and sold, the quantities and contract months must be designated, and each has a price associated with it. Contract months in options not only relate to the underlying futures contract, but also determine the expiry date. Futures options expiration dates are usually in the preceding month to the underlying futures month. Option traders need to articulate two more modifiers than are articulated in futures trading: strike price and whether the option is a put or a call.

The main difference between a futures contract and a futures option contract is that the latter permits traders to participate in futures markets without actually having to deal in the underlying commodity or financial instrument itself. When a trader buys a futures contract, he effectively owns the commodity. If exercised, the futures contract obliges the holder to take delivery of the commodity or instrument. If a futures options contract is exercised, the holder takes delivery of the futures contract, not the commodity. The options contract holder, in other words, becomes the futures contract holder.

There are three ways to get out of option positions: to let them expire worthless, to offset, and to exercise. Most often, options are offset. To offset an option means to trade it back to the market by taking an opposite position and the quantity, month, strike price and option type must be the same.

A futures option buyer has the right to exercise at any time, which means converting the option into a futures position. Most of the time an option is worth more when it is traded back to the market. However, as the expiration day approaches and/or the option becomes deep in the money, exercising may be the most profitable method of disposing of the option. Once the option is exercised, the futures position is assumed and the option no longer exists.

An option is left to expire and becomes worthless if it remains 'out of the money', in which case neither offsetting nor exercising it would be advisable, and the option holder would simply let it expire and limit his loss to the cost of the premium.[15]

NOTES

1. Daniel Kane, *Principles of International Finance*, London, Croom Helm, 1988, p. 281; Courtney, *Investor's Guide*, pp. 98, 101.
2. James T. Colburn, *Trading in Options on Futures*, New York, New York Institute of Finance, 1990, pp. 3-5.
3. Fink, *Futures Trading*, p. 618; Colburn, *Trading in Options*, p. 5.
4. Relly, *Investment Analysis*, p. 761ff; Hull, *Introduction*, p. 4; Fink, *Futures Trading*, p. 619.
5. Keith Redhead, *Introduction to Financial Futures and Option*, Cambridge, Mass., Woodhead Faulkner, 1990, p. 82.
6. Gitman, *Fundamentals*, p. 212.
7. Fink, *Futures Trading*, p. 630; Colburn, *Trading in Options*, pp. 14-17.
8. Colburn, *Trading in Option*, p. 8.
9. Ibid, p. VIII.
10. Gitman, *Fundamentals*, pp. 545-6; Courtney, *Investor's Guide*, p. 108.
11. Teweles, *Commodity Futures*, p. 212ff; Kane, *Principles*, p. 288.
12. Hull, *Introduction*, p. 181.
13. Ibid., p. 182.
14. Ibid., p. 185.
15. Colburn, *Trading in Option*, pp. 78-81.

CHAPTER SEVENTEEN

Options (*al-Ikhtiyārāt*) from the Islamic Legal Perspective

Arab writers have used different terms for options. The most commonly used term is the phrase *al-ʿamaliyyāt al-sharṭiyyah al-ājilah* (lit., deferred conditional transactions). Three types of options have been discussed by Arab writers: (simple) options, whether call or put, known as *ʿamaliyyāt sharṭiyyah basīṭah*; double options, *ʿamaliyyāt sharṭiyyah murakkabah*, which combine both call and put options and entitle the option holder to act in either or both capacities; and double quantity options, or *ʿamaliyyāt sharṭiyyah muḍāʿafah*. The latter are a peculiarity, it seems, of the Egyptian futures, in which the trader is granted the right to double the quantity of the underlying commodity so as to increase his profit, not merely through the option of whether or not to execute the contract, but by doubling the stipulated quantity of that contract at a predetermined price agreed upon at the time of contract.

Published materials on options and futures in Arabic are still scanty and no consistency in the use of terminology can yet be verified. I have here preferred the term *al-ikhtiyārāt,* used recently by ʿAbd al-Wahhāb Abū Sulaymān, simply because it is concise and strikes a note with the parallel term *al-khiyārāt*, which is a familiar theme of *fiqh* that we also need to explore in the following pages. Yet for reasons that will be explained later, in his article, 'Al-Ikhtiārāt: Darāsah Fiqhiyyah Taḥlīliyyah Muqāranah (Options: A Comparative Legal Analysis)', Abū Sulaymān has not discussed the varieties of options and, as a result, no specific terms have been identified for any of the three types of options mentioned above. Abū Sulaymān has, however, used three other related terms which merit recognition, namely, *ikhtiyār al-ṭalab*, *ikhtiyār al-dafʿ* and *fatrat al-ikhtiyār* for call option, put option, and option period respectively. By utilising Abū Sulaymān's terminology, we may designate *al-ikhtiyārāt al-basīṭah*, *al-ikhtiyārāt al-murakkabah* and *al-ikhtiyārāt al-muḍāʿafah* for simple options (or just options), double options and double quantity respectively—in preference, that is, to the longer phrases that have been used in earlier works.[1]

I have been able to consult the writings of only a handful of Arab writers on the subject of options, and they have all addressed the issue within the purview of the conventional fiqh doctrine of *al-khiyārāt* (options). The origins of *al-khiyārāt* are clearly traceable in the *Sunnah*, but the elaborate details and sub-divisions of *al-khiyārāt* into various types have all been developed, as a matter of initiative and *ijtihād*, in the juristic writings of the scholars. The basic concept of options, which occurs in the *Sunnah* and in the manuals of *fiqh*, was intended not so much as a new trading formula or a risk-management tool, but as a way to ensure propriety and fairness, as well as to protect the integrity of consent in the completion of contracts. The typical variety of *al-khiyārāt* validated by the *Sunnah* is the option of stipulation (*khiyār al-sharṭ*), which granted the buyer the option within a time frame (of three days or so following the conclusion of contract) to either ratify the contract or revoke it. The ruling of the *Sunnah* has evidently envisaged the eventuality where the buyer does not possess sufficient knowledge of the subject-matter he or she had agreed to buy. A sale of this type cannot be said to be reflective of the true intentions of the buyer, especially if the subject-matter turns out to be defective in a way that is not obvious to the naked eye. Following this, the options that Islamic law has granted are of two types, namely, those which are granted by the law itself regardless of any contractual stipulation, and options which materialise only as a result of a clear provision in the contract. The former variety is basically confined to the option of defect (*khiyār al-ʿayb*) and the option of viewing (*khiyār al-ru'yah*). The law thus grants the buyer an option on account of a material defect, in which case he is automatically entitled to seek revocation of contract on that basis, or when he sees the object he has bought for the first time. But it is the second type of options, that is, contractual options, such as the option of stipulation (*khiyār al-sharṭ*), or the option of identification (*khiyār al-taʿyīn*) that are of greater interest to our present purposes. All options, whether put, call or double, that are practised in conjunction with trading in stocks or in futures are, in fact, contractual options created by virtue of an agreement. *Al-khiyārāt,* in the Islamic law of contract, are generally seen to be anomalous in the sense that they tend to interfere with the integrity of contractual obligation. It is thus stated that once a contract is properly concluded, nothing should hinder its binding character or its enforcement. This is one aspect of the juristic discourse of the scholars on the subject of *al-khiyārāt* which is, however, not relevant for us here. The main future of the Islamic legal concept of *al-khiyārāt* that is of concern to us is that while recognising the basic freedom of contract, and also the binding nature of contract, Islamic law has in the meantime entitled the parties to stipulate that the contract so concluded will become effective only upon further ratification and approval. This is, in essence, the basic rationale of the *Sharīʿah* concept of *al-khiyārāt* that modern writers have utilised in their discourse on the validity or otherwise of trading in options. This approach is evidently based on the assumption that options are contractual stipulations that can be added and attached to an underlying contract. But there are certain aspects of option trading that do not find ready answers in the works of the scholars, and the theory of al-*khiyārāt* has fallen short of providing the necessary solutions. One such issue is whether or not it is lawful to charge a fee for granting an option, and whether an option can be bought and sold as a valuable instrument in its own right. The conventional discourse in *fiqh* envisages *al-khiyārāt* to be an aspect of the contract of sale, an ancillary or incidental aspect of that contract, but not a contract in its own right that could be evaluated and traded separately from the main contract. The issue here is addressed by some within the purview of the *fiqhī* concept of *ḍamān*, or compensation, in conjunction with al-*khiyārāt*. Say, for example, that one of the parties in a contract of sale (usually the seller) grants a privilege, or an option, to the other which might be disadvantageous to the former and he may therefore either grant it free of charge or ask for compensation. The scholarly debate then continues between those who consider such analogies relevant and valid to some of the rulings of *fiqh*, and those who do not, and this is partly why different responses have been recorded on the validity of charging a fee or a premium for options.[2]

An alternative approach has been taken by some writers who attempt to draw a parallel between options trading and the *fiqhī* concept of *al-ʿurbūn* (also rendered as *al-ʿurbān*). The term *ʿurbūn* refers to the earnest money that the seller takes from the buyer with the understanding that it becomes a part of the price in the event when the sale is ratified, but that it will belong to the seller in the event that the buyer fails to ratify his initial agreement. Among the leading schools of *fiqh*, only the Ḥanbalīs have validated *al-ʿurbūn* and the majority have ruled against it on the grounds that the seller has no right to keep the earnest money because it is the property of the buyer and must therefore be returned to him. Then there is the question of whether drawing a parallel between *al-ʿurbūn* (even if its validity is taken for granted) and options trading is accurate given that the basic purpose behind the two transactions is so different. Drawing an analogy between them could be seen as totally inappropriate and, indeed, in the final analysis, such an analogy will be no more than a discrepant analogy (*qiyās maʿ al-fāriq*), which is invalid.[3]

Another issue that has arisen in discussing options is the question of whether a sale is valid if one of the countervalues consists merely of granting a right, or a privilege, as opposed to a tangible asset (*māl*) purchased in exchange for a price. Here, some juristic detail does emerge as to whether a non-tangible asset, service or usufruct (*manfaʿah*), that has no concrete reality and existence at the time of contract, can be bought or sold in the same way as a tangible asset, or *māl*. Clearly, options partake in the nature of *manfaʿah* and may therefore not qualify as *māl*. Whereas the Shāfiʿīs and Ḥanbalīs include usufruct under the definition of property, the Ḥanafīs and Mālikīs do not. But the scholars of later periods (*al-muta'akhkhirun*) have generally included usufruct in the definition of *māl*.

The basic validity of *khiyār* is proven by the authority of a *ḥadīth* in which it is reported that Ḥabbān ibn Munqidh complained to the Prophet ﷺ that he was the victim of frequent cheating in sales, to which the Prophet ﷺ responded that, 'When you conclude a sale, you may say that there must be no fraud and you reserve for yourself an option lasting three days'.

قال رسول الله ﷺ اذا بعت فقل لا خلابه وأنت بالخيار ثلاثا .

But the option of stipulation that is granted by this *ḥadīth* is said to be only valid in regards to non-usurious sales. As for sales of usurable items such as currencies and barter sales of foodstuffs, they must be concluded without delay and they are not amenable to options. The option of stipulation is valid only with regard to contracts that are open to the possibility of cancellation, and we may thus preclude contracts such as marriage and divorce, or contracts which can be unilaterally repealed by either party, such as gifts or partnership, from the purview of this *ḥadīth*.

There is also the evidence of the *ḥadīth* of ʿAbd Allāh ibn ʿUmar to the effect that 'the parties to a sale are free to revoke their agreement before they part company except in a sale that is subjected to option'.

المتبايعان بالخيار ما لم يتفرقا الا بيع الخيار .

This *ḥadīth* confirms the substance of the previous *ḥadīth* on the basic validity of *khiyār*, but it does so in conjunction with the meeting of contract: it grants to both buyer and seller in an option sale the privilege of reserving for themselves the right to either revoke or ratify their initial agreement. They may, in other words, part company and leave the meeting of contract without breaking the conceptual continuity of that meeting if they have agreed on an option. The rationale for such an option may well be that the buyer may be uninformed and need time to consult another person, a relative or a business associate, to enable him to make a final decision.[4]

The leading *madhāhib* are in agreement on the validity of the option of stipulation (*khiyār al-sharṭ*) either by the buyer or seller, or both. An option may even be held in favour of a third party to approve the sale in order to make it effective and binding within a specified period of time. If both parties to the sale have stipulated options/conditions of their own, then the contract becomes effective if they both ratify it and it naturally collapses if they both revoke it. Should there be a disagreement as to whether the sale has been ratified or revoked, the plea in respect of its revocation shall prevail over that of ratification.

There is general agreement that the option period begins as of the moment of the conclusion of contract, but the scholars have differed as to the duration of a valid option of stipulation. The Ḥanafīs and Shāfiʿīs maintain that it should not exceed three days, partly because this is what the *ḥadīth* specifies, but also because *khiyār* is essentially *ultra vires* and no liberal recourse to it should therefore be encouraged. Imām Mālik has, on the other hand, taken a more flexible stance towards the understanding of the *ḥadīth* by saying that it mentions three days in a figurative sense merely to illustrate the concept. The actual duration of an option may thus be determined by relating the option period to the subject-matter of sale. The option period may thus be confined to three days in the case of the sale and purchase of animals and clothes, but it may be extended to a month or even two months in the case of buying a house. Imām ibn Ḥanbāl has held that an option may be for any length of time and that it is a matter entirely of agreement between the contracting parties. Even if the parties agree on an option of stipulation in principle without specifying any period for it, this is still valid according to Imām ibn Ḥanbal himself, although the ruling of the Ḥanbalī school, as Ibn Qudāmah has stated, is that it should be for a specified period so as to prevent conflict, uncertainty and *gharar*. This is also the view of the two disciples of Abū Ḥanīfah, Abū Yūsuf and al-Shaybānī. In validating an open-ended *khiyār*, Imām Ibn Ḥanbal has cited the *ḥadīth* to the effect that 'Muslims are bound by their stipulations unless it be a stipulation which declares unlawful what is permissible or permits what is unlawful'.

المسلمون على شروطهم الا شرطا احل حراما أو حرم حلالا .

The ownership of the subject-matter during the option period remains with the seller, who is responsible for loss or damage unless the buyer has actually taken possession of it, in which case responsibility for loss and damage will transfer to the buyer. However, according to Imām Abū Ḥanīfah, only the option holder is responsible for loss: if the buyer alone has stipulated the option he will be responsible. But the scholars have differed on this, as many tend to relate the question of responsibility for loss (*ḍamān*) to ownership, and generally maintain that *ḍamān* transfers to the buyer upon the transfer of ownership. Furthermore, in an option sale the buyer is normally not entitled to use the object for his benefit during the option period but he may use it for the purposes of investigation and testing.[5]

As for the validity or otherwise of charging a fee, or premium, for options, this is a matter that falls under the general subject of contractual stipulation, a subject that has invoked different responses from the *madhāhib*, despite the affirmative nature of the source evidence. The issue acquires a religious dimension when it is put in such terms as saying that contractual stipulations by the parties should not be allowed to circumvent or override the given mandates of the *Sharīᶜah* on contracts. The *Sharīᶜah* has determined the essential elements of a number of nominate contracts and any options/stipulations that are inserted therein should not exceed the basic framework that the law has laid down in relation to various contracts. The parties, in other words, are not at total liberty to stipulate what they please. Yet the basic validity of *khiyār* is not in doubt. We have already stated that the *Sunnah* entitles the parties to insert stipulations in contracts so as to meet their legitimate needs and what may be deemed to be of benefit to them. The liberty that is granted here is nevertheless subject to the general condition that contractual stipulations may not overrule the clear injunctions of the *Sharīᶜah* on *ḥalāl* and *ḥarām*. Provided that this limitation is observed, there is in principle no restriction on the nature and type of stipulation that the parties may wish to insert into a contract. The *Sunnah* has clearly granted this liberty in the interest of fairness and the overall integrity of transactions. The issue has invoked responses from the *madhāhib* that may vary in form but they generally tend to uphold the view that stipulations should be appropriate to and harmonious with the essence of contracts (*mulā'im li'l-ᶜaqd, muqtaḍā al-ᶜaqd*). This is the common Ḥanafī-Shāfiᶜī perspective on contractual stipulations, in which the latter are held to be valid when they are in harmony with the essence of a contract. It would thus be valid for the seller to ask the buyer, in a deferred sale, to provide a guarantor, or a surety in the form of a mortgage or a pawn. Provided that this is clearly stipulated and the parties have both agreed on it, it is binding on both sides.[6] The Mālikīs are even more explicit in validating these and other such stipulations that may have a financial value when, for example, the buyer stipulates that the goods must be transported to a certain locality, or that delivery or payment be postponed to a future date, and the like. There is, in other words, no objection, from the point of view of *Sharīʿah*, to any stipulations which entitle the parties to secure benefits.

In validating contractual stipulations, the Ḥanbalīs are the most liberal of the schools in laying emphasis on the basic freedom of contract and the parties' liberty to make stipulations as they please. Stipulations that fulfil a legitimate need, realise a benefit or convenience, or help to remove hardship and facilitate the easy flow of commercial transactions are generally valid as a matter of principle, the Ḥanbalīs maintain, and not by way of concessions or as a contrary to the norm (*khilāf al-qiyās*) as the Ḥanafīs and Shāfiʿīs tend to believe. To Ibn Taymiyyah and his disciple Ibn Qayyim al-Jawziyyah, the basic validity of contractual stipulations is not a matter of concession or exception to the normal rules. On the contrary, they are valid on the same Qur'ānic authority that validate contracts on the basis of mutual agreement.[7] In response to the question of whether certain types of stipulations might amount to a contract-within-a-contract and therefore fall within the purview of the *ḥadīth* that is prohibitive on this, Ibn Qayyim says that the *ḥadīth* here quoted is unreliable. The *ḥadīth* simply declares that 'the Prophet ﷺ prohibited a sale and [an overriding] condition',

نهى النبى ﷺ عن بيع وشرط .

and is not only spurious and defective from the standpoint of authenticity and transmission, but also in that it is in conflict with other more reliable *ḥadīth*, as well as with general consensus (*ijmāʿ*) and the normative rules of *Sharīʿah*. According to one *ḥadīth*, for example, the Prophet ﷺ bought a camel from one Jābir and agreed to Jābir's stipulation that he wished to ride the camel to Medina and deliver it afterwards. Then there is the *ḥadīth* in which the Prophet ﷺ has said: 'The one who sells a slave who owns property, the property shall belong to the seller unless the buyer stipulates otherwise'.

من ابتاع عبدا وله مال فماله للبائع الا ان يشترطه المبتاع .

Clearly, these *ḥadīth* have validated stipulations that were additional and extraneous to the sale, yet were approved of. According to yet another *ḥadīth*, the Prophet ﷺ has said: 'Whoever sells a palm tree that has borne fruit, the fruit belongs to the seller unless the buyer stipulates otherwise.'

من ابتاع نخلا بعد أن يثمر فثمرتها للبائع الا أن يشترطه المبتاع .

'This is nothing other than sale combined with [an extraneous] stipulation (*bayʿ wa sharṭ*) which is explicitly validated by authentic *Sunnah*', writes Ibn Qayyim. As for the conflict with *ijmāᶜ* (on the alleged *ḥadīth*), the consensus of the *ummah* affirms the permissibility of stipulations in the contract of sale in respect of taking a security deposit or a pawn, providing a guarantor, deferment (*al-ta'jīl*) and the option of stipulation. All of these are in the nature of combining sale with a stipulation and their validity is generally supported by *ijmāᶜ*.[8]

The affirmation outlined here relates not only to the parties' freedom to insert stipulations in contracts, but also allows monetary compensation or a fee to be asked for by the one who grants an option or a privilege to the other. If the seller is entitled to stipulate a security deposit or a pawn then it is a mere extension of the same logic that he may charge the buyer and impose a fee or demand for compensation in respect of such options and stipulations that are to the latter's advantage. When the buyer, for example, stipulates that he will ratify or revoke the contract within a week or a month, this may well prove to be costly to the seller and he may therefore charge a fee/compensation for granting the option. We can thus conclude that options may carry a premium and there should be no objection to this.

The fact that options are sold for a premium paid at the time of contract also differentiates options from futures in that at least one of the countervalues in options is payable at the time of contract, and this should, if anything, make the juristic hurdle somewhat easier. The option price (premium) is normally specified and paid up front; the option period which ends by the expiration date is also clearly specified, there remaining no uncertainty of the kind that might be classified as *gharar*. The option premium is paid in exchange for a right/privilege that is granted to the option holder and there is nothing objectionable in this.

The substance of my analysis here is sustained in the writings of at least three commentators whose works I have consulted and, although my research does not follow the approaches taken by them on certain issues, we tend to concur in our conclusions. I have consulted the works of Shahhat al-Jundī, Yūsuf Sulaymān and ᶜAlī ᶜAbd al-Qādir respectively, all of whom affirm the basic validity of options trading and come together on the conclusion that the option buyer pays for a right, or an advantage, and the seller who grants this is entitled to be paid for it. They have also drawn attention to the carefully regulated procedures of trading options which virtually eliminate uncertainty about the essential aspects of transactions, so much so that there is no likelihood of disputes arising between the parties. This analysis is then extended to all varieties of options, including double options and double quantity options, all of which may be seen as a manifestation of the valid exercise of the freedom of contract.[9]

Aḥmad Muḥayyuddīn Ḥassan has, on the other hand, taken a negative view of options trading on two grounds, the first of which is that the basic notion of *khiyār al-sharṭ* (the option of stipulation) is anomalous to the norm and is merely tolerated, which is why it is confined to three days. The way in which options are designed and traded, on the other hand, turns the restrictive terms of *khiyār al-sharṭ* into a basic permissibility, which marks a departure from the stated guidelines of *Sharīʿah*. This is in essence, as we noted earlier, the argument that the Ḥanafī and Shāfiʿī jurists have advanced on the subject, and it has, in fact, been addressed and effectively refuted in the writings of Ḥanbalī jurists. As noted above, Ibn Qayyim al-Jawziyyah, has departed from the majority position and reached the conclusion that options and contractual stipulations are valid as a matter of principle, and not by way of exception or as a departure from the norm, as Ḥassan asserts. The second objection that Ḥassan raises against options trading is that they are unfair and work to the distinct advantage of one party to the total detriment of the other. 'One of the contracting parties is granted open opportunity to realise profit at the expense of the other.' The option holder is granted the open choice of whether or not to finalise the sale, and he may pose as buyer or seller, or both, thereby allowing himself to maximise his profit etc. 'There is no doubt', Ḥassan glibly adds, that 'this is oppression and injustice (*ẓulm wa jawr*).'[10] This analysis is, however, inaccurate, since it is based on a wrong premise. For one thing, it should be obvious that the option holder does not always make profits, as Ḥassan suggests, but may make a loss and lose his premium as a result. Clearly, the option holder has not locked himself in a no-loss situation; Ḥassan has not acknowledged this. Another point is that the option holder may well be acting as a hedger who wishes to protect himself against exorbitant losses, and by buying options merely tries to minimise the prospects of a bigger loss. Finally, the issue of oppression and injustice is somewhat overstated here, simply because the parties enter an agreement and the option buyer pays for the advantage he is granted. The price that he pays is determined not by him or his agent, but by the exchange authorities, and the question of manipulation and unfair advantage is therefore not relevant.

ʿAbd al-Wahhāb Abū Sulaymān, a member of the Fiqh Academy of Jeddah (note that there are two Fiqh Academies in Saudi Arabia, of which the other is based in Mecca) has also passed a prohibitive judgement on options trading. His analysis of this transaction differs from the other commentators I mentioned above in that Abū Sulaymān has not discussed options trading in the general *fiqhī* context of *khiyārāt* (options), but has analysed it as a contract in its own right—that is, independently of its underlying contract. The author has not explained why he chose not to relate his discussion to the option of stipulation (*khiyār al-sharṭ*), or why he chose to dissociate options from the main contract or the underlying commodity over which they proceed for, indeed options are derivative instruments that derive their basic rationale from association with another transaction or contract. The notion of granting the trader a choice of whether to ratify or cancel an underlying contract is therefore essential to options. Thus relating option trading to *khiyār al-sharṭ* has the advantage that it covers the issues surrounding the underlying transaction, as well as addressing the question of whether or not an option can have a financial value of its own. In addition, Abū Sulaymān has neither acknowledged nor discussed the other writers on the subject, including the ones I mentioned earlier, who have discussed option trading in conjunction with *khiyārāt*, nor has he discussed the approach taken by them in their publications.

Having stated that an option is essentially a contract of sale in its own right, Abū Sulaymān then sets out to address the basic components of this contract, including the role, for example, of the brokers and the clearing-house, the countervalues involved, whether the subject-matter of sale in options qualifies for the juridical description of property (*māl*), the deferment period, and so forth. One of the key questions that has become the focus of Abū Sulaymān's discussion of the validity of options is whether it is lawful to attach a monetary value to an option, and whether the grantor of an option is within his rights to charge a fee for writing/granting an option. It is interesting to note that Abū Sulaymān's response to this question is clearly affirmative and he arrives at this through drawing an analogy with the sale of *ʿurbūn,* which is valid in Ḥanbalī law but which the majority have rejected. In Abū Sulaymān's words, 'charging a price for a call option whereby the buyer may then decide to exercise the option and make it a part of the price [sic], does not affect the validity of this contract—provided that it is valid in other respects—but it may be seen in the category of *ʿurbūn* sale (*min qabīl bayʿ al-ʿurbūn*), which consists of paying a part of the price and the buyer then stipulates that the deposit money should become a part of the price if he ratifies the sale but that it should belong to the seller otherwise'. In the event that the buyer decides not to ratify the sale, the deposit money in *ʿurbūn* becomes the property of the seller and the transaction is valid in either case—that is, whether the deposit money is kept by the seller or not, according to the Ḥanbalī *madhhab,* and the *Sharīʿah* validates this transaction.

Abū Sulaymān further adds that the fact that the price is specified and there is no ambiguity about the subject-matter's quantity or about terms also means that the transaction in question fulfils another basic requirement, which is that of a valid price. But then he adds, somewhat erroneously, that neither the price (*al-thaman*) nor the subject-matter (*muthman*) qualifies for the juridical description of *māl* (property), for the basic purpose of a sale is 'the exchange of one commodity for another and both must qualify as *māl*'. He then observes that 'the subject-matter of an option is a right (*ḥaqq*), and a right that is pure and simple (*al-ḥaqq al-mujarrad*) is neither a tangible commodity nor usufruct; it cannot therefore be the proper subject-matter of contract'.[11] This is a debatable statement, but the more fundamental error in Abū Sulaymān analysis is his disqualification of both of the contervalues in options from constituting *māl* proper. For the option price or premium is normally paid in cash, and there is no doubt that the price here is *māl*. The author repeats the same factual error in the next line on the same page when he writes that options trading is unlawful because 'neither the price nor the subject-matter (*al-thaman wa'l-muthman*) is taken into possession as they are both absent at the time of contract, and this turns the contract into *bayᶜ al-kāli' bi'l-kāli'* (or the sale of one debt for another). To validate a sale of this kind, it is necessary that at least one of the countervalues is prompt, and that the other, which is deferred, is accurately described so as to prevent disputes'. This statement is once again based on a wrong premise simply because one of the countervalues in options, namely the price or premium, is normally paid and taken into possession at the time of contract and the subject-matter of options is accurately identified. Following the registration of contract, the Options Clearing Corporation clears the relevant accounts of the parties to the transaction within twenty-four hours. Abū Sulaymān's statement here would be applicable to futures contracts but not to options. It seems that the author has perhaps failed to notice that in a futures contract nothing changes hands at the time of contract, but that this is not the case in options, where the premium is paid at the time of contract.

The rest of this chapter addresses the sale known as *bayᶜ al-ᶜurbūn*, which I have frequently mentioned, and which closely resembles options, especially that aspect of options relating to the payment of a non-returnable premium. *ᶜUrbūn* refers to a sale in which the buyer deposits earnest money with the seller as part payment of the price in advance, but agrees that if he fails to ratify the contract, he will forfeit the deposit money which the seller can then keep. The majority of scholars have held this to be invalid and considered it akin to misappropriating the property of others. Imām Aḥmad ibn Ḥanbal has, on the other hand, held it to be permissible, saying that ᶜUmar ibn al-Khaṭṭāb practised it, and that the latter's son, ᶜAbd Allāh ibn ᶜUmar, has also confirmed it to be valid. Among the followers of the Prophet's Companions (*ṭābiᶜūn*), certain prominent figures, including Saᶜīd ibn al-Musayyib, Ibn Sīrīn, Nāfiᶜ ibn al-Ḥārith and Zayd ibn Aslam, have also held it to be lawful.[12] The majority have, on the other hand, relied on a *ḥadīth* narrated by Ibn

ʿAbbās, and recorded in the *Muwaṭṭā* of Imām Mālik and in *Sunan Ibn Mājah,* which simply declares that 'the Prophet ﷺ prohibited the sale of *ʿurbūn*'.

أن النبي ﷺ نهى عن بيع العربون .

Imām Ibn Ḥanbal has, however, considered this *ḥadīth* to be weak, and in validating the *ʿurbūn* he has relied on the report of Nāfiʿ ibn al-Ḥārith, Caliph ʿUmar's officer in Mecca, which is to the effect that he bought from Safwān ibn Umayyah a prison house for the Caliph ʿUmar for 4,000 dirham on condition that if the Caliph approved of it, the deal would be final, otherwise he (Safwān) would be given 400 dirham (that is, about ten per cent of the actual price as compensation). In a sale of this kind, the buyer asks the seller to reserve the goods for him and agrees not to ask for the deposit back if he changes his mind. The Ḥanbalī school has validated this sale as it is devoid of vitiating elements. The majority have, on the other hand, prohibited the seller from taking any money for waiting or withholding the sale.[13]

In his analysis and comparison of the evidence for and against the *ʿurbūn* sale, al-Qaradāwī has stated that the opponents of *ʿurbūn* have relied on *ḥadīth*, and also on the argument that *ʿurbūn* is premised on a condition which entails the appropriation by the seller of the buyer's property without any exchange. As for the authenticity of this *ḥadīth*, al-Qaradāwī also concludes that it is unreliable, and that the evidence in it is contrary to another *ḥadīth*, recorded in *Nayl al-Awṭār* (vol. V, 162), to the effect that, 'The Messenger of God ﷺ was asked concerning the sale of *ʿurbān* (a variation of *ʿurbūn*) and he declared it permissible'.

أن رسول الله ﷺ سئل عن العربان في البيع فأحله .

But then this is also said to be a *mursal* (disconnected) *ḥadīth*, and its chain of transmitters includes a weak narrator. Having said this, al-Qaradāwī then observes that the issue should consequently be determined on rational grounds, and here we note that Imām Aḥmad ibn Ḥanbal has relied on the precedent of ʿUmar ibn al-Khaṭṭāb and has not considered *ʿurbūn* to fall into the category of unlawful appropriation. This ruling, al-Qaradāwī adds, is more suitable to our own times and in greater harmony with the spirit of *Sharīʿah*, which seeks to remove hardship and bring ease to people.[14] Here I may also refer to another prominent scholar, Muṣṭafā al-Zarqa, who has pointed out the utility of *ʿurbūn*, and therefore of options, in modern commerce and the support it has received in general custom and legislation. *ʿUrbūn* provides a useful formula that can be utilised to facilitate a credible commitment, or a surety that the buyer will not change his mind after finalising a sale but, if he did, then the seller could be compensated for a possible loss that might be caused as a result. The need for such an assurance is all the more evident in modern times, when large orders have to be entertained by making elaborate preparations that involve a chain of other subsidiary transactions, and which incur additional expenditures. It is quite likely that the seller who reserves his goods or manufactures them for the purpose, and waits until the buyer ratifies the sale, may lose the opportunity of selling his goods or may fail to sell them for a good price, in which case he should be entitled to compensation, and *ʿurbūn* responds to this need.[15]

I have argued earlier that the basic rationale of options resemble that of *ʿurbūn*, especially in the sense that both can be used as risk reduction strategies, or methods by which traders might wish to give themselves flexibility before committing themselves to large contracts. Suppose that a bakery owner wishes to expand his business and thinks that the current market price of $2.50 per bushel of wheat is reasonable. He may want to lock-in the current market price for six or nine months ahead, and yet because of the elements of uncertainty in the success of his expansion plan, he may choose to tread cautiously and decide to limit his possible losses to a small amount, while still being able to reserve the price level for the next several months. This he can do by means of buying a call option on, say, ten wheat contracts of 5000 bushels each, but instead of committing himself to the full price of such a large contract (i.e., $12,500 x 10 = $125,000), he may decide to pay an option premium of $100 per contract. This would mean that he would have limited his possible loss to only $1,000. The basic notion of *ʿurbūn* can also operate along similar lines: the buyer risks a small amount of money to give himself flexibility and also to limit his possible losses to a much smaller amount.

In conclusion, whichever formula we might choose, either that of options (*al-khiyārāt*) or *ʿurbūn*, options trading in general provides a beneficial mode of trading both as a risk reduction strategy and a means by which the seller can be compensated for the privilege he grants to the buyer. Although *khiyārāt* and *ʿurbūn* share the same rationale, and can both provide the necessary juristic support for options trading, they are nevertheless not identical and can each be utilised for their different purposes. I still prefer to utilise the theory of *khiyārāt* as a juridical premise for validating options. I say this not only because of the unequivocal support that is found for *al-khiyārāt* in the *Sunnah*, but also because the basic concept involved in the option of stipulation strikes a close note with options as a trading formula and a derivative instrument that is associated with an underlying contract. *Al-khiyārāt* are essentially predicated on the basic freedom of the individual in respect of legitimate contractual stipulations that are deemed to be of benefit, and this I believe offers a sound juridical foundation for validating options.

To sum up, this chapter has discussed the different approaches that Muslim scholars have taken in order to verify the validity or otherwise of options trading in Islamic law. While some have preferred to subsume trading in options under the Islamic legal concept of contractual stipulations, or *al-khiyārāt*, others have drawn an analogy with *ʿurbūn*, in which an intending purchaser lays down with the seller a deposit as good faith money, which is, however, non-returnable in the event that he does not proceed with the bargain. In yet a third approach, which to the best of my knowledge is taken by only one writer, Abū Sulaymān, options trading is considered as an independent transaction, that is to say, independently of its underlying assets. Research studies on the various questions that have been raised along the line are on the whole interesting, as we can see that some of the crucial issues, such as the validity of charging a fee for granting an option, and whether or not an option can be considered a saleable asset (*māl*), have on the whole received affirmative responses from these investigations. There is clearly no problem at all regarding the period for which an option is written, simply because the deferment of a bargain to a future date underscores the very essence of a contractual option or *khiyār*.

With regard to the length of the option period, we have noted that the Mālikī and the Ḥanbalī schools have taken a fairly liberal stance on the time-frame of the *khiyār*. There is of course no charging of interest involved here because the option premium is payable up front, that is, at the time of the contract. The Ḥanbalī scholars Ibn Taymiyyah and Ibn Qayyim al-Jawziyyah have evidently indicated the normative validity of the option of stipulation (*khiyār al-sharṭ*) that others have considered to be *ultra vires*. The conclusion drawn in this analysis, when applied to options trading, is that there is nothing inherently objectionable in granting an option, exercising it over a period of time, or charging a fee for it, and that options trading, like other types of trade, is permissible (*mubāḥ*) and, as such, it is simply an extension of the basic liberty that the Qur'ān has granted to the individual in respect of trading, civil transactions and contracts (2:275 and 5:1). Needless to say, options trading, like all kinds of commerce, can be distorted by malpractice and abuses, and the likelihood of this is perhaps great in options on futures and indeed all options on assets that involve a high level of speculative risk-taking. It is therefore essential that we take a vigilant attitude towards refining our safeguards against malpractice at all levels, including legislation, in-house regulatory procedures and the setting of quantitative position limits on traded options as well as on the underlying assets and instruments on which they proceed.

NOTES

1. Cf. ʿAbd al-Wahhab Ibrāhīm Abū Sulaymān, 'Al-Ikhtiārāt: Darāsah Fiqhiyyah Taḥlīliyyah Muqāranah', *Mujallah al-Buhūth al-Fiqhiyyah al-Muʿāṣarah*, n.15 (4th year), Jamadi al-Awwal 1413/October 1992, pp. 6-38. See also for earlier terminology on options al-Jundī, *Muʿāmalāt al-Burṣah*, pp. 133ff.

2. Cf. al-Jundī, *Muʿāmalāt*, pp. 162-3.

3. Cf. Abū Sulaymān, 'al-Ikhtiyārāt', pp. 32.

4. Ibn Rushd al-Qurṭubī, *Bidāyah*, II, 157ff; al-Shirāzī, *Muhadhdhab*, I, 343; al-Jundī, *Muʿāmalāt*, p. 141ff; Muḥammad Ḥasanayn, *Naẓariyyah Buṭlān al-ʿAqd fi'l-Fiqh al-Islāmī*, Algiers, al-Mu'assasah al-Wataniyyah li'l-Kitāb, 1988, pp. 55-56.

5. Ibn Juzay, *Qawānīn*, pp. 286-7; Ibn Qudāmah, *al-Mughnī*, III, 585; Ibn Rushd al-Qurṭubī, *Bidāyah*, II, 159; Ḥasanayn, *Naẓariyyah Buṭlān al-ʿAqd*, pp. 59-60.

6. Al-Sarakhsī, *al-Mabsūṭ*, XIII, 19; al-Kāsānī, *Badā'iʿ*, V, 171; al-Shirāzī, *al-Muhadhdhab*, I, 356.

7. Al-Ḥaṭṭāb, *Mawāhib al-Jalil li-Sharḥ Mukhtasar Khalīl*, Cairo, Maṭbaʿah al-Saʿādah, 1328AH, IV, 375; Ibn Qudāmah, *al-Mughnī*, IV, 217; Ibn Taymiyyah, *Naẓariyyah al-ʿAqd*, pp. 16, 152.

8. Ibn Qayyim, *Iʿlām*, II, 327.

9. Al-Jundī, *Muʿāmalāt*, p. 151ff; Yūsuf Sulaymān, 'Ra'y al-Tashrīʿ', in *al-Mawsūʿah al-ʿIlmiyyah*, V, 425; al-Qādir, 'Taʿqīb ʿalā Ra'y al-Tashrīʿ', in *al-Mawsūʿah al-ʿIlmiyyah*, V, 441.

10. Ḥasan, *ʿAmal*, pp. 268-71.

11. Abū Sulaymān, 'al-Ikhtiārāt', pp. 32-3.

12. Ibid., p. 33.

13. Ibid.

15. Ibn Rushd al-Qurṭubī, *Bidāyah*, II, 162; Ibn Qudāmah, *al-Mughnī*, IV, 256.

16. Ibn Qudāmah, *al-Mughnī*, IV, 258; al-Qaradāwī, *Sharīʿah al-Islām*, p. 114.

Conclusion

Those who have passed prohibitive judgements on futures and options have not only failed to produce decisive evidence in support of their positions but have done so on the assumption that futures trading has no social utility and has no bearing on the welfare (*maṣlaḥah*) of the people. Their arguments consist of dogmatic negations that fail to provide viable alternatives or explore reasonable solutions. Not one of the critics of futures and options has advanced a fresh perspective on them, and almost all of them have adopted the imitative approach of applying the *fiqh* rules of conventional sale to a new phenomenon. Some have drawn the conclusion that futures are unlawful because they fall short of fulfilling the requirements of *salam*, yet they do so without any effort on their part to see *salam* and futures as two distinct varieties of sale, despite their common features. Most critics have proscribed futures on account of the non-existence of the subject-matter of the sale and their failure to fulfil the requirement of taking the latter into possession (*qabḍ*). Added to this is the point that futures sales amount to the sale of one debt for another, which involves unnecessary risk that verges on gambling. The advocates of these views have quoted some *ḥadīth* in support of their arguments, yet these very arguments, and the manner in which they are related to the *ḥadīth*, are somewhat assumptive and less than convincing. They ignore the fact, for example, that the *ḥadīth* they rely on do not refer to futures but to conventional sales since futures were not known in the early days of Islam. While the critics have shown a tendency to hold on to the concrete instructions of these *ḥadīth*, there is no attempt on their part to relate their positions to the broad and general principles of *Sharīʿah* that might offer a more meaningful solution to some of the problems involved. To neglect the broader instructions of *Sharīʿah* on the principle of permissibility (*ibāḥah*), for example, and the parallel principle that prohibitions can only be established by means of decisive evidence, is simply unjustifiable. The same can be said of the tendency to turn a blind eye to the operational procedures of futures transactions, which are by no means a monolithic phenomenon, and each transaction needs to be carefully examined before a prohibitive judgement can be passed on it. Futures and options, also known as derivatives, are governed by a set of rules and procedures that are unprecedented, and which set them far apart from conventional sales, so much so that applying the manifest terms of a particular *ḥadīth* on *gharar* or on *qabḍ* to futures amounts to no more than the mechanical application of a certain idea to a different reality with no reasoning involved. The prohibitive judgements we have discussed do not even acknowledge the possibility that they might be speculative and doubtful; for they generally speak in definitive terms in declaring futures unlawful and contrary to the principles of *Sharīʿah*. Virtually none of the critics have made any reference to the Qur'ānic verse of *mudāyanah*, or debt (2: 282), which permits transactions involving future obligations for a specified period of time. It is all the more remarkable that neither the critics nor even those who have spoken in support of derivative trading have tried to relate their arguments to this particular passage of the Qur'ān. As stated earlier, the verse is primarily concerned with credit-based transactions that give rise to future obligations, and futures trading clearly falls within its ambit. It would appear that the tenacious hold of *taqlīd*, or imitation, comes in the way of direct recourse to the Qur'ān, so much so that people tend to look for answers not in the Qur'ān, but in the works of the jurists of the past who could only have dealt with the issues that were actually known to them. I take this opportunity to recall once again what Majd al-Dīn ʿAzzām observes, namely, that negative verdicts on futures are all based on speculative (*ẓannī*) evidence which is not in itself enough to justify a prohibition. A prohibitive ruling must be founded on direct and decisive evidence, and none of the critics are able to produce this.

I have argued in this work that trading in derivatives is not necessarily objectionable, provided that adequate measures are taken to ensure that it is for genuine reasons and that speculative risk-taking is kept down to acceptable levels. My affirmative stance is reflective not only of juristic considerations, but also of the realities of international relations and the prevailing economic order of our times. At present, Muslim countries and institutions are not the main actors in the global movement of prices and currencies, exchange rates or interest rates. However, they cannot escape the reality of being participants in international commerce, mainly in their capacities as the importers and consumers of capital goods, commodities and military hardware. In these circumstances it is essential that

Muslim countries and traders are able to protect themselves, by whatever means available, against adverse price movements in goods and currencies in the international market. This is to some extent possible through taking appropriate hedging positions in the derivatives market.

Those who declare derivative trading invalid on the grounds of purely imitative logic and speculative reasoning are in effect saying that Muslim traders and consumers should do nothing to protect themselves against adversity. To be complacent in the face of adverse economic realities, and to allow oneself to be the victim of circumstance, is neither prudent nor Islamic. There is simply no viable alternative to a pragmatic yet affirmative stance on derivative trading, for 'derivative products', as one commentator observed, 'are not investment but a means of managing exposure [to risk]'. Yet while derivatives are designed as risk management devices, they also partake in the risk. The answer, therefore, lies in adequate regulations and control procedures to manage the risk and turn it into advantage.[1]

There have been, of course, stories of financial debacles and phenomenal losses in the derivatives market that have received sensational media coverage and, as a result, equated trading in derivatives with high-powered gambling. The Orange County's losses of several billion dollars in interest rate derivatives, Procter and Gamble's losses in interest rate swaps and, more recently, the losses of Barings plc amounting to about $900 million at the hands of a single trader, Nick Leeson, in the Nekkei Stock Index futures, are all stark reminders of the hazards involved in derivatives trading, which can indeed bring countries, banks and individuals down to their knees. Reading the press coverage of these fiascos, one might be led to believe that there is something inherently wrong with derivatives. Yet like most sensationalised mass media episodes, the warnings that are given do not, on the whole, specify whether it is derivative trading as such or manifest mismanagement and abuse that is accountable for such disasters. When we examine the causes that led to these events, it turns out that in each case, derivatives were misused in clear violation of proper procedures. 'Every one of the fiascos involved', as one commentator noted 'speculative positions, not hedging.'[2] Indulgence in high risk speculation can be extremely harmful and, when it comes to trading in derivatives, there is simply no substitute for the careful observance of proper procedures. Reckless trading adventures can ruin people and businesses and not just in the derivatives. Speculation that is related to genuine hedging and seeks to protect a trading position may be said to be prudent and reasonable, especially when the underlying trade involves goods that are susceptible to price volatility. Under such circumstances, it may well be unreasonable to remain unprotected and exposed to the sort of risk that could be avoided through hedging in the derivatives market. Speculation that is purely based on a quick profit motive, without there being a real trading position to protect against the risk of financial loss, may generally be said to be unwarranted. It is this kind of speculation that appears to be a hallmark of each one of the financial disasters referred to above.

Those who equate commercial speculation with gambling and draw a direct analogy between them appear to show unwarranted dogmatism that is rooted in a *taqlīd*-oriented and shallow reading of the *Sharīʿah*. To say that speculation is forbidden in Islam is tantamount to being oblivious of the *Sharīʿah*: a careful examination of the *Sharīʿah* reveals that while proscribing *ribā'* and fixed return on capital, the *Sharīʿah* has given its full backing to profit-sharing and partnership in all areas of commerce. The Qur'ān prohibits *ribā'* but permits trading, and trading is generally predicated on profit–with the only difference that trading as envisaged in the Qur'ān must be on equitable terms. If one were to characterise the *Sharīʿah*'s philosophy on commercial transactions, one would say that it is to facilitate the equal apportionment of risk and reward between trading partners and entrepreneurs. Unlike interest-based transactions in which the profit is predetermined, fixed and essentially non-speculative, in the profit-sharing transactions envisaged by the *Sharīʿah*, the profit level remains undetermined and generally predicated on speculative risk-taking, which might well mean that higher risk is associated with greater profit. In an interest-based financial system, because the interest rate is usually fixed in advance, a relatively restrictive approach is taken towards speculation. When we compare this to the Islamic system of equity-based and partnership financing, trading and finance in the Islamic framework tend to be more inclined toward risk-taking and speculative enterprise.

It is admittedly difficult to differentiate speculation from hedging and investment, yet speculation is closely associated with profit and it is by definition 'the purchase and sale of an asset in the expectation of a gain from changes in the price of the asset'.[3] Speculation as such is an almost inalienable aspect of commercial activity, and there is an element of it in all kinds of investment, and even hedging. When the eventual return is determined and predicted in advance, the transaction in question is no longer speculative. But since the *Sharīʿah* prohibits *ribā'* and all interest-based transactions, it has left the door wide open to speculative enterprise. Islam's rejection of *ribā'* means, as Mohsin points out, that both capitalists and entrepreneurs, whose services are productive and essential to society, must assume risk and share rewards. Risk-taking and speculation are integral to the Islamic modes of commerce such as *muḍārabah* and *mushārakah*, yet the system emphasises the widest diffusion of risk and reward through the whole of society.[4] Iqbal and Fahim Khan have similarly observed that the Islamic economy assigns a more dynamic role to the entrepreneur and the financial institution in their capacities as parties to *muḍārabah* or partnership modes of transaction. This is in contrast to the role assigned to the interest-based financial institutions, which merely provide funds for investment, often by charging a fixed rate of interest that is averse to participation in business venture and involvement.[5]

Another feature of the *Sharīʿah* law of transactions that has a bearing on the Islamic economy is the prohibition of hoarding (*iḥtikār*), whether of money or of other assets and commodities, which evidently means that wealth must remain in circulation. Everyone who owns assets, including the state, is advised to engage their wealth in productive and profitable pursuits for the realisation of both personal profit and public welfare. There is much emphasis in the Qur'ān on the legitimate utilisation of the resources of the earth for the benefit of man. The realisation of benefit and the prevention of poverty and hardship are among the cardinal objectives of the economic and political agendas of Islamic government. This is the clear message of one of the well-known legal maxims of *Sharīʿah* which tells us that the basic criterion of judging the affairs of the head of state is whether or not he has succeeded in securing the *maṣlaḥah* or welfare of the people *(amr al-imām manʿūt bi'l-maṣlaḥah)*.

Another general objective of the Islamic economy articulated by Muslim economists in recent decades is 'broad-based economic well-being with full employment and optimum rate of economic growth'.[6] It is mainly due to this open-ended approach to commercial profit, risk capital and enterprise that Muslim economists have expressed the apprehension that the system might encourage profiteering. The interest rate is often fixed at ten or twelve per cent, but the profit can be fifty or a hundred per cent or even higher. The in-built speculative element in this is obviously greater, and gives rise to concern that the profit ratio might have to be passed on along the line and affect the consumer more severely than would be the case with a relatively marginal and, in any case, predictable size of interest rate. When this is read together with the fact that fixed interest is unacceptable and that credit financing in the Islamic system has to be interest-free, the fear arises of an inherent instability in this financial system. This concern was voiced in the 1981 Islamabad Seminar on the 'Monetary and Fiscal Economics of Islam' and was the subject of a paper presented to the seminar. It was subsequently stated in the seminar report that 'Muslim economists have now started applying themselves to the problem.' A suggestion was also made to the effect that the government might need to introduce profit-sharing ratios to replace the rate of interest in order to avert the destabilising effect that is expected of an open-ended and undetermined profit-sharing system.[7]

To facilitate a stable economy, the Islamic state would need to exert all its efforts to ensure stability in the value of money, and this would demand a number of other things, including the mobilisation of savings and avoidance of waste. The Islamic state is thus envisaged to be an active participant in productive economic activity and commerce. Since all loans must be interest-free, it is expected that a great deal of 'government spending would be financed either from the proceeds of taxes, or on a profit-sharing basis'.[8] The Islamic economy is participatory and dynamic and the state would need to realise a part of its budgetary requirements from profitable domestic and foreign trade.

This general characterisation of the Islamic state and economy leads to the conclusion that the state itself may need to utilise the derivatives market facility for hedging and risk-management purposes. When the trading and financial arms of the state, such as the central bank, commercial banks and other financial institutions, participate in a well-regulated derivatives market, they would be expected to exert a major influence on market direction and ensure the observance of prudent risk-control procedures by the market participants. This would hopefully discourage unnecessary speculation that was not related to real transactions in commodities and other beneficial trading activities.

The remaining part of this chapter draws attention to the experience of derivative trading in Malaysia. This country's participation in derivatives has been punctuated by self-questioning and doubts that have arisen from time to time about the acceptability in principle of derivatives. It is instructive to note at the outset that the issue has invoked a consistently affirmative yet cautious response from the leading personalities and institutions in Malaysia. I propose to discuss the Malaysian experience in some detail as it may in many ways be seen as a case study and a practical illustration of the views I have discussed and advocated in this study. One may disagree with certain aspects of the developments in Malaysia, yet one can hardly fail to note that Malaysia's experience in the trading of derivatives has been influenced by market realities and marked by the persistent advice of caution. I have already discussed the brief history of the Kuala Lumpur Commodity Exchange and the main developments that have taken place there since its inception in 1980. I have also discussed the salient points of the Futures Industry Act 1993 and the Futures Trading Act 1980. The discussion that follows is mainly concerned with the recent guidelines on derivatives issued by Bank Negara, the Central Bank of Malaysia, after an unhappy experience of losses in currency futures earlier in 1993. The new guidelines were issued on 12 January 1995 and were published in the media the following day, that is, well before the Barings debacle that happened a month or so later. This latter event also occurred at a time when public debate on the Bank Negara guidelines was attracting media attention. The Barings episode worked as a catalyst in bringing the issue into focus once again, and facilitated a double check, as it were, on the contents of the new guidelines.

An early Malaysian response to the Barings debacle and to the general question of the acceptability or otherwise of derivatives came from the Prime Minister, Dr. Mahathir, who was less than enthusiastic about derivatives and said in a press interview that those who wanted to conduct futures trading should concentrate on 'meaningful trading', adding that trade in derivatives was akin to gambling. With reference to the collapse of Barings plc, Dr. Mahathir said that 'he was not well-versed on the subject', but after the collapse of Orange Country in the United States, he had advised against derivatives trading. He added that Bank Negara's response was that if such activities could be regulated, it would be all right. When asked whether or not Malaysia should continue with the futures market, the Prime Minister said that in the futures market, there was meaningful trading, such as commodities trading, and that sometimes, one could even trade in the value of a currency, but he added that 'there are too many things being traded, including interest rates and others, which is not necessary and akin to gambling. We should only deal with items that are meaningful, such as commodities, where there must be commodities to deliver. We have been cheated before because of futures trading'.[9]

On the same day, when the Prime Minister spoke on derivatives, there was a press interview with the then Deputy Prime Minister, Anwar Ibrahim, who was also the Minister of Finance, in which he reflected on the contents of Malaysia's regulatory controls on derivatives. 'Malaysia's guidelines on derivatives trading are quite stringent and there is no need to overly react to the trading losses that led to the collapse of Britain's Merchant Bank Barings last weekend.' He said that the Barings episode, which involved estimated trading losses of $900 million, was a good lesson for Malaysia. 'We have been extremely cautious and we will continue to be so.' Derivatives as instruments or facilities are 'certainly acceptable'; what is important is that people should understand that derivatives are a new and sophisticated financial instrument. 'If we manage it carefully, abide by the rules and carry on on a small scale, it will not jeopardise business dealings.' Anwar added that based on initial reports, it seemed that the Barings fiasco occurred because of a lack of supervision and adherence to rules. However, in Malaysia, Bank Negara and the Securities Commission had drawn up guidelines and they did not foresee problems in dealing with derivative financial instruments.[10]

What was said here turned out to be right. The Barings collapse was due 'not to regulatory failure but to lack of internal control within the venerable 233-year-old bank'. The Investigators' report that was completed later in November 1995 blamed 'ineptitude and ignorance at the highest levels of Barings for the collapse of the bank'. As a result of the episode, Singapore tightened its control procedures and proposed 'confidential information-sharing with other exchanges, tighter rules for customer protection and the introduction of real-time clearing and settlement as well as critical risk-management systems'.[11] One of the glaring failures of the Barings Group—to check the reckless practices of Nick Leeson, the Head of Barings Futures, Singapore—was singled out by a *New Straits Times* reporter who wrote that 'in an exchange-traded contract, the profits and losses are settled daily at the clearing-house', and then posed the question: 'How did he [Leeson] raise the funds?'[12] It was further reported that the Barings Group breached a fundamental principle of proper internal control when they put Leeson in charge of both trading and settlement operations. These two functions should have been kept separate. This lapse was then compounded by 'Leeson's total lack of trading experience prior to his posting to Singapore'.[13] It then came as no surprise when in early December 1995, Leeson was convicted on charges of forgery and misrepresentation and sentenced to six and a half years imprisonment.

The full text of Bank Negara's guidelines on derivatives was published in the Malaysian media; it was preceded by the result of a survey that Bank Negara had earlier carried out on the extent of the Malaysian banks' involvement in derivative trading activities, which will be summarised presently.[14]

The Bank Negara guidelines on derivates are mainly addressed to licensed commercial banks and are on the whole supplementary to the futures Industry Act 1993. The guidelines were partly formulated in response to the increased number of applications made by commercial banks to trade in derivatives since the second half of 1994. Given the world-wide publicity given to losses and legal suits relating to derivatives at the time, Bank Negara decided to put on hold all applications made since September 1994 in order to review the Malaysian banks' involvement in derivatives.

The survey that Bank Negara conducted before issuing the new guidelines showed that of the thirty-seven licensed commercial and twelve licensed merchant banks, only sixteen licensed banks were involved in derivative trading related to interest rate swap, currency swap, currency options and interest rate options. Almost all of the derivative transactions undertaken by the banks involved simple and straightforward derivative products that have been widely used in the international financial markets. None of the banks was involved in the so-called 'exotics', which are combinations of or variations on the straightforward derivatives. The products are transacted mainly with non-bank customers who have underlying commercial transactions or with overseas banks by way of hedging the bank's own foreign exchange or interest rate exposure. The survey also showed that most derivative transactions are fully hedged, that is, the bank's exposure to interest rate or foreign exchange fluctuations have been offset by an opposite transaction. These hedges are generally conducted through back-to-back transactions with foreign banks and derivatives houses, thereby eliminating the exposure to market risk, that is, the risk of losses arising from adverse movements in interest rates and foreign exchange rates. Nevertheless, banks would still be exposed to credit risk just as they are in their normal lending operations. This is the risk of incurring losses when a counterparty or customer defaults.

The survey results indicate that derivative activities by licensed banks in Malaysia 'are not a major cause of concern as almost all transactions are fully hedged against interest rates and foreign exchange fluctuations ... Derivatives have not created new risks to the financial system'. The risks involved in derivative activities are identical to those faced by banks in their traditional activities such as lending and dealing in foreign exchange. It cannot be denied, however, that derivatives have, to some extent, highlighted existing risks by separating them out and pricing them individually. These risks include market risks arising from uncovered positions prior to maturity, currency or interest rate basis, liquidity risk which may arise if insufficient funds are available on settlement dates, and legal risk when contracts may not be enforceable in courts. The survey concluded with the following statement: 'The news of some companies incurring losses as a result of their foray into derivatives business should not overshadow the fact that derivatives are useful tools for managing risks if used prudently.'

The guidelines were issued in the form of a circular stipulating the conditions that a commercial bank would have to observe before Bank Negara's approval could be given for it to transact in a derivative product for the first time. It is thus implied that separate approval should be obtained whenever a commercial bank intends to transact in a particular derivative product. The following policy points were specified (the numbers are improvised for convenience):

1. Bank Negara will only consider applications on interest rate and currency-related derivatives. Equity-linked derivatives will only be considered on a case-by-case basis.

2. Any new derivative activity must be undertaken with the full knowl-

edge of the Bank's Board of Directors and be approved either by the Board, or a Committee designated by the Board to oversee derivative activities. It will be the Board's responsibility to put in place adequate risk management controls, sound measurement and monitoring systems, as well as comprehensive internal controls.

3. Derivative products can only be offered to customers who have an underlying commercial interest to hedge.

4. Commercial banks are required to educate their customers on the applicability of the relevant products to their requirements of risk management. Commercial banks must also be satisfied that their customers have fully understood the derivative product in which they propose to transact, and obtain a customers-signed letter of acknowledgement to that effect.

The guidelines also specify the type of information that a bank should submit in order to obtain Bank Negara's approval to transact. This must include:

1. An analysis of the risk associated with the proposed derivative activities.

2. Evidence that the proposed derivative activity has been approved by the bank's Board of Directors or the committee in charge of this task.

3. Information on the level of expertise that the bank has in handling the anticipated risks, and the qualifications and experience of the key personnel responsible for the banks overall derivative activities.

4. Evidence that the bank has sufficient capital to support potential losses from fluctuations in the value of uncovered derivative transactions and also default from customers.

The guidelines assign a supervisory role to Bank Negara to closely monitor the banks' involvement in derivative activities in the future by issuing further guidelines on specifying minimum standards on sound risk management practices, on appropriate public disclosure requirements in the treatment of accounts and on the adequacy of reserve capital for risk management purposes.

Although the circular applies specifically to commercial banks, Bank Negara has encouraged all parties concerned to observe the spirit of this circular and the guidelines that it contains on derivative trading activities.

The immediate response to these guidelines was generally positive and experts in the financial sector who were interviewed by media reporters observed that the new guidelines would restrict speculation. It was also noted that commercial banks that act as intermediaries for their clients were clearly accountable under the new rules and had been assigned a definite role in the orderly conduct of derivative trading activities. According to another commentator, commercial banks should clearly act as intermediaries for customers wishing to hedge and also ensure that the customer fully understood the nature of the transaction and the risk they were undertaking. The finance manager of a large corporation in Malaysia commented that corporations should naturally earn profit from their core businesses, and only use derivatives when they needed to, but normally, 'we have no business venturing into financial derivatives'. It is still useful for large corporations to limit their risks, when they are exposed to risk from fluctuations in currency exchange rates or interest rates, in order to protect their core business against losses that could be prevented through an intelligent approach to derivatives. The same commentator added: 'We did some interest rate swaps way back in 1987 and we were pretty successful.' A Forex dealer in a local bank said: 'We have been involved in currency swaps for a while now. What Bank Negara has issued is just a set of guidelines; we need to emphasise that the commercial banks must know the risk to which they and their clients might be exposed. Another commentator added that there were so many variants and the authorities could not be expected to give detailed guidelines on all of them. The Bank Negara guidelines were broad and general but they were adequate. According to yet another commentator, the Bank Negara guidelines were likely to have a restrictive effect on derivatives. To a market that is still not well-versed in derivative activities, the procedures laid down in these guidelines were helpful and some were even essential.'[15]

Clearly the most important feature of the Bank Negara guidelines is where it stated that 'derivative products can only be offered to customers who have an underlying commercial interest to hedge'. Given the basic framework and structure of derivatives trading, this is probably the most far-reaching guideline, which is specific enough yet not too rigid, by which to restrict speculative risk-taking in financial derivatives. This in a sense sums up the basic utility and rationale of the acceptable range of derivatives trading that I have advocated throughout this study. Commercial speculation is not a clear concept and hardly lends itself to an exclusive definition since the dividing line between hedging and speculation can often be a matter of opinion: what may seem excessive in one context may be seen differently in another context. Similarly, certain counters or items of trading, within or outside the same category of derivative products, may seem to be more speculative and exhibit greater price volatility than others. The Bank Negara policy directive, which restricts derivative trading to real hedging positions, imposes a financially sound and legally acceptable framework that can be supported by the substance of the *Sharīʿah* evidence I have presented in this research.

Throughout this presentation, I have maintained the view that trading in futures and options can be defended from the *Sharīʿah* perspective especially in commodities such as foodgrains, agricultural produce, oil products and other goods that are beneficial and necessary for the maintenance of normal economic transactions in society. To protect the farmer, the food processing plant or the producer of essential goods against violent price fluctuations, and facilitate efficiency and good planning through intelligent use of derivative facilities, falls within the ambit of measures that are necessary for the protection and realisation of public interest (*maṣlaḥah*).

With regard to the Bank Negara guidelines on financial derivatives, one may raise the objection that those transactions, such as currency and interest rate options and swaps, that are envisaged in these guidelines generally proceed on interest-bearing instruments and should therefore be proscribed. Although we still maintain the view that this research has mainly envisaged derivative trading in commodities, and that we should stay clear of derivatives trading which proceeds upon interest-bearing transactions, I am of the view nevertheless that hedging a real position against fluctuations in interest rates or currency exchange rates is guided by a different rationale: if the hedging transaction is only designed as a defensive device and risk management tool to avert or minimise exposure to financial loss over an existing position in a lawful trade, or *ḥalāl* merchandise, it may be validated by recourse to the rules of necessity and the legal maxim of *Sharīʿah* that 'necessities make the unlawful lawful'. Since the determination of interest rates and foreign currencies is normally beyond the control of any individual or institutional trader in Malaysia, or any other Muslim country for that matter, they are essentially helpless to change their predicament. The hedging position that they take in the derivative market therefore falls within the ambit of the rule of necessity. The same cannot be said, however, of engaging in speculative activity where financial derivatives are profit-driven, and entered into for the sole purpose of making a profit without there being an underlying transaction that can be protected against risk. It is hoped that by following a clearly defined objective, namely, to hedge a trading position against risk in a way that justifies the availability in principle of financial derivatives, the regulatory authorities will be able to minimise involvement in purely profit-motivated speculation. This is in fact the purport of another legal maxim of *Sharīʿah* which simply states that 'necessity is measured by the extent of its application—*al-ḍarūratu tuqdaru bi-qadrihā*'. The concession, in other words, that is granted on account of necessity ceases to apply when the necessity comes to an end.

The concession that is granted by the *Sharīʿah* for situations of necessity is a limited concession confined strictly to situations of real, and not assumed or liberally interpreted, necessity. I believe that the Bank Negara guidelines have gone a long way to confine derivative trading to the extent that is deemed necessary and beneficial. This is quite obvious from the emphatic tone of these guidelines and the diligence and co-operation that Bank Negara has solicited from the commercial banks and other participants in derivative trading in Malaysia. If there comes a time in the future when Malaysia and other Muslim countries become principal actors in the determination of currency and interest rates, then the rules of necessity we have proposed to evoke here will become redundant and no longer apply, in which case the situation may have to be reviewed and normal order restored.

To summarise, I have tried to expose the inherent weaknesses in the prohibitive arguments and judgements advanced on futures, refute them in detail, and then offer alternative proposals within the framework of both *Sharīᶜah* and social reality. The analysis proffered in this study concurs substantially and in various ways with the views and interpretations of the jurists, both classical and modern, who have seen the weaknesses of the literalist approach to the understanding of the relevant *ḥadīth*. With regard to the existence or non-existence of the subject-matter of a sale, or the requirement of taking it into in possession, we have noted that the underlying rationale of the *ḥadīth* on both of these issues, which relates more meaningfully to the commercial realities of our time, is to prevent *gharar* that emanates from the seller's inability or failure to make delivery. If this is effectively prevented and ensured, then the physical existence or possession of the subject-matter is no longer an issue. This analysis is supported, as I have shown, by many prominent jurists, including Ibn Taymiyyah, Ibn Qayyim al-Jawziyyah and, more recently, by ᶜAbd al-Razzaq al-Sanhūrī.

The issue of the sale of debts and the point that futures sales amount to what is stated as *bayᶜ al-kāli' bi'l-kāli'* is generally unspecified and obscure. Many prominent scholars have expressed doubt about the exact meaning of this transaction and the authenticity of the *ḥadīth* on its prohibition. We have discussed these views and also refuted the alleged *ijmāᶜ* or consensus in support of the prohibition in question, and then invoked the principle of permissibility *(ibāḥah)* on the subject. The affirmative view I have advanced here relates directly to the Qur'ānic verse of *mudāyanah* or indebtedness, which clearly validates transactions involving future obligations, and futures trading seems to fall within the manifest meaning of this verse.

With regard to the issue of speculation and gambling, I have argued that the facile equation of the one with the other that is often presumed is unjustified. I have discussed both these concepts in separate sections and reached the conclusion that gambling must be distinguished from commercial speculation, and that the issue we face in relation to futures trading is one of commercial speculation rather than gambling. Finally, with regard to commercial speculation, my position is that the main issue has always been one of degree and not of principle. The conclusion I have reached is that a cautious and well-regulated approach to commercial speculation in futures and options, such as the one taken in Malaysia, is advisable if it can serve the public interest or *maṣlaḥah*, and may, in some cases, even be vindicated within the ambit of the *Sharīʿah* principle of necessity (*ḍarūrah*).

NOTES

1. Robert Bladier, *The Star*, 15 March 1995, Business Section, p. 3.
2. Obiyatullah Ismath Bacha, 'Derivatives: an Overview', *Insight*, vol. 1 no. 5, September/ October 1995, p. 4.
3. Cootner, 'Speculation', *Modern Ecyclopedia of Social Sciences*, 1968.
4. Cf. Mohammad Mohsin, 'Sharīʿah Framework of Riba-Free Banks' in Ariff (ed.), *Monetary and Fiscal Economics of Islam*', Jeddah, King Abdul Aziz University, 1403/1982, p. 189.
5. Iqbal and Fahim Khan, *A Survey of Issue and a Programme for Research in Monetary and Fiscal Economics of Islam*, Islamabad, Institute of Policy Research, 1987, p. 28.
6. Cf. Umar Chapra, 'Money and Banking in an Islamic Economy', in Ariff (ed.) *Monetary and Fiscal Economics of Islam*, p. 146, note 2; I. and F. Khan, *A Survey of Issue*, p. 24, note 3.
7. Ibid., p. 72.
8. I. and F. Khan, *A Survey of Issue*, p. 85.
9. 'Futures Trading Should be Meaningful', *New Strait Times*, March 4, 1995, p. 2.
10. 'Anwar: Barings case a good lesson', *New Strait Times*, March 4, 1995, p. 12.
11. 'Singapore beefs up controls after fall of Barings', *New Strait Times*, November 21, 1995, p. 32.
12. Kula Shunmugan, 'Stringent guidelines likely for local derivative market', *New Strait Times*, March 1, 1995, p. 14.
13. 'Baring collapse could have been avoided, says report', *New Strait Times*, October 18, 1995, p. 21.
14. The text of the guidelines and survey report appeared in *The Star*, January 13, 1995, at Business p. 4, entitled 'The Guidelines on Derivative Activities'.
15. A roundup of anonymous interviews entitled 'Thumbs up for new guidelines', conducted by B. K. Sidhu *et al.*, *The Star*, January 13, 1995.

Glossary

aʿḍāʾ al-murāsilūn: associate members (in a futures market).
aʿḍāʾ al-samāsirah: clearing members (in a futures market).
ʿadah (pl. *ʿādāt*): custom, habit, usual practice.
aḥkām (pl. of *ḥukm*): laws, values, ordinances.
ahl al-raʾy: rationalists, partisans of personal opinion.
akl al-māl biʾl-bāṭil: unlawful consumption of the property of others.
ʿamaliyyāt sharṭiyya al-ajilah: deferred conditional transactions; options.
ʿamaliyyāt sharṭiyya murakkabah: double options.
ʿamaliyyāt sharṭiyya muḍāʿafah: double quantity options.
amīn: trustee.
ʿāmm: general, as opposed to specific.
ansab: sacrificing to stones.
ʿaqd: contract.
ʿaqd al-muʿallaq: contingent contracts.
ʿaqd al-muḍāf: deferred contracts.
ʿaqd al-munajjaz: prompt contracts.
ʿaraya: the sale of fresh dates in exchange for dry ones.
asbāb (pl. of *sabab*): causes, means, reasons.
aṣl fiʾl-ashyāʾ al-ibāḥah: phrase meaning that 'the norm for things is permissibility'.
ashyāʾ al-mustaqbala: future things.
aʿyan: unique objects.
ʿayb: defect; shortcoming.
ʿayn al-ḥādīrah: tangible asset.
azlām: divination by arrows.
bāṭil: null and void.
bayʿ al-dayn biʾl-dayn: debt clearance sale.
bayʿ al-duyūn: sale of debts.
bayʿ al-fāsid: voidable sale.
bayʿ al-ghāʾib: sale of the unseen.
bayʿ al-gharar: sale involving risk.

bayʿ al-ʿinah: deferred sale used to make a questionable gain.
bayʿ al-kāli' bi'l-kāli': sale of one debt for another.
bayʿ al-maʿdūm: sale of the non-existent object.
bayʿ al-maghṣūb: sale of a usurped object.
bayʿ al-majhūl: sale of the unknown.
bayʿ al-mu'ajjal: deferred sale.
bayʿ al-mūʿāṭāt: give and take sale.
bayʿ al-murābaḥah: cost plus profit sale.
bayʿatayn fī bayʿah: sale in which two prices are quoted, one prompt and the other deferred.
bayʿ bi-siʿr al-sūq: sale at the market price.
bayʿ ghayr al-mawjūd: sale of the non-existent.
bayʿ taḥt al-qaṭʿ: sale at the market price for a specified period of time.
bayʿ wa sharṭ: sale combined with a stipulation.
burṣah: bourse or money market.
burṣat al-ʿuqūd: lit. contracts market; the Egyptian Futures Market.
buṭlān: invalidity.
buyūʿ al-aʿyān: sales of special or unique objects.
buyūʿ al-ṣifāt: sale of goods by description.
ḍamān: liability for loss.
ḍarūrah: necessity.
ḍārūrī: essential, necessary.
dhimmah: personal responsibility or obligation.
fa'idah: utility; benefit.
faqīh: (pl. *fuqahā'*) jurist, one who is learned in *fiqh*.
farḍ: obligatory, obligation.
farḍ kafā'ī: collective obligation.
fāsid: irregular; corrupt.
faṣṣ: dice.
fatrah al-ikhtiyār: option period.
fatwā (pl. *fatāwa*): religious edict from a qualified scholar.
fiqh: Islamic law as developed by Muslim jurists.
faḍūlī: unauthorised person; uncommissioned agent.
fuqahā': jurists.
ghabn: manipulation.
ghālib: winner.
gharar: risk-taking.
gharar al-kathīr: excessive risk-taking.
gharar al-mutawassiṭ: moderate risk-taking.
gharar al-yasīr: minor risk-taking.
ghayr maḍmūn: not guaranteed.
ḥabal al-ḥabālah: sale of the offspring of an unborn animal.

ḥabs: retention.
ḥadīth: lit., speech; the reported sayings and teachings of Prophet Muhammad ﷺ.
ḥājjī: complementary.
ḥalāl: legitimate, allowed by Sharīʿah.
ḥaqq: a right.
ḥaqq al-mujarrad: a pure and simple right.
ḥaraj: hardship.
ḥarām: totally forbidden.
ḥaṣṣāt: sales, usually of clothes, in which the object was identified by throwing pebbles in the dark.
ḥawālah: letter of credit, transfer.
ḥaẓar: prohibition.
ḥikmah: rationale, wisdom.
ḥirāsah muḥkamah qawiyya bi'l-ḍamānāt: structure of guarantees.
ḥirz: custody.
ḥūkm: (pl. *aḥkām*) law, value or ruling of *Sharīʿah*.
ḥurriyya al-taʿāqud: freedom of contract.
ḥuṣūl: availability, acquisition.
ʿibādāt: devotional matters and rituals of worship.
ibāḥah: permissibility.
ibra' al-dayn: release of debt.
ijārah (pl. *ijārāt*): lease or hire.
ijmāʿ: consensus of scholars and jurists.
ijmāʿ al-nās: common consensus of the people.
ijmāʿan ẓanniyan: speculative consensus.
ijtihād: lit. exertion; independent reasoning by a qualified scholar to obtain legal rulings from the sources of *Sharīʿah*.
ikhtilāf: juristic disagreement.
ikhtiyārāt: options.
ikhtiyārāt al-basīṭah: simple options.
ikhtiyārāt al-murakkabah: double options.
ikhtiyārāt al-muḍāʿafah: double quantity options.
ikhtiyār al-ṭalab: call option.
ikhtiyār al-dafʿ: put option.
ʿillah: effective cause, or *ratio legis*, of a particular ruling.
irshād: moral guidance.
istiḥsan: to deem something good; juristic preference.
istiṣnāʿ: [contract of] manufacture.
jahālah: ignorance.
jahālah al-fāḥishah: excessive ignorance of something.
jā'iḥah: climatic disasters or disease.

juzāfan: as a lump sum.
kaʿb or kaʿbah: dice.
kaffārah (pl. *kaffārāt*): penance, expiation.
kafīl: guarantor.
karāhiyya: abomination, distaste for something.
khaṣṣ: specific or special.
khidāʿ: fraud.
khilāf al-qiyās: contrary to the norm.
khiyār al-ʿayb: option or defect.
khiyār al ru'yah: option of viewing.
khiyār al-sharṭ: option of stipulation.
khiyār al-taʿyīn: option of identification.
khiyārāt: options.
luzūm: enforceability.
madhhab: juristic or theological school.
madhāhib: pl. of *madhhab*.
maḍāmīn wa'l-malāqīḥ: loins and wombs [of animals].
maghlūb: loser.
mahr: dower, or groom's wedding gift to his bride.
mahr al-mithl: correctly apportioned dower.
majhūl: that which is unknown.
majhūl al-ḥāl: obscure; in an unknown condition or state.
maʿlūmiyya al-thaman: price-determination.
manfaʿah: usufruct.
maqāsah: clearance of mutual debts.
maqāṣid: (pl. of *maqṣūd*) goals and objectives.
maqdūr al-taslīm: able to be delivered.
maqṣūd al-shāriʿ: objective of the Lawgiver.
maṣlaḥah (pl. *maṣāliḥ*): consideration of public interest.
maṣlaḥah mursalah: unrestricted public interest.
mawāfiq al-qiyās: in accordance with norms.
mawqūf: suspended.
maysīr: game of chance.
muʿāmalāt: civil or commercial transactions.
muʿāmalāt mu'ajjalah: deferred transactions.
mūbāḥ: permissible.
muḍārabah: speculation.
mudāyanah: deferred liability contracts.
muftī: jurisconsult.
mujtahid (pl. *mujtahidūn*): legist competent to formulate independent tradition based opinions in legal or theological matters.
mukhāṭarah: risk-taking.

mulā'im li'l-ʿaqd: appropriate for a contract.
mulāmasah: sales, usually of clothes, concluded when the buyer touched the object.
munābadhah: sales, usually of clothes, concluded when the parties threw the objects to one another.
munqaṭiʿ: broken.
muqallidūn: imitators, followers of the opinions of others.
muqāmarah: gambling.
muqtadā al-ʿaqd: appropriate for a contract; requirement of a contract.
murābaḥah: sale of something at cost plus profit.
mursal: [of a *ḥadīth*] disconnected.
musabbab: legal effect [of a *sabab*, or cause].
musāwamah: cost price.
mushārakah: partnership, co-operation.
muslam fīh: the subject-matter of *salam*
musnad: *ḥadīth* with a continuous chain of narrators.
muta'akhkhirūn: [of scholars] those coming later.
mutawassiṭ: medium; moderate.
muṭlaq: absolute; unlimited, unrestricted.
muthman: subject of a sale.
muzāyadah: sale by auction.
nafādh: effectiveness.
nafaqah: maintenance.
nāfidh: effective.
nahy: prohibition.
naṣṣ qaṭʿī al-thubūt wa'l-dalālah: a text that is decisive in both meaning and transmission.
naṣṣ ṣaḥīḥ al-thubūt ṣarīh al-dalālah: a text that is authentic and conveys a clear meaning.
naẓariyya al-ajal: theory of deferment in contracts.
nuṣūṣ qaṭʿiyya: decisive injunctions.
qabḍ: possession.
qabḍ al-ḥaqīqī: actual possession.
qānūn: (pl. *qawānīn*): law.
qarḍ: loan.
qawāʿid kulliyyah: salient legal maxims.
qayd al-ḥisābī: account records.
qimār wa'l-maysīr: gambling and punting.
qiyās: analogy.
qiyās maʿ al-fāriq: discrepant analogy.
qutn: cotton.
qurʿah: throwing of lots.

raf[c] al-ḥaraj: removal of hardship.
ribā': usury.
rifq: gentleness; leniency.
rihān: betting.
rukn: essential requirement.
ruq[c]a al-ṣayārifah: promissory notes.
sabab: (pl. *asbāb*) cause, means of obtaining something.
sadd al-dharā'i[c]: blocking the means to something.
safātij: bills of exchange.
ṣaḥīḥ; valid, authentic.
salam: forward sale.
ṣarf: currency.
sha'n al-nuzūl: occasion of revelation.
Sharī[c]ah: Islamic law as contained in the divine guidance of the Qur'ān and *Sunnah*.
sharṭ al-fāsid: voidable stipulation or condition.
sharṭ al-luzūm: condition of enforceability.
sharṭ al-nafādh: condition of effectiveness.
sharṭ al-siḥḥah: condition of validity.
shibh al-salam: *salam* look-alike.
shirkah: partnership.
shirkat al-wujūh: credit partnership.
shurūṭ: (sing. *sharṭ*) conditions, pre-requisites.
ṣiḥḥah: validity.
si[c]r al-mithl: prevailing market price.
ṣukuk al-badā'i[c]: commodity coupons.
ṣulḥ: reconciliation.
Sunnah: the teaching and exemplary conduct of the Prophet Muhammad.
ta[c]abbudī: devotional.
ta[c]ām: foodstuffs.
ta[c]ām al-mu[c]ayyan: specified tangible foodstuffs.
ta[c]āwun: cooperation.
ṭābi[c]ūn: generation following the Companions.
tadāyantum: reciprocal deferred liability exchange.
tafarruq: separation or differentiation.
taḥrīm: total ban.
taḥsīnī: desirable.
ta'jīl: deferment.
takhliya: evacuation.
takhyīr: option; selection.
ta[c]līl: ratiocination.
tamyīz: identification.

taqābuḍ: taking possession.
taqlīd: imitation.
tasʿīr: price control.
tawātur: recurrent, continuous testimony.
tawāʿud: exchange of promises.
tawbah: repentance.
tawliya: sale at cost price.
taʿyīn: identification.
taysīr: facility, ease.
thaman: purchase price.
thaman al-musamma: specified price.
thaman al-mithl: the 'going rate' paid at which something is sold.
thiqqa: credibility.
thiqqāt: reliable narrators [of *ḥadīth*].
ummah: Muslim community at large.
ʿuqūd: contracts.
ʿuqūd al-ʿajilah: prompt contracts.
ʿuqūd al-muʿāwadah: contracts of exchange.
ʿuqūd al-tabarruʿ: charitable contracts.
ʿuqūd al-tamlīk: proprietary contracts.
ʿuqūd māliyya: pecuniary contracts.
ʿurbūn or *ʿurbān*: earnest money taken by seller.
ʿurf: custom, usage.
uṣūl al-fiqh: roots of Islamic Jurisprudence.
waḍīʿah: sale at lower than cost price.
wakālah: agency.
wakīl: agent.
wakīl ʿām: general representative.
waqf: charitable endowment.
waṣīy: executor.
waʿẓ: warning, kindly admonition.
ẓanni: speculative.
ẓulm wa jawr: oppression and injustice.

Bibliography

ʿAbd al-Salām, ʿIzz al-Dīn, *Qawāʿid al-Aḥkām fī Masalih al-Anam*, ed. Taha ʿAbd al-Rawuf Saʿd, Cairo: Maktabah al-Kulliyyat al-Azhariyyah, 1968.

Abū Zahrah, Muḥammad, *Uṣūl al-Fiqh*, Cairo: Dār al-Fikr al-ʿArabī, 1377/1958.

ʿAlī, Sami Wahba, *al-Burṣāt wa Taswiq al-Quṭn*, Cairo: Maṭbaʿah al-Risālah, 1966.

Alwi, Abdullah Haji Hassan, *Sales and Contracts in Early Islamic Commercial Law*, Islamabad: Islamic Research Institute, 1994.

Ariff, Muhammad (ed.), *Monetary and Fiscal Economics of Islam*, Jeddah: King Abdul Aziz University, 1403/1982.

Abū Dāwūd, *Sunan Abū Dāwūd*, Eng. trans. Ahmad Hasan, 3 vols., Lahore: Ashraf Press, 1984.

Abū Ḥabīb, Saʿdī, *al-Qāmūs al-Fiqhī Lughatan wa Istilahan*, Damascus: Dār al-Fikr 1402/1982.

Abū Sulaymān, ʿAbd al-Wahhāb Ibrāhīm, 'Aqd al-Tawrīd', manuscript due to appear in *al-Mawsūʿah al-Fiqhiyyah al-Iqtisadiyyah*. I wish to record my appreciation to the author for providing me with a copy of his manuscript (October 1994).

——'Al-Ikhtiyyarāt: Darasah Fiqhiyyah Taḥlīliyyah Muqāranah', in *Mujallah al-Buḥuth al-Fiqhiyyah al-Muʿāṣarah*, No.15 (4th year), Jamadi al-Awwal 1413/October 1992, pp. 6-38.

Al-Āmidī, Sayf al-Dīn, *al-Iḥkām fī Uṣūl al-Aḥkām*, ed. ʿAbd al-Razzāq ʿAfīfī, Beirut: al-Maktab al-Islāmī, 1402/1982.

Al-ʿArabī, ʿAbd Allāh, *ʿAradāt al-Ahwadhi bi-Sharḥ Ṣaḥīḥ al-Tirmidhī*, Beirut: Dār al-Kutub al-ʿIlmiyyah, n.d.

Al-ʿAsqalānī, Aḥmad b. ʿAlī b. Ḥajar, *Fatḥ al-Bārī bi-Sharḥ Ṣaḥīḥ al-Bukhārī*, ed. Taha ʿAbd al-Rauf Saʿd, Cairo: Maktabah al-Kulliyyat al-Azhariyyah, 1978.

ʿAtr, Nūr al-Dīn, *al-Muʿāmalāt al-Maṣrafiyyah wa'l-Ribawiyyah wa ʿIlajuha fi'l-Islām,* Beirut: Mu'assasat al-Risālah, 1406/1986.

Al-ʿAṭṭār, ʿAbd al-Nāṣir Tawfiq, *Naẓariyyah al-Ajal fī al-Iltizam fi'l-Sharīʿah al-Islāmiyyah wa'l-Qawanin al-ʿArabiyyah*, Cairo: Maṭbaʿah al-Saʿādah, 1978.

Bacha, Obiyatullah Ismath, 'Derivatives: An Overview', in *Insight*, vol.1, no. 5, September 1995, pp. 2-6.

Amīr Bādshāh (Muḥammad Amīn known as Amīr Bādshāh), *al-Taysīr Sharḥ al-Taḥrīr*, Beirut: Dār al-Kutub al-ʿIlmiyyah, 1983.

Al-Baghāwī, Abū Muḥammad al-Ḥusayn, *Sharḥ al-Sunnah*, Damascus: al-Maktab al-Islāmī, 1974.

Al-Bāji, Abū al-Walīd Sulaymān, *al-Muntaqā Sharḥ al-Muwaṭṭā*, Beirut: Dār al-Kitāb al-ʿArabī, 1332 AH.

Bakken, Henry H., 'Futures Trading', in *Encyclopedia Americana*, vol. XII, p. 208.

Al-Baʿlī, ʿAbd al-Ḥamīd Maḥmūd, *Ḍawābiṭ al-ʿUqūd fi'l-Fiqh al-Islāmī*, vol. 1, Cairo: Matabiʿ al-Ittiḥād al-Duwali li'l-Bunūk al-Islāmiyyah, n.d.

Bayt al-Tamwil al-Kuwaitī, *al-Fatāwā al-Sharʿiyyah fi'l-Masā'il al-Iqtisadiyyah*, 2nd edn, Kuwait, 1405/1985.

Al-Buhūtī, Manṣūr b. Idrīs, *Kashshāf al-Qannaʿ*, ed. Muṣṭafā Hilal, Riyad: Maktabah al-Ḥadīthah, n.d.

Al-Bukhārī, Muḥammad b. Ismāʿīl, *Ṣaḥīḥ al-Bukhārī*, Eng. trans. Muḥammad Muḥsin Khān, 6th edn, Lahore: Kazi Publications, 1986.

Chapra, Umar 'The Role of the Stock Exchange in an Islamic Economy', in Sheikh Ghazali Abod *et al.* (ed.), *An Introduction to Islamic Finance*, Kuala Lumpur: Quill Publishers, 1992.

——'Money and Banking in an Islamic Economy', in M. Ariff (ed.), *Monetary and Fiscal Economics of Islam*, Jeddah: King Abdul Aziz University, 1403/1982, pp.145-187.

Colburn, James T., *Trading in Options on Futures*, New York: New York Institute of Finance, 1990.

The Commodity Futures Act, Malaysia, 1980

The Commodity Trading Act, Malaysia, 1985.

Cootner, 'Speculation, hedging and arbitrage', in *Modern Encyclopedia of Social Sciences*, London, 1968.

Courtney, David and Bettelheim, *An Investor's Guide to the Commodity Futures Markets*, London: Butterworths, 1986.

Al-Ḍarīr, Shaykh Siddīq, *al-Gharar wa Atharuh fi'l-ʿUqūd fi'l Fiqh al-Islāmī*, Cairo: Dār al-Nashr al-Thaqafah, 1386/1967.

Al-Dihlawī, Shāh Waliyyullāh b. ʿAbd al-Raḥīm, *Ḥujjāt Allāh al-Bālighah*, Cairo: Dār al-Turath, 1355 AH.

Encyclopedia Britannica

The Encyclopedia of Islam, new edn, Leiden: E. J. Brill, 1965.

Encyclopedia of Religion and Ethics, ed. James Hastings, New York, T&T Clark, 1908.
The Financial Times, London.
Fink, Robert E. & Feduniak, Robert B., *Futures Trading. Concepts and Strategies*, New York: New York Institute of Finance, 1988.
Firdaus, Jamaluddin *et al.*, 'The Kuala Lumpur Commodity Exchange', unpublished paper, Kuala Lumpur: International Islamic University, 1994.
The Futures Industry Act, Malaysia, 1993.
Ghazali, Sheikh Abod, Syed Omar Syed Agil, Aidit Ghazali, comps., *An Introduction to Islamic Finance*, Kuala Lumpur: Quill Publishers, 1992.
Al-Ghiyati, Muḥammad Yūnus, *Bayᶜ Milk al-Ghayr fi'l-Qānūn al-Madani wa'l Fiqh al-Islāmī*, Tanta: Maktabah Jāmiᶜah Tanta, 1986.
Gitman, Lawrence J. & Michael D. Joehnk, *Fundamentals of Investing*, 3rd edn, New York: Harper and Row, 1988.
Gup, Benton, *The Basics of Investing*, 3rd edn, New York: John Wiley, 1986.
Ḥamoud, Samī Ḥassan, *Taṭwīr al-Aᶜmal al-Maṣrafiyyah bima Yattafiq wa al-Sharīᶜah al-Islāmiyyah*, 2nd edn, Oman: Maṭbaᶜah al-Sharq, 1402/1982.
Ḥasan, Aḥmad Muḥayyudin Aḥmad, *ᶜAmal Sharīkāt al-Istithmār al-Islāmiyyah fī al-Sūq al-ᶜAlamiyyah*, Jeddah: al-Dār al-Saᶜudiyyah li'l-Nashr wa'l-Tawzīᶜ, 1407/1986.
Ḥassanayn, Muḥammad, *Naẓariyyah Buṭlān al-ᶜAqd fi'l-Fiqh al-Islāmī*, Algiers: al-Mu'assasah al-Wataniyyah li'l-Kitāb, 1988.
Al-Ḥaṭṭāb, Abū ᶜAbd Allāh, *Muwāhib al-Jalil li Sharḥ Mukhtasar Khalīl*, Cairo: Maṭbaᶜah al-Saᶜādah, 1328 AH.
Hull, John, *Introduction to Futures and Options Markets*, Englewood Cliffs; N.J.: Prentice Hall, 1991.
Ḥusayn, Aḥmad Farraj, *al-Milkiyyah wa Naẓariyyah al-ᶜAqd fi'l-Sharīᶜah al-Islāmiyyah*, Alexandria: Dār al-Jāmiᶜiyyah, 1986.
Ibn ᶜĀbidīn, Muḥammad Amīn, *Ḥāshiyat al-Radd al-Mukhtār ᶜalā'l-Durr al-Mukhtār* (known as *Ḥāshiyat Ibn ᶜAbidīn*), 2nd edn, Cairo: Maṭbaᶜah al-Bābī al-Ḥalabī, 1386/1966.
Ibn Ḥanbal, Aḥmad, *Fihris Aḥādīth Musnad al-Imām Aḥmad b. Ḥanbal*, compiled by Abū Hājir Zaghlūl, Beirut: Dār al-Kutub, 1405/1985.
Ibn Ḥazm, Muḥammad ᶜAlī b. Aḥmad, *al-Muḥallā*, ed. A. G. Sulaymān al-Bandarī, Beirut: Dār al-Kutub al-ᶜIlmiyyah, 1408/1988.
Ibn al-Humam, Kamal al-Dīn, *Fatḥ al-Qadīr*, Cairo: Muṣṭafā al-Bābī al-Ḥalabī, 1389/1970.
Ibn Juzay, Muḥammad b. Aḥmad al-Gharnāṭi, *Qawānīn al-Aḥkām al-Sharᶜiyyah*, Cairo: ᶜĀlam al-Fikr, 1975.

Ibn Kathīr, Abū'l-Fidā'ī Ismāᶜīl, *Tafsīr al-Qur'ān al-ᶜAzīm*, Cairo: Dār al-Kitāb al-Miṣrī, 1408/1988.

Ibn Mājah, Muḥammad b. Yazīd al-Qazwīnī, *Sunan Ibn Mājah*, Istanbul: Cagri Yayinlari, 1401/1981.

Ibn Qudāmah, Muwaffaq al-Dīn Abū Muḥammad al-Maqdisī, *al-Mughnī*, Cairo: Dār al-Manār, n.d.; and Cairo: Maktabah al-Qahirah, 1969.

Ibn Taymiyyah, Taqī al-Dīn, *Naẓariyyah al-ᶜAqd*, Beirut: Dār al-Maᶜrifah, 1317 AH.

——*Majmūᶜah Fatāwā Shaykh al-Islām Ibn Taymiyyah*, compiled by ᶜAbd al-Raḥmān b. al-Qāsim, Beirut: Mu'assasah al-Risālah, 1398.

Ismail, Abdul Halim, 'The Deferred Contracts of Exchange in Al-Qur'an,' in Ghazali *et. al.*, *An Introduction to Islamic Finance*, Kuala Lumpur: Quill publishers 1992, pp. 284-314.

Al-Jassas, Abū Bakr Aḥmad b. ᶜAlī al-Rāzī, *Aḥkām al-Qur'ān*, ed. Muḥammad al-Sadiq Qamhawi, Beirut: Dār Iḥyā' al-Turath al-ᶜArabī, 1985.

Al-Jawziyyah, Ibn Qayyim, *Iᶜlām al-Muwaqqiᶜīn ᶜan Rabb al-ᶜĀlamīn*, Cairo: Maktabah al-Kulliyyat al-Azhariyyah, 1968.

——*ᶜAwn al-Maᶜbūd Sharḥ Sunan Abī Dāwūd*, ed. ᶜAbd al-Raḥmān Muḥammad ᶜUthman, 3rd edn, Cairo: Dār al-Fikr, 1399/1979.

——*Al-Furusiyyah*, ed. Muḥammad Nizam al-Fatih, Madīnah Munawarah: Maktabah Dār al-Turath, 1410/1990.

Al-Jazīrī, ᶜAbd al-Raḥmān, *al-Fiqh ᶜalā al-Madhāhib al-Arbaᶜah*, 5th edn, Cairo: Al-Maktabah al-Tijāriyyah al-Kubra, n.d.; and Istanbul: Hakikat Kitaberi, 1991.

Al-Jundī, Muḥammad al-Shahat, *Muᶜāmalāt al-Burṣah fi'l-Sharīᶜah al-Islāmiyyah*, Cairo: Dār al-Nahdah al-ᶜArabiyyah 1409/1988.

Al-Jurjānī, Sayyid Sharif, *Kitāb al-Taᶜrifāt*, Istanbul: al-Astanah, 1327 AH.

Kamali, Mohammad Hashim, *Principles of Islamic Jurisprudence*, 2nd revised edition, Cambridge: The Islamic Texts Society, 1991.

Kane, Daniel, *Principles of International Finance*, London: Croom Helm, 1988.

Al-Kāsānī, ᶜAla'uddīn, *Badā'iᶜ al-Ṣanā'iᶜ fī Tartīb al-Shara'iᶜ*, Cairo: Maṭbaᶜah al-Jamaliyyah, 1328/1910.

Kāzīm, Murad, *al-Burṣah, Jihazuha, Anwaᶜuha, ᶜAmaliyatuha*, Damascus: Maṭbaᶜah al-Thubat, n.d.

Khan, Muhammad Akram, 'Commodity Exchange and Stock Exchange in An Islamic Economy', *The American Journal of Islamic Social Sciences* 5 (1988), pp. 89-102.

Khan, Muhammad Fahim *et al.*, *A Survey of Issues and a Programme for Research in Monetary and Fiscal Economics of Islam*, Islamabad: Institute of Policy Research, 1981.

Al-Khaṭīb, ᶜAbd al-Karīm, *al-Siyāsah al-Māliyyah fi'l-Islām wa Sillatuha bi'l-Muᶜamat al-Muᶜasarah*, 2nd edn, Cairo: Dār al-Fikr al-ᶜArabī, 1976.

Al-Khaṭṭabī, Abū Sulaymān Harad b. Muḥammad, *Maᶜālim al-Sunan*, ed. Muḥammad Hamīd al-Faqi, Cairo: Maṭbaᶜah al-Sunnah al-Muḥammadiyyah, 1368/1949.

Kolb, Robert W. *Understanding Futures Markets*, Glenview (Illinois): Scott, Foresman & Co., 1985.

Kuala Lumpur Commodity Exchange Manual of Floor Procedures, Kuala Lumpur, 1985.

Madkūr, Muḥammad Salām, *al-Fiqh al-Islāmi: al-Madkhal wa'l-Amwal wa'l-Ḥuqūq wa'l-ᶜUqūd*, 2nd edn, Cairo: Maṭbaᶜah al-Fajalah, 1955.

Mahmassānī, Ṣubḥī, *Al-Mawjibāt wa'l-ᶜUqūd fi'l-Sharīᶜah al-Islāmiyyah*, 3rd edn. Beirut: Dār al-ᶜIlm li'l-Malāyin, 1983.

Majlis al-Majmaᶜ al-Fiqhī al-Islāmī, 'Sūq al-Bada'iᶜ (al-Burṣah)', in *Qararat Majlis al-Majmaᶜ al-Fiqhī al-Islāmī*, Mecca: Rabitah al-ᶜAlam al-Islāmī, 1985, pp. 120-25.

Malaysian Business, Kuala Lumpur.

Mālik, Ibn Anas, *al-Muwaṭṭa'*, ed. ᶜAbdal-Wahhāb ᶜAbd al-Latif, Beirut: Dār al-Maᶜrifah, 1399/1979.

Mallat, Chibli (ed.), *Islamic Law and Finance*, London: Graham & Trotman, 1988.

Maniᶜ, ᶜAbd Allāh b. Sulaymān, 'Hukm al-ᶜUrf fī Iᶜtibar Qabḍ al-Shik Qabḍ li-Muhtawah', Jeddah: al-Majmaᶜ al-Fiqh al-Islāmī (Resolution No. 7), 1989.

Al-Marghinānī, Burhān al-Dīn, *The Hidāya*, tr. Charles Hamilton, Lahore: Premier Book House, 1982.

Al-Mawsili, ᶜAbd Allāh b. Maḥmud b. Mawdūd, *al-Ikhtiyar li-Taᶜlil al-Mukhtar*, ed. Taha Muḥammad al-Zayri, Cairo: al-Maṭbaᶜah al-Munīriyyah, 1950.

Al-Mawsūᶜah al-Fiqhiyyah, Kuwait: Wizārat al-Awqāf Wa'l-Shu'ūn al-Islāmiyyah, 1408/1987.

Al-Mawsūᶜah al-ᶜIlmiyyah wa'l-ᶜAmaliyyah li'l-Bunūk al-Islāmiyyah Cairo: al-Ittiḥād al-Duwali li'l-Bunūk al-Islāmiyyah, vol. 5, 1402/1982.

Mayo, Herbert B., *Investments: An Introduction*, Chicago: Dryden Press, 1984.

Al-Miṣrī, Rafiq Yūnus, *al-Maysir wa'l-Qimār al-Musabaqat wa'l-Jawa'iz*, Damascus: Dār al-Qalam, 1413/1993.

Mohammed, Noor, 'Principles of Islamic Contract Law', *Journal of Law and Religion*, 6 (1988).

Mohsin, Mohammed, 'A Profile of Riba-free Banking', in Muhammad Ariff (ed.), *Monetary and Fiscal Economics of Islam*, Jeddah: King Abdul Aziz University, 1403/1982, pp.187-224.

Al-Mubārakfūrī, Abū al-ᶜAlī Muḥammad ᶜAbd al-Raḥmān, *Tuḥfah al-Ahwazi bi-Sharḥ Jamiᶜ al-Tirmidhī*, 2nd edn, Cairo: al-Maktabah al-Salafiyyah, 1965.

Mujallah al-Aḥkām al-ᶜAdliyyah (known as the *Mejelle*), Eng. trans. C. R. Tyser, Lahore: Law Publishing Co., 1967.

Musa, Muhammad Yusuf, 'The Liberty of Individual in Contracts and Conditions According to Islamic Law', *Islamic Quarterly* 2 (1955), pp. 68-85.

Mūsā, Muḥāmmad Yūsuf, *al-Buyūᶜ wa'l-ᶜAmaliyyat al-Māliyyah al-Muᶜasarah*, Cairo: Dār al-Kitāb al-ᶜArabī, 1954.

Muslim, Abū al-Ḥusayn ibn al-Ḥajjāj al-Nīshāpūrī, *Mukhtaṣar Ṣaḥīḥ Muslim*, ed. Muḥammad Nāṣir al-Dīn al-Albānī, 4th edn, Beirut: al-Maktab al-Islāmī, 1402/1982.

Al-Nawawī, Abū Zakariyya Muḥyī'l-Dīn Yaḥyā b. Sharaf, *al-Majmūᶜ Sharḥ al-Muhadhdhab*, Cairo: Idarah al-Tibāᶜah al-Munīriyyah, 1345/1925.

——*Al-Wafi fī Sharḥ al-Arbaᶜīn Ḥadīth al-Nawawiyyah*, compiled by Muṣṭafā al-Naqa', 2nd edn, Damascus: Mu'assassah ᶜUlūm al-Qur'ān, 1982.

New York Institute of Finance, *Futures. A Personal Seminar*, New York: New York Institute of Finance, 1989.

New Strait Times, Kuala Lumpur.

Niazi, Liaquat Ali Khan, *Islamic Law of Contract*, Lahore: Research Cell, 1990.

Parker R. J., 'The Role and Organisation of the Clearing House', paper presented at Kuala Lumpur Commodity Exchange workshop, Johor Bahru, 28 September 1985.

Parker R. J. & Salihin Ramli, 'The Clearing House Procedures', paper presented at Kuala Lumpur Commodity Exchange workshops, Johor Bahru, 28 September 1985.

Al-Qādir, ᶜAlī ᶜAbd, 'Taᶜqīb ᶜalā Ra'y al-Tashrīᶜ fī Masā'il al-Burṣah', in *al-Mawsūᶜah al-ᶜIlmiyyah wa'l-ᶜAmaliyyah li'l-Bunūk al-Islāmiyyah*, Cairo: Al-Ittihad al-Duwali li'l-Bunūk al-Islāmiyyah, 1402/1982.

Qadri, Anwar Ahmad, *Islamic Jurisprudence in the Modern World*, 2nd edn, Lahore: Shah Muhammad Ashraf, 1981.

Al-Qaradāwī, Yūsuf, *Bayᶜ al-Murābaḥah li'l-Amir bi'l-Shira'*, 2nd edn, Cairo: Maktabah Wahbah, 1407/1987.

——*Sharīʿah al-Islām Salihah li'l-Tatbiq fī Kull Zaman wa Makah*, Cairo: Dār al-Sahwah, 1393 AH.

Al-Qarāfī, Shihāb al-Dīn, *Kitāb al-Furūq*, Cairo: Maṭbaʿah Dār al-Iḥyā' al-Kutub al-ʿArabiyyah, 1346 AH.

Al-Qurṭubī, Abū ʿAbd Allāh Muḥammad, *al-Jāmiʿ li-Aḥkām al-Qur'ān* (known as *Tafsīr al-Qurṭubī*), 3rd edn, Cairo: Dār al-Kutub al-ʿArabiyyah, 1387/1967.

Al-Qurṭubī, Abū'l-Walīd Muḥammad b. Rushd, *Bidāyat al-Mujtahid wa Nihāyat al-Muqtaṣid*, 5th edn, Cairo: Muṣṭafā al-Bābī al-Ḥalabī 1401/1981.

Rahim, Sir Abdur, *Principles of Muhammadan Jurisprudence*, Lahore: All Pakistan Legal Decisions, 1977.

Rayner S. E., *The Theory of Contracts in Islamic Law*, London: Graham & Trotman, 1991.

Al-Rāzī, Fakhr al-Dīn Muḥammad b. ʿUmar, *Tafsīr al-Kabīr*, Beirut: Dār al-Fikr, 1398/1978.

Rebell, Arthur L. *et al.*, *Financial Futures and Investment Strategy*, Homewood: Dow Jones-Irwin, 1984.

Redhead, Keith, *Introduction to Financial Futures and Options*, Cambridge, Mass: Woodhead Faulkner, 1990.

Relly, Frank K., *Investment Analysis and Portfolio Management*, 2nd edn, Chicago: The Dryden Press, 1985.

Rosenthal, Franz, *Gambling in Islam,* Leiden: E.J. Brill, 1975.

Ibn Rushd, Muḥammad ibn Aḥmad. *al-Muqaddimāt al-Mumahhidāt*, Cairo: Maṭbaʿah al-Saʿādah, 1325 AH.

Al-Ṣabūnī, ʿAbd al-Raḥmān *et al.*, *al-Madkhal al-Fiqhī wa Tārīkh al-Tashrīʿ al-Islāmī*, Cairo: Maktabah Wahbah 1402/1982.

Sahnun, ʿAbd al-Salām b. Saʿīd b. Ḥabīb al-Tanukhi, *al-Mudawwanah al-Kubrā li'l-Imām Mālik b. Anas*, Beirut: Dar al-Maʿrifah, n.d.

Salleh, Nabil A., 'Financial Transactions and the Islamic Theory of Obligation & Contracts', in C. Mallat (ed.), *Islamic Law and Finance*, London: Graham & Trotman 1988, pp. 13-31.

——'Definition and Formation of Contract under Islamic and Arab Law', *Arab Law Quarterly,* 5 (1990), p. 100-117.

Al-Sālūs, ʿAlī Aḥmad, *al-Muʿāmalāt al-Māliyyah al-Muʿasarah fī Daw' al-Sharīʿah al-Islāmiyyah*, Kuwait:Maktabah al-Falah, 1406/1986.

Al-Ṣanānī, Muḥammad b. Ismāʿīl, *Subul al-Salām Sharḥ Bulugh al-Maram*, Cairo: al-Maktabah al-Tijāriyyah al-Kubra, 1353 AH.

Al-Sanhūrī, ʿAbd al-Razzāq, *Maṣādir al-Ḥaqq fi'l-Fiqh al-Islāmī*, Cairo: Maʿhad al-Darasāt al-ʿArabiyyah al-ʿĀliyyah, 1956.

Al-Sarakhsī, Shams al-Dīn, *al-Mabsūṭ*, Beirut: Dār al-Maʿrifah, 1406/1986.

Al-Shāfiʿī, Muḥammad b. Idrīs, *al-Risālah*, ed. Aḥmad Muḥammad Shakir, Cairo: Muṣṭafā al-Bābī al-Ḥalabī, 1940.

——*Al-ʿUmm*, Bulaq: al-Maṭbaʿah al-Kubra 1321/1901.

Shalabī, Muḥammad Muṣṭafā, *al-Fiqh al-Islāmī bayn Mithāliyyah wa'l-Wāqiʿiyyah*, Cairo: Dār al-Jāmiʿah, 1982.

Al-Sharbīnī, Muḥammad al-Khaṭīb, *Mughnī al-Muḥtāj*, Cairo: Muṣṭafā al-Bābī al-Ḥalabī, 1958.

Al-Shāṭibī, Abū Isḥāq Ibrāhīm, *al-Muwāfaqāt fī Uṣūl al-Aḥkām*, ed. Shaykh ʿAbd Allāh Dirāz, Cairo: al-Maṭbaʿah al-Tijāriyyah al-Kubra, n.d.

Al-Shawkānī, Yaḥyā b. ʿAlī, *Irshād al-Fuhūl min Taḥqīq al-Ḥaqq ilā ʿIlm al-Uṣūl*, Cairo: Dār al-Fikr, n.d.

——*Nayl al-Awṭār Sharḥ Muntaqā al-Akhbār*, Cairo: Muṣṭafa al-Bābī al-Ḥalabī, n.d.

Al-Shirāzī, Ibrāhīm b. ʿAlī b. Yūsuf, *al-Muhadhdhab fi'l-Madhhab*, Cairo: Muṣṭafa al-Bābī al-Ḥalabī, 3rd printing, 1396/1976.

Siddiqi, Muhammad Nejatullah, *Insurance in an Islamic Economy*, Leicester: The Islamic Foundation, 1985.

Smith, Gene, 'Commodity Market', in *Encyclopedia Americana*, vol. VII, p. 391.

Siraj, Muḥammad Aḥmad, *al-Niẓām al-Maṣrafī al-Islāmī*, Cairo: Dār al-Thaqāfah li'l-Nashr wa'l-Tawzīʿ, 1410/1989.

SFC Finance Co. v. *K. Masri*, All England Law Reports 1 (1986) 44.

The Star, Kuala Lumpur.

Sulaymān, Aḥmad Yūsuf, 'Ra'y al-Tashrīʿ al-Islāmi fī Masā'il al-Burṣah', in *al-Mawsūʿah al-ʿIlmiyyah wa'l-ʿAmaliyyah li'l-Bunūk al-Islāmiyyah*, Cairo: al-Ittiḥād al-Duwali li'l-Bunūk al-Islāmiyyah, vol. V, 1402/1982, pp. 384-410.

Teweles, R. J. & Frank J. Jones, *The Commodity Futures Game*, 2nd edn, New York: Mc Graw Hill Book Co., 1987.

Al-Tirmidhī, Abū ʿĪsā Muḥammad, *Sunan al-Tirmidhī*, Istanbul: Cagri Yayinlari, 1981.

Wilson, Rodney, 'Islamic Financial Instruments', *Arab Law Quarterly* 6 (1991), pp. 205-15.

Zaman, Raquibuz, 'The Operation of Modern Financial Markets for Stocks and Bonds and Its Relevance to an Islamic Economy', *The American Journal of Islamic Social Sciences*, 3 (1986), 125.

Al-Zarqa, Muṣṭafā Aḥmad, *al-Madkhal al-Fiqhī al-ʿAm*, 3 vols., Damascus: Dār al-Fikr, 1967-68.

Al-Zaylaʿi, ʿUthman b. ʿAlī, *Tabyin al-Haqa'iq Sharḥ Kanz al-Daqa'iq*, Cairo: Bulaq 1313 AH.

Index

Abbasids, 153
ʿAbd al-Bāsiṭ, Badr al-Mutawalli, 170-6
ʿAbd Allāh ibn ʿUmar, 114, 194, 201
ʿAbd al-Qādir, ʿAlī
 on 'sell not what is not with you', 115
 response to prohibitive judgements on futures, 160-2
 views on options trading, 198
ʿAbd al-Salām, ʿIzz al-Dīn, 100
Abī Wahshiyah, Jaʿfar ibn, 112
 absent, sale of the. See sale of the unseen
 absolute meanings of Qur'ānic verses, specifying, 80
Abū Bakr, 153
Abū Dāwūd, 111
Abū Ḥabīb, Saʿdī, 152
Abū Ḥanīfah, 133. See also Ḥanafī school
Abū Hurayrah, 2
Abū Sulaymān, ʿAbd al-Wahhāb, 191-2, 199-201
Abū Yūsuf
 position on duration of option period, 195
 position on manufacturing contract, 133
 account records, 123
al-aʿḍā' al-munḍammūn, 52
al-aʿḍā' al-murāsilūn, 52
al-aʿḍā' al-samasirah. See clearing members
agency, 25, 136, 176-7
 brokerage activity as, 169
 on behalf of both parties in a contract, 176
 specific and general representation, 177
 when the rules of lease and hire apply, 176
aggregate trading positions, 56
agricultural commodities, 12
agricultural futures, 183
ahl al-ra'y, 79
Aḥmad ibn Ḥanbal. See also Ḥanbalī school
 on *bayʿ al-kāli' bi'l-kāli'*, 127-8
 on market price, 96
 on *al-ʿurbūn*, 201-2
 on delaying delivery, 107
 on duration of option period, 195
 on possession before sale, 119
 on postponing delivery of object of sale, 141
 on sale of debt prior to maturity in forward sale, 127
 on 'sell not what is not with you' (*ḥadīth*), 111
 on stipulations in contracts, 76
ajal. See deferment period
akl māl al-ghayr bi'l bātil, 90
al-ʿamaliyyāt al- sharṭiyyah al-ājilah, 191
al-ʿaqd al-muʿallaq, 135
al-ʿaqd al-muḍāf. See deferred contract

al-ʿaqd al-munajjaz, 135
al-ʿAṭṭār, 142
al-Awzāʿī, on sale of commodities in lump sum, 174
al-azlām, 151
Alexandria Cotton Company, 50
Alexandria futures market, 49-53
    delivery, 159
ʿamaliyyāt sharṭiyyah muḍāʿafah, 191
American-type options, 186
amīn, 177
ʿāmm meanings of Qur'ānic verses, specifying, 80
analogies, 193-4
ʿaqd al-muḍāf. See deferred contract
ʿaqd al-quṭn mutawassiṭ al-tīlah, 52-53
ʿaqd al-quṭn ṭawīl al-tīlah, 52-53
Arabs
    common commercial practices of, 2-3
    use of deferred transactions, 139
ʿarayā, 82
arbitragists, 38
arrows, divination by, 151
asbāb. See causes
associate members, 52
asymmetry in options contract, 188
'at the money' options, 187
attorneys, 176
auction, 143
availability, 86
Āyah al-Mudāyanah, 138-44
    occasion of revelation of, 142
ʿayb (defect), 81
ʿayn, 140, 175
ʿayn al-ḥāḍirah, 131
ʿAzzām, Majd al-Dīn
    on *ḥadīth* of *bayʿ al-kāli' bi'l-kāli'*, 128
    views on futures trading, 170-6

Bādshāh, Amīr, 82
al-Baghāwī, 113
Bahrain, Commercial Code of, 138
al-Bāji, Abū'l-Walīd, 88, 114
barter sale, 141
bāṭil. See void contractual stipulations
al-Batti, ʿUthmān, 174
bayʿ al-ʿaynah, 88
bayʿ al-dayn. See debt clearance sale
bayʿ al-ghā'ib. See sale of the unseen
bayʿ al-juzāf, 88
bayʿ al-kāli' bi'l-kāli', 125
    analysis of *ḥadīth* on, 128, 175
    prohibition of, 127-8, 175
bayʿ al-maʿdūm. See non-existent objects
bayʿ al-maghṣūb. See usurped objects
bayʿ al-majhūl, 89
bayʿ al-mu'ajjal. See deferred sales
bayʿ al-ʿurbūn. See *al-ʿurbūn*
bayʿ bi siʿr al-sūq. See market price
bayʿ qabl al-qabḍ, 88. See also possession
bayʿ taḥt al-qaṭʿ, 53
al-bayʿatayn fī bayʿah, 88
bayʿ al-muʿatat, 154
benefit, 171. See also *maṣlaḥah*
bequest, 135
betting, 153
bills of exchange, acceptance of, 2
bonds, 150
Bourses Act, 50
Bourses Committee, 50-51
Bretton Woods fixed exchange rate system, 183
brokers, 60, 169
bucketing, 48, 57
burṣāt al-ʿuqūd. See Egyptian Futures Market
buyer, role in futures contract, 6
Buyids, 153
buyūʿ al-aʿyān, 113
buyūʿ al-ṣifāt, 113

Cairo, 49
call options, 186
cancellation, option of. See also option of stipulation

as an anomalous stipulation, 77
in options sale, 185
in sale of the unseen, 105
cash market
compared to futures market, 32
contracts as, 74
relationship with futures market, 38-39
CBOE (Chicago Board of Options Exchange), 185
CBOT See Chicago Board of Trade
CFTC (Commodity Futures Trading Commission), 27, 46-48
charitable contracts, 85, 100, 106
charitable endowments (*waqf*), 136
Chicago Board of Options Exchange (CBOE), 185
Chicago Board of Trade (CBOT), 3
bibliography of publications on futures market, 150
history, 31
Chicago, 3
churning, 47
clearance of mutual debts, 126
clearing margins, 36
clearing members, 52
clearing-houses, 23, 34-38
in cotton exchange of Alexandria, 51
customer and house accounts, 34
example illustrating operation procedures, 36-37
guarantee and surplus funds, 36
members of, 34
offsetting procedure, 37-38
Options Clearing Corporation, 185
performance guarantees, 28, 34
role in elimination of risk-taking, 94, 130
collective duty of *ijtihād*, 82
commenda, 136
commerce, 171
commercial papers
use of by early Arabs, 2
commission fees, 8. See also premiums
Commodities Trading Act 1985, 54
Commodities Trading Commission, 54
Commodity Brokers' Association, 50
commodity coupons
documentary evidence of weight of commodity, 123
use of in Umayyad rule, 2
Commodity Exchange Act, 48
Commodity Exchange Authority, 9
commodity futures exchange, 30
origins, 4
Commodity Futures Trading Commission (CFTC), 27, 46-48
commodity prices, fluctuations in, 3. See also price
Compensation Fund, 54
compensation. See *ḍamān*
complementary benefit, 171
compulsory registration of transactions, 47
condition of enforceability, 89
conflicts, prevention of, 77-78
consensus
can originate from customs, 80
decisive and speculative, 175
popular consensus, 175
consent, 137
consequences and causes of a contract, distinguishing between, 136
contingent contracts, 135
contract notes, 58-59
contracts. See also futures contract
cannot be used to inflict harm, 106-7
classification of, 135, 136
conditions for validity, 172
conventional, 22-28
freedom of, 74-77
period, 185
positions of the four schools on, 76
prompt, 164
stipulations, 75-76, 196-7
suspended, 177
varieties of present at advent of Islam, 139

contracts of exchange, 100
contractual options, 192
contract-within-a-contract, 197
controlled nature of futures contract, 26-27
conventional contracts, 22-28
corporations, conferring membership privileges to, 33
corruption, 86
cost plus profit sale, 85
cost-efficiency of futures trading, 17
cotton exchange of Alexandria, 49-53
Cotton Price Stabilisation Fund, 51
cotton, 49-53
  sale before possession, 122
countervalues, 134
covered writers, 187
CPO (crude palm oil), 53
credit partnership, 161
cross-trading, 32, 48, 57
cumulative contracts, 85
currency for currency, sale of, 120, 141
custody, 121
custom (*ʿurf*), 79-81
  role of in Egyptian Civil Law, 137
  role of in interpretation of the Qur'ān, 80
  stipulations validated by, 77
customer accounts, 34

daily limit, 43, 149
  imposed by Egyptian legislation, 169
  regulating speculation with, 156
daily range, 43, 149
daily settlement. See marking-to-the-market
ḍamān, 114, 161, 193
  sale before possession, 121
  transfer of, 196
  al-Daraqutnī
  ḥadīth on *bayʿ al-kālī' bi'l-kālī'*, 128
al-Ḍarīr, Ṣiddīq
  on effective risk-taking, 88
  on 'sell not what is not with you' (*ḥadīth*), 115
  position of on sale of debts, 128
  position of on sale of non-existent objects, 91
ḍārūrī benefit, 171
dayn, 139. See also debt clearance sale
  ʿayn, distinguishing between, 140, 175
  differences on interpretation of, 142
debt clearance sale, 125-30
  debt transfer, 127
  deferment of debts, 142
  Fakhr al-Rāzī's position on, 141
  offsetting transaction, resemblance of to, 129
  to third parties, invalidity of, 107
decisive consensus, 175
decisive text, 66
defects, 81
deferment period, 134
deferred contract, 25. See also deferred sales
  forward sale, discussion on whether deferred contract qualifies as, 165
  futures contract compared to, 26
  positions of the schools of law on, 136
  Qur'ānic verse concerning, 138-44
  situations in which deferment is valid, 93
deferred liability transactions, 2
deferred sales, 25, 131-44
  ʿayn and *dayn* in transactions, 140
  conditions for validity of, 134
  deferment of debts, 142
  deferment of one countervalue only, 140-1
  delaying delivery of the object of the sale, 141
  preventing risk-taking in, 86
definitive prohibitions, 171
deliverability, 86, 106-8
delivery, 10-11

agricultural commodities, 12
in forward sale, 25
Ibn Taymiyyah's and Ibn Qayyim's position on, 107
postponing, 77, 107-8, 141
taking possession (*qabḍ*) and, 117
derivative instruments, 58
description of objects in sale of the unseen, 104
elimination of uncertainty with, 161, 167
desirable benefit, 171
devotional matters and *muʿāmalāt*, 78
al-Dhahabi, 111
dice, 152
difference of opinion (*ikhtilāf*), 162
disciplinary regulations, 46-48
discounts for lower grades, 10-11
discrepant analogies, 193-4
divination by arrows, 151
divorce, 136
documentation
importance of, 138
transactions which do not require, 140
warehouse receipts, 123
double options, 186, 191
double quantity options, 191
dowry, 81, 95
Dubai Law of Contracts, 138

ease, 70-74
in the *Sunnah*, 73
Qur'ānic directives for, 72-73
economics, 171
effective causes, 78-79
of prohibition of sale before possession (*qabḍ*), 120
effective risk-taking, 88
Egyptian Civil Law, 137
Egyptian Cotton Committee, 52
Egyptian Futures Market, 49
delivery, 159
regulating speculation, 169
enforceability, 89
equity securities, 184
essential benefit, 171
European-type options, 186
evacuation, 117, 121
excessive risk-taking, 87-90
Exchange Management Company, 55
executor, 26
executorship, 135
exercise date, 183
exercise price, 26, 183, 185
expiration date, 183
exploitation, prevention of, 77-78

Fair Letter, 1
false trading, 57, 60
farḍ kafā'ī (collective duty), 82
farmers, 38
fasād (corruption), 86
fāsid. See irregular contractual stipulations
fatrat al-ikhtiyār, 191
fatwā, originating from customs (*ʿurf*), 80
FCMs (Futures Commission Merchants), 32, 36-37
fictitious sales, 57
financial futures, 183
Fiqh Academy of Jeddah, 92, 199
position on sale before possession, 120
Fiqh Academy of Mecca
views of on futures trading, 162-6
fiqh, influence of social customs on, 162
firms, conferring membership privileges to, 33
floor brokers, 31
churning and front-running, preventing, 47
example illustrating operation procedures, 37
fluctuations in commodity prices, 3
alleviated by use of futures, 16
Cotton Price Stabilisation Fund, 51
KLCE daily limits for, 56
fluctuations in commodity prices,

3,149
foodstuffs, 68-69
possession of before sale, 118-9
football, 148
foreign currencies, 12
forward sale
delivery dates, 25
futures market, differences from, 5
ignoring elements of risk in, 85
inflexibility of, 24
length of deferment, 127
possession not required before, 122
postponing price to a future date, 175
sale of debt prior to maturity, 127
sale of non-existent objects, 23
subject-matter in, 133
to-arrive contracts, 4
validity of, 3, 77, 113
when deferred contracts do not qualify as, 165
fraudulent manipulation, 74
fraudulent trading, 48, 57
freedom of contract, 74-77
freedom of stipulation in contracts, 75
front-running customer orders, preventing, 47
fruit, sale of unripe, 87
fungible commodities, 24
selling before ownership, permissibility of, 113
taking possession of (*qabḍ*), 122
fuqahā, 71
futures broker licences, 59-60
Futures Commission Merchants (FCMs), 32
example illustrating operation procedures, 36-37
futures contract. See also futures trading
commission fees, 8
conventional contracts, differences from, 22-28
debt clearance sale, 125-30
deferred contract compared to, 26
five types of, 12
forward sale, differences from, 5
history, 1-6
margin, 9-10
matching, 35
measurement and weighing, 123
options contract, differences from, 186, 189
options on futures, 187-9
prevailing market prices, 96
registration of, 7-8
sale before possession, 122-4
specification, 6-7
standardisation, 24
standardised deferment periods, 94
stocks, compared with, 8-9, 150
subject-matter in, 102
termination of, 23
unlimited number can be created, 7
futures exchange, 30-33
cash market compared, 32
members, 31
pits, 31
structure, 32
Futures Industry Act, 58
futures options. See options on futures
futures trading. See also futures contract
as a risk transfer mechanism, 148
beneficial uses of, 15-20, 164
cotton exchange of Alexandria, 49-53
delivery, 10-11, 108, 118
disadvantages of, 163
economic effects, 148
Fiqh Academy of Mecca, position of on, 162-6
flexibility of, 6
history, 1-6
offsetting transaction, 129
Options Clearing Corporation, 185
possession, 167
possibility of making profit and loss, 143

price volatility and, 149
prohibitive judgements on, 159-60
risk-taking, 92, 94
rules introduced to ensure orderly trading, 5
sale of non-existent objects, application of concept to, 91-92
speculation in, 155
speculative aspects of, regulating, 27
stocks, compared with, 8-9, 150

gambling, 25-26, 151-7. See also risk-taking
betting, 153
compared to insurance, 152
defined, 151-2
difference from speculation, 147
implications on sale of unseen and unknown, 90
maysīr, meaning of, 152-3
risk-taking and, 153-5
similarities with futures trading, 163
general representation, 177
general meanings of the Qur'ān, specifying, 80
ghabn. See fraudulent manipulation
ghālib, 152
gharar. See risk-taking
ghayr-maḍmūn, 114
gifts, 136
give and take sale, 154
GNMAS, 12
going long, meaning of, 7
goods tradable in futures markets, 32
grades, delivery, 10
grantors, 184
covered and uncovered, 187
guarantee funds, 36
guarantees, 161
guarantors, 129

ḥabal al-ḥabālah. See unborn animals
Ḥabbān ibn Munqidh, 194
ḥabs, 121
ḥadīth, local factors in collection of, 162
ḥājjat al-nās (public needs), 85
ḥājjī benefit, 171
Ḥakim ibn Ḥizām, 23
'sell not what is not with you' (*ḥadith*), 112, 160
ḥalāl. See lawful and unlawful
Ḥanafī school
basis for position on option of cancellation, 105
contracts, 76
custom (*ʿurf*), use of, 81
deferred sale, conditions for validity of, 134
ownership of object of sale, 112-3
position on contractual stipulations, 196
position on deferred sale, 133
position on duration of option period, 195
position on sale before possession, 120
position on sale of the unseen, 89, 90, 103-106
valid, irregular and void contractual stipulations, 76-77
Ḥanbalī school
delivery, delaying, 107-8
determination of price, 95-96
Egyptian civil law, influence of in, 137
freedom of stipulation in contracts, 75
market price, legitimacy of sale at, 90
non-existent objects, sale of, 100-101
position on clearance of debt sale, 126
position on contractual stipulations, 197
position on deferred sale, 132
position on sale before possession, 121
principle of permissibility (*ibāḥah*), application of, 67

risk-taking, four-part classification of, 93-94
al-ḥaraj. See hardship
ḥarām. See lawful and unlawful
hardship, removal of, 70-74. See also leniency
ignoring risks in contracts, 85
Ḥassan, Aḥmad Muḥayyuddīn, 198-9
al-ḥaṣṣāt, 87
ḥawālah, 2
hedgers, 38-40
hedging, 2. See also spreading
in futures market, 17
risk management and reduction, 183
risk transferral with, 39
Hidāya, 119
ḥirāsah muḥkamah qawiyyah bi'l-ḍ amānāt, 161
hire. See lease and hire
al-ḥirz, 121
holding periods for futures contracts, 28
horse racing, 153
house accounts, 34
ḥūkm. See consequences
Hunt, Baker, 149
ḥurriyyah al-taʿāqud. See contracts, freedom of
ḥuṣūl (availability), 86
Hutchinson, 149

ʿibādāt, 78
ibāḥah. See permissibility
IBM stock, 184
Ibn ʿAbbās, ʿAbd Allāh
deferred sale, confining to one countervalue only, 140-1
expiation and repentance, 70-71
on possession (*qabḍ*), 118-9, 174
Ibn ʿĀbidīn
definition of risk-taking, 84
definition of sale and deferred sale, 132
Ibn al-ʿArabī, definition of qimār, 152
Ibn al-Humam, 112
Ibn Bāz, ʿAbd al-ʿAzīz, 165
Ibn Ḥazm
definition of risk-taking, 85-86
on sale before possession, 121
Ibn Ḥabbān, 111
Ibn Juzay
on sale of the unseen, 104
tolerance of minor risk-taking, 87
Ibn Kathīr
on deferred contracts, 142
on the *āyah al-mudāyanah*, 140
Ibn Masʿūd, ʿAbd Allāh, 80
Ibn Qayyim al-Jawziyyah
Egyptian civil law, influence of in, 137
on existence of subject-matter of a sale, 100
on *maysīr*, 151
on presumtion of impermissibility, 66
on sale of 'what is not with you', 113-4
position on contractual stipulations, 197
position on deferred sale, 132
position on delaying delivery, 107-108
position on sales in which exact price is unknown, 95
sale of non-existent objects, 91
Ibn Qudāmah
on debt clearance sale, 127
on *ḥadīth* of *bayʿ al-kāli' bi'l-kāli'*, 128
on sale before possession, 121, 173
on sale of what the seller does not own, 112
position on duration of option period, 195
Ibn Rushd al-Qurṭubī
on conditions of a valid forward sale, 127
on excessive risk-taking, 87
on requirements of a sale, 22

on sale before possession, 120
Ibn Sīrīn, 201
Ibn Taymiyyah, Taqī al-Dīn
contracts and stipulations, 76
definition of risk-taking, 86, 90
Egyptian civil law, influence of in, 137
on existence of subject-matter of a sale, 100
on *ḥadīth* of *bay*ᶜ *al-kālī' bi'l-kālī'*, 128
on relationship between risk-taking and gambling, 153-5
on sale of the unseen, 105, 154
on sale 'of what is not with you', 114
on the evils of gambling, 151
position on contractual stipulations, 197
position on deferred sale, 132
position on delaying delivery, 107
position on sale before possession, 121
position on sales in which exact price is unknown, 95
relationship between means and legal consequences, 74
sale of debt prior to maturity in forward sale, 127
ibrā' al-dayn, 136
ignorance of object of sale, 88-89
ijārah. See lease and hire
*ijmā*ᶜ. See consensus
ijtihād, 79
ikhtilāf, 162
*ikhtiyār al-daf*ᶜ. See put option
ikhtiyār al-ṭalab. See call option
al-ikhtiyārāt. See options trading
ᶜ*illah*. See effective causes
illicit gain, 77. See also usury
Illinois-Michigan canal, 3
immovable objects, sale before possession, 120
'in the money' options, 187
ᶜ*inah*, 126, 132
Imām al-Shāfiᶜī's exclusion of from the purview of usury, 174
ineffective risk-taking, 88
inflation, combatting with futures, 16
injustice, prevention of, 77-78
insurance
compared to gambling, 152
excessive risk-taking in, 94
futures as, 16-17
intellect. See reason
interest rate options, 181
interest. See usury
interest-earning assets, 12
international relations, 171
International Tin Council (ITC), 33
International Union of Islamic Banks, 170
inventories, writing options against, 183
investing, 147
Iraqi civil code, 137
irregular contractual stipulations, 76, 77
īṣā', 135
Islamic law
accomodating social changes, 79
custom, 79-81
ease and the removal of hardship, 70-74
principle of permissibility, 66-70
ursuing of benefits in, 82
reason, role of, 78
risk taking (*See* risk-taking)
*istiṣnā*ᶜ. See manufacture, contract of
ITC (International Tin Council), 33
*Ittihād al-Iskandariyyah li'l-Maḥāṣīl al-*ᶜ*Āmmah*, 50

Jābir, 107
postponing delivery of object of sale, 141
*Jamā*ᶜ*ah Samāsirah al-Badā'i*ᶜ, 50
Japan, 1
al-Jassas, 71
Jordan's Civil Code, 138
al-Jundī, Shahat
views of on futures trading, 166-8
views on options trading, 198

al-Jurjānī, Sayyid Sharīf, 152
juristic disagreement, 162
jurists, 71
juzāfan, 119, 121

kafīl, 129
kāli', 128
Kansas City Board of Trade, 13
memberships, 33
al-Kāsānī, ʿAla'uddīn
definition of risk-taking, 86
on deliverability of subject matter of sale, 106
on ignorance of object of sale, 88-89
on ownership of subject-matter of sale, 112
on sale before possession, 120
on seller acquiring ownership after the sale, 22-23
position on sales in which exact price is unknown, 95
KATS, 59
al-Khaṭīb, ʿAbd al-Karīm
on *ḥadīth* of 'sell not what is not with you', 112
views of on futures trading, 168-70
al-Khaṭṭabī, 113
khiyār al-ʿayb, 192
khiyār al-ru'yah, 90, 192
khiyār al-sharṭ. See option of cancellation; option of stipulation
khiyār al-taʿyīn, 192
al-khiyārāt, 192
use of concept of to validate options trading, 193, 203
khiyār wa ajal. See option and deferment
Kitāb al-ʿUmm, 105
KLCE Gazette, 56
KLCE. See Kuala Lumpur Commodity Exchange
KLFM (Kuala Lumpur Futures Market), 58
KLIBOR (Kuala Lumpur Interbank Offered Rates), 58
KLOFFE See Kuala Lumpur Options and Futures Exchange
KLOFFE's Automated Trading System, 59
Kuala Lumpur Commodity Exchange, 53-57
conditions for clearing membership, 55
membership at, 55
trading limits, 56-57
Kuala Lumpur Futures Market, 58
Kuala Lumpur Interbank Offered Rates, 58
Kuala Lumpur Options and Futures Exchange, 12, 57-60
contract notes, 58-59
derivative instruments, 58
KLOFFE's Automated Trading System, 59
trading and local members, 58
Kuwait's Commercial Code, 138

Lajnah al-Quṭn al-Miṣriyah, 52
Lajnat al-Burṣāh, 50-51
land, 150
lawful and unlawful
definitive and speculative prohibitions, 171
effective causes, inquiry into, 78-79
meanings contained within the purview of a prohibition, 111-2
necessity makes the unlawful lawful, 71
necessity of clear injunctions for establishing unlawfulness, 143
presumption of permissibility, 67-68
reason, role of in establishing rulings concerning, 78
'the Prophet (Allāh bless him and give him peace) prohibited', meaning of, 86
unlawfulness, declaration of as sole prerogative of Allāh, 70

Ẓāhirī school's understanding of, 75
lease and hire, 25, 136
risk-taking can affect contract of, 85
when rules of apply to agency (*wakālah*), 176
Leggat, J., 6
Leiter, 149
leniency. See also hardship,
ḥadīth concerning, 73
in sale involving commodity coupons, 2
letter of credit, acceptance of, 2
liability for loss, 114
licences, 60
LIFFE (London International Financial Futures Exchange), 33
livestock futures, 11
LME (London Metal Exchange), 33
loans, 135, 139
local members (KLOFFE), 58
localities, influence of on fiqh, 162
London International Financial Futures Exchange (LIFFE), 33
London Metal Exchange (LME), 33
long (buyer in futures contract), 6
long fibre cotton contract, 52-53
long hedge example, 39-40
long sales in options, 187
lotteries, 153
lump sum
foodgrains bought in, 119
sale before possession, 121
sale of commodities in, 174
luzūm, 89

Madkūr, Muḥammad Salām, 75
maʿdūm. See non-existent objects
maghlūb, 152
mahr al-mithl, 95
maintenance margin, 9
Makdūr, Muḥammad Salām, 75
Malaysia, introduction of futures and options in, 54
Malaysian Futures Clearing Corporation, 55
Mālik, Imām. See also Mālikī school
contracts of exchange and charitable contracts, 100
on deferment period, 134
on sale of commodities in lump sum, 174
position on debt clearance sale, 125
position on duration of option period, 195
prohibition of commodity coupons, 2
Mālikī school. See also Mālik, Imām
custom (*ʿurf*), use of, 81
deferred sale, conditions for validity of, 134
freedom of contract, 76
on deliverability of subject-matter in charitable contracts, 106
position on contractual stipulations, 196
position on deferred sale, 132
position on duration of option period, 195
position on sale before possession, 120
position on sales in which exact price is unknown, 95
reverse mortgage, 127
sale of the unseen, position on, 90, 101, 103-6
maʿlūmiyyah al-thaman. See price, determination of
manfaʿah, 194
manufacture, contract of, 25-26, 133
lawfulness of, 99
possession not required before, 122
sale of non-existent objects, 78
maqāsah (clearance of mutual debts), 126
maqāṣid. See objectives of Islamic law
maqdūr al-taslīm. See deliverability
margin transactions, 9-10
margins

clearing margins, 36
purpose of, 177
market fluctuations, 3
market price, sale at, 88, 95-96
legitimacy of in Ḥanbalī school, 90
marking-to-the-market
allows small initial margins, 10
clearing-houses, 23, 34-38
example illustrating clearing-house operation procedures, 36-37
interferes with concept of fixed price, 26
London Metal Exchange's adoption of, 33
performance guarantees, 28, 34
risk management, 44-45
marriage, 67, 68
Marwān ibn al-Ḥakam, 2
maṣlaḥah
beneficial uses of futures, 15-20
can originate from customs, 80
maṣlaḥah al-mursalah (unrestricted public interest), 76
realisation of as basis of Islamic law, 172
in sale involving commodity coupons, 2
use of in legalisation of price control, 78
mass media, 150
matching of futures contracts, 35
maturity of options, 183
mawqūf. See suspended sale
maysīr. See gambling
measurement
as a mode of possession of foodstuffs, 123
of fungible foodgrains, 122
medieval juristic opinions, 70
Medinan market compared to modern markets, 115
medium fibre cotton contract, 52-53
members of clearing-houses, 34
members of futures exchanges, 31, 33
compulsory registration of transactions, 47
Kuala Lumpur Commodity Exchange, 55
types of in futures market of Alexandria, 52
metallurgical commodities, 12
metals, 150
MFCC (Malaysian Futures Clearing Corporation), 55
Mid-America Commodity Exchange, 13
Mīna al-Baṣal, 49, 50
Minister of Primary Industries, 54
Minneapolis Grain Exchange, 13
minor risk-taking, 87-90
Al-Mīzān, 111
moderate risk-taking, 87
modern law, 137-8
moveable objects, sale of before possession, 120
muʿāmalāt
overriding the presumption of permissibility, 66, 171
presumption of permissibility, 67-68
reason, role of in establishing rulings concerning, 78
al-Mubārakfūrī, 113
al-maḍāmīn wa'l-malāqīh, 88
muḍārabah, 136
al-Mudawwanah, 126
al-Mudāyanah, Qur'ānic *āyah*, 138-44
occasion of revelation of, 142
muftīs, 71
Mughnī al-Muḥtāj, 126
mukhāṭarah. See risk-taking
mulā'im li'l-ʿaqd, 196
mulāmasah, 87, 90, 154
Mullā ʿAlī Qārī, 113
munābadhah, 87, 90, 154
muqāmarah. *See* gambling
al-muqāyadah, 141
muqtadā al-ʿaqd, 76, 196
murābaḥah (cost plus profit sale), 85
Mūsā, Muḥāmmad Yūsuf, 93, 115
on determination of price, 96
musabbab, 74

al-musāwamah, 143
mushāhadah, 121
muṭlaq meanings of Qur'ānic verses, 80
mutual consent, 137
Muwaṭṭa', 2
al-muzāyadah, 143

Nāfiʿ ibn al-Ḥārith, 201
al-Nasā'ī, 111
Nasīf, ʿAbd Allāh ʿUmar, 165
naṣṣ qaṭ'ī al-thubūt wa'l dalālah, 66
National Futures Association (NFA), 47
al-Nawawī, Yaḥyā ibn Sharaf
on sale of the unseen, 104
ruling of lawfulness of sale involving commodity coupons, 2
Nayl al-Awṭār, 173-4
Naẓariyyah al-Ajal, 142
necessity makes the unlawful lawful, 71
New York Futures Exchange, 33
New York Stock Exchange Index, 12
newspapers, 150
NFA (National Futures Association), 47
non-existent objects, sale of, 90-93
al-Jundī's acceptance of validity of, 166
al-Sanhūrī's categorisation of into four types, 91
application of concepts of to futures trading, 91-92
Ibn Taymiyyah's and Ibn Qayyim's opinions on, 100
in forward sale, 23
in Kuwait's Commercial Code, 138
in manufacturing contract, 78
three types of, 101-3
non-tangible assets, 194

objectives of Islamic law, 70
changing rulings to achieve, 82
OCC (Option Clearance Corporation), 188
offsetting, 32, 129
example illustrating procedure, 37-38
options, 189
oils, 150
oppressive practices in futures trading, 163
option and deferment, 135
Option Clearance Corporation (OCC), 188
option of cancellation, 77, 105
option of defect, 192
option of identification, 192
option of stipulation, 192, 195
option of viewing, 90, 103, 192
option period, 191, 195
Options Clearing Corporation, 185
options on futures, 187-9
advantages of, 188
options trading
calls, puts and doubles, 185-6
cancellation of options, 185
converting options into futures positions, 189
exercising options, 189
expiration date, 186
expiring options, 189
futures contract, differences from, 186, 189
al-khiyārāt, use of concept of to validate, 193
malpractice, likelihood of, 204
monetary value, attaching to options, 200
objections raised against, 199-201
offsetting options, 189
option dealers, 184
premiums, 184, 193, 198
price, 183
reasons for popularity of, 183-4
as risk-management tool, 182
subject-matter of, 200
two types of in Islamic law, 192
types of, 191
uses of options, 183

writers, 184
al-ʿurbūn, using as an analogy for, 193-4
original margin, 9
'out of the money' options, 187
over the counter options, 189
ownership, 22. See also 'sell not what is not with you'
Ḥanafī position on, 112-3

palm oil, sale before possession, 123
partnership, 33, 161, 136
Patten, 149
pecuniary contracts, 77
performance guarantees, 28, 34
period loans, 135
perishable goods, precluded from futures trading, 32
permissibility, principle of, 66-70
civil transactions, 171
overriding the presumption of permissibility, 66
Qur'ānic proofs of, 67
Ẓāhirī school's rejection of, 75
Persians, 153
pits, 31
planning, made possible with use of futures, 16
popular consensus, 175
position limits, 156
position traders, 40
possession
in banking transactions, 123
in barter sale, 141
evacuation, 121
in futures trading, 167
ḥadīth concerning, 118-9
measurement and weighing, 123
prohibition of sale before, reason for, 120
risk-taking in sale before, 120
in sale involving commodity coupons, 2
sale prior to taking, 88, 117-24
various meanings of, 121
postponing delivery, 77
Powers, Dr. Mark, 54
precious stones, 150
premiums, 198
for higher grades, 10-11
in options, 184
validity of, 196
prevailing custom. See custom
prevailing market price, 96, 176
price
control (*tasʿīr*), 78
Cotton Price Stabilisation Fund, 51
determination of, positions of the schools on, 90, 95-96
distortion of, 163-4
exercise and settlement prices, 26
fluctuations in, using hedging to minimise risks of, 40
futures as indicators of, 17-18
futures as moderators of, 19
manipulation of, 48, 57
market (*See* market price)
matching, 35
options contract, 183
postponing to a future date in forward sale, 175
prevailing market price, 96, 176
trading limits, to prevent excessive changes in, 43-44
volatility of, and futures trading, 149
principal-to-principal settlements, 33
professional speculators, 40. See also speculators; speculation
profit, cumulative transfer of to customer, 172
prohibitions. See lawful and unlawful
promissory notes, acceptance of, 2
prompt contracts, 135, 164
public needs, ignoring risks in contracts because of, 85
Public Productivity Corporation of Alexandria, 50
put options, 186

qabḍ. See possession
Qānūn al-Burṣāh, 50
al-Qarafi, 89
qarḍ (loans), 135, 139
al-Qaradāwī, Yūsuf
  criticism of Mālikī position on deferred sales, 132
  on *ḥadīth* 'sell not what is not with you', 111
  on principle of permissibility, 66
  on reason for prohibition of sale 'of what is not with you', 115
  on *ᶜurbūn*, 202
Qatar Civil and Commercial Law, 138
al-qayd al-ḥisābī, 123
qimār. See gambling
qiyās maᶜ al-fāriq, 194
al-qurᶜah, 153
Qur'ān
  āyah al-Mudāyanah, 138-44
  evidence from for the legality of sale, 142
  occasion of revelation of verses, 142
  prohibition of *maysīr*, 151
  role of custom (*ᶜurf*) in interpretation of, 80
  taking outside Muslim lands, 79

rafᶜ al-ḥaraj. See hardship
random walk approach, 18
rare items, 150
ratiocination, 77-79
ration. See reason
rationalists, 79
al-Rāzī, Fakhr, 141
RBD palm olein, 53
reason, role of in Islamic law, 78
reconciliation, 136
registration of contracts, 7-8
regularisation of market, 15-16
regulation of trading, 46-48
release of debt, 136
repentance, 71
representation. See agency
requirements of contracts, 76, 196
responsibility for loss, 196
retention, 121
reverse mortgage, 127
reverse transactions, 118
ribāᶜ. See usury
al-rifq. See leniency
rihān, 153
risk management
  hedging, transferring risk with, 39
  marking-to-the-market, 44-45
  options on futures, 188
  options, 203
  spreading, 45-46
  trading limits, 43-44
  with futures, 16, 19, 148
  al-ᶜurbūn, 203
risk-taking
  clearing-houses, role of in elimination of, 94, 130
  in deferred contract, 26
  defined, 84-86
  excessive and minor, 87-90
  four-part classification of, 93-94
  gambling and, 153-5
  in insurance, 152
  legality of manufacturing contract, 78
  prevention of conflicts, 77
  sale before possession, 120
  sale involving exchange of debts, 125
  sale of the unknown, difference from, 89
  unavoidability of, 146
  uncertainty eliminated with description of subject-matter, 161
Romans, 153
Rosenthal, Franz, 152
round the clock trading, 13
Royal Exchange of London, 1
rubber, 53, 122
ruqᶜ al-ṣayārifah (promissory notes), 2

sabab. See causes
sadd al-dharā'iᶜ, 132

safātij (bills of exchange), 2
Sufyān ibn Sa'īd al-Thawri, 74
ṣaḥīḥ. See valid contractual stipulations
Saʿīd ibn al-Musayyib, 201
salam. See forward sale
sale
  before possession (*See* possession)
  definition of, 131
  prohibition of certain types of, 143
  Qur'ānic evidence for the legality of, 142
  risk-taking in (*See* risk-taking)
sale of the unknown, 89
sale of the unseen, 90-93, 103-6
  Ḥanafī and Shāfiʿī positions on, 89
  involvement in unlawful appropriation, 154
  moderate risk-taking in, 88
  option of viewing, 90
sale of 'what is not with you', 110-5
sale-at-the-market-price, 53
Salmān ibn Yāsar
  prohibition of commodity coupons, 2
al-Sanʿānī, 112
al-Sanhūrī, 91, 93
sale of the unseen, position on, 101-2
al-Sarakhsī
  definition of risk-taking, 85
  on option of cancellation, 105
  on sale before possession, 120
  option and deferment, 135
  position on sales in which exact price is unknown, 95
ṣarf. See currency for currency
scalpers, 41
screen-based trading, 35
Securities Exchange Commission (SEC), 46
securities markets, 43
securities, difference from options, 184
'sell not what is not with you' (*ḥadīth*), 110-5
  al-Khaṭīb's understanding of, 168
  chain of transmission, discrepancies in, 111
  interpretations of, 112-5
  use of to declare certain types of deferred contract invalid, 165
seller
  delivery notices, 10
  role in futures contract, 6
selling short, meaning of, 7
separation, 121
settlement price, 26
al-Shāfiʿī, Muḥammad ibn Idrīs
  exclusion of *ʿinah* from the purview of usury, 174
  on deferment of debts, 142
  on *ḥadīth* of *bayʿ al-kāli' bi'l-kāli'*, 128
  position on sale before possession, 119
  position on selling what one does not own, 113, 114
Shāfiʿī school
  contingent and deferred contracts, 136
  contracts, 76
  custom (*ʿurf*), use of, 81
  position on clearance of debt sale, 126
  position on contractual stipulations, 196
  position on deferred sales, 132-3
  position on duration of option period, 195
  position on sale of the unseen, 89, 90, 103-6
  position on sales in which exact price is unknown, 95
sha'n al-nuzūl, 142
al-Sharbīnī, 104
Sharīʿah Counsel to the Finance House of Kuwait, 170
Sharīʿah. See Islamic law
Sharja, 138
sharṭ al-luzūm (condition of enforceability), 89
sharṭ al-nafādh, 120

al-sharṭ al-fāsid. See voidable stipulations
al-Shāṭibī, Abū Isḥāq Ibrāhīm, 20
on difference between laws of devotion and *muʿāmalāt*, 78
on disadvantages in *maṣāliḥ*, 20
on pursuing of benefits in Islamic law, 82
al-Shawkānī, Yaḥyā ibn ʿAlī, 75
ḥadīth on *bayʿ al-kāli' bi'l-kāli'*, 128
on sale before possession, 121, 173-4
al-Shaybānī, 195
shibh al-salam, 172
al-Shirāzī, 104
Shirkah al-Quṭn al-Iskandariyyah, 50
shirkāt al-wujūh, 161
short (seller in futures contract), 6
short sales in options, 187
Siddiqi, 152
ṣiḥḥah. See validity of sales
simple options, 191
siʿr al-mithl, 176
social changes, 79
socialism, impact of on Egyptian futures market, 51
soil, sale of what is hidden in, 88
specific objects, sale of, 113
specific representation, 177
specification, 86
speculation, 146-50. See also gambling
defined, 147
differences from gambling and investing, 147
in futures trading, 155
lawfulness of, 156
liquidity in the market provided by, 168
low margin requirements and, 150
regulating, 27, 156, 169
unreality of transactions in futures trading, 167
speculative consensus, 175
speculative prohibitions, 171
speculators, 38-41
provide futures market with liquidity, 30
strategies used by, 40
spreading, 45-46
Standard and Poor's 500 Stock Index, 12
standardised contracts, 24, 103
stipulation in contracts
contract-within-a-contract, 197
freedom of, 75, 196-7
optional cancellations, 77
voidable, 77
stock indices, 12
stocks, 8-9, 150
straddle, 45-46
strike price, 183
subject-matter of sales, 99-103
description of eliminates uncertainty, 161
forward sale, 132
in Egyptian Civil Law, 137
in Iraqi civil code, 137
in Jordan's Civil code, 138
in options trading, 200
in Qatar Civil and Commercial Law, 138
non-existence of, 168
of futures sale, 166-7
ownership of during option period, 195
responsibility for loss of, 196
ṣukuk al-badā'iʿ. See commodity coupons
Sulaymān, Aḥmad Yūsuf, 96
prohibitive judgement on futures trading, 159
views on options trading, 198
ṣulḥ, 136
Sunduq Muwāzanah Asʿār al-Quṭn, 51
surplus funds, 36
suspended sale, 106, 177
symmetry in futures contract, 188

taʿāwun, 139, 176
tabarruʿāt. See charitable contracts
al-tafarruq, 121

taḥrīm. See lawful and unlawful
taḥsīnī benefit, 171
ta'jīl, 136
takāful insurance, 94
takhliya (evacuation), 117, 121
takhṣīs (specification), 86
taʿlīl (ratiocination), 77-79
tamyīz, 121
tangible objects, 131, 194
taqābuḍ. See possession
taqlīd, 166
tasʿīr. See price, control
taslīm. See delivery
tawātur, 175
tawbah (repentance), 71
al-tawliyah, 143
taʿyīn, 121
taysīr. See ease
termination of contracts, 23
al-thaman. See price
thaman al-mithl, 95
thiqqah, 161
throw sales 87, 90
throwing of lots, 153
al-Tirmidhī, 111
to-arrive contracts, 4
touch sales 87, 90
trade forms, 56
trade. See sale
trading licences, 60
trading limits, 43-44
  Kuala Lumpur Commodity Exchange, 56-57
trading members (KLOFFE), 58
trading regulation, 46-48
transactions. See also sale
  example illustrating clearing-house operation procedures, 36-37
  presumption of permissibility, 69-70
  ratiocination, 77-79
  witnessing of, 139
trustees, 177
two bargains in one, 88

Umar ibn al-Khaṭṭāb, 201
Umayyad rule, use of commodity coupons during, 2
unborn animals, sale of, 87, 91, 154
uncertainty eliminated with description of subject-matter, 161
uncovered writers, 187
United Arab Emirates Federal Civil Code, 138
unlawful. See lawful and unlawful
unrestricted public interest, 76
unripe fruit, sale of, 87, 91
unseen. See sale of the unseen
ʿuqūd al-ʿajilah, 164
ʿuqūd al-muʿāwadah (contracts of exchange), 100
ʿuqūd al-muʿāwaḍāt al-māliyyah (cumulative contracts), 85
ʿuqūd al-tabarrū. See charitable contracts
ʿuqūd māliyyah (pecuniary contracts), 77
al-ʿurbūn, 201-3
  prohibition of, analysis of *ḥadīth* on, 202
using as an analogy for options, 193-4
utility of in modern commerce, 202
ʿurf. See custom
usufractuary contracts, 136, 194
usurped objects, 106
usury
  futures trading free of, 143-4
  illicit gain, 77
  interest in to-arrive contracts, 4
  non-permissibility of contracts over interest-bearing instruments, 164

valid contractual stipulations, 76, 77
validity of sales, 89
Value Line Index, 12
void contractual stipulations, 76, 77
voidable sales, 106
voidable stipulations, 77

al-waḍīʿah, 143
wakālah. *See* agency

waqf, 136
warehouse receipts. See commodity coupons
wash sales, 57
waṣīy. See executor
weighing
  as a mode of possession of foodstuffs, 123
  of fungible foodgrains, 122
wheat contracts, 13
witnesses, 80, 139
  transactions which do not require, 140
worship. See devotion
writers, 184
  covered and uncovered, 187

Ẓāhiri school
  definition of risk-taking, 84-85
  position on sale before possession, 121
  position on sales in which exact price is unknown, 95
  the norm of prohibition, 75
Zaid ibn Thābit, 2
al-Zarqa, Muṣṭafā, 202
Zayd ibn Aslam, 201